SOURCES

SOURCES

An Anthology of Contemporary
Materials Useful for Preserving
Personal Sanity While Braving the
Great Technological Wilderness

Edited by
THEODORE ROSZAK

HARPER COLOPHON BOOKS
Harper & Row, Publishers
New York, Hagerstown, San Francisco, London

SOURCES

Introductory material, editorial notes and compilation copyright © 1972 by Theodore Roszak. All rights reserved. Printed in the United States of America. No part of this book may be used or reproduced in any manner without written permission except in the case of brief quotations embodied in critical articles and reviews. For information address Harper & Row, Publishers, Inc., 49 East 33rd Street, New York, N.Y. 10016.

FIRST EDITION: HARPER COLOPHON BOOKS 1972

LIBRARY OF CONGRESS CATALOG NUMBER: 77–183200

STANDARD BOOK NUMBER: 06-091000-3

Designed by C. Linda Dingler

CONTENTS

INTRODUCTION

The Human Whole and
Justly Proportioned

Soon after the end of World War II, Dwight Mac-
Donald, writing under the title "Marxism is Obsolete," produced a shrewd design for redrawing the
political map of the world. He suggested that
the traditional left-right dichotomy be retired in
favor of a new polarity between what he called
"progressives" and "radicals." The touchstone that
would tell the two apart? Their attitude toward
science, industrial development, and ethical responsibility.

Had MacDonald's proposal become the ABC of
postwar life, doubtless we should be living in a
world of saner political discourse today. It didn't.
Instead, a political consciousness suited to our
times has had to struggle into existence belatedly,
fitfully, and along unlikely routes; primarily by way
of generational conflict during the middle and late
sixties.

Since this is a book of readings, let me, at the
outset, take the liberty of quoting MacDonald at

From *The Root Is Man: Two Essays in Politics* (Alham-
bra, Calif., 1953). Reprinted by permission of the author.

length. His might as well be the first borrowed text of this anthology since it provides a concise, preliminary survey of the terrain which the writers to follow will be explaining.

. . . both the old Right and the old Left have almost ceased to exist as historical realities, and their elements have been recombined in the dominant modern tendency: an inegalitarian and organic society in which the citizen is a means, not an end, and whose rulers are anti-traditional and scientifically minded. Change is accepted in principle—indeed, the unpleasant aspects of the present are justified precisely as the price that must be paid to insure a desirable future . . . . The whole idea of historical process, which a century ago was the badge of the Left, has become the most persuasive appeal of the apologists for the status quo.

In this Left-Right hybrid, the notion of Progress is central. . . . By "Progressive" [should] be understood those who see the present as an episode on the road to a better future; those who think more in terms of historical process than of moral values; those who believe that the main trouble with the world is partly lack of scientific knowledge and partly the failure to apply to human affairs such knowledge as we do have; those who, above all, regard the increase of man's mastery over nature as good in itself and see its use for bad ends, as atomic bombs, as a perversion. . . .

"Radical" would apply to the as yet few individuals— mostly anarchists, conscientious objectors, and renegade Marxists like myself—who reject the concept of Progress, who judge things by their present meaning and effect, who think the ability of science to guide us in human affairs has been overrated and who therefore redress the balance by emphasizing the ethical aspects of politics. They, or rather we, think it is an open question whether the increase of man's mastery over nature is good or bad in its actual effects on human life to date, and favor adjusting technology to man, even if it means as may be the case a technological regression, rather than adjusting man to technology. . . . We feel that the firmest ground from which to struggle for that human liberation which was the goal of the old Left is the ground not of History but of those non-historical values (truth, justice, love, etc.) which Marx has made unfashionable among socialists. . . .

I might add that the Radical approach, as I understand it at least, does not deny the importance and validity of science in its own proper sphere, or of historical, sociological and economic studies. Nor does it assert that the only reality is the individual and his conscience. It rather defines a sphere which is outside the reach of scientific investigation, and whose value judgments cannot be proved (though they can be demonstrated in appropriate and completely unscientific terms); this is the traditional sphere of art and morality. The Radical sees any movement like socialism, which aspires towards an ethically superior kind of society, as rooted in that sphere, however its growth may be shaped by historical process. This is the sphere of human, personal interest, and in this sense, the root is man.

So we are long past due for a new radicalism— one that comes to grips with the formidable paradox its opponent presents. We deal today with a status quo animated by demonic dynamism—an elitism that appropriates the surface features of revolution: the zeal for innovation, contempt for the past and the nonscientific, the passion to experiment and make over, to subject all things to rational analysis, to invent the future boldly and spread the benefits (or at least the mystique) of industrial progress. Thus, an establishment that *moves*—and with breathtaking pace.

What a strange beast it is, this patrician technocracy that makes total war on tradition in the name of development, growth, progress. Even our "conservatives" these days restrict themselves to the "tradition" of corporate industrialism: nothing older than the railroads, the Bessemer furnace, and the holding company. Industrial haze clouds their historical horizons; they see nothing on the far side of the smoke. The appeal to scientific values, the appeal to the future; these, once the ideological colors of revolution, now pass into the invidious service of the "new industrial state." There is, let us admit it, no revolutionary movement on earth today which is reshaping human society and the face of nature as vastly, as precipitously as the American business community. Metternich, speaking for conservatism old style, proclaimed himself "the rock from which the waves recoil." But our jet-set managers, administrators, entrepreneurs, and systems analysts are a storm beating at every coast. Of course, such change makers have no interest in changing the distribution of social power to their disadvantage. *Plus ça change, plus c'est la même chose*. But in every other spectacular and unsettling respect, they are the earthshakers of contemporary history.

This should not be surprising. It was in the cards. The innovative passion has ruled bourgeois society for centuries, though often concealed beneath a superficial stolidity of social manner and banality of taste. Prudish and mediocre the middle class may have been and so an easy target for bohemian jibes; but world beaters nonetheless.

Recall the famous passage in *The Communist Manifesto* which rehearses at length—and celebrates!—the "most revolutionary part" capitalism has played in world history. Strangely, Marx did not anticipate that capitalist society, so inherently devoted to innovation, might for this very reason be superbly placed to dominate the future. For why should a social class as resourceful and experimental as the industrial bourgeoisie not be capable of surmounting whatever "contradictions" its dynamics might generate? Inefficiency, civic disruption, maldistribution of resources, inadequate social coordination, the "breakdowns in communication" that were in former times called injustice—these are hardly intractable problems for those who invented industrialism and brought it to maturity. Why should they not be able to hire the brains to unsnarl the economic knots, mollify discontent, and outflank the opposition? In brief, why should not capitalism be capable of transforming itself into technocracy?

More sadly still, Marx failed to see that—once having endorsed the fundamental values of industrialism—his socialist alternative might have no choice but to let its dynamic capitalist competitor pace it along the course of history. The two contenders may bear different banners, but they are in the same race, striving for the same prizes: Big System Efficiency, Big System Productivity, Big System Social Integration, Conquest of Nature, Total Secularization of Consciousness, The Fat Silly Life. Of necessity, the runners fall into step with one another; and though they collaborate to keep their fans involved and cheering, at a distance it becomes somewhat difficult to tell them apart.

The irony of the situation is great. For generations, radical intellectuals and avant-garde artists have assumed that it was their peculiar task to provide the cultural ginger that would jolt the hidebound establishment. Still today many young artists, aspiring to *épater les bourgeois,* specialize ingeniously in shock tactics—only to find that the first people on the scene to cover their creative birth pangs with rave notices are the trendy young men from *Esquire, Time,* and *Playboy,* and that such applause and cash as comes their way derives from solid, middle class swingers and respectable foundations which grow constantly more shock-proof. "Progress," "daring invention," "breakthrough"—these are the orthodoxies of superindustrialism. Change—runs the cliché—is the only constant in our world. Western society, mainly in the years since World War II, has crossed a line of the mind beyond which "anything goes" and nothing (except the inhibition of progress) is any longer unthinkable. We have crossed that line by virtue of the dynamism long inherent in bourgeois industrialism. What is it innovative artists call their work— "experiments"? The term is borrowed from the scientist and technician. It is they—not the artist—who have addicted us to the exhilaration of risk, daring, and discovery. Avant-gardism is largely the artist's somewhat cripplegaited effort to get into step with the dizzying pace of industrial change, and there has been no end to cheap tricks used to achieve novelty for novelty's sake. "Don't ask if it's good; just ask if it's new." It is technological, not artistic values that undergird such a standard of cultural taste. (There is, however, another "avant-garde" whose essence has been, not novelty of form, but the perennial wisdom, "shocking" only as the old truth obtruded among the latest assemblage of polite lies.)

"Anything goes"—what better motto for the bedlam of contemporary western culture? A thrill a minute. No holds barred. Experimentation galore. Never a dull moment—the whirligig celebrated by its boosters as a "multiplying of our options." But there is no health in such a routinized excess—though there *is* much wealth to be made by it. A straining against the limits, a desperate pressing toward extremes no longer sensed to be extreme at all, a confabulation with once unimaginable prospects: symptoms, all these, of cultural disintegration, no question about it. Mind at the end of its tether. "Things fall apart, the center cannot hold. . . ."

The scientists and the promethean engineers, these lieutenants of the technocracy have done the most to transform our culture into the push-button Tower of Babel we inhabit. They have habituated us to apocalyptic vistas. Nothing too big, too bizarre, too mind-boggling to be dared. Matter, we have learned, is a vibrant jelly of energy; the universe a burst balloon of galactic fragments; thought itself a mere feedback in the cerebral electronics; life a chemical code soon to be deciphered; all seeming law nothing but the large-scale likelihoods of basic chaos. No absolutes. Nothing sacred. Any day now homunculus in a test tube—cyborgs made to order—interstellar tourism—the doomsday bomb. Why not? What is possible is mandatory.

A great intellectual adventure, all this. But sooner or later the exhilarating breakthroughs enfuel the engines of Juggernaut. No glory for the technician's boldness without the attendant blame. For knowledge *is* power. And power is politics—somebody's politics—as it turns out, *anybody's* politics who pays the way. A tragic perversion of noble intentions? To a degree. But at Los Alamos on August 5, 1945, there were physicists who rushed to order champagne dinners when news came that the thing had worked. "Worked!" The original sin to which science was born: *hubris*—at last become pandemic. "We have now," the head of a prominent think-tank announces, "or know how to acquire the technical capability to do very nearly anything we want . . . if not now or in five years or ten years, then certainly in 25 or in 50 or in 100."

"And ye shall be as gods. . . ."

Our presidents still take oaths upon bibles; our astronauts read us scripture from outer space. But the mark of the beast is upon the appetites and aspirations that most govern our collective conduct: demonic imbalance—endless distraction by unholy infinities of desire: to produce and devour without limit, to build big, kill big, control big. Anything goes—but where anything goes, nothing counts. No natural standard gives discipline. Mephisto's strategy with Faust: to make absence of restraint matter more than presence of purpose, to make liberation nihilism's bait. Until at last, even the man in the street takes the unthinkable in stride, perhaps tries his own hand at a Faustian turn or two. Was not Buchenwald administered by bank clerks —by *good* bank clerks, responsible employees with clean fingernails? And My Lai massacred by last year's high-school basketball stars: nice boys, "not at all like that . . . really"? Listen as you pass along the streets, watch the front pages of newspapers. Salesgirls and mechanics banter glibly during coffee breaks about universal extermination— school kids pass jokes about the death of God ("No, God is not dead; he is alive and hiding out in Argentina")—real estate speculators take out property options on Mars—pop singers exhaust all the rhymes for "alienation"—ladies in the laundromat exchange opinions on brain transplantation while folding sheets—movie stars tell the world how to live with the bomb—

"And what rough beast . . . slouches toward Bethlehem to be born . . . ?"

So walls long defended are overthrown. Terrors of the earth move in next door and pretend to be our neighbors. The genocidal lunacies of De Sade dress up as respectable politics and run for president. Dr. Moreau wins the Nobel Prize for biological research. The temptations of St. Anthony are published as children's literature. Granted, I can cite you no golden age from whose height we have slipped. The walls that held the horrors out—the age-old repertory of repressions—in reality *created* the horrors, which are but parts of ourselves, cut off, disowned, turned gangrenous: nightmare shapes that wear our faces. The horrors were no less beyond the walls than inside, but *no less inside either* if habituation to horror becomes the new sanity. And already we see that "thinking the unthinkable" has become a high-salaried profession, a business that proceeds as usual.

If we admit the madness into our presence, it must be to acknowledge it for what it is, to call it by name, *to live our way through it and out the other side*. A risky venture. Yet "resisting madness can be the maddest way of being mad" (Norman O. Brown).

But here, in this volume, we give no attention to the nightmares. They have been by now often enough recounted: Kafka . . . Eliot . . . Beckett . . . Artaud . . . Genet. . . .

Let us sound only good vibrations, though they are often, seemingly, as bizarre as the bad. For *these too* now seep into the mainstream of debate, subtly but insistently; styles of life, modes of perception, revitalized traditions undeniably far-fetched and starry-eyed. The call goes out for "paradise now" (though it makes for poor theater); Paul Goodman invokes a "neolithic conservatism"; Gary Snyder tells us that "college kids doing it the way they do in New Guinea is modern politics"; many youngsters take out citizenship in Woodstock Nation, which seems to be a *diaspora* of handicraft-mendicant communitarians making its way world-wide by hitchhiking, underground press, and telepathy. But what else should the new radicalism be *but* far-fetched and starry-eyed? The magnitude of the crisis invites a vastness and variety of cultural improvisation. It is a time for eclectic samplings and explorations; perhaps even the cabalistic and occult have their part to play, for who can say where the saving vision—or a glimmer of it—may not lie hidden? The only response to the one-dimensional consciousness of technocratic society: a renaissance of the imagination. Already one senses a rising restlessness and spirit of adventure even in the safely integrated middle classes. How else to explain the spread of the psychic "growth centers"? (God knows, *all* that soul searching can't be evaporating into fun and games.) How long, then, before the prophecies of Blake are read into the Congressional Record and the Canticle of the Sun becomes the platform of the opposition? Before revolution becomes revelation, and the politics of time become the politics of eternity? (No rhetorical question, that —but a prayer, I suppose.)

Easy enough to make light of this growing countercultural appetite for the exotic and outlandish; easier still to scandalize its deviation from serviceable rationality. "There can be no appeal from reason," said the sober father Freud (who praised his children for never believing in fairy tales) as if indeed our Lady Reason had not shared many strange beds in her time. *Whose* Reason? Did not Blake warn us against a kind of "Reasoning Power in Man" which is

. . . a false Body, in Incrustation over my Immortal
Spirit, a Selfhood which must be put off & annihilated
always?

Sand against the holy wind, he called such single-
visioned logicality and proclaimed true vision *fourfold:* Reason, Energy, Imagination, and the union
of these three raising all to a higher power from
which even enraptured utterance falls mutely away.
So then, *Whose* Reason? The war-scholar's methodi-
cal lie, or the humane poet's "angelic raving"?

But, you see? The sure sign of cultural disintegration: all the familiar old dichotomies lose definition,
as if they had only always been the sound of one
hand clapping. Matter-energy—mind-body—reason-
feeling—reality-fantasy—mad-sane—the boundaries
blur into paradox. "I would rather be mad with the
truth than sane with lies" (Bertrand Russell).

Yet the task is not simply to counterbalance: madness against madness, villainy against villainy, extreme against extreme. "Two extremes:" Pascal
reminded, "to exclude reason, to admit nothing but
reason."

(An old vaudeville gag we do well to bear in
mind:

"They said that Edison was crazy. They said that
Pasteur was crazy. They said my Uncle Jake was
crazy . . ."

"Your Uncle Jake . . . ?"

"Yeah. He really *was* crazy.")

If we take ourselves to the deep end to fish the
dark waters, it is for some forgotten principle of
wholeness: Blake's "marriage of heaven and hell";

Abraham Maslow's "hierarchical integration"; L. L. Whyte's "unitary culture"; Dane Rudhyar's "planetarized consciousness." What, after all, is the evil of "Satan's mathematick holiness"? That it *imperializes* consciousness—like the white man who claims to "discover" the world, imposes "civilization" at gunpoint, obliterates the culture of "savage" peoples—and then? Then settles down to build a hubcap factory.

Single-vision must be embraced, but its monopoly broken. We must see. We must see *through*. We must see through *to*. (Thus Blake: "I question not my Corporeal or Vegetative Eye any more than I would question a Window concerning a Sight. I look *thro'* it and not *with* it.")

It is the problem of Jack-in-the-box. The box is also a part of the whole. But Jack thinks it *is* the whole. Jack is an idolator; he lets the lesser reality displace the greater. Yet knock at the side of Jack's box-universe and invite him out to play, and he thinks it is the voice of Satan, of Old Adam, of the murdering Id, the criminal passions. Nonetheless, poor Jack *must* come out, for so narrow a world does not become him, and he despairs therein.

All realities are real. But sanity's reality is bigger, more vividly experienced in all its sectors, more discriminately ordered. Thus, we must have the human whole and justly proportioned.

What are these the sources *for*? I suppose for the only revolution I can foresee within this technocratic order still strong with contrived consensus: an accelerating disaffiliation and internal restructuring which will in time become the new society shaped and tested within the shell of the old. There is a frontier of the mind which needs pioneering if we are to subvert the orthodoxies of Big Science, Big Technique, Big War to which industrial culture is addicted. Never underestimate the power of that addiction. But also—study the eyes of our fellow citizenry, trapped in their glass-box towers, their "escape machine" automobiles that escape to nowhere but endless freeways and Disneyland wilderness, their suburban Sargassos, their idiot affluence and Playboy deliriums, trying desperately to believe what the hired experts tell them: that *this,* this counterfeit of life, is the whole meaning of Progress, Reason, Reality. They *don't* believe it! Their eyes show it. They hate what they have been made; but will hate still more those who mock their moral embarrassment. They grow ugly with thwarted aspiration. But how else for them to live? Within what *other* reality?

Here is an addiction not to be cured by fierce denunciation or the blowing up of well-insured capitalist property. Ugly will not be made beautiful by increase of ugliness. And beauty—the beauty of human souls reclaimed and illuminated—is the banner and power of *our* revolution. A beautiful politics. Despite the bastards.

The technocracy will not be overthrown. It will be displaced—inch by inch—by alternative realities imaginatively embodied. Already our society is honeycombed with experiments—some of them mentioned in the "survival kit" at the end of this anthology. To take a nice example from abroad of this revolution-by-displacement: the good natured Dutch *Kabouters* whose whole politics is the here-and-now generation of an "alternative society," e.g., they occupy abandoned buildings, renovate them for the city's poor, and then form the new inhabitants into tenants' unions. They also run for office (and poll a handsome vote) but campaign by way of *Ludiek* (playfulness). The strategy of the court jester, it would seem. Charm and wit, cunning and invention—within the interstices. *Kabouter* means "pixy": little, elusive folk who come in the night and make better, like the shoemaker's elves.

Of course, displacement takes time. But history moves so fast these days. And always remember: barring the war, history is on our side—not that it pays to care too much for such things. For we are young. And they are old. Strange, is it not? How they keep growing older and older and older . . . While we . . . grow younger . . . and younger . . . .

About the selections in this volume:

Imagine what you read here is arranged in five concentric circles, but each circle defined by no more than the emphasis of the author's thoughts and flowing into the next. Thus, five expanding stages of liberation: person, body, community, whole earth, transcendance.

Few of the writers in this volume can be fairly represented by a single sample of their work. Many of them could have appeared at length in each of the book's five sections, or supplied a book of their own to replace the section. And needless to say, there are the many others—a score of names rushes to your mind and mine—who might have appeared here and don't. What can any anthologist say in his defense but that here are the things that seemed to jell and to be sufficient within reasonable limits?

I have decided to use relatively contemporary writers; men and women, that is, who have been with us during the last few decades. (Buber is, I think, the oldest of the contributors here.) To reach back further takes one into an ancestry too vast for reckoning.

I have also tried not to let already well-known figures monopolize the book; and where such do appear, I have mostly drawn on less prominent examples of their writing.

Finally, I have cast a wide net that draws in many kinds of contributors: poets and scholars, psychiatrists and philosophers, academics of several varieties, activist ideologues and natural scientists—the better to show how diverse and often unlikely our sources must be. It occurs to me that there could easily have been more poetry; perhaps the volume might as well have been a poetry anthology, but that was not what I was after.

If this effort is a success, it will provide the elements of what is, to my way of thinking, an emerging vision of life and will be all of a piece. Though perhaps the wholeness of the design is less in what the writers overtly say than in their tone and spirit —the refusal to entertain old dichotomies, the vigorous sense of the person and of ethical purpose, the lively respect for the psychic deeps, the disinterest in conventional ideals of power, productivity, establishment politics. There are obviously many timely issues not discussed here in any direct fashion: arms race, Third World, black power, Vietnam, women's liberation, "the other America," etc. But such was not the purpose of the volume. Rather, I wanted to piece together, mosaic-fashion, a consciousness expansively at work among us and within which old conundrums may find unanticipated solutions in the generation to come. If you come away from these texts more inclined to read the world about you by light of a vision that is personalist, communitarian, unitary, nonviolent, and pansacramental, then the book has served its purpose.

SOURCES

J. PERSON

I

Master Meng said: There was once a fine forest on the
    Ox Mountain,
Near the capital of a populous country.
The men came out with axes and cut down the trees.
    Was it still a fine forest?

Yet, resting in the alternation of days and nights,
    moistened by dew,
The stumps sprouted, the trees began to grow again.
Then out came goats and cattle to browse on the young
    shoots.
The Ox Mountain was stripped utterly bare.
And the people—seeing it stripped utterly bare—
Think the Ox Mountain never had any woods on it at all.

II

Our mind too, stripped bare like the mountain,
Still cannot be without some basic tendency to love.
But just as men with axes, cutting down the trees every
    morning,
Destroy the beauty of the forest,
So we, by our daily actions, destroy our right mind.

Day follows night, giving rest to the murdered forest,
The moisture of the dawn spirit

From *Mystics and Zen Masters* (New York, Farrar,
Straus & Giroux, Inc., 1961). Copyright © 1961, 1962, 1964,
1966, 1967 by the Abbey of Gethsemani. This poem is based
on a literal translation from the Chinese, from *Mencius on
the Mind* by I. A. Richards (New York: Humanities Press).
Reprinted by permission of Farrar, Straus & Giroux, Inc. and
Humanities Press Inc.

Awakens in us the right loves, the right aversions.
With the actions of one morning we cut down this love,
And destroy it again. At last the night spirit
Is no longer able to revive our right mind.

Where, then, do our likes and dislikes differ from those
   of animals?
In nothing much.
Men see us, and say we never had in us anything but
   evil.
Is this man's nature?

     (Adapted by Thomas Merton from the "Ox
Mountain Parable" of Meng Tzu.)

Begin with the person and you make an end of
ideology, an end of political rhetoric generally. To
ideology and rhetoric belongs the discussion of collectivities, "social forces," and "the course of history"—the macrocosmic principles of things. But the
person clings fiercely to the private moment and
spontaneous gesture, the inexpressible and the unexpected—and so slips through the finest mesh of
principle. What is true "in general" is seldom true
"in person."

System and abstraction, the air-drawn inevitabili-
ties of numbers, logics, proofs: word-worlds all
these, often useful enough, right and real as long as
the word is made flesh, can wince and bleed, can
tremble with mortality. But again and again, language—the cerebral shadow of life—goes into business on its own. We give way to a "life of the mind"
that never minds the unruliness of real experience:
life as it is lived day by day choking on its own
stifled cry for recognition. The person is devoured

by a brain-born cancer of ghostly generalities. Then we have "policy" as devoid of people as a city planner's park.

"The root is man," says Dwight MacDonald, "here and not there, now and not then." More precisely: the root is you—and me—in all our intractable peculiarness. These social multitudes that leaders lead —nations, publics, movements, classes, castes, races, sexes—are at bottom only you and me and him and her. And each of us is a face and a name and a life of our own. We appear on the political stage *in person* or best call off the show.

A rough rule-of-thumb: the more statistical the mode of discourse, the less its personal relevance. Unique beings do not quantify, except for the marginal pieces and parts of their needs and functions. The administrative belly never digests us whole. To speak of a "gross national product" without saying what is produced and what the human use of it is —to speak of "full employment" without asking if the work people do is *worth* doing—to speak of "deterrence," "revolutionary terror," "law and order" without an accounting of the blasted flesh, the broken heads, the butchered innocents—all this is a juggling of illusions. Most politics is compounded of such reified hallucinations.

How do we find our way back through the labyrinth of language to our essential identity? There is no counting the ways: what follows here is but a varied sample—a Trappist monk on the uses of solitude, a psychiatrist on the dream-life, an anthropologist on psychedelic experience, an Indian holy man on the deceptions of the ego. There are a thousand doors to open, and they are being opened. The passion to ransack the long-locked chambers of personality is already strong among us and leads to many a foolish excess—"blow your mind"—"let it all hang out"—"kicking the jambs"—"it is forbidden to forbid." A messy but inevitable stage. Before the painter sets to work, he heaps and smears his palette with perhaps a chaotic multiplicity of colors, the many possibilities of a harmony yet to be created. But the palette is not the canvas, needless to say.

Thomas Merton. *Rain and the Rhinoceros*

Is there not in all of us an organic need for seclusion? As if self-knowledge was a seed requiring subterranean privacy if it is to unfold. Surely it is impossible to imagine what human culture would be like without the treasures of insight the shamans, saints, and sages have brought back to us from the secrecy of wild places.

Thomas Merton was uniquely suited to discuss the contribution of solitude to personal growth. A Trappist monk who frequently spent long intervals in hermitical isolation, he only seemed to grow wiser and more relevant to his age as his seclusion deepened. There are few public men who have stayed as urgently close to the realities of the contemporary world as Merton did, alone and in prayer in the quiet of the Kentucky woods.

LET ME say this before rain becomes a utility that they can plan and distribute for money. By "they" I mean the people who cannot understand that rain is a festival, who do not appreciate its gratuity, who think that what has no price has no value, that what cannot be sold is not real, so that the only way to make something *actual* is to place it on the market. The time will come when they will sell you even your rain. At the moment it is still free, and I am in it. I celebrate its gratuity and its meaninglessness.

The rain I am in is not like the rain of cities. It fills the woods with an immense and confused sound. It covers the flat roof of the cabin and its porch with insistent and controlled rhythms. And I listen, because it reminds me again and again that the whole world runs by rhythms I have not yet learned to recognize, rhythms that are not those of the engineer.

I came up here from the monastery last night, sloshing through the cornfield, said Vespers, and put some oatmeal on the Coleman stove for supper. It boiled over while I was listening to the rain and toasting a piece of bread at the log fire. The night became very dark. The rain surrounded the whole cabin with its enormous virginal myth, a whole

world of meaning, of secrecy, of silence, of rumor.
Think of it: all that speech pouring down, selling
nothing, judging nobody, drenching the thick mulch
of dead leaves, soaking the trees, filling the gullies
and crannies of the wood with water, washing out
the places where men have stripped the hillside!
What a thing it is to sit absolutely alone, in the
forest, at night, cherished by this wonderful, unin-
telligible, perfectly innocent speech, the most comforting speech in the world, the talk that rain makes
by itself all over the ridges, and the talk of the
watercourses everywhere in the hollows!

Nobody started it, nobody is going to stop it. It
will talk as long as it wants, this rain. As long as it
talks I am going to listen.

But I am also going to sleep, because here in this
wilderness I have learned how to sleep again. Here
I am not alien. The trees I know, the night I know,
the rain I know. I close my eyes and instantly sink
into the whole rainy world of which I am a part,
and the world goes on with me in it, for I am not
alien to it. I am alien to the noises of cities, of people, to the greed of machinery that does not sleep,
the hum of power that eats up the night. Where
rain, sunlight and darkness are contemned, I cannot
sleep. I do not trust anything that has been fabricated to replace the climate of woods or prairies. I
can have no confidence in places where the air is
first fouled and then cleansed, where the water is
first made deadly and then made safe with other
poisons. There is nothing in the world of buildings
that is not fabricated, and if a tree gets in among

the apartment houses by mistake it is taught to grow chemically. It is given a precise reason for existing. They put a sign on it saying it is for health, beauty, perspective; that it is for peace, for prosperity; that it was planted by the mayor's daughter. All of this is mystification. The city itself lives on its own myth. Instead of waking up and silently existing, the city people prefer a stubborn and fabricated dream; they do not care to be a part of the night, or to be merely of the world. They have constructed a world outside the world, against the world, a world of mechanical fictions which contemn nature and seek only to use it up, thus preventing it from renewing itself and man.

Of course the festival of rain cannot be stopped, even in the city. The woman from the delicatessen scampers along the sidewalk with a newspaper over her head. The streets, suddenly washed, became transparent and alive, and the noise of traffic becomes a plashing of fountains. One would think that urban man in a rainstorm would *have* to take account of nature in its wetness and freshness, its baptism and its renewal. But the rain brings no renewal to the city, only to tomorrow's weather, and the glint of windows in tall buildings will then have nothing to do with the new sky. All "reality" will remain somewhere inside those walls, counting itself and selling itself with fantastically complex determination. Meanwhile the obsessed citizens plunge through the rain bearing the load of their obsessions, slightly more vulnerable than before, but still only barely aware of external realities. They do not see that the streets shine beautifully, that they themselves are walking on stars and water, that they are running in skies to catch a bus or a taxi, to shelter somewhere in the press of irritated humans, the faces of advertisements and the dim, cretinous sound of unidentified music. But they must know that there is wetness abroad. Perhaps they even *feel* it. I cannot say. Their complaints are mechanical and without spirit.

Naturally no one can believe the things they say about the rain. It all implies one basic lie: *only the city is real.* That weather, not being planned, not being fabricated, is an impertinence, a wen on the visage of progress. (Just a simple little operation, and the whole mess may become relatively tolerable. Let business *make* the rain. This will give it meaning.)

Thoreau sat in *his* cabin and criticized the railways. I sit in mine and wonder about a world that has, well, progressed. I must read *Walden* again, and see if Thoreau already guessed that he was part of what he thought he could escape. But it is not a matter of "escaping." It is not even a matter of protesting very audibly. Technology is here, even in the cabin. True, the utility line is not here yet, and so G.E. is not here yet either. When the utilities and G.E. enter my cabin arm in arm it will be nobody's fault but my own. I admit it. I am not kidding anybody, even myself. I will suffer their bluff and patronizing complacencies in silence. I will let them think they know what I am doing here.

They are convinced that *I am having fun.*

This has already been brought home to me with a wallop by my Coleman lantern. Beautiful lamp: It burns white gas and sings viciously but gives out a splendid green light in which I read Philoxenos, a sixth-century Syrian hermit. Philoxenos fits in with the rain and the festival of night. Of this, more later. Meanwhile: what does my Coleman lantern tell me? (Coleman's philosophy is printed on the cardboard box which I have (guiltily) not shellacked as I was supposed to, and which I have tossed in the woodshed behind the hickory chunks.) Coleman says that the light is good, and has a reason: it "*Stretches days to give more hours of fun.*"

Can't I just be in the woods without any special reason? Just being in the woods, at night, in the cabin, is something too excellent to be justified or explained! It just *is*. There are always a few people who are in the woods at night, in the rain (because if there were not the world would have ended), and I am one of them. We are not having fun, we are not "having" anything, we are not "*stretching our days,*" and if we had fun it would not be measured by hours. Though as a matter of fact that is what fun seems to be: a state of diffuse excitation that can be measured by the clock and "stretched" by an appliance.

There is no clock that can measure the speech of

this rain that falls all night on the drowned and lonely forest.

Of course at three-thirty A.M. the SAC plane goes over, red light winking low under the clouds, skimming the wooded summits on the south side of the valley, loaded with strong medicine. Very strong. Strong enough to burn up all these woods and stretch our hours of fun into eternities.

And that brings me to Philoxenos, a Syrian who had fun in the sixth century, without benefit of appliances, still less of nuclear deterrents.

Philoxenos in his ninth *memra* (on poverty) to dwellers in solitude, says that there is no explanation and no justification for the solitary life, since it is without a law. To be a contemplative is therefore to be an outlaw. As was Christ. As was Paul.

One who is not "alone," says Philoxenos, has not discovered his identity. He seems to be alone, perhaps, for he experiences himself as "individual." But because he is willingly enclosed and limited by the laws and illusions of collective existence, he has no more identity than an unborn child in the womb. He is not yet conscious. He is alien to his own truth. He has senses, but he cannot use them. He has life, but no identity. To have an identity, he has to be awake, and aware. But to be awake, he has to accept vulnerability and death. Not for their own sake: not out of stoicism or despair—only for the sake of the invulnerable inner reality which we cannot recognize (which we can only *be*) but to which we awaken only when we see the unreality of our vulnerable shell. The discovery of this inner self is an act and affirmation of solitude.

Now if we take our vulnerable shell to be our true identity, if we think our mask is our true face, we will protect it with fabrications even at the cost of violating our own truth. This seems to be the collective endeavor of society: the more busily men dedicate themselves to it, the more certainly it becomes a collective illusion, until in the end we have the enormous, obsessive, uncontrollable dynamic of fabrications designed to protect mere fictitious identities—"selves," that is to say, regarded as objects. Selves that can stand back and see themselves having fun (an illusion which reassures them that they are real).

Such is the ignorance which is taken to be the axiomatic foundation of all knowledge in the human collectivity: in order to experience yourself as real, you have to suppress the awareness of your contingency, your unreality, your state of radical need. This you do by creating an awareness of yourself as *one who has no needs that he cannot immediately fulfill.* Basically, this is an illusion of omnipotence: an illusion which the collectivity arrogates to itself, and consents to share with its individual members in proportion as they submit to its more central and more rigid fabrications.

You have needs; but if you behave and conform you can participate in the collective power. You

can then satisfy all your needs. Meanwhile, in order
to increase its power over you, the collectivity increases your needs. It also tightens its demand for
conformity. Thus you can become all the more committed to the collective illusion in proportion to becoming more hopelessly mortgaged to collective
power.

How does this work? The collectivity informs and
shapes your will to happiness ("have fun") by pre-
senting you with irresistible images of yourself as
you would like to be: having *fun that is so perfectly
credible that it allows no interference of conscious
doubt*. In theory such a good time can be so convincing that you are no longer aware of even a
remote possibility that it might change into something less satisfying. In practice, expensive fun always admits of a doubt, which blossoms out into
another full-blown need, which then calls for a still
more credible and more costly refinement of satisfaction, which again fails you. The end of the cycle
is despair.

Because we live in a womb of collective illusion,
our freedom remains abortive. Our capacities for
joy, peace, and truth are never liberated. They can
never be used. We are prisoners of a process, a
dialectic of false promises and real deceptions ending in futility.

"The unborn child," says Philoxenos, "is already
perfect and fully constituted in his nature, with all
his senses, and limbs, but he cannot make use of
them in their natural functions, because, in the

womb, he cannot strengthen or develop them for such use."

Now, since all things have their season, there is a time to be unborn. We must begin, indeed, in the social womb. There is a time for warmth in the collective myth. But there is also a time to be born. He who is spiritually "born" as a mature identity is liberated from the enclosing womb of myth and prejudice. He learns to think for himself, guided no longer by the dictates of need and by the systems and processes designed to create artificial needs and then "satisfy" them.

This emancipation can take two forms: first that of the active life, which liberates itself from enslavement to necessity by considering and serving the needs of others, without thought of personal interest or return. And second, the contemplative life, which must not be construed as an escape from time and matter, from social responsibility and from the life of sense, but rather, as an advance into solitude and the desert, a confrontation with poverty and the void, a renunciation of the empirical self, in the presence of death, and nothingness, in order to overcome the ignorance and error that spring from the fear of "being nothing." The man who dares to be alone can come to see that the "emptiness" and "uselessness" which the collective mind fears and condemns are necessary conditions for the encounter with truth.

It is in the desert of loneliness and emptiness that the fear of death and the need for self-affirmation are seen to be illusory. When this is faced, then anguish is not necessarily overcome, but it can be accepted and understood. Thus, in the heart of anguish are found the gifts of peace and understanding: not simply in personal illumination and liberation, but by commitment and empathy, for the contemplative must assume the universal anguish and the inescapable condition of mortal man. The solitary, far from enclosing himself in himself, becomes every man. He dwells in the solitude, the poverty, the indigence of every man.

It is in this sense that the hermit, according to Philoxenos, imitates Christ. For in Christ, God takes to Himself the solitude and dereliction of man: every man. From the moment Christ went out into the desert to be tempted, the loneliness, the temptation and the hunger of every man became the loneliness, temptation and hunger of Christ. But in return, the gift of truth with which Christ dispelled the three kinds of illusion offered him in his temptation (security, reputation and power) can become also our own truth, if we can only accept it. It is offered to us also in temptation. "You too go out into the desert," said Philoxenos, "having with you nothing of the world, and the Holy Spirit will go with you. See the freedom with which Jesus has gone forth, and go forth like Him—see where he has left the rule of men; leave the rule of the world where he has left the law, and go out with him to fight the power of error."

And where is the power of error? We find it was after all not in the city, but in *ourselves*.

Today the insights of a Philoxenos are to be sought less in the tracts of theologians than in the meditations of the existentialists and in the Theater of the Absurd. The problem of Berenger, in Ionesco's *Rhinoceros*, is the problem of the human person stranded and alone in what threatens to become a society of monsters. In the sixth century Berenger might perhaps have walked off into the desert of Scete, without too much concern over the fact that all his fellow citizens, all his friends, and even his girl Daisy, had turned into rhinoceroses.

The problem today is that there are no deserts, only dude ranches.

The desert islands are places where the wicked little characters in the *Lord of the Flies* come face to face with the Lord of the Flies, form a small, tight, ferocious collectivity of painted faces, and arm themselves with spears to hunt down the last member of their group who still remembers with nostalgia the possibilities of rational discourse.

When Berenger finds himself suddenly the last human in a rhinoceros herd he looks into the mirror and says, humbly enough, "After all, man is not as bad as all that, is he?" But his world now shakes mightily with the stampede of his metamorphosed fellow citizens, and he soon becomes aware that the very stampede itself is the most telling and tragic of all arguments. For when he considers going out into the street "to try to convince them," he realizes that he "would have to learn their language." He looks in the mirror and sees that *he no longer resembles anyone*. He searches madly for a photograph of people as they were before the big change. But now humanity itself has become incredible, as well as hideous. To be the last man in the rhinoceros herd is, in fact, to be a monster.

Such is the problem which Ionesco sets us in his tragic irony: solitude and dissent become more and more impossible, more and more absurd. That Berenger finally accepts his absurdity and rushes out to challenge the whole herd only points up the futility of a commitment to rebellion. At the same time in *The New Tenant* (*Le Nouveau Locataire*) Ionesco portrays the absurdity of a logically consistent individualism which, in fact, is a self-isolation by the pseudo-logic of proliferating needs and possessions.

Ionesco protested that the New York production of *Rhinoceros* as a farce was a complete misunderstanding of his intention. It is a play not merely against *conformism* but about *totalitarianism*. The rhinoceros is not an amiable beast, and with him around the fun ceases and things begin to get serious. Everything has to make sense and be totally useful to the totally obsessive operation. At the same time Ionesco was criticized for not giving the audience "something positive" to take away with them, instead of just "refusing the human adventure." (Presumably "rhinoceritis" is the latest in human adventure!) He replied: "They [the spectators] leave in a void—and that was my intention. It is the business of a free man to pull himself out of this void by his own power and not by the power of other people." In this Ionesco comes very close to Zen and to Christian eremitism.

"In all the cities of the world, it is the same," says Ionesco. "The universal and modern man is the man in a rush (i.e., a rhinoceros), a man who has no time, who is a prisoner of necessity, who cannot understand that *a thing might perhaps be without usefulness;* nor does he understand that, at bottom, it is the useful that may be a useless and back-breaking burden. If one does not understand the usefulness of the useless and the uselessness of the useful, one cannot understand art. And a country where art is not understood is a country of slaves and robots. . . ." (*Notes et Contre Notes,* p. 129) Rhinoceritis, he adds, is the sickness that lies in wait "for those *who have lost the sense and the taste for solitude.*"

The love of solitude is sometimes condemned as "hatred of our fellow men." But is this true? If we push our analysis of collective thinking a little further we will find that the dialectic of power and need, of submission and satisfaction, ends by being a dialectic of hate. Collectivity needs not only to absorb everyone it can, but also implicitly to hate and destroy whoever cannot be absorbed. Paradoxically, one of the needs of collectivity is to reject certain classes, or races, or groups, in order to strengthen its own self-awareness by hating them instead of absorbing them.

Thus the solitary cannot survive unless he is ca-

pable of loving everyone, without concern for the
fact that he is likely to be regarded by all of them
as a traitor. Only the man who has fully attained his
own spiritual identity can live without the need to
kill, and without the need of a doctrine that permits
him to do so with a good conscience. There will always be a place, says Ionesco, *"for those isolated
consciences who have stood up for the universal
conscience"* as against the mass mind. But their
place is solitude. They have no other. Hence it is
the solitary person (whether in the city or in the
desert) who does mankind the inestimable favor of
reminding it of its true capacity for maturity, liberty
and peace.

It sounds very much like Philoxenos to me.

And it sounds like what the rain says. We still
carry this burden of illusion because we do not dare
to lay it down. We suffer all the needs that society
demands we suffer, because if we do not have these
needs we lose our "usefulness" in society—the usefulness of suckers. We fear to be alone, and to be
ourselves, and so to remind others of the truth that
is in them.

"I will not make you such rich men as have need
of many things," said Philoxenos (putting the words
on the lips of Christ), "but I will make you true rich
men who have need of nothing. Since it is not he
who has many possessions that is rich, but he who
has no needs." Obviously, we shall always have
some needs. But only he who has the simplest and
most natural needs can be considered to be without
needs, since the only needs he has are real ones, and

the real ones are not hard to fulfill if one is a free man!

The rain has stopped. The afternoon sun slants through the pine trees: and how those useless needles smell in the clear air!

A dandelion, long out of season, has pushed itself into bloom between the smashed leaves of last summer's day lilies. The valley resounds with the totally uninformative talk of creeks and wild water.

Then the quails begin their sweet whistling in the wet bushes. Their noise is absolutely useless, and so is the delight I take in it. There is nothing I would rather hear, not because it is a better noise than other noises, but because it is the voice of the present moment, the present festival.

Yet even here the earth shakes. Over at Fort Knox the Rhinoceros is having fun.

John Haines. "Poem of the Forgotten"

John Haines has been for some years an Alaskan homesteader, living about seventy miles outside Fairbanks, hunting, fishing, trapping, gathering wild berries, writing poems . . . .

> I came to this place,
> a young man green and lonely.

From *Winter News* (Middletown, Conn.: Wesleyan University Press, 1964). Copyright © 1964 by John Haines. Reprinted by permission of the publisher.

Well quit of the world,
I framed a house of moss and timber,
called it a home,
and sat in the warm evenings
singing to myself as a man sings
when he knows there is
no one to hear.

I made my bed under the shadow
of leaves, and awoke
in the first snow of autumn,
filled with silence.

Kilton Stewart. *Dream Exploration Among the Senoi*

To "know thyself," said Socrates, is the whole meaning of philosophy. But the self most of us know is no more than the wide-awake, sharply-focused, daylight fraction of our identity. Every morning, as soon as the alarm clock marshalls us to job or school, each of us undertakes a psychically obliterating discipline. Systematically, ruthlessly, but subliminally, we erase our dream life, until no more than faded images remain. And by day's end, even these are lost to us. How much of ourselves is thus roughly discarded with our sleep and dream experience? How much of our essential identity, of our personal destiny, do we

From *Creative Psychology and Dream Education* (New York: Stewart Foundation for Creative Psychology), pp. 23–36. Reprinted by permission of Mrs. Clara Stewart Flagg, widow.

daily amputate in this way so that we might put on the orthodox consciousness society requires of us?

In the Hindu and Buddhist traditions, dream-mind and sleep-mind share equally with waking-mind in the composition of human identity. Thus, the mantric seed-syllable AUM (OM) synthesizes the three modes of consciousness: A, being wakefulness (*jagarat*), U, being the dream (*svapna*), and M, being deep sleep (*susupti*). Finally, "OM as a whole represents the all-encompassing cosmic consciousness (*turiya*) on the fourth plane, beyond words and consciousness . . ." (Lama Govinda). How tissue-thin our conventional western psychology seems by comparison. It is largely a mapping of the articulate surface, of the outer cerebral shell.

One need not go to these rich oriental traditions, however, to find a sophisticated appreciation of the role played by the dream- and sleep-minds in shaping the person. Many primitive groups have fashioned oneirologies that far surpass even those of Freud and Jung. Jungians like Kilton Stewart have, however, been willing to learn from the primitives.

Iꜰ ʏou should hear that a flying saucer from another planet had landed on Gualangra, a lonely mountain peak in the Central Mountain Range of the Malay Peninsula a hundred years ago, you would want to know how the space ship was constructed and what kind of power propelled it, but most of all you would want to know about the people who navigated it and the society from which they came. If they lived in a world without crime and war and destructive conflict, and if they were comparatively free from chronic mental and physical ailments, you would want to know about their methods of healing and education, and whether these methods would work as well with the inhabitants of the earth. If you heard further that the navigators of the ship had found a group of 12,000 people living as an isolated community among the mountains, and had demonstrated that these preliterate people would utilize their methods of healing and education, and reproduce the society from which the celestial navigators came, you would probably be more curious about these psychological and social methods that conquered space inside the individual, than you would about the mechanics of the ship which conquered outside space.

As a member of a scientific expedition traveling through the unexplored equatorial rain forest of the Central Range of the Malay Peninsula in 1935, I was introduced to an isolated tribe of jungle folk, who employed methods of psychology and interpersonal relations so astonishing that they might have come from another planet. These people, the Senoi, lived in long community houses, skillfully constructed of bamboo, rattan and thatch, and held away from the ground on poles. They maintained themselves by practicing dry-land, shifting agriculture, and by hunting and fishing. Their language, partly Indonesian and partly Mon-Kamian, related them to the peoples of Indonesia to the south and west, and to the Highlanders of Indo-China and Burma, as do their physical characteristics.

Study of their political and social organization indicates that the political authority in their communities was originally in the hands of the oldest members of patrilineal clans, somewhat as in the social structure of China and other parts of the world. But the major authority in all their communities is now held by their primitive psychologists whom they call *halaks*. The only honorary title in the society is that of *Tohat*, which is equivalent to a doctor who is both a healer and an educator, in our terms.

The Senoi claim there has not been a violent crime or an intercommunal conflict for a space of two or three hundred years because of the insight and inventiveness of the *Tohats* of their various communities. The foothill tribes which surround the Central Mountain Range have such a firm belief in the magical powers of this Highland group that they give the territory a wide berth. From all we could learn, this attitude of the Lowlanders is a very ancient one. Because of their psychological knowledge of strangers in their territory, the Senoi said they could very easily devise means of scaring them off. They did not practice black magic, but allowed the nomadic hill-folk surrounding them to think that they did if strangers invaded their territory.

This fear of Senoi magic accounts for the fact that they have not, over a long period, had to fight with outsiders. But the absence of violent crime, armed conflict, and mental and physical diseases in their own society can only be explained on the basis of institutions which produce a high state of psychological integration and emotional maturity, along with social skills and attitudes which promote creative, rather than destructive, interpersonal relations. They are, perhaps, the most democratic group reported in anthropological literature. In the realms of family, economics, and politics, their society operates smoothly on the principle of contract, agreement and democratic consensus, with no need of police force, jail or psychiatric hospital to reinforce the agreements or to confine those who are not willing or able to reach consensus.

Study of their society seems to indicate that they have arrived at this high state of social and physical cooperation and integration through the system of psychology which they have discovered, invented and developed, and that the principles of this system of psychology are understandable in terms of Western scientific thinking.

It was the late H. D. Noone, the Government Ethnologist of the Federated Malay States who introduced me to this astonishing group. He agreed with me that they have built a system of interpersonal relations which, in the field of psychology, is perhaps on a level with our attainments in such areas as television and nuclear physics. From a year's experience with these people working as a research psychologist, and another year with Noone in England integrating his seven years of anthropological research with my own findings, I am able to make the following formulations of the principles of Senoi psychology.

Being a pre-literate group, the principles of their psychology are simple and easy to learn, understand, and even employ. Fifteen years of experimentation with these Senoi principles have convinced me that all men, regardless of their cultural development, might profit by studying them.

Senoi psychology falls into two categories. The first deals with dream interpretation; the second with dream expression in the agreement trance or cooperative reverie. The cooperative reverie is not participated in until adolescence and serves to initiate the child into the status of adulthood. After adolescence, if he spends a great deal of time in the trance state, a Senoi is considered a specialist in healing or in the use of extra-sensory powers.

Dream interpretation, however, is a feature of child education and is the common knowledge of all Senoi adults. The average Senoi layman practices the psychotherapy of dream interpretation on his family and his associates as a regular feature of education and daily social intercourse. Breakfast in the Senoi house is like a dream clinic, with the father and older brothers listening to and analyzing the dreams of all the children. At the end of the family clinic the male population gathers in the council, at which the dreams of the older children and all the men in the community are reported, discussed, and analyzed.

While the Senoi do not of course employ our system of terminology, their psychology of dream interpretation might be summed up as follows: Man creates features or images of the outside world in his own mind as part of the adaptive process. Some of these features are in conflict with him and with each other. Once internalized, these hostile images turn man against himself and against his fellows. In dreams man has the power to see these facets of his psyche, which have been disguised in external forms, associated with his own fearful emotions, and turned against him and the internal images of other people. If the individual does not receive social aid through education and therapy, these hostile images, built up by man's normal receptiveness to the outside world, get tied together and associated with one another in a way which makes him physically, socially and psychologically abnormal.

Unaided, these dream beings, which man creates to reproduce inside himself the external socio-physical environment, tend to remain against him the way the environment was against him, or to become disassociated from his major personality and tied up in wasteful psychic, organic, and muscular tensions. With the help of dream interpretation, these psychological replicas of the socio-physical environment can be redirected and reorganized and again become useful to the major personality.

The Senoi believes that any human being, with the aid of his fellows, can outface, master, and actually utilize all beings and forces in the dream universe. His experience leads him to believe that, if you cooperate with your fellows or oppose them with good will in the day time, their images will eventually help you in your dreams, and that every person should and can become the supreme rulor and master of his own dream or spiritual universe, and can demand and receive the help and cooperation of all the forces there.

In order to evaluate these principles of dream interpretation and social action, I made a collection of the dreams of younger and older Senoi children, adolescents, and adults, and compared them with similar collections made in other societies where they had different social attitudes toward the dream and different methods of dream interpretation. I found through this larger study that the dream process evolved differently in the various societies, and that the evolution of the dream process seemed to be related to the adaptability and individual creative output of the various societies. It may be of interest to the reader to examine in detail the methods of Senoi dream interpretation:

The simplest anxiety or terror dream I found among the Senoi was the falling dream. When the Senoi child reports a falling dream, the adult answers with enthusiasm, "That is a wonderful dream, one of the best dreams a man can have. Where did you fall to, and what did you discover?" He makes the same comment when the child reports a climbing, traveling, flying or soaring dream. The child at first answers, as he would in our society, that it did not seem so wonderful, and that he was so frightened that he awoke before he had fallen anywhere.

"That was a mistake," answers the adult-authority. "Everything you do in a dream has a purpose, be-

yond your understanding while you are asleep. You
must relax and enjoy yourself when you fall in a
dream. Falling is the quickest way to get in contact
with the powers of the spirit world, the powers laid
open to you through your dreams. Soon, when you
have a falling dream, you will remember what I am
saying, and as you do, you will feel that you are
traveling to the source of the power which has
caused you to fall.

"The falling spirits love you. They are attracting
you to their land, and you have but to relax and
remain asleep in order to come to grips with them.
When you meet them, you may be frightened of
their terrific power, but go on. When you think you
are dying in a dream, you are only receiving the
powers of the other world, your own spiritual power
which has been turned against you, and which now
wishes to become one with you if you will accept it."

The astonishing thing is that over a period of
time, with this type of social interaction, praise, or
criticism, imperatives, and advice, the dream which
starts out with fear of falling changes into the joy
of flying. This happens to everyone in the Senoi
society. That which was an indwelling fear of anxiety, becomes an indwelling joy or act of will; that
which was ill esteem toward the forces which
caused the child to fall in his dream, becomes good
will toward the denizens of the dream world, because he relaxes in his dream and finds pleasurable
adventures, rather than waking up with a clammy
skin and a crawling scalp.

The Senoi believe and teach that the dreamer—

the "I" of the dream—should always advance and attack in the teeth of danger, calling on the dream images of his fellows if necessary, but fighting by himself until they arrive. In bad dreams the Senoi believe real friends will never attack the dreamer or refuse help. If any dream character who looks like a friend is hostile or uncooperative in a dream, he is only wearing the mask of a friend.

If the dreamer attacks and kills the hostile dream character, the spirit or essence of this dream character will always emerge as a servant or ally. Dream characters are bad only as long as one is afraid and retreating from them, and will continue to seem bad and fearful as long as one refuses to come to grips with them.

According to the Senoi, pleasurable dreams, such as of flying or sexual love, should be continued until they arrive at a resolution which, on awakening, leaves one with something of beauty or use to the group. For example, one should arrive somewhere when he flies, meet the beings there, hear their music, see their designs, their dances, and learn their useful knowledge.

Dreams of sexual love should always move through orgasm, and the dreamer should then demand from his dream lover the poem, the song, the dance, the useful knowledge which will express the beauty of his spiritual lover to the group. If this is done, no dream man or woman can take the love which belongs to human beings. If the dream character demanding love looks like a brother or a sister, with whom love would be abnormal or incestuous in reality, one need have no fear of expressing love in the dream, since these dream beings are not, in fact, brother or sister, but have only chosen these taboo images as a disguise. Such dream beings are only facets of one's own spiritual or psychic make-up, disguised as brother or sister, and useless until they are reclaimed or possessed through the free expression of love in the dream universe.

If the dreamer demands and receives from his love partner a contribution which he can express to the group on awakening, he cannot express or receive too much love in dreams. A rich love life in dreams indicates the favor of the beings of the spiritual or emotional universe. If the dreamer injures the dream images of his fellows or refuses to cooperate with them in dreams, he should go out of his way to express friendship and cooperation on awakening, since hostile dream characters can only use the image of people for whom his good will is running low. If the image of a friend hurts him in a dream, the friend should be advised of the fact, so he can repair his damaged or negative dream image by friendly social intercourse.

Let us examine some of the elements of the social and psychological processes involved in this type of dream interpretation:

First, the child receives social recognition and esteem for discovering and relating what might be called an anxiety-motivated psychic reaction. This is the first step among the Senoi toward convincing the child that he is acceptable to authority even when he reveals how he is inside.

Second, it describes the working of his mind as rational, even when he is asleep. To the Sonoi it is just as reasonable for the child to adjust his inner tension states for himself as it is for a Western child to do his homework for the teacher.

Third, the interpretation characterizes the force which the child feels in the dream as a power which he can control through a process of relaxation and mental set, a force which is his as soon as he can reclaim it and learn to direct it.

Fourth, the Senoi education indicates that anxiety is not only important in itself, but that it blocks the free play of imaginative thinking and creative activity to which dreams could otherwise give rise.

Fifth, it establishes the principle that the child should make decisions and arrive at resolutions in his night-time thinking as well as in that of the day, and should assume a responsible attitude toward all his psychic reactions and forces.

Sixth, it acquaints the child with the fact that he can better control his psychic reactions by expressing them and taking thought upon them, than by concealing and repressing them.

Seventh, it initiates the Senoi child into a way of thinking, which will be strengthened and developed throughout the rest of his life, and which assumes that a human being who retains good will for his fellows and communicates his psychic reactions to them for approval and criticism, is the supreme ruler of all the individual forces of the spirit—subjective—world whatsoever.

Man discovers his deepest self and reveals his

greatest creative power at times when his psychic processes are most free from immediate involvement with the environment and most under the control of his indwelling balancing or homeostatic power. The freest type of psychic play occurs in sleep, and the social acceptance of the dream world would, therefore, constitute the deepest possible acceptance of the individual.

Among the Senoi the child accumulates good will for people because they encourage on every hand the free exercise and expression of that which is most basically himself, either directly or indirectly, through the acceptance of the dream process. At the same time, the child is told that he must refuse to settle with the denizens of the dream world unless they make some contribution which is socially meaningful and constructive as determined by social consensus on awakening. Thus his dream reorganization is guided in a way which makes his adult aggressive action socially constructive.

Among the Senoi where the authority tells the child that every dream force and character is real and important, and in essence permanent, that it can and must be outfaced, subdued, and forced to make a socially meaningful contribution, the wisdom of the body operating in sleep, seems in fact to reorganize the accumulating experience of the child in such a way that the natural tendency of the higher nervous system to perpetuate unpleasant experiences is first neutralized and then reversed.

We could call this simple type of interpretation dream analysis. It says to the child that there is a manifest content of the dream, the root he stubbed his toe on, or the fire that burned him, or the composite individual that disciplined him. But there is also a latent content of the dream, a force which is potentially useful, but which will plague him until he outfaces the manifest content in a future dream, and either persuades or forces it to make a contribution which will be judged useful or beautiful by the group, after he awakes.

We could call this type of interpretation suggestion. The tendency to perpetuate in sleep the negative image of a personified evil is neutralized in the dream by a similar tendency to perpetuate the positive image of a sympathetic social authority. Thus, accumulating social experience supports the organizing wisdom of the body in the dream, making the dreamer first unafraid of the negative image and its accompanying painful tension state, and later enabling him to break up that tension state and transmute the accumulated energy from anxiety into a poem, a song, a dance, a new type of trap, or some other creative product, to which an individual or the whole group will react with approval (or criticize) the following day.

The following further examples from the Senoi will show how this process operates:

A child dreams that he is attacked by a friend, and, on awakening, is advised by his father to inform his friend of this fact. The friend's father tells his child that it is possible that he has offended the dreamer without wishing to do so, and allowed a malignant character to use his image as a disguise in the dream. Therefore, he should give a present to the dreamer and go out of his way to be friendly toward him, to prevent such an occurrence in the future.

The aggression building up around the image of the friend in the dreamer's mind thereby becomes the basis of a friendly exchange. The dreamer is also told to fight back in future dreams, and to conquer any dream character using the friend's image as a disguise.

Another example of what is probably a less direct tension state in the dreamer toward another person is dealt with in an equally skillful manner. The dreamer reports seeing a tiger attack another boy of the long house. Again, he is advised to tell the boy about the dream, to describe the place where the attack occurred and, if possible, to show it to him so he can be on his guard, and in future dreams kill the tiger before it has a chance to attack him. The parents of the boy in the dream again tell the child to give the dreamer a present, and to consider him a special friend.

Even a tendency toward unproductive fantasy is effectively dealt with in the Senoi dream education. If the child reports floating dreams, or a dream of finding food, he is told that he must float somewhere in his next dream and find something of value to his fellows, or that he must share the food he is eating; and if he has a dream of attacking someone he must apologize to them, share a delicacy with them, or make them some sort of toy. Thus, before aggression and jealousy can influence social behavior, the tensions expressed in the permissive dream state become the hub of social action in which they are discharged without being destructive.

My data on the dream life of the various Senoi age groups would indicate that dreaming can and does become the deepest type of creative thought. Observing the lives of the Senoi it occurred to me that modern civilization may be sick because people have sloughed off, or failed to develop, half their power to think. Perhaps the most important half. Certainly, the Senoi suffer little by intellectual comparison with ourselves. They have equal power for logical thinking while awake, considering their environmental data, whereas our capacity to solve problems in dreams is infantile compared to theirs.

In the adult Senoi a dream may start with a waking problem which has failed solution, with an accident, or a social debacle. A young man brings in some wild gourd seeds and shares them with his group. They have a purgative effect and give everyone diarrhea. The young man feels guilty and ashamed and suspects that they are poisonous. That night he has a dream, and the spirit of the gourd seeds appears, makes him vomit up the seeds, and explains that they have value only as a medicine, when a person is ill. Then the gourd spirit gives him a song and teaches him a dance which he can show his group on awakening, thereby gaining recognition and winning back his self-esteem.

Or, a falling tree which wounds a man appears in his dreams to take away the pain, and explains that it wishes to make friends with him. Then the tree spirit gives him a new and unknown rhythm which he can play on his drums. Or, the jilted lover is visited in his dreams by the woman who rejected him, who explains that she is sick when she is awake and not good enough for him. As a token of her true feeling she gives him a poem.

The Senoi does not exhaust the power to think while asleep with these simple social and environmental situations. The bearers who carried out our equipment under very trying conditions became dissatisfied and were ready to desert. Their leader, a Senoi shaman, had a dream in which he was visited by the spirit of the empty boxes. The song and music this dream character gave him so inspired the bearers, and the dance he directed so relaxed and rested them, that they claimed the boxes had lost their weight and finished the expedition in the best of spirits.

Even this solution of a difficult social situation, involving people who were not all members of the dreamer's group, is trivial compared with the dream solutions which occur now that the Senoi territory has been opened up to alien culture contacts.

Datu Bintung at Jelong had a dream which succeeded in breaking down the major social barriers in clothing and food habits between his group and the surrounding Chinese and Mohammedan colonies. This was accomplished chiefly through a dance which is dream prescribed. Only those who did his dance were required to change their food habits and wear the new clothing, but the dance was so good that nearly all the Senoi along the border chose to do it. In this way, the dream created social change in a democratic manner.

Another feature of Datu Bintung's dream involved the ceremonial status of women, making them more nearly equals of the men, although equality is not a feature of either Chinese or Mohammedan societies. So far as could be determined this was a pure creative action which introduced greater equality in the culture, just as reflective thought has produced more equality in our society.

In the West the thinking we do while asleep usually remains on a muddled, childish, or psychotic level because we do not respond to dreams as socially important and include dreaming in the educative process. This social neglect of the side of man's reflective thinking, when the creative process is most free, seems poor education.

Among the Senoi, the terror dream, the anxiety dream, and the simple pleasure dream, as well as muddled dreams of vague inconsequential happenings, such as a meaningless repetition of the day's activities, largely disappear before puberty. From puberty on, the dream life becomes less and less fantastic and irrational, and more and more like reflective thinking, problem solving, exploration of unknown things or people, emotionally satisfying social intercourse, and the acquiring of knowledge from a dream teacher or spirit guide. However dull or unimportant an individual may be, he can always count on receiving a hearing from his family members and from the larger group through his dreams.

There would seem to be a rational basis for the

Senoi ideology and practice if we accept the view that man's psycho-physical structure is not merely altered as experience accumulates, but must be re-organized in line with some principle of inner homeostatic balance.

The internalized social order, which largely makes up the intellectual structure of the individual, does not integrate well with man's power to reorganize and unify his accumulating experience, unless the individual maintains a feeling of good will toward the members of his society, whose images are being internalized as the process of socialization takes place.

If the social authorities, who have a counterpart in the psychic structure of the individual, listen to his dreams with appreciation and respond with criticism, praise and imperatives or directives, the homeostatic processes have the power to reorganize the elements of the mind, as well as those of the body, in a way which keeps both the body and the mind healthy, and permits of a type of social inter-action which does not obtain in societies where man is not encouraged and directed to reorganize his accumulating experience in dreams.

Civilized man pays little attention to the thinking he has the power to do in his sleep through dreams. Western society is rife with war, crime and wasteful economic conflict, insanity, neurosis and chronic psychogenic physical ills. The Senoi make their dreams the major focus of their intellectual and so-cial interest, and have solved the problem of violent crime and destructive economic conflict, and largely eliminated insanity, neurosis and psychogenic illness. They have done this without the help of a written language, or of the scientific method as we think of it.

Carlos Casteneda. *The Psychedelic Allies*

Techniques of consciousness alteration may be—along with grammatical speech—the oldest of all technologies. No society has been without its ritualized repertory of exercises and chemical means for elevating perception and sensibility into an extraordinary new key: fasting, ascetic self-torment, smoke inhalation, self-hypnosis, dizziness, holding the breath until faint—the variety of means defies accounting. Some Greco-Roman oracles swung through the air to achieve vertigo, thus seeking a giddy "high" that still tantalizes every child on a park swing. Even simple intoxication was once regarded as ecstatic communion with the divine; the art of fermenting beverages—man's first chemistry—is among the most ancient inventions, and in most cultures has been enveloped by a sense of sacred revelation: *in vino veritas*.

Here, then, is a tradition that darkly counterpoints the political and economic history of man:

From *The Teachings of Don Juan* (Berkeley and Los Angeles: University of California Press, 1968), pp. 32–34, 56–60. Reprinted by permission of the Regents of The University of California.

a deep and indispensable soil of psychic shape-shifting from which a wealth of human self-knowledge grows. It has been, invariably, in moments of trance or dizzy transport that men and women have approached nearest the gods and been inspired (*breathed into*) by creative powers greater than their normal own.

Significantly, our society is among the few that has no well-developed mystical discipline. The mainstream of Christianity—despite the great ecstatic saints—is theological: discursive, literalist, logical, a talking about God rather than a sacramental awareness. Hence, the creeds, dogmas, inquisitions, and persecutions. However, since the advent of the scientific revolution, the consciousness-shaping chemicals most encouraged in our culture have been, not those that entrance, but those that enforce awakeness, mental precision, the severely logical mindfulness of mathematician and chess player. Coffee, tea, and chocolate: all appear in the age of Newton and sweep the society. Along with the new stay-awake pharmaceuticals, they are still the mainstay of our daily routine. Even alcohol has to be delayed until "after hours."

Little wonder, then, that use of the psychedelics, or even of marijuana, should be seen as an affront to official consciousness. High industrial society cannot afford to see its mental concentration blurred. Potheads make rotten systems analysts; as the Vietnam war shows us, they make even worse killers.

The recent, eager unearthing of the psychedelic tradition signifies a revolution in consciousness. It revives the longing for sacramental experience.

Unhappily, we are left with little in the way of lore or discipline with which to surround the experience; it easily degenerates into mere psychic fireworks. Carlos Casteneda was uniquely fortunate in this respect. His introduction to psychedelia came under the tutelage of don Juan, a Yaqui Indian *brujo* (shaman) who was able to integrate the drugs with an ancient folk wisdom. Casteneda spent six years as don Juan's apprentice. Here are the notes for only three days of that remarkable adventure; but in them we see what brilliant philosophical elaboration our so-called primitive ancestors bestowed on the psychedelic exploration of human nature.

Sunday, August 20, 1961

Last night don Juan proceeded to usher me into the realm of his knowledge. We sat in front of his house in the dark. Suddenly, after a long silence, he began to talk. He said he was going to advise me with the same words his own benefactor had used the first day he took him as his apprentice. Don Juan had apparently memorized the words, for he repeated them several times, to make sure I did not miss any:

"A man goes to knowledge as he goes to war, wide-awake, with fear, with respect, and with absolute assurance. Going to knowledge or going to war in any other manner is a mistake, and whoever makes it will live to regret his steps."

I asked him why was it so and he said that when a man has fulfilled those four requisites there are no mistakes for which he will have to account; under such conditions his acts lose the blundering quality of a fool's acts. If such a man fails, or suffers a defeat, he will have lost only a battle, and there will be no pitiful regrets for that.

Then he said he intended to teach me about an "ally" in the very same way his own benefactor had taught him. He put strong emphasis on the words "very same way," repeating the phrase several times.

An "ally," he said, is a power a man can bring into his life to help him, advise him, and give him the strength necessary to perform acts, whether big or small, right or wrong. This ally is necessary to enhance a man's life, guide his acts, and further his knowledge. In fact, an ally is the indispensable aid to knowing. Don Juan said this with great conviction and force. He seemed to choose his words carefully. He repeated the following sentence four times:

"An ally will make you see and understand things about which no human being could possibly enlighten you."

"Is an ally something like a guardian spirit?"

"It is neither a guardian nor a spirit. It is an aid."

"Is Mescalito your ally?"

"No! Mescalito is another kind of power. A unique power! A protector, a teacher."

"What makes Mescalito different from an ally?"

"He can't be tamed and used as an ally is tamed and used. Mescalito is outside oneself. He chooses to show himself in many forms to whoever stands in front of him, regardless of whether that person is a brujo or a farm boy."

Don Juan spoke with deep fervor about Mescalito's being the teacher of the proper way to live. I asked him how Mescalito taught the "proper way of life," and don Juan replied that Mescalito *showed* how to live.

"How does he show it?" I asked.

"He has many ways of showing it. Sometimes he shows it on his hand, or on the rocks, or the trees, or just in front of you."

"Is it like a picture in front of you?"

"No. It is a teaching in front of you."

"Does Mescalito talk to the person?"

"Yes. But not in words."

"How does he talk, then?"

"He talks differently to every man."

I felt my questions were annoying him. I did not ask any more. He went on explaining that there were no exact steps to knowing Mescalito; therefore no one could teach about him except Mescalito himself. This quality made him a unique power; he was not the same for every man.

On the other hand, the acquiring of an ally required, don Juan said, the most precise teaching and the following of stages or steps without a single deviation. There are many such ally powers in the world, he said, but he was familiar with only two of them. And he was going to lead me to them and their secrets, but it was up to me to choose *one* of them, for I could have only one. His benefactor's ally was in la yerba del diablo (devil's weed), he said, but he personally did not like it, even though his benefactor had taught him its secrets. His own ally was in the humito (the little smoke), he said, but he did not elaborate on the nature of the smoke.

I asked him about it. He remained quiet. After a long pause I asked him:

"What kind of a power is an ally?"

"It is an aid. I have already told you."

"How does it aid?"

"An ally is a power capable of carrying a man beyond the boundaries of himself. This is how an ally can reveal matters no human being could."

"But Mescalito also takes you out of the boundaries of yourself. Doesn't that make him an ally?"

"No. Mescalito takes you out of yourself to teach you. An ally takes you out to give you power."

I asked him to explain this point to me in more detail, or to describe the difference in effect between the two. He looked at me for a long time and laughed. He said that learning through conversation was not only a waste, but stupidity, because learning was the most difficult task a man could undertake. . . . Thus he saw no point in talking about knowledge. He said that certain kinds of knowledge were too powerful for the strength I had, and to talk about them would only bring harm to me. He apparently felt there was nothing else he wanted to say. He got up and walked toward his house. I told him the situation overwhelmed me. It was not what I had conceived or wanted it to be.

He said that fears are natural; that all of us experience them and there is nothing we can do about it. But on the other hand, no matter how frightening learning is, it is more terrible to think of a man without an ally, or without knowledge.

Saturday, April 8, 1962

In our conversations, don Juan consistently used or referred to the phrase "man of knowledge," but never explained what he meant by it. I asked him about it.

"A man of knowledge is one who has followed truthfully the hardships of learning," he said. "A man who has, without rushing or without faltering, gone as far as he can in unraveling the secrets of power and knowledge."

"Can anyone be a man of knowledge?"

"No, not anyone."

"Then what must a man do to become a man of knowledge?"

"He must challenge and defeat his four natural enemies."

"Will he be a man of knowledge after defeating these four enemies?"

"Yes. A man can call himself a man of knowledge only if he is capable of defeating all four of them."

"Then, can anybody who defeats these enemies be a man of knowledge?"

"Anybody who defeats them becomes a man of knowledge."

"But are there any special requirements a man must fulfill before fighting with these enemies?"

"No. Anyone can try to become a man of knowledge; very few men actually succeed, but that is only natural. The enemies a man encounters on the path of learning to become a man of knowledge are truly formidable; most men succumb to them."

"What kind of enemies are they, don Juan?"

He refused to talk about the enemies. He said it would be a long time before the subject would make any sense to me. I tried to keep the topic alive and asked him if he thought *I* could become a man of knowledge. He said no man could possibly tell that for sure. But I insisted on knowing if there were any clues he could use to determine whether or not I had a chance of becoming a man of knowledge. He said it would depend on my battle against the four enemies—whether I could defeat them or would be defeated by them—but it was impossible to foretell the outcome of that fight.

I asked him if he could use witchcraft or divination to see the outcome of the battle. He flatly stated that the results of the struggle could not be foreseen by any means, because becoming a man of knowledge was a temporary thing. When I asked him to explain this point, he replied:

"To be a man of knowledge has no permanence. One is never a man of knowledge, not really. Rather, one becomes a man of knowledge for a very brief instant, after defeating the four natural enemies."

"You must tell me, don Juan, what kind of enemies they are."

He did not answer. I insisted again, but he dropped the subject and started to talk about something else.

*   *   *

Sunday, April 15, 1962

As I was getting ready to leave, I decided to ask him once more about the enemies of a man of knowledge. I argued that I could not return for some time, and it would be a good idea to write down what he had to say and then think about it while I was away.

He hesitated for a while, but then began to talk.

"When a man starts to learn, he is never clear about his objectives. His purpose is faulty; his intent is vague. He hopes for rewards that will never materialize, for he knows nothing of the hardships of learning.

"He slowly begins to learn—bit by bit at first, then in big chunks. And his thoughts soon clash. What he learns is never what he pictured, or imagined, and so he begins to be afraid. Learning is never what one expects. Every step of learning is a new task, and the fear the man is experiencing begins to mount mercilessly, unyieldingly. His purpose becomes a battlefield.

"And thus he has stumbled upon the first of his natural enemies: Fear! A terrible enemy—treacherous, and difficult to overcome. It remains concealed at every turn of the way, prowling, waiting. And if the man, terrified in its presence, runs away, his enemy will have put an end to his quest."

"What will happen to the man if he runs away in fear?"

"Nothing happens to him except that he will never learn. He will never become a man of knowledge. He will perhaps be a bully, or a harmless,

scared man; at any rate, he will be a defeated man.
His first enemy will have put an end to his crav-
ings."

"And what can he do to overcome fear?"

"The answer is very simple. He must not run
away. He must defy his fear, and in spite of it he
must take the next step in learning, and the next,
and the next. He must be fully afraid, and yet he
must not stop. That is the rule! And a moment will
come when his first enemy retreats. The man begins
to feel sure of himself. His intent becomes stronger.
Learning is no longer a terrifying task.

"When this joyful moment comes, the man can
say without hesitation that he has defeated his first
natural enemy."

"Does it happen at once, don Juan, or little by
little?"

"It happens little by little, and yet the fear is
vanquished suddenly and fast."

"But won't the man be afraid again if something
new happens to him?"

"No. Once a man has vanquished fear, he is free
from it for the rest of his life because, instead of
fear, he has acquired clarity—a clarity of mind
which erases fear. By then a man knows his desires; he knows how to satisfy those desires. He can
anticipate the new steps of learning, and a sharp
clarity surrounds everything. The man feels that
nothing is concealed.

"And thus he has encountered his second enemy:
Clarity! That clarity of mind, which is so hard to
obtain, dispels fear, but also blinds.

"It forces the man never to doubt himself. It gives him the assurance he can do anything he pleases, for he sees clearly into everything. And he is courageous because he is clear, and he stops at nothing because he is clear. But all that is a mistake; it is like something incomplete. If the man yields to this make-believe power, he has succumbed to his second enemy and will fumble with learning. He will rush when he should be patient, or he will be patient when he should rush. And he will fumble with learning until he winds up incapable of learning anything more."

"What becomes of a man who is defeated in that way, don Juan? Does he die as a result?"

"No, he doesn't die. His second enemy has just stopped him cold from trying to become a man of knowledge; instead, the man may turn into a buoyant warrior, or a clown. Yet the clarity for which he has paid so dearly will never change to darkness and fear again. He will be clear as long as he lives, but he will no longer learn, or yearn for, anything."

"But what does he have to do to avoid being defeated?"

"He must do what he did with fear: he must defy his clarity and use it only to see, and wait patiently and measure carefully before taking new steps; he must think, above all, that his clarity was only a point before his eyes. And thus he will have overcome his second enemy, and will arrive at a position where nothing can harm him anymore. This will not be a mistake. It will not be only a point before his eyes. It will be true power.

"He will know at this point that the power he has been pursuing for so long is finally his. He can do with it whatever he pleases. His ally is at his command. His wish is the rule. He sees all that is around him. But he has also come across his third enemy: Power!

"Power is the strongest of all enemies. And naturally the easiest thing to do is to give in; after all, the man is truly invincible. He commands; he begins by taking calculated risks, and ends in making rules, because he is a master.

"A man at this stage hardly notices his third enemy closing in on him. And suddenly, without knowing, he will certainly have lost the battle. His enemy will have turned him into a cruel, capricious man."

"Will he lose his power?"

"No, he will never lose his clarity or his power."

"What then will distinguish him from a man of knowledge?"

"A man who is defeated by power dies without really knowing how to handle it. Power is only a burden upon his fate. Such a man has no command over himself, and cannot tell when or how to use his power."

"Is the defeat by any of these enemies a final defeat?"

"Of course it is final. Once one of these enemies overpowers a man there is nothing he can do."

"Is it possible, for instance, that the man who is defeated by power may see his error and mend his ways?"

"No. Once a man gives in he is through."

"But what if he is temporarily blinded by power, and then refuses it?"

"That means his battle is still on. That means he is still trying to become a man of knowledge. A man is defeated only when he no longer tries, and abandons himself."

"But then, don Juan, it is possible that a man may abandon himself to fear for years, but finally conquer it."

"No, that is not true. If he gives in to fear he will never conquer it, because he will shy away from learning and never try again. But if he tries to learn for years in the midst of his fear, he will eventually conquer it because he will never have really abandoned himself to it."

"How can he defeat his third enemy, don Juan?"

"He has to defy it, deliberately. He has to come to realize the power he has seemingly conquered is in reality never his. He must keep himself in line at all times, handling carefully and faithfully all that he has learned. If he can see that clarity and power, without his control over himself, are worse than mistakes, he will reach a point where everything is held in check. He will know then when and how to use his power. And thus he will have defeated his third enemy.

"The man will be, by then, at the end of his journey of learning, and almost without warning he will come upon the last of his enemies: Old age! This enemy is the cruelest of all, the one he won't be able to defeat completely, but only fight away.

"This is the time when a man has no more fears, no more impatient clarity of mind—a time when all his power is in check, but also the time when he has an unyielding desire to rest. If he gives in totally to his desire to lie down and forget, if he soothes himself in tiredness, he will have lost his last round, and his enemy will cut him down into a feeble old creature. His desire to retreat will overrule all his clarity, his power, and his knowledge.

"But if the man sloughs off his tiredness, and lives his fate through, he can then be called a man of knowledge, if only for the brief moment when he succeeds in fighting off his last, invincible enemy. That moment of clarity, power, and knowledge is enough."

Meher Baba. *Undoing the Ego*

For all its recent popularization, eastern mysticism has scarcely begun to make its influence felt on the mainstream of western thought, let alone on our living values. With the exception of the off-beat Gestaltists and Jungians, even our psychologists have not attempted to integrate its transcendent conception of identity. Little wonder. The western ego—even in its wild and woolly version as the Freudian id—is indeed a tough nut to crack. Its psychic genealogy runs back through

From *God to Man and Man to God* (London: Victor Gollancz, 1955). Reprinted by permission of Della de Leon.

the Christian notion of soul: the atomic self, final and isolated, stuffed sausage-like into its bag of corruptible skin, claiming tenacious property rights in personal salvation. When the Vedic-Buddhist critique of self-hood tells us this beleaguered ego is an illusion, we quickly interpret this, not as an invitation to free and expand our identity, but as a nihilistic assault upon the person. Yet for Meher Baba, as for all eastern mystic teachers, the impoverished ego we cling to is nothing less than "the root-cause of the chaos which precipitates itself in wars." Thus, he insisted that the transformation of identity must be an integral and primary part of any healthy social change.

To face the Truth is to realize that life is one in and through its many manifestations and to lose the limiting self in the realization of unity. . . . Economic adjustment is impossible unless people realize that there can be no effectively planned and cooperative action in economic matters until self-interest gives place to self-giving love.

Here is a motif we will return to in many later selections, and especially in E. F. Schumacher's efforts to liberate economics from its commitment to greed and competitive envy.

Meher Baba (Merwan Sheheriarji Irani), who died in 1969, has become one of the most widely known Indian holy men in the western world. It is difficult to catch the spirit of the man on the printed page, not only because, like all mystics, his teachings must be experienced by way of a spiritual discipline, but also because, since the year 1925, he neither wrote nor spoke, but lived under a vow of total silence. The only communication he allowed himself, even during his several teaching tours of Europe and America, was by way of an alphabet board on which he would "dictate" to his closest disciples. His way of life and his personal presence were intended to be his principle language. In this way he hoped to achieve a clairvoyant universality which would allow him to contact all people regardless of caste, sex, nation, or religious connection.

The conclusion of the discourse that follows—an analysis of the ego—may have an authoritarian ring to western ears. We have no widely-respected counterpart in our society of the spiritual master (guru) to whom the individual can entrust himself wholly without fear of exploitation. Bear in mind that the master Meher Baba refers to is not the *führer* of a mass movement, but a teacher who selflessly cultivates a very few deeply personal relationships, rather like those that held between Socrates and his pupils. Unfortunately, Meher Baba's following, like that of so many eastern holy men, often weakens toward cultic adulation, which is the winding sheet of the visionary powers.

In the prehuman stage, consciousness has experiences that are not explicitly brought into relation with a central "I." For instance, a dog is angry, but does not feel "I am angry." But even a dog learns through experiences acting upon each other as a result of the mechanical tension of connected imprints or *sanskaras;* this, however, is different from the intelligent synthesis of experiences through the development of I-consciousness. The first step in submitting the working of isolated impressions to intelligent regulation consists in bringing them in relation with the centre of consciousness, which appears as the explicit limited ego. The consolidation of the ego-consciousness is defined from the beginning of human consciousness.

The Origin of the Ego

Human consciousness would be no more than a repository of the accumulated imprints of varied experiences did it not also contain the principle of ego-centred integration in the attempt to organize and understand experience. The process implies capacity to hold different experiences together as parts of a unity and the capacity to evaluate them by mutual relation. The integration of the opposites of experience is a condition of emancipating consciousness from the thraldom of compulsions and repulsions which tend to dominate consciousness irrespective of valuation: and the early attempts in securing such integration are through the formation of the ego as its control.

The ego emerges as an explicit accompaniment of all the happenings of mental life to fulfil a certain need. The part played by the ego in human life may be compared with the function of the ballast in a ship. The ballast keeps the ship from too much oscillation; without it, the ship is likely to be too light and unsteady and in danger of being over-turned. The psychic energy would be caught up in the mazes of dual experience and would be frittered away were there no provisional nucleus to bind to-gether the active tendencies born of the relatively independent instincts inherited from animal-con-sciousness. The formation of the ego serves the pur-pose of giving a certain amount of stability to con-scious processes, and secures a working equilibrium which makes for an organized life.

It would, therefore, be a mistake to imagine that, as the ego arises only to vanish, it fulfils no need in the long journey of the soul. Though the ego is not meant to be permanent since it can be transcended and outgrown through spiritual endeavour, the phase of ego-formation must nevertheless be looked upon as a necessary evil for the time being.

The ego thus fulfils a certain need in the progress of consciousness; but since it takes its shelter in the false idea of being the body, it is a source of illusion. It is of the essence of the ego that it should feel separate from the rest of life by contrasting itself with other forms of life. Thus, though inwardly try-ing to complete and integrate individual experience, the ego creates division between external and in-ternal life in the attempt to feel and secure its own existence; and this division cannot but have its re-verberations in the inner individual life over which it presides.

The Ego a Seat of Conflicts

While striving to establish unity and integration in experience, the ego can never realize this objective; and though it establishes a certain kind of balance, this is only provisional. The incompleteness of its attainments is evident from the internal conflict which is never absent as long as experience exists only from the point of view of the ego. From moment to moment, the mind passes through a series of conflicts. The minds of great persons as well as the minds of common people are harassed by conflicting desires. Sometimes the conflict is so acute that the person concerned yields to psychic pressure, with the result that there is either a partial or total breakdown or a complete derangement of the mind. There is no vital difference between the normal man and the so-called abnormal man. Both face the same problems; but the one more or less successfully solves his problems and the other does not.

The ego attempts to solve its inner conflicts through false valuations and wrong choice. It is characteristic of the ego that it takes what is unimportant as important and what is important as unimportant. Thus power, fame, wealth, ability and other attainments and accomplishments are taken delight in by the ego and are clung to by it. Spirituality the ego fights against. For example, if a person experiences bodily or mental discomfort while doing work of spiritual importance, the ego desires to restore that comfort even at the cost of giving up the spiritual work. Bodily and mental comfort as well as other worldly attainments are necessary, but not important. Many things come to the ego as necessary which are not in themselves important, so that the ego represents a fundamental principle of ignorance. . . .

Hidden Conflicts

In fact, the conflicts upon ordinary things are rarely brought to the surface of consciousness, so that they cast a shadow on life, from, as it were, behind a screen. Such conflicts have to be brought to the surface of consciousness and faced. This process should not degenerate into imagining conflicts where there are none. The sure indication of a hidden but real conflict is the sense that the whole of the heart is not in the thoughts or actions that happen to be dominant at the moment, and there is a vague feeling of a narrowing down or restriction of life. On such occasions, an attempt should be made to analyse the mental state through inward attention and such analysis will bring to light the hidden conflicts.

The most important requirement for the satisfactory resolution of conflicts is the motive power or inspiration that comes from a burning longing for the Truth. Mere analysis may aid choice, but the choice will remain a barren intellectual preference, unless it is vitalized by zeal for the Truth that appeals to the depths of human personality. Psychology has done much to reveal the sources of conflict; but it has yet to discover the method of awakening inspiration or supplying the mind with that which makes life worth living.

To establish love for the Truth is the beginning of right valuation, and the beginning of the undoing of the constructions of the ego exhibits itself through false valuation. Any action that expresses the true values of life contributes towards the disintegration of the ego, which is a product of ages of ignorant action. Life cannot permanently be imprisoned within the ego; it must make efforts towards ultimate Truth. In the ripeness of evolution comes the discovery that life cannot be understood and lived fully so long as it moves upon the pivot of the ego: and man is, therefore, driven by the logic of his own experience to find the true centre of experience and to reorganize his life in the Truth. This brings about the wearing out of the ego and its replacement by truth-consciousness. The false nucleus of consolidated *sanskaras* disappears in the integration and fulfilment of life.

The Ego an Affirmation of Separateness

The ego as an affirmation of separateness takes many forms. It may take the form of self conscious memory expressing itself in such recollections as, "I did this and I did that, I felt this and I felt that". It also takes the forms of ego-centred hopes expressed through plans, "I shall do this", "I shall do that", "I shall feel this", "I shall feel that", "I shall think that".

Or the ego has a strong feeling of being some one in particular and asserts its separateness from others. While provisionally serving a useful purpose in the development of consciousness, the ego, as an affirmation of separateness, constitutes the chief hindrance to the spiritual emancipation and enlightenment of consciousness.

The ego affirms separateness through craving, hate, anger, fear or jealousy. When a person craves for the company of others, he is conscious of being separate from them and feels his own separate existence in an intensive manner. The feeling of separation from the other is most acute where there is unrelieved craving. In hate and anger also the other person is excluded from one's own being and regarded as hostile to the thriving of the ego. Fear is a subtle form of affirming separateness and exists where the consciousness of quality is unabated. Fear acts as a curtain between the "I" and the "you" and not only nourishes distrust of the other but brings about a shrinking and withdrawal of consciousness so as to exclude the being of another from one's own life. To fear God and his manifestations is to strengthen duality; to love them is to weaken it.

The feeling of separateness finds most poignant expression in jealousy. There is a deep and imperative need in the human soul to love and identify itself with others; this is not fulfilled where there is craving or hate, anger or fear. In jealousy, in addition to the non-fulfillment of this deep need there is the conviction that another has successfully identi-

fied itself with the person whom one sought: there is
therefore an irreconcilable protest against both for
being in a relationship designed for oneself. All exclusive feelings such as craving, hate, anger, fear or
jealousy bring about a narrowing of life and contribute to the limitation of consciousness: they are
instrumental to the affirmation of separateness and
feed the ego.

The Reduction of the Ego Through Love

Every thought, feeling or action that springs from
the idea of exclusive or separate existence binds the
soul, all experiences—small or great—and all aspirations—good or bad—create a load of impressions and
nourish the sense of the "I". The only experience
that makes for the reduction of the ego is the experience of love, and the only aspiration that makes
for the elimination of separateness is the longing for
becoming one with the Beloved. Craving, hatred,
anger, fear and jealousy are exclusive attitudes that
create a gulf between oneself and others; love alone
helps towards the bridging over of this self-created
gulf and breaks through the separative barrier of
false imagination. The lover, too, longs; but he longs
for union with the Beloved; and in seeking or experiencing union with the Beloved the sense of the
"I" declines. In love, the "I" does not think of its
own preservation. The ego is the affirmation of separateness from the other: and love is the affirmation
of oneness with the other: the ego can be dissolved
only through love.

Explicit and Implicit Ego

The problem of erasing the ego from consciousness is complicated because the roots of the ego are
in the sub-conscious mind in the form of latent
tendencies. The limited ego of explicit consciousness is only a small fragment of the ego. The ego is
like the iceberg floating in the sea, of which about
one-eighth is visible. Only a small portion of the ego
becomes manifest in consciousness as an explicit "I":
the major portion remains submerged in the dark
and inarticulate sanctuaries of the sub-conscious
mind.

. The *explicit ego* which finds its manifestation in
consciousness is by no means a harmonious whole
but an arena for conflicts of opposing tendencies. It
has a limited capacity for this, however, for two
persons have to be at least on speaking terms if they
are to enter into a quarrel, otherwise they have no
common ground. In the same manner two tendencies entering into conscious conflict must have a
common ground; otherwise they remain submerged
in the sub-conscious mind, until modified through
the tensions exerted by the activities of the conscious mind.

Although the ego is essentially heterogeneous, the
explicit ego of consciousness is less so than the *implicit ego* of the sub-conscious mind, and operates
as a formidable whole as against the isolated
sub-conscious tendencies that seek to emerge in
consciousness. The organized ego of explicit con-

sciousness thus becomes a repressive barrier, which indefinitely prevents the several constituents of the implicit ego from getting access to consciousness. All problems of the ego can be tackled through intelligent and conscious action, and, therefore, a complete annihilation of the ego is possible only when all the constituents of the ego pass through intelligent consciousness.

The action of the intelligent consciousness is important, but not in itself sufficient. Even the components of the implicit ego of the sub-conscious mind have to be brought to the surface of consciousness to become parts of the explicit ego and to be submitted to the action of intelligent consciousness. If this is to be achieved, there has to be weakening of the explicit ego in such a manner that it allows the emergence in consciousness of those desires and tendencies that could not hitherto find admittance in the arena of consciousness. This release of inhibited tendencies brings about additional confusion and conflict in the explicit ego; therefore, the process of the disappearance of the ego is often accompanied by intensified conflicts in the arena of the conscious mind rather than by any easing of conflicts. However, at the end of the uncompromising struggle lies the poise and harmony that come after the dissolution of the structure of the ego. . . .

The ego is activated by the principle of self-perpetuation and has a tendency to live and grow through any means not closed to it. If the ego is curtailed in one direction, it seeks compensating expansion in another, and, if overpowered by spir-

itual actions, it may even fasten upon this very
force brought into action for the ousting of the ego.
If a person attempts to cultivate humility to relieve
himself of the monstrous weight of the ego and
succeeds in doing so, the ego can with surprising
alacrity get transferred to this attribute of humility
itself. It feeds itself through attachment to such
assertions as "I am spiritual", as, in primary stages, it
achieves the same end by "I am not interested in
spirituality". Thus arises the ego that feels separateness through the attainment of things considered
highly desirable and unworldly. But this type of
spiritual ego is as binding as the crude ego.

In fact, in the more advanced stages of the Path,
the ego does not seek its strengthening through open
methods, and uses the means that are available for
securing the elimination of the ego. These tactics
are like guerilla warfare and are the most difficult
to counteract. The elimination of the ego from
consciousness is necessarily an intricate process. The
nature of the ego itself is very complicated and
needs divine grace to overcome it. Since the ego
has almost endless possibilities of securing its existence and creating self-delusions, the aspirant finds
it impossible to cope with its ever fresh forms, and
can hope to be successful with the tricks of the ego
only through the grace of a Master. . . .

Inferiority, Superiority, Equality, Unity

The ego subsists upon possessions such as power,
fame, wealth, ability and accomplishments. It cre-

ates and recognizes what is distinctively "mine". However, in spite of all the things it claims as "mine", it feels empty and incomplete and seeks to fortify itself through further acquisitions. It brings its varied possessions into comparison with those of others and uses its possessions for self-display at the cost of others. Yet the ego is dissatisfied despite its possessions, and seeks to derive satisfaction by a more intense sense of possession. Thus the ego as an affirmation of separateness lives through the idea of "mine".

The ego wants to feel separate and unique, and seeks self-expression either in the role of one better than others or as inferior to them. Either role may serve. As long as there is the ego, there is the background of duality, and the mental operations of comparison and contrast with others cannot be ended. Therefore, even where a person feels a sense of equality with another, this feeling is not securely established, and marks a point of transition between the two attitudes of the ego, rather than a permanent freedom from the distinction between "I" and "thou". This pseudo equality, may be made articulate in the formula "I am not in any way inferior or superior to the other", which will be seen to be a negative assertion of the ego. The balance between the "I" and the "thou" is disturbed by a superiority or inferiority complex: and the idea of equality arises to restore this balance. The negative assertion of the ego in the form of equality is, however, utterly different from the sense of unity, and the conditions of co-operative life are fulfilled only

where the idea of equality is replaced by the realization of unity. . . .

Surrender to the Master

When a person comes into contact with the Master and recognizes him as being in the state of ego-
less perfection, his self-surrender is distinguished
from the inferiority feeling because accompanied
by the awareness that the Master has basic unity
with the disciple. Such self-surrender is not an expression of loss of confidence, but of confidence in
the final overcoming of obstacles through the help
of the Master. The appreciation of the divinity of
the Master is the manner in which the Higher Self
of the disciple expresses its sense of dignity.

To bring about a rapid dissolution of the feelings
of superiority and inferiority, the Master may stir
both feelings in alternation. If the disciple is losing
heart and giving up the search, he may arouse deep
self-confidence; if he is egoistic he may create situations in which the disciple has to accept his own
incapacity or futility. Thus the Master wields his
influence over the disciple to expedite the stages
through which the ego passes before its disappearance.

The superiority feeling and the inferiority feeling
have to be brought into relation with each other,
and may require a psychic situation in which they
will be allowed to have their play without requiring
the repression of the one to secure the expression of

the other. When the soul enters into a vital relation with the Master, the feelings concerned with the senses of inferiority and superiority are both brought into play and counteract each other. With the dissolution of these opposites there comes the breaking down of the separative barriers of the ego in all forms; with the breaking down of the barriers, there arises divine love; and with the arising of divine love, the feeling of "I", as distinguished from "thou", dissolves in the sense of unity.

So that a car should move towards its destination a driver is necessary, but the driver may cultivate strong attachments for the things he encounters on the way, and may not only halt at intervening places but get lost in the sideways in pursuit of things that appeal to him. He may keep the car moving without coming nearer the goal; he may even get further away from it. Something like this happens when the ego assumes the control and direction of consciousness.

If consciousness is to be emancipated from its limitations and rendered adequate for serving the purpose for which it came into existence, it must draw its directive momentum not from the ego but from some other principle. In other words, the driver who is ignorant of the ultimate destination must be exchanged for another driver, free from the influence of the things he encounters on the way, one who keeps his attention on the goal of non-duality. The shifting of the centre of interest from unimportant to important values is comparable to the transfer of power from the ignorant driver to the driver who knows the destination.

Integration Around a False Idea

Had the ego been nothing but a medium for the integration of human experience, it would have been possible for man to get established in the Truth merely by carrying it actively further; but while playing a part in the progress of consciousness, the ego represents an active principle of ignorance which prevents spiritual development. The ego attempts the integration of experience around the false idea of separateness. And having taken an illusion as a foundation for the construction of its edifice only succeeds in building one illusion upon another.

As long as human experience is within the limitation of duality, its integration is the condition of a rational and significant life. But the ego as a nucleus of integration has to be renounced because of its alliance with ignorance. There arises an imperative need to have a new centre for integration, free from the basic ignorance of a separateness, which allows scope for the incorporation of the values inaccessible to the ego-centre. Such a new centre is provided by the Master who represents the absolute Truth. The shifting of interest from unimportant to important values is facilitated by allegiance and self-surrender to the Master who becomes the new nucleus for integration.

Union with the Master and Realization
of the Truth

The Master is an affirmation of the unity of all
life; allegiance to the Master, therefore, brings about
a gradual dissociation from the ego-nucleus which
affirms separateness. After this crisis in the life
of man, all mental activity has a new reference in
the light of its relation to the Master as the manifestation of the infinite Truth. The person hence-
forth experiences his acts as no longer initiated
from the limited "I", but inspired by the Truth. He
is no longer interested in the well-being of the limited self, but only in the Master as representing
universal and individual life. He offers all his experiences and desires to the Master, reserving neither
the good nor the evil for the limited "I", thus stripping the ego of its contents. This bankruptcy of the
ego does not interfere with the process of integration, which is created around the new centre established by the Master. When the ego-nucleus is bankrupt and devoid of any power or being, the Master
as Truth is firmly established in consciousness as
the guiding and animating principle. This is at once
the attainment of union with the Master and the
realization of the Infinite Truth.

As the ego gradually adjusts itself to the spiritual
requirements of life through the cultivation of humility, selflessness and love or whole-hearted surrender and offering to the Master, it suffers drastic

curtailment in being, and it not only offers increasingly reduced resistance to spiritual enfoldment, but
undergoes a radical transformation that causes the
ego, as an affirmation of separateness, completely to
disappear. The intermediate steps of the reduction
of the ego and the softening of its nature are comparable to the trimming and the pruning of the
branches of a tree, whereas the final step of the
annihilation of the ego amounts to the uprooting of
the tree. When the ego disappears entirely, there
arises the knowledge of the True Self. Thus, the long
journey of the soul consists in developing from
animal consciousness the explicit self-consciousness
of the limited "I", then in transcending the "I", and,
through the medium of the Master, to be initiated
into the consciousness of the Supreme and Real Self,
as an everlasting and Infinite "I am" in which there
is no separateness, which includes all existence.

MANAS. *The Mists of Objectivity*

The antithesis of the personal is the objective,
the single mode of consciousness our scientific
culture regards as a reliable guide to reality. In
this essay from the philosophical journal MANAS,
the author reviews the liabilities that follow from
the unlimited expansion of the objective style to
all aspects of life. Since its beginning in 1947,
MANAS has conducted some of the most search-

From *MANAS*, May 5, 1965. Reprinted by permission of
the publisher.

ing discussions of science and society to be found in our periodical literature. The balance and sensitivity of the selection that follows are typical of the journal's fare.

THIS ESSAY was to be called "The Myth of Objectivity," but it seemed that the word "myth" ought to be saved for better purposes. In the growing usage of the present, myth is a light to the field of experience. It is a kind of fulcrum for the deliberated acts of human beings. It helps to identify and range the elements of the human situation according to their role and value in the drama of self-discovery.

Until very recently, "objectivity" signified a state of intellectual blessedness peculiar to modern thought. You propped up the thing you wanted to know about, got far enough away from it to count its arms and legs, made tabulations of the frequencies of its various "behaviors," exposed it to various stimuli to learn about its reactions; and then, if sufficient samples were available, you cut it up, hoping for information about its inner structure and dynamics.

A formal account of the rise in importance of objectivity would take us back to Galileo. Following the lead of Kepler, Galileo distinguished even more clearly between the objective qualities of things, such as their size and weight, and the attributes which result from the sensibility and intelligence of the human being who looks at them. The idea was to eliminate any possibility of equivocation concerning the "real" world, which meant

—for the purposes of physics at least—getting rid of whatever could not be precisely defined in physical terms. This became known as the correct way to read the "Book of Nature." As A. E. Burtt summarized the result: "From being a realm of substances in qualitative and teleological relations, the world of nature had definitely become a realm of bodies moving mechanically in space and time."

It seems likely that this stripping of nature of all but physically measurable qualities would have remained no more than a handy methodological device, save for the extraordinary success of the mathematical manipulations of matter and force by the first "natural philosophers"—who became, thereby, the founders of modern science. Newton's laws *worked!* The world machine (despite Newton's objections) soon took the place of God and all purposive intelligence in nature. You didn't have to wrestle with theological imponderables any more, but could study the Book of Nature and prove your readings as you went along with the wonderful objectivity of mathematical demonstrations. In his *History of Materialism* (New York: Harcourt Brace Jovanovich, 1925), Frederick Lange describes what happened:

From the triumph of this purely mathematical achievement there was curiously developed a new physics. Let us carefully observe that a purely mathematical connection between two phenomena such as the fall of bodies and the motion of the moon, could only lead to that great generalization in so far as there was presupposed a common and everywhere operative material cause of the phenomena. The course of history has eliminated this unknown material cause, and has placed the mathematical law itself in the rank of physical causes. The collision of the atoms shifted into an idea of unity, which as such rules the world without any material mediation. What Newton held to be so great an absurdity that no philosophic thinker could light upon it, is prized by posterity as Newton's great discovery of the harmony of the universe!

The broader cultural effects of the enthronement of scientific objectivity, and of the worship of "fact," are brilliantly summarized by Carl Becker in his *Heavenly City of the Eighteenth-Century Philosophers:*

. . . [In the twentieth century] natural science became science, and scientists rejected, as a personal affront, the title of philosopher, which formerly they had been proud to bear. The vision of man and his world as a neat and efficient machine, designed by an intelligent Author of the Universe, gradually faded away. Professors of science ceased to speak with any assurance of the laws of nature, and were content to pursue, with unabated ardor, but without any teleological implications whatever, their proper business of observing and experimenting with the something which is the stuff of the universe, of measuring and mastering its stress and movement. "Science," said Lloyd Morgan, "deals exclusively with changes in configuration, and traces the accelerations which are observed to occur, leaving to metaphysics to deal with the underlying agency, if it exist. . . ."

Science has taught us the futility of troubling to understand the "underlying agency" of the things we use. We have found that we can drive an automobile without knowing how the carburetor works, and listen to a radio without mastering the secret of radiation. . . .

In dismissing the underlying agency with a casual shrug, we are in good company. The high priest of science, even more than the common man, is a past master of this art. It is one of the engaging ironies of modern thought that the scientific method, which it was once fondly hoped would banish mystery from the world, leaves it every day more inexplicable than ever . . . the essential quality of the modern climate of opinion is factual rather than rational.

This was written in 1932. It is now beginning to dawn on us more emphatically that a world defined in terms of its supposed "objective facts" is a world to which we cannot successfully relate in human terms. The human being inside every one of us is undeniably some kind of "underlying agency"— which science systematically and by design ignores. The three-hundred-year experiment by which Western man attempted to achieve absolute certainty by barring from the "real" world the non-objective facts of subjective experience has not worked. The assumption that you can get an adequate account of the nature and needs of human beings through statistical description of human behavior has not worked either. And the political proposition that justice can be done by establishing a system based upon a "scientific" reading of history has broken down.

We are beginning to recognize that a theory of knowledge which claims objectivity to be the only criterion of truth is a theory which turns its supporters into arrogant, fanatical men. They think they *know*.

Now the fact of the matter is that they do *not*

know. They understand neither the good nor the evil of which the human heart is capable. They do not know the difference between *being* an organism and *having* one. They make no definitions which distinguish between appetite and aspiration. To them, "Socratic ignorance" is a meaningless expression. Access to cybernetic techniques of suppressing subjective "error" has not helped the present government of the United States to illuminate what the country ought to do about its unbearable problems in Vietnam. The great mechanical brains we call computers are the climactic achievement of what we may hope is the final attempt to make "objective"—and therefore capable of technical manipulation—the problems of human beings. They won't work—not, at least, for this end. The problems of human beings are living, inner, moral and intellectual problems. They are not "objective," and they can't be made so without killing and cutting them up into manageable ("dead") parts.

Well, then, is "objectivity" good for nothing at all? We should say that a purely objective truth can say nothing of final importance to human beings. Objective truth is filled with counsels concerning what to do about man as an object, but it is totally silent on what man himself ought to do as subject. And man is *first* subject, *then* object.

After all the facts are in about the "objective situation," you still have to *choose*. And there is a whole universe of reality—mostly unexplored reality —which ought to affect such human decision and choice. The objective world may be some kind of analogue of the subjective world, but *it is not the same world*. Objective truth is a great boon to the practical needs of mankind, but only if it is understood that the so-called "practical" needs are not man's only needs. By the claim that only objective truth is "real," truth becomes, for human purposes, no longer truth but obsession.

What is an "objective truth" anyway? The simplest definition we can think of is that it is a truth which is intrinsically the same for all men. It can apply, therefore, only to the parts of all men which are the same. But the important parts of all men are the parts that are *not* the same. Objective truths can say nothing about the individuality of human beings.

Of course, in order to "handle" or "manage" people, we devise tricky little techniques to make judgments about them. We make them fill out forms before they can get jobs. We grade their papers in school. Geniuses have been known to get very bad grades because the objective criteria of the tests employed did not cover the symptoms of genius, or were actually designed to discourage any such deviations from the mediocre norms of mass education. Further, if you have a properly docile population of students, exams intended to disclose originality are bitterly resented. The students prefer to deal with what is *expected* of them.

Another approach would say that "objective truth" is something that one man can really *give* to another. Or you can hire somebody to collect the objective truth you need at the moment, such as the knowledge needed for building a house or a city hall. Objective truth, in short, is the kind of truth you can put into handbooks. It is the kind of truth you can use without understanding how it was obtained. . . .

When you think about this situation, you begin to see that the pretense of settling all important matters by reference to "facts" is a great razzle-dazzle which has no legitimate connection with authentic processes of deliberative thought and intelligent decision-making. The old scientific slogan, "Facts, justly arranged, interpret themselves," is the key to this confusion. The joker is the phrase, "justly arranged," since any arrangement involving fitness or appropriateness depends upon subjective considerations. A just arrangement of facts is an arrangement according to philosophical and ethical—that is, *human*—criteria. Such criteria are reached by human beings in their inner lives as subjective and moral agents. The development of those criteria is the only important project of an association of civilized human beings, since the use they make of whatever "facts" they have, or think they have, is finally determined by the ruling moral attitudes of the people involved.

What shapes ethical criteria? This simple question has a simple answer. A man's feelings about his own nature and worth and the nature and worth of other people, his ideas of right and wrong, good and evil, in all personal and social relationships, shape his ethical criteria.

The next question is: How do people change or

improve their ideas about themselves and others?
And the answer is, they do it only by strenuous
effort. They do it through the conscious search for
truth—a task that can never be delegated to anyone else. Without subjective criteria, objective truth
isn't truth—it isn't anything at all, except a meaningless jumble of unrelated appearances. We should
all of us know by now, from a study of the history of
Western thought, that the claimant to "objective
truth" without a subjective (philosophical, metaphysical, and ethical) foundation is a completely
deluded person. His thinking is filled with un-
examined assumptions.

Are, then, "objective facts" no good at all? It
would be foolish to suggest this. The quest for
objectivity, if honestly pursued, inevitably instructs
us in the futility of arriving at real knowledge by
this means. A man soon learns that assembling an
array of facts, or approximate facts, is in some cases
possible and in other cases not, but that, either way,
the decisive problem is always gaining assent for
the moral implications with which the investigator
started out, or which began to emerge as he worked
on the project.

One of the interesting things about the development of physical science in the twentieth century is
the gradual withdrawal of scientific authority from
the cult of objectivity. The Logical Positivists, as is
well known, long ago abandoned hope of reaching
"truth" by means of inductive investigation, and
grow a little irritated when anyone suggests that
scientists have any responsibility in this direction.

What seems probable, however, is that attempts at objective (scientific) description are analogues of the search for truth, and that a man who has some experience in this direction is likely to have acquired a decent humility in relation to all attempts to get actual knowledge.

Some years ago, Pierre Duhem, a theoretical physicist and philosopher of science, showed that without a philosophical foundation in metaphysics, science could never be anything more than a kind of elite technology. In an article published in *Science* for April 23, 1954, Duhem wrote of physical science:

Concerning the very nature of things, or the realities hidden under the phenomena we are studying, a theory conceived on the plan we have just drawn teaches us absolutely nothing.

Physical theory by itself, Duhem maintained, could never accomplish explanation, but only representation and classification. He said that the nature of ultimate reality was beyond the scope of physical science, although it might provide a kind of parallelism in its account of physical structure. Duhem continues:

Physical theory never gives us the explanation of experimental laws; it never reveals realities hiding under sensible appearances; but the more complete it becomes, the more we apprehend that the logical order in which theory orders experimental laws is the reflection of an ontological order, the more we suspect that the relations it establishes among the data of perception correspond to real relations among things, and the more we feel that theory tends to be a natural classification.

This, indeed, from the point of view of the quest for knowledge, is the justification of physical science:

the physicist is compelled to recognize that it would be unreasonable to work for the progress of physical theory if this theory were not the increasingly better defined and more precise reflection of a metaphysics; the belief in an order transcending physics is the sole justification of physical theory.

The interesting thing about a statement of this sort by a theoretical physicist is its candid return to Platonic idealism as the basis of a theory of knowledge. This is not a tendency limited to physical scientists, although it obtains special importance from the fact that the physicists were primarily responsible for isolating the measurable, external qualities of nature and proposing that reliable definitions of "reality" could be had in no other way. Today, the entire movement of serious thought is in the direction of restoring the primacy of subjective perception. This is certainly the central significance of the work of the humanistic psychologists; it is an obvious requirement of Erich Fromm's assignment of responsibility to the individual for his own transformation (the therapeutic "leap").

It is natural to ask: But won't such high claims for the subjective side of human existence lay us open to the hazards of uncontrolled emotionalism? Surely we ought not to jettison the hard-won disciplines of scientific impersonality and impartial devotion to truth?

This comment seems exactly right. Science *was*

born from a love of truth. The spirit of scientific method must be preserved, if we are not to lose the value of some three hundred years of hungering and striving for knowledge. And it is perfectly possible to recognize the rediscovery of subjective reality as a climactic achievement of science itself—making it possible once again for men of science to be serious philosophers. What we lose from this development is only the delusion that from endless collection of "objective" facts we can finally construct a "sure-thing" science of man; and we gain, to take its place, a growing awareness of the subjective potentialities of human beings.

Abraham H. Maslow. *I—Thou Knowledge*

Abraham Maslow was one of the founders of humanistic psychology, which might be described as the effort to tell academic psychologists what the moral philosophers, poets, dramatists, prophets, novelists, statesmen, judges, seasoned newspaper reporters, and just about every decently intelligent man, woman, child, and dog knew all along. Namely, that people are neither machines nor performing rats in a maze. In short, another bone-wearying attempt to undo the

From *The Psychology of Science: A Reconnaissance* (New York: Harper & Row, 1966), pp. 102–4, 107–110, 112–114, 115–117. Copyright © 1966 by Abraham H. Maslow. Reprinted by permission of the publisher.

learned follies of scientism. Maslow's psychology was distinguished by his eagerness to integrate the insights of art and mysticism (especially the Taoist tradition) into his work, to take seriously the claims of transcendent consciousness, and to draw his image of sanity from the example of history's great souls rather than from Pavlov's sad menagerie. All this despite his own early background in Watsonian behaviorism. The book from which this selection comes, *The Psychology of Science,* is one of Maslow's finest and freest efforts; a unique contribution to the reconstruction of the sciences.

HISTORICALLY SCIENCE first concerned itself with physical impersonal, inanimate things—planets, falling objects—and with equally impersonal mathematics. It went on to study living things in the same spirit, and finally about a century ago it deliberately brought the human being into the laboratory to study him in the same ways that had already proved so successful. He was to be studied as an object dispassionately, neutrally, quantitatively, in controlled experimental situations. The choice of "problem" tended to be whatever was susceptible to handling in this way. (Of course, at the same time an entirely different kind of psychology was evolving among psychiatrists in the clinic, out of an entirely different tradition and with different laws, rules, and methods.)

The "scientific" study of the human being was simply a more difficult, more exasperating application of the methodology of physics, astronomy, biology, etc., to an irritatingly unsuitable object. He was a special case, so to speak, a peripheral example on the edge of impersonal scientific method. I propose that instead of this impersonal centering point we take the human person as the starting or centering point. Let us try to take knowledge of the person as the model case from which to create paradigms or models of methodology, conceptualization, and *Weltanschauung*, of philosophy and epistemology.

What are the consequences (for the moment) of taking as the ultimate bit of knowledge that which occurs in the I-Thou, interpersonal, Agapean-love relationships between two people. Let us think of this knowledge as "normal," "basic," routine, as our basic measuring stick to judge how "knowledgy" any bit of knowledge is. Examples, not always reciprocal, are a friend knowing a friend, two persons loving each other, a parent knowing a child, or a child knowing a parent, a brother knowing a brother, a therapist knowing a patient, etc. In such relationships it is characteristic that the knower is involved with what he knows. He is not distant; he is close. He is not cool about it; he is warm. He is not unemotional; he is emotional. He has empathy, intuition for the object of knowledge, i.e., he feels identified with it, the same as it, to some degree and in some manner identical with it. He cares.

The good mother can often communicate better with her child than pediatricians or psychologists can. If these doctors have any sense, they use her as an interpreter or translator, and often enough they ask, "What is he trying to say?" Long time friends, especially married ones, understand each other, predict and communicate with each other in ways totally mysterious to spectators.

The ultimate limit, the completion toward which this kind of interpersonal knowledge moves, is through intimacy to the mystical fusion in which the two people become one in a phenomenological way that has been best described by mystics, Zen Buddhists, peak experiencers, lovers, estheticians, etc. In this experience of fusion a knowing of the other comes about through *becoming* the other, i.e., it becomes experiential knowledge from within. I know it because I know myself, and it has now become part of myself. Fusion with the object of knowledge permits experiential knowledge. And since experiential knowledge is the best kind of knowledge for many human purposes, a good mode of cognizing an object is to move toward fusion with it. And certainly since a good move toward fusion with anyone is to care for him and even to love him, we wind up with a "law" of learning and cognizing: Do you want to know? Then care!

Less extreme than mystical fusion is the therapeutic growth relationship. I confine myself here to all the insight-uncovering, Taoistic, nondirective therapies, e.g., Freud, Rogers, existential therapy. Much has been written about transference, encounter, unconditional positive regard, and the like, but all have in common the explicit awareness of the necessity of a particular kind of relationship that dispels fear, that permits the one receiving therapy to see himself more truly and thus gives him control over self-approved and self-disapproved aspects of himself. . . .

Knowing persons is complicated by the fact that so much of their motivational lives is interpersonal. The basic needs are satisfied or frustrated generally by other people. If you are trying to understand another person, it is better if he feels unthreatened with you, if he feels you accept, understand, and like him, perhaps even love him, if he feels that you respect him, and if he feels that you do not threaten his freedom to be himself. If on the other hand you dislike him or disrespect him, if you feel contempt or disapproval, if you look down on him, or if you "rubricize" him, i.e., if you refuse to see him as an individual, then the person will close off much of himself and refuse to let himself be seen. . . . He may even with secret malice deliberately give you wrong information. This happens often enough to ethnologists, psychotherapists, sociologists, public opinion pollers, child psychologists, and many others. . . .

We have been taught and retaught that *the* path to reliable knowledge is always the same whether you wish to study molecules or men. And now we are being told that maybe there are different paths for these two kinds of study. Occasionally there is even an implication that maybe the technique for studying humans may be generalized one day so as to *include* the study of molecules, so that we may even wind up again with a monistic epistemology but with a different centering point!

Something of this sort, this acquiring of knowledge through an interpersonal relationship of intimacy between knower and known, also happens, perhaps in lesser degree, in other areas of science. Ethology comes to mind at once. But all forms of knowledge derived "clinically" by physicians share some of these characteristics also. So does social anthropology. So do many branches of sociology, political science, economics, history, and possibly all the social sciences. Perhaps also we could add all or many of the linguistic sciences.

But I wish to make a more important point. It is not necessary to "choose up sides" or to vote a straight party ticket. It is true that we could make a hierarchy of sciences or of all areas of knowledge, ranging from greatest to least involvement in a relationship. But I wish to raise the more radical question: can *all* the sciences, *all* knowledge be conceptualized as a resultant of a loving or caring interrelationship between knower and known? What would be the advantages to us of setting this epistemology alongside the one that now reigns in "objective science"? Can we simultaneously use both?

My own feeling is that we can and should use both epistemologies as the situation demands. I do not see them as contradictory but as enriching each other. There is no reason not to include both weapons in the armory of any knower who wants to know *anything*. We must entertain the possibility that even the astronomer or geologist or chemist might be able to perceive more wholly even that which is least personal. I mean the conscious, verbalized, formulated possibility, because I am already convinced that some astronomers and some chemists, etc., secretly relate to their "problems" in ways analogous to those of lovers to their loved ones.

"Love for" the Object of Study

The meaning of "love for" the object to be known, understood, and appreciated has to be seen more clearly in its complexities. At the least it must mean "interest in" the object of study. It is difficult to see or hear that which is totally uninteresting or boring. It is also difficult to think about it, to remember it, to keep oneself at the job, to stick to it. All the defensive and resistive powers of the person can be mobilized into action when one is forced by some external pressure to study something totally uninteresting. One forgets, one thinks of other things, the mind wanders, fatigue sets in, intelligence seems to diminish. In a word, one is likely to do a poor job unless one is minimally interested in the task and drawn to it. At least a little passion (or libidinizing) seems to be needed.

True, it is possible to be dutiful, and even a child will do many jobs in school without interest or with only external interest in order to please the teacher. But such children bring up other problems, too profound to go into here, of training of the character, of the enriching of autonomy, of the dangers of mere docility. I mention them because I do not wish to fall into the black-white dichotomy that is so easy here. In any case there is little question about the simple statement that for the best learning, perceiving, understanding, and remembering of a person, it is desirable to be interested, involved, to have "a little bit of love," to be at least a little fascinated and drawn.

So far as the scientist is concerned, he knows that this is true for him if only because scientific study especially needs patience, stubbornness, stick-to-it-iveness, unswerving concentration on the task, the fortitude to overcome inevitable disappointments, etc. This is a minimal statement. What is really needed for long-time scientific success is passion, fascination, obsession. The fruitful scientist is the one who talks about his "problem" in about the same spirit as he does about the woman he loves, as an end rather than as a means to other ends. Rising above all distractions and becoming lost in his work means that he is not divided. All his intelligence is available for the one purpose that he is entirely given to. He gives it everything he's got.

This can be meaningfully called an act of love, and there are certain definite advantages in such a phrasing. Similarly it is meaningful to expect better work from the one who loves his work and his problem. This is why I think it will help us, even as scientists in the strictest sense, to study carefully the paradigm of "knowledge through love" that we can see most purely in lovers or in the parent-child relationship or, suitably translated into naturalistic terms, in theological and mystical literature. . . .

Fusion-Knowledge

These love relationships that can go over into the mystic experience of fusion with the world give us our end point (*beyond* knowledge through love for the object) of knowledge by fusion with the object, by becoming one with it. This can then be considered for theoretical purposes to become experiential knowledge, knowledge from within, by *being* what we are knowing. At least this is the ideal limit to which such knowledge approaches or tries to approach.

This is not so far-out as it may sound. A respectable way of studying schizophrenia is to try to *be* schizophrenic temporarily by the use of appropriate chemicals, or to have been schizophrenic and recovered. One can then more easily identify with the schizophrenic. One of the most loved and respected of the neobehavioristic rat psychologists, Edward Tolman, admitted once in defiance of his own official theorizing that when he wanted to predict what a rat would do, he tried to identify with the rat, to feel like one, and then to ask himself, "Now what would I do?" Much of what we know about Communists has been taught us by reformed Communists, who can remember how it felt to be one. The same would be true for John Birchers, and I await eagerly such a retrospective account of how it felt to be a John Bircher.

Another kind of example, following the same

paradigm in a different field, is that of the ethnologist. You can learn many facts about a tribe that you dislike or by whom you are disliked, but there are definite limits to what you can then get to know. In order to know your Indians rather than merely to know about them, you have to melt into the culture to some extent. If you "become" a Blackfoot Indian, then you can answer many questions simply by introspection.

Even at the impersonal extreme it is possible to differentiate the two feels of looking through a telescope. One can peep through the telescope at the moon, like a peeping Tom (spectator, outsider) peeping through a keyhole at the alien, the distant, the other, the far away (which we are not and never can be). Or you can sometimes forget yourself, get absorbed, fascinated, and be out there in the middle of what you are looking at, *in* that world rather than outside it peering in. This can be likened to the difference between being a member of a family and being an orphan out in the dark cold street, wistfully looking in through the window at the warm family inside. Colin Wilson's books are full of examples of outsiders and wistful peepers.

Similarly one can be within the microscopic world, or one can be outside it, looking with your eye through the microscope at the slide that is an object out there. You can listen to organ music judiciously, calmly examining it to hear how good it is and whether it is worth the money you paid for the ticket. Or you can suddenly get caught up by it and become the music and feel it pulse through your insides, so that you are not in some other place. If you are dancing and the rhythm "gets you," you can slip over to being inside the rhythm. You can identify with the rhythm. You can become its willing instrument.

Two Kinds of Objectivity

The term "scientific objectivity" has, in effect, been preempted by the physics-centered theorists of science and bent to the use of their mechanomorphic *Weltanschauung*. It was certainly necessary for astronomers and physicists to assert their freedom to see what was before their eyes rather than having truth determined a priori by the church or the state. This is the kernel of sense in the concept of "value-free science." But it is this generalization, uncritically accepted today by many, that has crippled so many human and social scientists. . . .

Classically, "scientific objectivity" has been most successfully achieved when its objects were most distant from human aspirations, hopes, and wishes. It is easy to feel uninvolved, detached, clear-eyed, and neutral if one is studying the nature of rocks or heat or electrical currents. One doesn't identify with a moon. One doesn't "care" about it as one does about one's child. It is easy to take the laissez-faire attitude with oxygen or hydrogen and to have non-interfering curiosity, to be Taoistically receptive, to let things be themselves. To be blunt about it, it is easy to be neutrally objective, fair, and just when you don't care about the outcome, when you can't identify or sympathize, when you neither love or hate.

But what happens with this framework of ideas and attitudes when we move over into the human and social realm, when we try to be objective about people we love or hate, about our loyalties or values, about our very selves? We are then no longer laissez-faire, impersonal, uninvolved, unidentified, without stakes. Accordingly it becomes far more difficult to be "laissez-faire objective" or "not-caring objective." Now there are new hazards.

In the effort to achieve "scientific," i.e., uninvolved, laissez-faire, don't-care objectivity, the anthropologist, for instance, may buy the whole package that he mistakenly ties to this kind of objectivity. He may become scientistic rather than scientific, may feel it necessary to drown his human feelings for the people he studies, may quantify whether necessary or not, and may wind up with accurate details and a false whole. (The best approach to reading in ethnology is still a discreet mix of technical monographs, the better travel reports, and the impressionistic writings of the more poetic and humanistic anthropologists.) . . .

Briefly stated, my thesis is: if you love something or someone enough at the level of Being, then you can enjoy its actualization of itself, which means that you will not want to interfere with it, since you love it as it is in itself. You will then be able to perceive it in a noninterfering way, which means leaving it alone. This in turn means that you will be able to see it as is, uncontaminated by your selfish

wishes, hopes, demands, anxieties, or preconcep-
tions. Since you love it as it is in itself, neither will
you be prone to judge it, use it, improve it, or in
any other way to project your own values into it.
This also tends to mean more concrete experiencing
and witnessing; less abstracting, simplifying, organizing, or intellectual manipulation. Leaving it
alone to be itself also implies a more holistic, global
attitude and less active dissecting. It adds up to
this: you may be fond enough of someone to dare
to see him just as he is; if you love something the
way it is, you won't change it. Therefore you may
then see it (or him) as it is in its own nature, un-
touched, unspoiled, i.e., objectively. The greater
your Being-Love of the person, the less your need
to be blind.

Michael Glenn. *Radical Therapy: A Manifesto*

The privacy of the person is but half of human
reality. The person blends naturally into community. Eventually, the claims of fellowship make
themselves felt *from within our own sense of
identity*, even in conditions of withdrawal. Jesus
returned from the wilderness; the Buddha came
down from his mountain retreat; St. Francis took
to the road to find ears for his message. Even

From *The Radical Therapist*, April–May 1970. Reprinted
by permission of the publisher.

in monastic isolation, the primary duty of the brothers is to pray for the souls of mankind. The person can only be provisionally parted off from others.

The search for personal identity is the province of psychotherapy: the doctoring of souls, which in our day becomes, inevitably, a profession now skilled in many ingenious techniques. But self-discovery, lacking the social dimension, is to human liberation as masturbation is to love. We unburden our own personality only in league with our fellows, for how much of what gnaws at our heart is guilt or outrage related to special privilege, unmerited advantage, egoistic aggression, citizenly failure?

Nevertheless, much therapy today is essentially masturbatory. There is every temptation to wrap the sick soul in infantile self-indulgence and every reward to be had for such casuistic distraction—beginning with lush fees. In this perverted sense of the term, the technocracy is well on its way to being the most "therapeutic" society in history. Already in the Soviet Union, where the technocratic hand is still amateurishly heavy, the punishment for dissent is now, as a matter of course, called "therapeutic detention"; political prisons have assumed the disguise of psychiatric hospitals —and well before 1984.

Fortunately, a growing number of young therapists are alert to the dangers. Here, for example, is the manifesto Michael Glenn wrote for the initial issue of *The Radical Therapist* in 1970. The statement serves as an appropriate bridge from the discussion of person and body to the discussion of community that follows.

IN THE midst of a society tormented by war, racism and social turmoil, therapy goes on with business as usual. In fact, therapists often look suspiciously at social change and label as "disturbed" those who press towards it. Concerned with maintaining and justifying current practices, therapy avoids moving towards making life more meaningful for all people. All this is no secret. Many people in and out of therapy fields agree the situation is intolerable. Why then does it persist?

Therapists by training, what we have been taught is increasingly irrelevant, and even destructive. Our notions of therapy are obsolete: elitist, male-centered, and obsessional. Our modes of practice are often racist and exploitive. Clinging to concepts often outmoded and rarely questioned, we insulate ourselves from the society around us and support the status quo. And we can do this very successfully. The therapist in this society is safe: he lives near the top of the heap, pursuing moneyed comforts, influence, and prestige, while the rest of society is racked by violence and war. He buys land and boats while others die in the streets. Often he even seems unaware of the bias he perpetuates or of the oppression he enacts in the name of "liberation." Expert as he may be at analyzing intrapersonal forces, he is often ignorant about forces controlling the larger society in which he lives. This must be exposed and clarified.

Therapy today has become a commodity, a means of social control. We reject such an approach to people's distress. We reject the pleasant careers with which the system rewards its adherents. The social system must change, and we will be workers towards such change. But to be true instruments of change, therapy and therapists must be liberated from their own forms of oppression. . . .

Therapy has political as well as professional aspects. Radical insights within the therapy fields can alter the way we define and carry out our work. Radical insights into the larger social order can show therapy's place within that order, and suggest how it can be a more effective force for change. At the outset, we acknowledge the uneasy tension between the words RADICAL and THERAPIST. Yet many of us live daily with this tension and know only too well that it must be clarified.

Just as all people are potentially patients, so all are potentially therapists. All can attack the roots of emotional distress. We invite support from all concerned people, not just from a professional elite. We repudiate divisions among ourselves on the bias of sex, class, training, and status: we are more alike than different. Our common task is transforming therapy into a more effective popular system which can free those in distress instead of oppressing them.

We shall pursue the following points:

1 Liberating Therapy, Therapists, and Others

Therapy is dominated by gradualist models which bolster the status quo. Even well-meaning people

today find themselves trapped in a frustrating, de-
humanizing system, from which they see no solution. The revolutionary spirit of the founders of
therapy—Pinel, Freud, Reich—has been weeded out.
Intending to liberate people from their neurosis,
therapists today further "adjustment," social control,
and the commercialized society. In spite of evidence
from therapists themselves, the system remains un-
responsive, bulky, privileged and stiff. Therapy notions are a tangle of midwife myths, fantasy, and
outright bias. Therapy practice serves the free enterprise system. But contemporary therapy demands
contemporary ideas. Sensitive to notions of "coun-
ter-transference," therapists can be amazingly blind
to their own class, race, and sex bias; and to the historical moment in which they live.

Therapy's goals need clarification. Many today
are in emotional distress and seek help. What kind
of "help" will they get? From whom? Towards what
end? At what fee? Under what system? With what
orientation? And who will guarantee the competent
concern of their "therapist"?

Therapy today is a class phenomenon: a luxury
for the well-to-do. Most people receive no such
help, or are consigned to hurried, inexperienced
therapists who rely mainly on drugs. At home with
the affluent, therapy extends itself with suspicion
to other social groups, and often tries only to regulate or determine their development. Therapists
universally retreat behind the safety of a one-up
"impartial" stance. The situation is unsatisfactory.

Therapy's insights must be reevaluated and altered, and then made available to people in ways which serve their goals. As a commodity on an open market-place though, therapy is ultimately degrading.

Nor is it enough to pursue a medical model and try to develop popular programs to "treat the masses." Therapists must understand their place in the changing social and political reality: thus therapy must become more politically aware. No therapist, no person, can claim detachment from his social context. Each human act is a social and moral statement: a political fact. It then becomes important which values we hold and which of them comes first. This awareness must structure all radical therapy today: for liberation from within has to be accompanied by liberation from without.

2 *Developing New Training Programs*

Therapists are groomed for elitist, frequently escapist, and exploitive careers. Professional associations and journals legitimize such training, and the mass media touts its necessity. Yet current training perpetuates outmoded systems. In an age when everything is under question, therapy training bears down all the harder on those it teaches, as if this will abolish doubt. Hierarchical systems obviate change; and training programs, like practice, tend to stultify and wound many people. The system is slow to respond to popular needs.

Artificial barriers are created everywhere: between senior and junior staff, between therapists from various disciplines, between "professionals" and laymen. Institutional rigidity represses the need for alteration, and men of good will are lost year after year within their labyrinthine tangles.

Training programs keep therapists apart and encourage false professionalism. Course-work in other relevant fields is lacking in every discipline. Psychiatrists lack training in psychology; social workers lack training in simple drug-use; psychologists lack training in sociology. All therapists lack training in politics, art, history, and economics, which they vitally need today. Therapy is not a medical specialty, nor is it a branch of the social sciences. It is a field all its own, dealing with relationships between people; and as such it demands its own orientation and its own training programs which draw on the experience of all pertinent disciplines.

We need new training programs, not amended or expanded versions of what we already have. We need ten times as many therapy workers. We need to make better use of community resources and extend to more people the insights now available to the few. We need, not more of the same, but a wholly new approach. Finally, we need to examine the fee system which allows some therapists to obtain excessive wealth at people's expense.

Training must be de-mystified and made more open, more responsive, and more creative. New experiments are already beginning to challenge and redefine our notion of therapy. We encourage them and look forward to their results.

3 Elaborating a New Psychology of Men and Women, and New Concepts of Family and Community Life

The ways we live intimately with one another are changing. Yet much of this is poorly understood. We must look into ways in which unquestioned male-dominate ideas have influenced therapy, especially therapy of women. Men and women must both be liberated from rigid sex-stereotypes in order to develop their own potential. Deviance as a social diagnosis must not be confused with neurotic behavior.

We need to know much more about all this, for our old ideas are no longer appropriate. The nuclear family, so long revered and unchallenged, now appears as simply the most common alternative for achieving needs for intimacy and raising children. We need to evaluate the other alternatives. Similarly, we need to investigate the changing notions of men and women, as well as alternate modes of living. But unless we ourselves are freed from dogma and bias, we will never understand others who experiment with new ways. Instead we will see dangerous "sickness" everywhere.

4 Encouraging the Development of More Responsive Therapy Programs Under Client-Control

Despite all the talk about "community mental health," therapists have done little towards considering the real health needs of communities. The community mental health movement is a fraud. It has never been in popular hands. Affording a crucible of power to ambitious professionals, it often offers but another form of oppression to the people. Professionals' needs for wealth, prestige, and influence are satisfied, while distress in the community goes on as before. Bringing a skill in understanding human feelings to the community, he must learn to offer it as his clients need it, not as he would give it. More sensible forms of therapy, controlled by and responsive to community needs, must be devised and offered.

The community is its people: not the therapists, or the university, or the research teams, or big business, or the government. Therapists who enter the community may consider themselves part of it: but they cannot claim to know what is best for it. They cannot shape its needs. As radical therapists, our task is exposing the nature of current practices and pursuing innovations in therapy services: decentralized, democratic, non-institutional, and popular. We can identify and channel grievances, and help stimulate action. This way we join the search for new ways of serving the community's needs.

More than communities are being violated.
Therapists define what is appropriate and what is
not, even while claiming to be "disinterested." They
operate as forces for social control, weeding out
deviance with the label of "mentally ill." Wherever
it functions as an agent of the system, encouraging
conformity, helping people "adjust" to the realities
of exploitation, antiquated roles, and a casual de-
humanizing ethic, therapy is an instrument of oppression. Such "therapy" institutionalizes and stig-
matizes those whom society will not tolerate, numbs
minds, tranquilizes and anti-depresses, electro-
shocks, disenfranchizes, ostracizes, psychologizes,
and treats people as commodities and things. We
oppose this from the core of our being. We denounce all "therapy" which dehumanizes and vio-
lates our brothers and sisters.

5 *Encouraging New Techniques*

We encourage the search for self-realization,
singly and in groups, with the eventual goal of
growth within communities. Growth can be individual as well as collective. We support new techniques and innovations in therapy, but we decry
their use as middleclass escapist outlets or as vehicles for profiteering by some in our field. Effective
techniques should be popularly available.

New forms of therapy are important in our move
towards liberation. They deserve sympathetic and
critical evaluation, freed from insistence that whatever exists now is best. So long as innovations are

honest and open and are not used to exploit people, we are interested in them. Moves toward group and communal experience, as well as individual growth, can help free us from inner as well as outer forms of repression.

At the same time, we are alarmed by the use of insights from therapy fields to extend institutional and governmental control, through required psychological tests for employee-applicants, inappropriate in depth interviews, and the use of therapists as consultant-engineers for third parties such as corporations, the military, and universities. Psychological innuendo in advertising is also questionable on moral grounds, and must be reexamined. Therapy cannot escape responsibility for the over-sexualization of every commodity on the market; and for the under-sexualization of sex itself.

6 Confronting the Way Our Society Functions

We are concerned with the social milieu in which we all live, and with its effect on psychological well-being. Thus we join the crusade against violation of our natural resources: whether through encroachment on our minds by advertising, the mass media, stereotyped education, and out-dated cultural myths; or through the blatant destruction of our environment's wholesomeness through air- and water-pollution, overpopulation, chemical and industrial waste, and unlivable cities. Our technology might create an environment free from scarcity and want, clean and aesthetically pleasing. Instead, it destroys whatever it touches.

Just as the rivers and lakes are destroyed by an arrogant, unfeeling technology, so our sense of humanness is barraged daily by the mass media. Advertising and the consumer-economy make every person a thing. The measure of success becomes accumulated objects, wealth, and notoriety; not the well-being of one's family and self, community and world. We must realize that many people called "mentally ill" have been socially traumatized by our society, which creates and exacerbates emotional suffering. While we do not pretend that all mental suffering is socially caused, we are alert to the social and political roots of much of it. Failing to pursue this would be negligence and complicity.

Beyond the environmental ruin and the consumer-economy lies the constant presence of war. Breaking out now on many fronts at once, war's results are always the same: destruction of people, killing and maiming, disruption of family and community life, violence, brutality, senseless suffering. The internal ills our society now experiences have already "brought the war home." What we practice internationally, we now suffer nationally and locally. We are all affected by such brutality, and by the ultimate madness of our nuclear weapons. Unless we as therapists and people can look beyond "professional" issues and approach the social and political roots of suffering, we act as unknowing agents for the established order. . . .

While drawing on therapeutic tradition, we should

de-professionalize and de-mystify therapy work. Our view of existing institutions is radically critical: but then it is no secret how bad things have become. We will make people aware of the situation, and pursue programs for change. In this exciting venture, we invite support and participation from all who help us redefine therapy and make it more a responsive, meaningful human pursuit.

Denise Levertov. "During the Eichmann Trial: When we look up"

> When we look up
> Each from his being
> *Robert Duncan*

He had not looked,
pitiful man whom none

pity, whom all
must pity if they look

into their own face (given
only by glass, steel, water

barely known) all
who look up

to see—how many
faces? How many

seen in a lifetime? (Not those
that flash by, but those

into which the gaze wanders
and is lost

and returns to tell
Here is a mystery,

a person, an
other, an I?

Count them.
Who are five million?)

'I was used from the nursery
to obedience

all my life . . .
Corpselike

obedience.' Yellow
calmed him later—

'a charming picture'
yellow of autumn leaves in

Wienerwald, a little
railroad station
nineteen-o-eight, Lemburg,

yellow sun
on the stepmother's teatable

Franz Joseph's beard
blessing his little ones.

It was the yellow
of the stars too,

stars that marked
those in whose faces

you had not
looked. 'They were cast out

as if they were
some animals, some beasts.'

'And what would disobedience
have brought me? And

whom would it have served?'
'I did not let my thoughts

dwell on this—I had
seen it and that was

enough!, (The words
'slur into a harsh babble')

'A spring of blood
gushed from the earth.'
Miracle

unsung. I see
a spring of blood gush from the earth—

Earth cannot swallow
so much at once

a fountain
rushes towards the sky

unrecognized
a sign—.

Pity this man who saw it
whose obedience continued—

he, you, I, which shall I say?
He stands

isolate in a bulletproof
witness-stand of glass,

a cage, where we may view
ourselves, an apparation

telling us something he
does not know: we are members

one of another.

II. BODY

1. Man has no Body distinct from his Soul; for that call'd Body is a portion of Soul discern'd by the five senses, the chief inlets of Soul in this age.
2. Energy is the only life, and is from the Body; and Reason is the bound or outward circumference of Energy.
3. Energy is Eternal Delight.

The ancient tradition that the world will be consumed in fire at the end of six thousand years, is true, as I have heard from Hell.

For the cherub with his flaming sword is hereby commanded to leave his guard at the tree of life; and when he does, the whole creation will be consumed and appear infinite and holy, whereas it now appears finite & corrupt.

This will come to pass by an improvement of sensual enjoyment.

(William Blake, from "The Marriage of Heaven and Hell.")

Incorrigibly, we speak of body as an "it": "it" is not "us," but a thing we own, possess externally, an article of personal property.

"Body, my horse, my house, my hound . . ."

My body—*your* body—the form is grammatically correct, psychologically disastrous: For who is the "I" apart from my body? Can we even begin to conceive of ourselves *apart* from the body—except as *another* ghostly or invisible body? What most people think of as "soul" is but a spectral image of their physique, still abroad in space, the senses functioning, the frame weightless, perhaps glowing, invulnerable to harm, deathless—but *still* the body.

"How can we tell the dancer from the dance . . . ?"

Yet to say (in truth) that we *are* our body, that personality is undivided organism, that identity ramifies subtly through every cell, down finely through the rhythms of the metabolism—this smacks still of heresy, an affront to the Christian notion of "soul." Even our medical science, though non-religious, has but renamed the soul, called it "brain," and rejects the idea of organic unity, which is, originally and still, of mystic apprehension. Thus, today we have leading surgeons who toil ingeniously to peel and preserve the live brain out of its cranial shell, perhaps to transplant it (or the whole head) to another body, and so to achieve us a replaceable-parts immortality. Item: report from the *Times* of London:

MELBOURNE, SEPTEMBER 15 [1970]: A leading American surgeon claimed here today that human brain transplants are now medically feasible, but he said that the whole head would probably have to be grafted at the same time. Professor David Hume, chief of the department of surgery at the Medical College of Virginia and a pioneer of organ transplants, said . . . that the donor of the brain in such an operation would, in fact, be the recipient, as the mind would take over the body to which it was grafted, "The person whose brain was transplanted would retain his personality, as the brain is a memory bank," he said.

How revealing, this surgical psychology: "You" are your head, or rather are *in* your head—a "ghost in a machine." Head is *head*quarters policing the unruly and incompetent body, dosing it on sleeping pills, wake-up pills, sex pills, excretion pills, uppers, downers, etc. "Your" body is a vehicle which "you-in-your-head" pilot about. When body wears out, "you" need but trade it in for a later model (obtained *where*, one wonders). Eventually—who can doubt it?—we shall have better bodies (fiberglass, aluminum, no-scratch plastic) mass produced by subsidiaries of General Motors-Ford-Chrysler, every year a new improved model.

The self-body (mind-body, soul-body, spirit-body) schism is particularly pronounced in western society ("I think, therefore I am," but not—why not? —"I shit, therefore I am"), but it is very nearly universal, part of a religious psychology so ancient and dispersed that perhaps the sensed dichotomy, even though muted, must always be an adjunct of human nature—perhaps. The shamanic vision has invariably taken the form of a flight of the spirit, the body being put off and left behind, an encumbering garment. A powerful image of liberation, this, one that effectively distances the dread of death. And surely there is a germ of the truth hidden here: perhaps that the whole—the vital pattern of personality—is indeed more than the sum of its perishing parts.

But our habit is to purchase that truth at the expense of the body, ignoring that even our science no longer divorces matter from energy, but treats nature as so many shifting patterns of basic stuff. So body becomes cage, prison, dead weight. And its mortality becomes, not a defining feature of humanity, but a curse we would escape. There are few religious traditions which, like the Tantric cakra-yoga, have learned to regard body as the *unique* instrument on which the music of liberation may be played.

We have only barely begun to know ourselves *in* the body, *through* the body, *as* the body. Science, though casting out disembodied entities like soul, is no help in the matter, since it is fundamentally ascetic. As Walter Kaufmann observes, the empiricism of modern science has become "empiricide," a killing off of immediate sensory experience in favor of mathematical and theoretical abstractions: head-knowing. On the other hand, we suffer with various kinky erotic obsessions which can now be easily packaged for merchandizing as "sexual freedom," but do nothing to redeem the body from its fallen state, being but another lot of abstractions— "sex in the head."

Fortunately, here and there—mainly in the growth centers of the Human Potentials Movement—people have begun at last to experiment with organismic therapies (gestalt, sensory awareness, structural integration, trust-touch-and-tenderness) that may yet make us sane and whole. It is by way of these integrative psychiatric yogas that we are finding our way back to the life and death meaning of organism. Perhaps in this—as Norman O. Brown suggests—lies the meaning of body's resurrection.

Or, as Sri Aurobindo has put it:

The obstacle which the physical represents to the spiritual is no argument for the rejection of the physical; for in the unseen providence of things our greatest difficulties are our best opportunities. Rather, the perfecting of the body also should be the last triumph.

Norman O. Brown. *The Resurrection of the Body*

"Our real choice," Norman Brown has written, "is between holy and unholy madness. . . . Freud is a measure of our unholy madness, as Nietzsche is the prophet of the holy madness, of Dionysus, the mad truth."

Life Against Death was Brown's exploratory descent into "the unholy madness": the dominion of death-in-life which is called "history." Doubtless his thesis—Freud's thesis amplified and sounded unflinchingly to its depths—is correct: the dark side of civilized achievement has been instinctual repression, the ruthless degradation of the body. Doubtless too the body must be redeemed and given its prelapsarian dignity if Eros and Thanatos are at last to make their peace within us. But Brown leaves us with the question,

From *Life Against Death* (Middletown, Conn.: Wesleyan University Press, 1959). Copyright © 1959 by Wesleyan University. Reprinted by permission of the publisher.

now made the more pointed by his study: where is the line to be drawn between sick repression and that loving discipline for lack of which energy dissipates, giving life no shape?

THE PATH of sublimation, which mankind has religiously followed at least since the foundation of the first cities, is no way out of the human neurosis, but, on the contrary, leads to its aggravation. Psychoanalytical theory and the bitter facts of contemporary history suggest that mankind is reaching the end of this road. Psychoanalytical theory declares that the end of the road is the dominion of death-in-life. History has brought mankind to that pinnacle on which the total obliteration of mankind is at last a practical possibility. At this moment of history the friends of the life instinct must warn that the victory of death is by no means impossible; the malignant death instinct can unleash those hydrogen bombs. For if we discard our fond illusion that the human race has a privileged or providential status in the life of the universe, it seems plain that the malignant death instinct is a built-in guarantee that the human experiment, if it fails to attain its possible perfection, will cancel itself out, as the dinosaur experiment canceled itself out. But jeremiads are useless unless we can point to a better way. Therefore the question confronting mankind is the abolition of repression—in traditional Christian language, the resurrection of the body.

We have already done what we could to extract from psychoanalytical theory a model of what the resurrected body would be like. The life instinct, or sexual instinct, demands activity of a kind that, in contrast to our current mode of activity, can only be called play. The life instinct also demands a union with others and with the world around us based not on anxiety and aggression but on narcissism and erotic exuberance.

But the death instinct also demands satisfaction; as Hegel says in the *Phenomenology*, "The life and knowledge of God may doubtless be described as love playing with itself; but this idea sinks into triviality, if the seriousness, the pain, the patience and the labor of the Negative are omitted." The death instinct is reconciled with the life instinct only in a life which is not repressed, which leaves no "unlived lines" in the human body, the death instinct then being affirmed in a body which is willing to die. And, because the body is satisfied, the death instinct no longer drives it to change itself and make history, and therefore, as Christian theology divined, its activity is in eternity.

At the same time—and here again Christian theology and psychoanalysis agree—the resurrected body is the transfigured body. The abolition of repression would abolish the unnatural concentrations of libido in certain particular bodily organs— concentrations engineered by the negativity of the morbid death instinct, and constituting the bodily base of the neurotic character disorders in the human ego. In the words of Thoreau: "We need pray for no higher heaven than the pure senses can furnish, a purely sensuous life. Our present senses are

but rudiments of what they are destined to become."
The human body would become polymorphously
perverse, delighting in that full life of all the body
which it now fears. The consciousness strong enough
to endure full life would be no longer Apollonian
but Dionysian—consciousness which does not observe the limit, but overflows; consciousness which
does not negate any more.

If the question facing mankind is the abolition of
repression, psychoanalysis is not the only point of
view from which the question can and should be
raised. We have already indicated that the question
is intrinsic to Christian theology. The time has come
to ask Christian theologians, especially the neo-
orthodox, what they mean by the resurrection of the
body and by eternal life. Is this a promise of immortality after death? In other words, is the psychological premise of Christianity the impossibility of
reconciling life and death either in "this" world or
the "next," so that flight from death—with all its
morbid consequences—is our eternal fate in "this
world" and in "the next"? For we have seen that
the perfect body, promised by Christian theology,
enjoying that perfect felicity promised by Christian
theology, is a body reconciled with death.

In the last analysis Christian theology must either
accept death as part of life or abandon the body.
For two thousand years Christianity has kept alive
the mystical hope of an ultimate victory of Life over
Death, during a phase of human history when Life
was at war with Death and hope could only be
mystical. But if we are approaching the last days,

Christian theology might ask itself whether it is only the religion of fallen humanity, or whether it might be asleep when the bridegroom comes. Certain it is that if Christianity wishes to help mankind toward that erasure of the traces of original sin which Baudelaire said was the true definition of progress, there are priceless insights in its tradition—insights which have to be transformed into a system of practical therapy, something like psychoanalysis, before they are useful or even meaningful.

The specialty of Christian eschatology lies precisely in its rejection of the Platonic hostility to the human body and to "matter," its refusal to identify the Platonic path of sublimation with the ultimate salvation, and its affirmation that eternal life can only be life in a body. Christian asceticism can carry punishment of the fallen body to heights inconceivable to Plato; but Christian hope is for the redemption of that fallen body. Hence the affirmation of Tertullian: *"Resurget igitur caro, et quidem omnis, et quidem ipsa, et quidem integra*—The body will rise again, all of the body, the identical body, the entire body." The medieval Catholic synthesis between Christianity and Greek philosophy, with its notion of an immortal soul, compromised and confused the issue; only Protestantism carries the full burden of the peculiar Christian faith. Luther's break with the doctrine of sublimation (good works) is decisive; but the theologian of the resurrected body is the cobbler of Görlitz, Jacob Boehme. . . .

Whatever the Christian churches do with him,

Boehme's position in the Western tradition of mystic hope of better things is central and assured. Backward he is linked, through Paracelsus and alchemy, to the tradition of Christian gnosticism and Jewish cabalism; forward he is linked, through his influence on the romantics Blake, Novalis, and Hegel, with Freud. We have argued that psychoanalysis has not psychoanalyzed itself until it places itself inside the history of Western thought—inside the general neurosis of mankind. So seen, psychoanalysis is the heir to a mystical tradition which it must affirm. . . .

Boehme, like Freud, understands death not as a mere nothing but as a positive force either in dialectical conflict with life (in fallen man), or dialectically unified with life (in God's perfection). Thus, says Benz, "Our life remains a struggle between life and death, and as long as this conflict lasts, anxiety lasts also." In Boehme's concept of life, the concept of play, or love-play, is as central as it is in Freud's; and his concept of the spiritual or paradisical body of Adam before the Fall recognizes the potent demand in our unconscious both for an androgynous mode of being and for a narcissistic mode of self-expression, as well as the corruption in our current use of the oral, anal, and genital functions. It is true that Boehme does not yet accept the brutal death of the individual physical body, and therefore makes his paradisical body ambiguously immaterial, without oral, anal, and genital organs; and yet he clings obstinately to the body and to bodily pleasure, and therefore says that Adam was "magically" able to eat and enjoy the "essence" of things, and "magically" able to reproduce and to have sexual pleasure in the act of reproduction. Boehme is caught in these dilemmas because of his insight into the corruption of the human body, his insight that all life is life in the body, and, on the other hand, his inability to accept a body which dies. No Protestant theologian has gone further; or rather, later Protestantism has preferred to repress the problem and to repress Boehme. . . .

Psychoanalysis accepts the death of the body; but psychoanalysis has something to learn from body mysticism, occidental and oriental, over and above the wealth of psychoanalytical insights contained in it. For these mystics take seriously, and traditional psychoanalysis does not, the possibility of human perfectibility and the hope of finding a way out of the human neurosis into that simple health that animals enjoy, but not man.

As Protestantism degenerated from Luther and Boehme, it abandoned its religious function of criticizing the existing order and keeping alive the mystical hope of better things; in psychoanalytical terminology, it lost contact with the unconscious and with the immortal repressed desires of the unconscious. The torch passed to the poets and philosophers of the romantic movement. The heirs of Boehme are Blake, Novalis, Hegel, and, as Professor R. D. Gray has recently shown, Goethe. (See his

Goethe The Alchemist.) These are the poets whom
Freud credited with being the real discoverers of
the unconscious.

Not only toward the mystics but also toward the
poets psychoanalysis must quit its pretension of
supramundane superiority. Instead of exposing the
neuroses of the poets, the psychoanalysts might
learn from them, and abandon the naive idea that
there is an immense gap, in mental health and intellectual objectivity, between themselves and the
rest of the world. In the world's opinion, in the
eyes of common sense, Novalis is crazy, and Ferenczi also: the world will find it easier to believe
that we are all mad than to believe that the psychoanalysts are not. And further, it does not seem to be
the case that the psychoanalytical mode of reaching
the unconscious has superannuated the poetic, or
artistic, mode of attaining the same objective. Anyone conversant both with modern literature and
with psychoanalysis knows that modern literature is
full of psychoanalytical insights not yet grasped, or
not so clearly grasped, by "scientific" psychoanalysis.
And anyone who loves art knows that psychoanalysis has no monopoly on the power to heal. What
the times call for is an end to the war between
psychoanalysis and art—a war kept alive by the
sterile "debunking" approach of psychoanalysis to
art—and the beginning of cooperation betwen the
two in the work of therapy and in the task of making the unconscious conscious. A little more Eros
and less strife.

Modern poetry, like psychoanalysis and Protestant

theology, faces the problem of the resurrection of the body. Art and poetry have always been altering our ways of sensing and feeling—that is to say, altering the human body. And Whitehead rightly discerns as the essence of the "Romantic Reaction" a revulsion against abstraction (in psychoanalytical terms, sublimation) in favor of the concrete sensual organism, the human body. "Energy is the only life, and is from the Body. . . . Energy is Eternal Delight," says Blake. . . .

The "magical" body which the poet seeks is the "subtle" or "spiritual" or "translucent" body of occidental mysticism, and the "diamond" body of oriental mysticism, and, in psychoanalysis, the polymorphously perverse body of childhood. Thus, for example, psychoanalysis declares the fundamentally bisexual character of human nature; Boehme insists on the androgynous character of human perfection; Taoist mysticism invokes feminine passivity to counteract masculine aggressivity; and Rilke's poetic quest is a quest for a hermaphroditic body. There is an urgent need for elucidation of the interrelations between these disparate modes of articulating the desires of the unconscious. Jung is aware of these interrelations, and orthodox psychoanalysts have not been aware of them. But no elucidation results from incorporation of the data into the Jungian system, not so much because of the intellectual disorder in the system, but rather because of the fundamental orientation of Jung, which is flight from the problem of the body, flight from the concept of repression, and a return to the path of sublimation. Freudianism must face the issue, and Freud himself said: "Certain practices of the mystics may succeed in upsetting the normal relations between the different regions of the mind, so that, for example, the perceptual system becomes able to grasp relations in the deeper layers of the ego and in the id which would otherwise be inaccessible to it."

Joseph Needham's interest in what we have called body mysticism, an interest which underlies his epoch-making work *Science and Civilization in China*, reminds us that the resurrection of the body has been placed on the agenda not only by psychoanalysis, mysticism, and poetry, but also by the philosophical criticism of modern science. Whitehead's criticism of scientific abstraction is, in psychoanalytical terms, a criticism of sublimation. His protest against "The Fallacy of Misplaced Concreteness" is a protest on behalf of the living body as a whole: "But the living organ of experience is the living body as a whole"; and his protest "on behalf of value" insists that the real structure of the human body, of human cognition, and of the events cognized is both sensuous and erotic, "self-enjoyment." Whitehead himself recognized the affinity between himself and the romantic poets; and Needham of course recognizes the affinity between the philosophy of organism and mysticism. Actually Needham may be exaggerating the uniqueness of Taoism. The whole Western alchemical tradition, which urgently needs re-examination, is surely "Whiteheadian" in spirit, and Goethe, the last of the alchemists, in his "Essay on the Metamorphosis of Plants" produced the last, or the first, Whiteheadian scientific treatise. Goethe, says a modern biologist, "reached out to the reconciliation of the antithesis between the senses and the intellect, an antithesis with which traditional science does not attempt to cope."

Perhaps there are even deeper issues raised by the confrontation between psychoanalysis and the philosophy of organism. Whitehead and Needham are protesting against the inhuman attitude of modern science; in psychoanalytical terms, they are calling for a science based on an erotic sense of reality, rather than an aggressive dominating attitude toward reality. From this point of view alchemy (and Goethe's essay on plants) might be said to be the last effort of Western man to produce a science based on an erotic sense of reality. And conversely, modern science, as criticized by Whitehead, is one aspect of a total cultural situation which may be described as the dominion of death-in-life. The mentality which was able to reduce nature to "a dull affair, soundless, scentless, colourless; merely the hurrying of material endlessly, meaninglessly"—Whitehead's description—is lethal. It is an awe-inspiring attack on the life of the universe; in more technical psychoanalytical terms, its anal-sadistic intent is plain. And further, the only historian of science who uses psychoanalysis, Gaston Bachelard, concludes that it is of the essence of the scientific spirit to be mercilessly ascetic, to eliminate human enjoyment from our relation to nature, to eliminate the human senses, and finally to eliminate the human brain:

It does indeed seem that with the twentieth century there begins a kind of scientific thought in opposition to the senses, and that it is necessary to construct a theory of objectivity *in opposition to* the object. . . . It follows that the entire use of the brain is being called into question. From now on the brain is strictly no longer adequate as an instrument for scientific thought; that is to say, the brain is the *obstacle* to scientific thought. It is an obstacle in the sense that it is the coordinating center for human movements and appetites. It is necessary to think *in opposition to* the brain.

Thus modern science confirms Ferenczi's aphorism: "*Pure intelligence* is thus a product of dying, or at least of becoming mentally insensitive, and is therefore *in principle madness.*"

What Whitehead and Needham are combating is not an error but a disease in consciousness. In more technical psychoanalytical terms, the issue is not the conscious structure of science, but the unconscious premises of science; the trouble is in the unconscious strata of the scientific ego, in the scientific character-structure. Whitehead called the modern scientific point of view, in spite of its world-conquering success, "quite unbelievable." Psychoanalysis adds the crucial point: it is insane. Hence there is unlikely to be any smooth transition from the "mechanistic" point of view to the "organismic" point of view. It is unlikely that problems generated in the mechanistic system will lead to organismic solutions. The two points of view represent different instinctual orientations, different fusions of life and death. It is even doubtful that the adoption of an organismic point of view under present conditions would be a gain; it might be a relapse into naive animism. . . . Psychoanalytical therapy involves a solution to the problem of repression; what is needed is not an organismic ideology, but to change the human body so that it can become for the first time an organism— the resurrection of the body. An organism whose own sexual life is as disordered as man's is in no position to construct objective theories about the Yin and the Yang and the sex life of the universe.

The resurrection of the body is a social project facing mankind as a whole, and it will become a practical political problem when the statesmen of the world are called upon to deliver happiness instead of power, when political economy becomes a science of use-values instead of exchange-values— a science of enjoyment instead of a science of accumulation. In the face of this tremendous human problem, contemporary social theory, both capitalist and socialist, has nothing to say. Contemporary social theory (again we must honor Veblen as an exception) has been completely taken in by the inhuman abstractions of the path of sublimation, and has no contact with concrete human beings, with their concrete bodies, their concrete though repressed desires, and their concrete neuroses.

To find social theorists who are thinking about the real problem of our age, we have to go back to the Marx of 1844, or even to the philosophers influencing Marx in 1844, Fourier and Feuerbach. From

Fourier's psychological analysis of the antithesis of work and pleasure Marx obtained the concept of play, and used it, in a halfhearted way to be sure, in some of his early utopian speculations. From Feuerbach Marx learned the necessity of moving from Hegelian abstractions to the concrete senses and the concrete human body. Marx's "philosophic-economic manuscripts" of 1844 contain remarkable formulations calling for the resurrection of human nature, the appropriation of the human body, the transformation of the human senses, and the realization of a state of self-enjoyment. Thus, for example, "Man appropriates himself as an all-sided being in an all-sided way, hence as total man. [This appropriation lies in] every one of his human relationships to the world—seeing, hearing, smell, taste, feeling, thought, perception, experience, wishing, activity, loving, in short, all organs of his individuality." The human physical senses must be emancipated from the sense of possession, and then the humanity of the senses and the human enjoyment of the senses will be achieved for the first time. Here is the point of contact between Marx and Freud: I do not see how the profundities and obscurities of the "philosophic-economic manuscripts" can be elucidated except with the aid of psychoanalysis. . . .

Psychoanalytical thinking has a double relation to the dialectical imagination. It is, on the one hand (actually or potentially), a mode of dialectical consciousness; on the other hand, it contains, or ought to contain, a theory about the nature of the dialectical imagination. I say "actually or potentially" because psychoanalysis, either as a body of doctrine or an experience of the analysand, is no total revelation of the unconscious repressed. The struggle of consciousness to circumvent the limitations of formal logic, of language, and of "common sense" is under conditions of general repression never ending. . . . "Dialectical" are those psychoanalysts who continue this struggle; for the rest, psychoanalytical terminology can be a prison house of Byzantine scholasticism in which "word-consciousness" is substituting for consciousness of the unconscious.

And even if we take Freud as the model of psychoanalytical consciousness, we have argued that at such crucial points as the relation between the two instincts and the relation between humanity and animality, Freud is trapped because he is not sufficiently "dialectical." Nevertheless, the basic structure of Freud's thought is committed to dialectics, because it is committed to the vision of mental life as basically an arena of conflict; and his finest insights (for example, that when the patient denies something, he affirms it) are incurably "dialectical." Hence the attempt to make psychoanalysis out to be "scientific" (in the positivist sense) is not only vain but destructive. Empirical verification, the positivist test of science, can apply only to that which is fully in consciousness; but psychoanalysis is a mode of contacting the unconscious under conditions of general repression, when the unconscious remains in some sense repressed. To put the matter another way, the "poetry" in Freud's thought cannot be purged away, or rather such an expurgation is ex-

actly what is accomplished in "scientific" textbooks
of psychology; but Freud's writings remain unex-
purgatable. . . .

The key to the nature of dialectical thinking may
lie in psychoanalysis, more specifically in Freud's
psychoanalysis of negation. There is first the theorem
that "there is nothing in the id which can be compared to negation," and that the law of contradiction does not hold in the id. Similarly, the dream
does not seem to recognize the word "no." Instead
of the law of contradiction we find a unity of opposites: "Dreams show a special tendency to reduce
two opposites to a unity"; "Any thing in a dream
may mean its opposite." We must therefore entertain the hypothesis that there is an important connection between being "dialectical" and dreaming,
just as there is between dreaming and poetry or
mysticism. Furthermore, in his essay "The Antithetical Sense of Primal Words" Freud compares
the linguistic phenomenon of a hidden (in the
etymological root) identity between words with
antithetical meanings; he reveals the significant fact
that it was the linguistic phenomenon that gave him
the clue to the dream phenomenon, and not vice
versa. It is plain that both psychoanalysis and the
study of language (philosophical and philological)
need a marriage or at least a meeting.

And, on the other hand, Freud's essay "On Negation" may throw light on the nature of the "dialectical" dissatisfaction with formal logic. Negation is
the primal act of repression; but it at the same time
liberates the mind to think about the repressed

under the general condition that it is denied and thus remains essentially repressed. With Spinoza's formula *omnis determinatio est negatio* in mind, examine the following formulations of Freud: "A negative judgment is the intellectual substitute for repression; the 'No' in which it is expressed is the hall-mark of repression. . . . By the help of the symbol of negation, the thinking process frees itself from the limitations of repression and enriches itself with the subject-matter without which it could not work efficiently." But: "Negation only assists in undoing one of the consequences of repression—the fact that the subject-matter of the image in question is unable to enter consciousness. The result is a kind of intellectual acceptance of what is repressed, though in all essentials the repression persists."

We may therefore entertain the hypothesis that formal logic and the law of contradiction are the rules whereby the mind submits to operate under general conditions of repression. As with the concept of time, Kant's categories of rationality would then turn out to be the categories of repression. And conversely, "dialectical" would be the struggle of the mind to circumvent repression and make the unconscious conscious. But by the same token, it would be the struggle of the mind to overcome the split and conflict within itself. It could then be identified with that "synthesizing" tendency in the ego of which Freud spoke, and with that attempt to cure, inside the neurosis itself, on which Freud came finally to place his hope for therapy. As an attempt to unify and to cure, the "dialectical" consciousness would be a manifestation of Eros. And, as consciousness trying to throw off fetters of negation, the "dialectical" consciousness would be a step toward that Dionysian ego which does not negate any more.

What the great world needs, of course, is a little more Eros and less strife; but the intellectual world needs it just as much. A little more Eros would make conscious the unconscious harmony between "dialectical" dreamers of all kinds—psychoanalysts, political idealists, mystics, poets, philosophers—and abate the sterile and ignorant polemics. Since the ignorance seems to be mostly a matter of self-ignorance, a little more psychoanalytical consciousness on all sides (including the psychoanalysts) might help—a little more self-knowledge, humility, humanity, and Eros. We may therefore conclude with the concluding words of Freud's _Civilization and Its Discontents:_

> Men have brought their powers of subduing the forces of nature to such a pitch that by using them they could now very easily exterminate one another to the last man. They know this—hence arises a great part of their current unrest, their dejection, their mood of apprehension. And now it may be expected that the other of the two "heavenly forces," eternal Eros, will put forth his strength so as to maintain himself alongside of his equally immortal adversary.

And perhaps our children will live to live a full life, and so see what Freud could not see—in the old adversary, a friend.

Kay Johnson. *Proximity*

Most of what passes at present for sexual liberation is either masturbatory fantasy, mainly intended to supplement the junior executive standard of consumption, or compulsive genital virtuosity. In either case, there is little understanding of what Freud meant by *Geschlect*. The permissive society includes such a deal of antisexual sexuality.

On the other hand, there is the whole-body eroticism which many parents of the last few generations seem to have allowed their children to enjoy to a marked degree (the positive aspect of permissiveness) and which characterizes the sensual congestion of the Rock festivals. "Some chemical interchange from skin to skin," Kay Johnson calls it.

UNIVERSAL SPIRITUAL & PHYSICAL EXPRESSION OF LOVE POSSIBLE WITHOUT SIN, FORNICATION, OR ADULTERY . . .

So I have a game that I pretend, when I'm not allowed to pretend love, when no one else will pretend love with me. It's true I fall in love much more often than any one person is supposed to do. It's

From *Journal for the Protection of All Beings* No. 1, edited by Michael McClure, Lawrence Ferlinghetti, and David Maltzer. (San Francisco: City Lights Books, 1961.) Copyright © 1961 by City Lights Books. Reprinted by permission of the publisher. This selection is complete as published in the *Journal;* the many elipses it contains are the author's punctuation.

true that if I can be alone with any one person for an hour or two, I can achieve falling in love with him or her. But this is desperate, and they won't believe it, and they won't play it, my game of universal love. So I just go along, painting it.

For if they come again, I'm all trembling.

For when I see them again, my eyes cry "Lover!" And they are all ashamed and embarrassed in front of me, for the husbands have wives and the wives have husbands already, and they do not understand this thing that I must do to them, having already done it to myself, for them.

They see me, and they run from me. They run because in that moment, their eyes acclaim me, in that moment my eyes gave myself to them, entered them, and in that moment, their eyes were opened . . . and their eyes cried, being open . . . and I painted this. Yea, and when I painted the husband, the wife bought the painting, saying it was for her alone. And when I painted the wife, the husband came wearing such a cold anger that I could not paint him at all.

And of those who are single, they are terrified.

For each wants to think that I speak only to him personally, and each wants to think that I want to possess him personally, and he only, and that the invitation in my eyes is for him personally, and not for everyone as much as it is for him. Each thinks that there is just *one* consummation of this love, that this love must bear its union in a physical, sexual consummation, and that if this cannot take place . . . the love was a lie, and it was not true.

And they resent me for it and they run from me, because of it.

But what in the hell do people think Friendship is, if it is not love, if it is not the whole love, the complete love, the completely being in love, complete as with a lover. . . .

Yes, as proof of this thing, as proof of the reality of it, I could physically and mentally and emotionally sleep with everyone of them, as Saint Francis kissed the leper, I could kiss each one of them, I could unite sexually with each one of them. But how can I stop with one? I cannot stop with one. I cannot even have one at a time. I want all of them. Everyone manages to stop with one. They get one lover, and they stop with one. You have no idea the amount of will power this takes for them. They call it "infidelity," this overt expression of universal love, when it's expressed physically. But if souls love, the bodies are opened as easily, the bodies are only the houses the souls live in. If the soul is given, the body is open as easily. The soul is the key to it all, and where the soul is given, the body is open as easily.

And here's the trouble of it all.

They find if they let the soul flow out, the body is opened as easily, and everyone has no fidelity any longer, and everyone truly deep down in their soul, wants to love everyone of them, as Saint Francis kissed the leper, I could everyone, and if we were all released from the barriers of our imaginations, the whole world would turn to an ecstatic holocaust . . . and we would all be throwing our-

selves upon the bodies of each other constantly, un-
discriminately.

Because this is the nature of us.

Only a few wild ones dare give in to it.

The rest of us play at it, play at it, I say, only.

These are called flirtations. We play at it, we joke,
we kid each other about it.

Thus must the souls be damned, thus must the
souls be damned up, lest they flow, for if they flow,
then the bodies flow too, and have no power to stop
themselves . . . thus would our souls and bodies go
fornicating everywhere. . . .

Thus are people afraid of the love of the soul, thus
must they damn their souls up separately within
them, thus must they lock the soul in, thus must they
deny it. . . .

For where the soul is completely given, where it
is open, the body stands open as well . . . and to
realize the potentiality for the essential whoredom
of each of us . . . this is the monster that might
threaten to undo us, this is the guilt that must be
kept hidden. . . .

So heroically we inhibit, we pretend it is not so.
And to achieve love on top of this denial of love,
this takes a saint. But take our clothes off, and we
are all saints in our most simple and passionate love
for each other. . . . Remove our inhibitions, and
the love of man for man and the love of man for
woman and the love of woman for woman and the
love of woman for man is all the most basic reality
our souls and bodies have been created for . . .
this touching of each other on our skins, the phys-

ical warmth of another body, this is what we were created for. Even the warmth of an animal, even a dog's lapping in our mouths with his solicitous tongue, there is pleasure there that he loves us and touches us, we could take pleasure in it, we could kiss the animal back, on his tongue, with our tongue. Our tongues are willing, our hearts are willing, but something tells us this is wrong, this touching of wet tongues between two animals, this love, and so we have convinced ourselves it is repulsive, that we do not want to be got wet by his tongue, that it is an imposition of him to want to lap us up, and we will not surrender to it, no we will not surrender to any kind of love. And how we do succeed at this! Lordy, we succeed so that we draw away instinctively from a dog's wet tongue. We succeed to such an extent that we do not want his muddy paws on our clean clothes. We succeed to such an extent we have really convinced ourselves that our dresses, our white slacks, should not be over-run by dog hairs, by fleas, by animal smells, nor our skin even by his touch. . . .

We convince ourselves we don't like cats at all.

They, more than the dogs, are too openly sensuous. Do you know what they overtly do when they come and sit on your stomach at night? Do you know the rhythm they have, how with their paws they innocently knead your stomach and dare purr at the same time and rub themselves, their whole selves, against you, indecently as love and sensuality itself. . . .

Yea, should we give in to one, should we dare give

into one, and love just one little animal, we should
be undone for every dog and cat approaching us,
we should be utterly undone for every human being
approaching us. . . .

For the soul has been sublimated into sex.

Who did it, if Freud did not do it? Every yearn-
ing of the soul of man for man or the soul of woman
for man or the soul of man for woman or of woman
for woman, has been sublimated into a sexual significance, and this is all today that we are conscious
of when we say love, when we say sensuality.

The dog, the cat, when they rub us with their
flesh, yes, with their flesh, when the cat kneads and
purrs, when the dogs want to kiss us in the mouths
. . . oh the sensual and beautiful soul of the animal,
it's not the full sexual union of its sexual organs with
yours it's asking for . . . but simply closeness, the
closeness of its little sensual soul, which IS its body
. . . the touching of the skin . . . the lying down
close to each other and curled up against each
other . . . the transmitting of warmth from skin to
skin, the transmitting of kisses and moisture . . .
the lying close to each other for a long time . . .
exchanging of something electrical, a charge that
leaps from skin to skin . . . this touching of skins
as friends lie down together, as friends want to be
holding each other's hands, want to be putting an
arm across a shoulder, want to be somehow un-
accountably sitting close, next to each other.

This is in itself, fulfillment.

This is something which is not known, today.

This is something Freud had no idea of, that

where there is love, there is no lust connected to the sexual organ, the lust is for looking, the lust is for proximity, the lust is for touching of the hand, the skin, the lust is for the interchange of some cosmic, electrical energy . . . and it is done, it is accomplished simply by proximity . . . by the sharing and exchanging of warmth, by the touching of skin to skin, it is done by body warmth, as a child, when it wants to be loved wants the body warmth of its mother, the skin contact.

The sexual organs have a different kind of love all by themselves. But the love simply of the skin for another skin, of one bodily warmth for another warmth, of the contact of one being for the contact of another being, this is a spiritual sensuosity . . . which does not *seek* to consummate itself, by the use of the sexual organs, which is satisfied innocently and fully and completely, simply by the sharing of warmth, by the skin contact, by the kiss, by moisture. . . .

And the soul is fully and innocently contented in this contract. *It* is contented, where there is the love of the soul. But where there is not the love of the soul, then the sexual organs rise and open in their own private lust, having nothing to do with the soul. Having private laws of their own.

And even where there is the love of the soul, all innocent and natural, society in its very fear of sexuality, *proclaims* that sex is what's wanted after all. So we aim for it, as if it were a target, and we will not be contented, no we will not *allow* ourselves to be contented, until we thrust our arrows in that red place, in the target's sexual centre.

But it is not sexual union the soul is after. It is some chemical interchange from skin to skin, from being to being, from proximity to proximity, from sitting next to each other, from sleeping in the same bed. From the clasping of hands, from the touching of skins.

Paul Goodman. *Polarities and Wholeness: A Gestalt Critique of "Mind," "Body," "External World"*

Gestalt means "figure," "form," perhaps better still "pattern." Starting as a theory of perception, Gestalt psychology taught the spontaneous, pattern-making activity of the senses (mainly eye, ear, and touch) which insists always on weaving atoms of data into well-shaped wholes. From this, naturally enough, followed a theory of learning based on the importance of insight—the sudden, unaccountable "falling-into-place" of scattered experience which befalls us like a sense of recognition.

Had Gestalt gone no further, this much would have buried the old behaviorism with its *tabula rasa* conception of mind. The perceiving-learning psyche, we now know (and should never have

From *Gestalt Therapy: Excitement and Growth in the Human Personality* by Frederick Perls, M.D., Ph.D., Ralph F. Hefferline, Ph.D., and Paul Goodman, Ph.D. (New York: Julian Press, 1951; Dell paperback, 1963). Reprinted by permission of The Julian Press, Inc.

forgotten) is a participant *maker* of experience, not a passive recipient. But in the hands of men like Frederick Perls (the school's most notable practitioner in America) Gestalt has at last become a psychiatric therapy in which the pattern-making potentialities of the senses are extended to the organism generally.

Because of its emphasis on the spontaneous and wholistic, its willingness to deal in the mysteries of organic self-adjustment, Gestalt has blended nicely with numerous mystical and oriental psychologies. Obviously, yoga and the Zen-Taoist vision of nature are closely related. These richly assimilative qualities have made Gestalt, in one version or another, by far the most prominent therapy in the growth centers now springing up across America. Not the least important of the school's contributions has been its closing of the mind-body schism and its ingenious use of physical technique as basic psychotherapy.

Paul Goodman needs no introduction for his work as a social philosopher. Goodman the novelist and poet is perhaps slightly less well-known. Goodman the Gestalt-Therapist is certainly least known of all. Yet his contribution in 1951 to the volume *Gestalt Therapy* (his coauthors were Ralph Hefferline and Frederick Perls) stands as one of the most persuasive theoretical statements of Gestalt principles. A small portion of the book is given here: that having to do with the Gestalt solution of the mind-body "problem."

We draw attention to the following neurotic dichotomies, some of which are universally prevalent, some of which have been dissolved in the history of psychotherapy but are still otherwise assumed, and some of which (of course) are prejudices of psychotherapy itself.

"*Body*" and "*Mind*": this split is still popularly current, although among the best physicians the psychosomatic unity is taken for granted. We shall show that it is the exercise of a habitual and finally unaware deliberateness in the face of chronic emergency, especially the threat to organic functioning, that has made this crippling division inevitable and almost endemic, resulting in the joylessness and gracelessness of our culture.

"*Self*" and "*External World*": this division is an article of faith uniformly throughout modern western science. It goes along with the previous split, but perhaps with more emphasis on threats of a political and inter-personal nature. Unfortunately those who in the history of recent philosophy have shown the absurdity of this division have mostly themselves been infected with either a kind of mentalism or materialism.

"*Emotional*" (subjective) and "*Real*" (objective): this split is again a general scientific article of faith, unitarily involved with the preceding. It is the result of the avoidance of contact and involvement and the deliberate isolation of the sensoric and motoric functions from each other. (The recent history of statistical sociology is a study in these avoidances raised to a fine art.) We shall try to show that the real is intrinsically an involvement or "engagement."

"*Infantile*" and "*Mature*": this split is an occupational disease of psychotherapy itself, springing from the personalities of the therapists and from the social role of the "cure": on the one hand a tantalizing preoccupation with the distant past, on the other the attempt to adjust to a standard of adult reality that is not worth adjusting to. Traits of childhood are disesteemed the very lack of which devitalizes the adults; and other traits are called infantile that are the introjections of adult neuroses.

"Biological" and *"Cultural"*: this dichotomy, which is the essential subject-matter of anthropology to eliminate, has in recent decades become entrenched precisely in anthropology; so that (not to mention the idiotic racialisms of one side) human nature becomes completely relative and nothing at all, as if it were indefinitely malleable. We shall try to show that this is the result of a neurotic fascination with artifacts and symbols, and the politics and culture of these, as if they moved themselves.

"Poetry" and *"Prose"*: this split, unitarily involved with all the preceding, is the result of neurotic verbalizing (and other vicarious experience) and the nausea of verbalizing as a reaction against it, and it leads some recent semanticists and inventors of languages of science and "basic" languages to disesteem human speech as though we had enough other media of communication. There are not, and there is a failure of communication. Universal terms, again, are taken as mechanical abstractions rather than expressions of insight. And correspondingly, poetry (and plastic art) becomes increasingly isolated and obscure.

"Spontaneous" and *"Deliberate"*: more generally, it is believed that the unsought and inspired belongs to special individuals in peculiar emotional states; or again to people at parties under the influence of alcohol or hasheesh; rather than being a quality of all experience. And correspondingly, calculated behavior aims at goods that are not uniquely appropriated according to one's fancy, but are in turn only good for something else (so that pleasure itself is endured as a means to health and efficiency). "Being oneself" means acting imprudently, as if desire could not make sense; and "acting sensibly" means holding back and being bored.

"Personal" and *"Social"*: this common separation continues to be the ruination of community life. It is both the effect and cause of the kind of technology and economy we have, with its division of "job" and "hobby," but no work or vocation; and of timid bureaucracies and vicarious "front" politics. It is to the credit of the therapists of interpersonal relations to try to heal this split, yet even this school, anxiously controlling the animal and sexual factors in the field, likewise usually comes to formal and symbolic rather than real communal satisfactions.

"Love" and *"Aggression"*: this split has always been the result of instinctual frustration and self-conquest, turning the hostility against the self and esteeming a reactive passionless mildness, when only a release of aggression and willingness to destroy the old situations can restore erotic contact. But in recent decades this condition has been complicated by a new high esteem given to sexual love

at the same time as the various aggressive drives are especially disesteemed as anti-social. The quality of the sexual satisfaction may perhaps be measured by the fact that the wars we acquiesce in are continually more destructive and less angry.

"Unconscious" and *"Conscious":* if taken absolutely, this remarkable division, perfected by psychoanalysis, would make all psychotherapy impossible in principle, for a patient cannot learn about himself what is unknowable to him. (He is aware, or can be made aware, of the distortions in the structure of his actual experience.) This theoretical split goes with an underestimation of the reality of dream, hallucination, play, and art, and an overestimation of the reality of deliberate speech, thought, and introspection; and in general, with the Freudian absolute division between "primary" (very early) thought-processes and "secondary" processes. Correspondingly, the "id" and the "ego" are not seen as alternate structures of the self differing in degree—the one an extreme of relaxation and loose association, the other an extreme of deliberate organization for the purpose of identification—yet this picture is given at every moment of psychotherapy. . . .

Creative Adjustment: "Organismic Self-Regulation"

With regard to the working of the organic body, there has recently been a salutary change in theory in this respect. Many therapists now speak of "organismic self-regulation," that is, that it is not necessary deliberately to schedule, to encourage or inhibit, the promptings of appetite, sexuality, and so forth, in the interests of health or morals. If these things are let be, they will spontaneously regulate themselves, and if they have been deranged, they will tend to right themselves. But the suggestion of the more total self-regulation, of all the functions of the soul, including its culture and learning, its aggression and doing the work that is attractive, along with the free play of hallucination, is opposed. The possibility that if these things are let be, in contact with the actuality, even their current derangements will tend to right themselves and come to something valuable, is met with anxiety and rejected as a kind of nihilism. (But we reiterate that the suggestion is a spectacularly conservative one, for it is nothing but the old advice of the Tao, "stand out of the way.")

Instead, every therapist knows—how?—what the "reality" is to which the patient ought to conform, or what the "health" or "human nature" is that the patient ought to realize. How does he know it? It is only too likely that by the "reality-principle" is meant the existing social arrangements, for note that with regard to physical phenomena no such need to conform is felt at all, but physical scientists generally freely hypothesize, experiment, and fail or succeed, quite without guiltiness or fear of "nature," and thereby they make ingenious machines that can "ride the whirlwind," or foolishly stir it up. . . .

From the point of view of psychotherapy, when

there is good contact—e.g., a clear bright figure freely energized from an empty background—then there is no peculiar problem concerning the relations of "mind" and "body" or "self" and "external world." Every contacting act is a whole of awareness, motor response, and feeling—a cooperation of the sensory, muscular, and vegetative systems—and contacting occurs at the surface-boundary *in* the field of the organism/environment.

We say it in this odd way, rather than "at the boundary between the organism and the environment," because . . . the definition of an animal involves its environment: it is meaningless to define a breather without air, a walker without gravity and ground, an irascible without obstacles, and so on for every animal function. The definition of an organism is the definition of an organism/environment field; and the contact-boundary is, so to speak, the specific organ of awareness of the novel situation of the field, as contrasted, for instance, with the more internal "organic" organs of metabolism or circulation that function conservatively without the need of awareness, deliberateness, selection or avoidance of novelty. In the case of a stationary plant, a field of organism/soil, air, etc., this *in*-ness of the contact-boundary is fairly simple to conceive: the osmotic membrane is the *organ of the interaction* of organism and environment, both parts being obviously active. In the case of a mobile complicated animal it is the same, but certain illusions of perception make it more difficult to conceive. The illusions . . . are simply that the mobile wins attention against the stationary background, and the more tightly complicated wins attention against the relatively simpler. But at the boundary, the interaction is proceeding from both parts.

(The verbal embarrassments here are deep in our language. Consider the confusion of usual philo sophic speech in this context, when we say "inner" and "outer." "Inner" means "inside the skin," "outer" means "outside the skin." Yet those who speak of the "external world" mean to include the body as part of the external world, and then "internal" means "inside the mind," inside the mind but not inside the body.)

Now again, as Freud and especially William James pointed out, consciousness is the result of a delaying of the interaction at the boundary. . . . And we can see at once that consciousness is functional. For if the interaction at the contact-boundary is relatively simple, there is little awareness, reflection, motor adjustment, and deliberateness; but where it is difficult and complicated, there is heightened consciousness. Increasing complexity of sensory organs means that there is need of more selectivity, as an animal becomes more mobile and adventures among more novelties. Thus, with increasing complexity we may conceive of the series: phototropism becomes conscious seeing, and this becomes deliberate attending; or osmosis becomes eating and this becomes deliberate food-taking.

Let us consider various possibilities at the contact-boundary as the interaction variously works out:

(1) If the equilibrium is easily established,

awareness, motor adjustment, and deliberateness are relaxed: the animal lives well and is as if asleep.

(2) If the tensions on both sides of the boundary have been difficult to equilibrate, and therefore there has been much deliberateness and adjustment, but now there is a relaxation: then there is the beautiful experience of esthetic-erotic absorption, when the spontaneous awareness and muscularity drinks in and dances in the environment as if self-oblivious, but in fact feeling the deeper parts of the self responding to heightened meaning of the object. The beauty of the moment comes from relaxing deliberateness and expanding in an harmonious interaction. The moment is recreative and again ends in loss of interest and sleep.

(3) The situation of danger: if the boundary becomes intolerably overworked because of environmental forces that must be rejected by extraordinary selectivity and avoidance; and

(4) The situation of frustration, starvation, and illness: if the boundary becomes intolerably tense because of proprioceptive demands that cannot be equilibrated from the environment.

In both these cases, of excess of danger and frustration, there are temporary functions that healthily meet the emergency *with the function of protecting the sensitive surface*. These reactions may be observed throughout the animal kingdom, and are of two kinds, subnormal or supernormal. On the one hand, panic, "mindless" flight, shock, anesthesis, fainting, playing dead, blotting out a part, amnesia: these protect the boundary by temporarily desensitizing it or motorically paralyzing it, waiting for the emergency to pass. On the other hand, there are devices to cushion the tension by exhausting some of the energy of tension in the agitation of the boundary itself, e.g., hallucination and dream, lively imagination, obsessive thought, brooding, and with these motor restlessness. The subactive devices seem to be adapted to protecting the boundary from environmental excess, shutting out the danger; the superactive have to do rather with proprioceptive excess, exhausting the energy—except that when, in starvation or illness, the danger-point is reached, fainting occurs.

We have thus come to another function of consciousness: to exhaust energy that cannot reach equilibrium. But note that this is again, as in the primary function, a kind of delaying: previously the delay consisted of heightened awareness, experimentation, and deliberateness in order to solve the problem; here it is delay for the sake of rest and withdrawal, when the problem cannot otherwise be solved. . . .

There are thus at the boundary of contact these two processes to meet emergencies: blotting out and hallucination. They are, let us emphasize, healthy *temporary* functions in a complicated organism/environment field.

Now at last we are in a position to explain the astonishing notion of "Mind" as against both "Body" and "External World," in place of the rather *prima facie* conception that we have been developing, of consciousness as a contact-function in a difficult organism/environment field.

This *prima facie* conception which, in modern but not greatly superior trappings, is like Aristotle's sensitive and rational soul, offers no peculiar scientific difficulties. There are definite observable and experimentable functional relations between this entity and others. There are, for example, criteria for "good contact," such as the singleness, clarity, and closure of the figure/background; grace and force of movement; spontaneity and intensity of feeling. Also the formal similarity of the observed structures of awareness, motion, and feeling in the whole; and the lack of contradiction, of the several meanings or purposes. And variations from the norm of "good contact" can be shown, analytically and experimentally, to involve both effectual and causal relations with environmental and somatic abnormalities.

Nevertheless, we must now show that the notion of "mind" as a unique isolated entity *sui generis* is not only genetically explicable but is in a sense an unavoidable illusion, *empirically given in average experience*.

For let us consider still another possibility at the contact-boundary. Conceive that instead of either the reestablishment of equilibrium or blotting-out and hallucination in a temporary emergency excess of danger and frustration, there exists a chronic low-tension disequilibrium, a continual irk of danger and frustration, interspersed with occasional acute crises, and never fully relaxed. This is a dismal hypothesis, but it is unfortunately historical fact for most of us. . . .

In the chronic low-grade emergency that we have been describing, what dispositions of the contact-boundary tend to the possible simplicity of the field? Both of the emergency functions, deliberate blotting-out and undeliberate hyper-activity are called into play, as follows: in a reaction which is different from that in the acute emergency, the attention is turned away from the proprioceptive demands and the sense of the body-as-part-of-the-self is diminished. The reason for this is that the proprioceptive excitations are the more controllable threat in the mutually aggravating troubles. Toward the more direct environmental threat, on the other hand, the attention is heightened to meet the danger, even when there is no danger. But what is given by such attentiveness is "alien," it is irrelevant to any felt awareness of oneself, for the proprioceptive has been diminished. And in the attentiveness, the senses (receptors) do not reach out expansively, but rather shrink from the expected blow; so, if the process is long continued, the state of deliberate alertness to danger becomes rather a state of muscular readiness than of sensory acceptance: a man stares, but does not thereby see any better, indeed soon he sees worse. And with all this, again, goes a habitual readiness to take flight, but without actually taking flight and releasing the muscular tension.

To sum up, we have here the typical picture of neurosis: *underaware proprioception and finally perception, and hypertonus of deliberateness and muscularity. . . .*

In the situation of chronic low-grade emergency that we have been describing, sense, the initiation of movement, and feeling are inevitably presented as "Mind," a unique isolated system. Let us review the situation from this point of view:

(1) Proprioception is diminished or selectively blotted out (for instance, by clenching the jaw, tightening the chest or the belly, etc.). Thus the functional relation of the organs and consciousness is not immediately felt, but the excitations that come through must be "referred" (and then abstract theories, like this present one, are invented).

(2) The unity "desired-perceived" is split; the sensation does not reach out either beforehand or responsively, the figure loses liveliness. Thus the functional unity of organism and environment is not immediately aware and motoric. Then the "External World" is perceived as alien, "neutral" and therefore tinged with hostility, for "every stranger is an enemy." (This accounts for a certain obsessional and paranoid "sterilizing" behavior of positivist science.)

(3) The habitual deliberateness and unrelaxed self-constriction color the whole foreground of awareness and produce an exaggerated feeling of the exercise of "Will," and this is taken to be the pervasive property of the self. When "I will to move my hand," I feel the willing but I do not feel my hand; but the hand moves, therefore the willing is something somewhere, it is in the mind.

(4) The safe play of dream and speculation are maximized and play a disproportionate role in the self-awareness of the organism. Then the delaying, calculative, and restorative functions of the boundary are taken as the chief and final activities of mind.

What we are arguing, then, is not that these conceptions, Body, Mind, World, Will, Ideas are ordinary errors that may be corrected by rival hypotheses and verification; nor, again, that they are semantical misnomers. Rather, they are given in immediate experience of a certain kind and can lose their urgency and evidential weight only if the conditions of that experience are changed. . . .

The "unavoidable misconception," in a chronic low-grade emergency, that there is such a thing as "Mind" becomes more frightening when one begins to suffer from psychosomatic ailments.

Firmly planted in his loved or despised mind, our man is unaware that he is deliberately controlling his body. It is his *body,* with which he has certain external contacts, but it is not *he;* he does not feel himself. Assume, now, that he has many things to cry about. Every time he is stirred to the point of tears, he nevertheless does not "feel like crying," and he does not cry: this is because he has long habituated himself not to be aware of how he is muscularly inhibiting this function and cutting off the feeling—for long ago it led to being shamed and even beaten. Instead, he now suffers headaches, shortness of breath, even sinusitis. (These are now more things to cry about.) The eye muscles, the

throat, the diaphragm are immobilized to prevent
the expression and awareness of the coming crying.
But this self-twisting and self-choking in turn arouse
excitations (of pain, irritation, or flight) that must
in turn be blotted out, for a man has more important arts and sciences for his mind to be busy
with than the art of life and the Delphic self-
knowledge.

Finally, when he begins to be very ill, with severe
headaches, asthma, and dizzy spells, the blows
come to him from an absolutely alien world, his
body. He suffers *from* headache, *from* asthma, and
so forth; he does not say, "I am making my head
ache and holding my breath, though I am unaware
how I am doing it or why I am doing it."

Good. His body is hurting him so he goes to a
doctor. And supposing the affection is as yet
"merely functional," that is, there are not yet any
gross anatomical or physiological ravages: the doctor decides there is nothing wrong with him and
gives him aspirin. For the doctor too believes that
the body is an affectless physiological system. Great
institutions of learning are founded on the proposition that there are a body and a mind. It is estimated that more than 60% of visitors to medical
offices have nothing the matter with them; but they
obviously have *something* the matter with them.

Luckily, however, sickness rates high among the
things that must be attended to, and our man now
has a new lively interest. The rest of his personality
becomes more and more the background for a consuming interest in his body. The mind and body

become at least acquaintances, and he speaks of "*my* headaches, *my* asthma, etc." Sickness is the unfinished situation par excellence, it can be finished only by death or cure.

To conclude . . . let us make a few further remarks about the genesis of the concept of the External World.

If we return to the psychoanalytic theory of Freud, we find that along with the body and the various kinds of the "mental," he spoke of Reality, and then of the "reality-principle," which he contrasted with the "pleasure-principle" as the principle of painful self-adjustment to safe functioning.

It can be shown, we think, that he conceived of reality in two different ways (and did not understand the relation between them). In one way, the mind *and* the body are parts of the pleasure-system, and reality is primarily the social "External World" of other minds and bodies painfully constraining one's pleasures by deprivation or punishment. In the other way, he meant the "External World" given in perception, including one's own body, and opposed to the imaginary elements of hallucination and dream.

The social External World he thought of especially in connection with the so-called helplessness and delusional omnipotence of the human infant. The infant lies there isolated, has ideas of its own omnipotence, and yet is dependent for everything except the satisfactions of its own body.

But let us consider this picture in its total social context and it will be seen to be the projection of an adult situation: the repressed feelings of the adult are attributed to the child. For how is the infant essentially helpless or isolated? It is part of a field in which the mother is another part. The child's anguished cry is an adequate communication; the mother *must* respond to it; the infant needs fondling, she needs to fondle; and so with other functions. The delusions of omnipotence (to the extent that they exist and are not adult projections), and the rages and tantrums of infinite abandonment, are useful exhaustions of the surface-tension in periods of delay, in order that inter-functioning can proceed without past unfinished situations. And ideally considered, the growing apart of the infant and the mother, the disruption of this field into separate persons, is *the same as* the increase of the child in size and strength, his growing teeth and learning to chew (and the drying up of the milk and the turning of the mother to other interests), and his learning to walk, talk, etc. That is, the child does not learn an alien reality, but discovers-and-invents his own increasing reality.

The bother, of course, is that the ideal condition does not obtain. But then we must say, not that the child is essentially isolated and helpless, but that he is soon made so, thrown into a chronic emergency, and eventually he conceives of an external social world. And what is the situation of the adult? In our societies that have no fraternal community, one exists in and grows deeper into this same isolation. Adults treat one another as enemies and their children as alternately slaves or tyrants. Then, by projection, the infant is inevitably seen to be isolated and helpless and omnipotent. The safest condition is then seen, truly, to be a breaking, a disconnection, from the continuity with the original unitary field.

(The passional attributes of the External World of science reveal the same projections. The world of "facts" is at least neutral: does this not reflect the sigh of relief at getting out of the family home and coming into contact with reasonable beings, even if they are only things? But of course, it is also indifferent; and try as one will, one cannot milk out of "naturalism" an ethics, except the stoic apathy. Natural resources are "exploited": that is, we do not participate with them in an ecology, rather *we* use *them*, a safe attitude that leads to much inefficient behavior. We "conquer" nature, we are the master of nature. And persistently, conversely, there is the strain that it is "Mother Nature.")

Michael McClure. *Revolt*

Michael McClure's defense of "the old body spirits" may be somewhat fanciful physiology; but it is a persuasive rhapsody on Reichian psychological themes. Paradoxically, the new radicalism grounds itself in the healthy conservatism of bodily instinct. The revolt is, then, against "the overlay of unnaturality," in behalf of "the physical urges of the meat": the wisdom of the body.

And the politics of the matter? "Worldly revolt of the individual," McClure observes, "comes from an interior revolt that has sought out health and natural physical processes subtle and gross."

COMING UPON some words that begin a writing of mine I was moved by an impulse to write an essay upon the meaning of revolt, and to make an investigation and exploration of it. The lines that intrigued me are erotic and Universal and I meant but to begin with them and to track down one physiological meaning.—The lines were the first stanza of a poem titled RANT BLOCK.

For a basic relevant meaning of revolt to us as many-celled meat creatures I move to seek into a lower phylum of the animal kingdom—to the phylum that is the first to have so many common characteristics with us. This phylum has as I do 3 layers of flesh: Ectoderm—or outer skin, endoderm—or inner stomach skin, and for the first time in the evolutionary ladder there is the third layer of flesh—mesoderm or muscle and organ flesh. This phylum of beasts is the phylum Platyhelminthes—or flatworms. It is the main branching on the tree of evolution of beasts of many cells. Planaria—small flat black worms with triangular heads living in icy streams —are the first beasts to have the 3 layers of meat as all animals after them have, including myself. In addition they are the first animals to be bilaterally symmetrical as most creatures evolved after them are.

These tiny spirits move in cold water and seek out the tinier beasts they prey upon—to whom they are raptors or dragons of prey—and they fall upon these desires of their hunger and swallow them whole, or fasten upon them with their bellymouths and shake them to pieces that they may be ingested in particles thru their maw.

These are the first higher beasts—also they have the first definite upper and lower surfaces to their body, and the first large eye-organs and complexities of nervous system and digestion. These are our farthest close-cousins.

The planaria black worms are said to reproduce both sexually (they are bisexually hermaphroditic) —and asexually. But I believe a qualitative point in evolution is reached. I say that they perhaps only reproduce sexually and that the asexual reproduction should be called revolt. Or, for the image of what I say, I seek to call the asexual division *revolt*. (Hermaphroditic sexual reproduction is normal by means of a penis and womb-sac and is enacted with a bisexual hermaphroditic partner. . . .)

The asexual reproduction or revolt is spectacular. Each planaria creature is divided at points along its body into sub-individuals that are points of possible division in revolt or asexual division BUT there is no morphological or physiological organic sign of these places of revolt—neither on the outside nor inside of the animal. They are physical spirit divisions of resentment and sub-individuality. Simply, there are invisible lines where it is predictable that a revolt may take place and along which a planaria will divide into two. The planaria to the rear will grow a new head and necessary organs and swim away complete after the division.

The revolt takes place in this manner: the tail end of the beast tightens itself upon an object in the water and vigorously shakes from itself the head end . . . disavowing itself of the domination of the old head-end that has made all decisions with its brain and eyes. The sub-individual, become individual itself, now is headless and self-decisive. In turn the individuals of itself may revolt from the new growing head in their time. AHH!

I wish to make a fantasy as an image: . . . The Head which is the major receptacle of sensory impressions and sense organs in the higher beasts is most clear at birth or at its first growing, but gradually or quickly it fills with preconception and becomes locked in a vision of the outer world and of itself. The Head makes patterns and phorms of the environment and of the filling of its desires in regards to the flowing of circumstances surrounding it—and by the nature of its meat these patterns or nervous synapses and chains of synapses become set and less at liberty to make swift change and new decision. The Head finally may act by self-image of itself, by a set and unchanging vision that ignores the demands of its Body that is following with its load of lesser conscious desires and needs and protoplasmic instincts and intuitions. The Head is chief and The Body follows.

With planaria the "Comedy" is that gut *and* the mouth belong to the Body—they are on the body and not on the head. In evolution from this point the mouth moves up into the Head and asserts that there is a more single spirit in control of all behind it. Mouth and Head control Gut in evolution after planaria. But the old body spirits of revolt remain as tiny voices in all animals.

My fantasy stops. No—here is a little more: the reward for eradication of the sub-individuals in higher evolutionary creatures is co-ordination. Beasts higher than the planaria but still in the phyla beneath ours have no concept of Time and they must be totally co-ordinated to spring upon their desires that pass with speed *in* Space. There cannot be argument from darkness within their meat. They must be co-ordinated to leap.

The goal of revolt at all times is the search for health or naturality, a desire to fill out the normal physiological processes that give pleasure of fullness and expansion. The problems of the earth—or the enactions of life itself are Desire and Hunger. And the basis of all revolt is in one phase or another Sexuality. The Erotic impulse is the impulse to destroy walls and join units together into larger and larger structures. This is the heat of Romance!! To make love structures, then, old visions, self-images, phorms and patterns must be disavowed or destroyed—anything that chains life to a search that has changed to preconception of goals and reality must go—for that is a threat to the meat itself. . . .

Freud, Jung and Reich assert the sexual beginning of life and of neurosis. Freud is the dark poet of the real and the conceptual-real. Jung is an anagogic poet leading out to flight of fantasy and imaginative cohesion of instincts and memories. Freud is like Shelley, and Jung is like Keats who makes idylls of beauty. Reich is the creator of true romance and a sexological pioneer of Freud and a golden medievalist. The value of these men to the individual who is not analyst is their value as sexologists. In sex lies both the complexities of desire and fulfillment and the meanings of revolt which is a physiological process of seeking for naturality of the physical processes.

To the Elizabethans the body was the *Bulk* and to men who conceive of the body as Bulk there is no differentiation of the body and Spirit—it is the bulk that performs the actions of the spirit—no matter how fine or how gross the nature of the gesture. In the simple black spirits of our lower cousins there are less complexities of desire moving to fulfillment. Sub-Individual revolts from Chief-Head and divides to the fullfillment of his desire. He pulls away and becomes himself Chief by growing his head himself: an act and demonstration of physical-spirit as much as is his violent capturing of the tiny beast that satisfies his hunger. Size does not matter—and does matter!—but there is no proportion to gauge the intensity of desire.

For the swart flat worm as he moves on his thready cilia and strand of mucous there is no Time and no Society that he acts against—the background of his acts made with his total meat-spirit is the organization of his body and all the lesser individuals of it. Physiologically and morphologically it is a simpler universe of clearer beauty and simpler Good and Bad. Light and sight are themselves more evident being degrees of light and dark and they combine without complexities with the tellings of other fine senses upon the cheeks of the beast and turn him directly to his desires and flights.

Against the meanings the Head has assumed in millions of millions of years are matched the needs of the sub-spirits darting behind. . . .

Revolt in the highest animals, the animals that must live in Time for their survival, can no longer take place by division of the meat spirit itself. For success I must remain one and whole by the nature of my evolved meat. My revolt must be of total meat&spirit—and yet it must fight the passing vision that is made or frozen into a concrete manner of seeing, and I must drive attitude and preconception from myself and remain as close as possible to the freshness of evolved and primal urges. There is a single SELF now and I know it and feel it. And that self is genetic and real and is NOT the overlay of assumed patterns of synapses and dead actions that are physically layered on me by circumstance. Though the propensities for weakness and strength, that are also genetic, allow for the imprint of circumstance and environment. This needs must be and is truly beautiful.

Revolt is the striving for SUCCESS, a search for basic naturality and freshness of physical processes when the spirit and almost voiceless tiny cries of the organs and tissues rebel against the overlay of unnaturality. As a Mammal I deal with the layering of attitude within myself that I have accumulated and that tend to remain there by inertia. My spirit calls for freshness of experience and chance to build love. THAT IS THE INTERIOR!

ON THE EXTERIOR—I stride in a Universe of greater complexity than the planaria, and, because of the complexities the Universe *seems* to impose on me, there is greater necessity for formulations—and those can become Attitude. If the formulations remain when the reasons for them are gone I can become burdened and live in a vision that has past . . . if I do, there is no freshness of experience and I must revolt.

In addition: I live in Society that wilfully and through previous agreement and tradition will force upon me patterns of existence. Some of these patterns are dissipative and hysterical and pointed toward the weakening of my spirit. And some are made with good intent, and some are to twine me in love-structures of Society that I may or may not prefer to be joined to. . . .

Revolt is a striving to a regimen that is conceived of as athletic and physical. Its function is to uncover and keep alive the natural physical urges of the meat. Among the natural processes are sex, desire for awareness and desire for pleasure. And perhaps these are not divisible but all erotic. There is no need to make instincts or godhoods of them except to divide them or place them together to speak of them. And there is no need for the godhood of the Erotic but to give it a passing name. We are free to divide, Personify, invent, and place all things together as we choose; that is a manifestation of liberty.

A classical division is INTELLECT and BODY. Intellect is a function of the body—but it gives us at moments the usable fantasy that it may stand separate from Body and judge or guide it.

EMOTIONS and DESIRES, like words, are physical parts of the body composed of infinities of tissues and nerves and actions of the body-physical.

We are nothing if we are not the sum total of our physique and the history of the actions of our physique—that we carry with us in body and in memory.

FEEDBACK is unused energy or desire that was not fulfilled in a gesture we needed to perform. Feedback is a part of our physique and history. Feedback nourishes attitudes and strengthens patterns that become strong and, in turn, lead to weakness and dissipation. It is an interior and cyclical occurrence that refeeds itself—the cycle of it must be broken for liberty.

The Intellect used as an arbitrary division and joyful game in regimen *with* the Body can remind it to circumvent or ellipse patterns and stop the flow of feedback by breaking a cycle of actions composing an attitude. And the use of the Intellect can be athletic and physical as it is a part of the athletic and physical body. Regimen is a willful use of all forces to achieve an end with economy of exertion. The idea of intellect must be arbitrary and open to change, and must not become itself an attitude. Definition and personification must change constantly. INTELLECT MUST CHANGE CONSTANTLY AS

BODY CHANGES CONSTANTLY, AND THE PICTURE OF BODY MUST CHANGE AS THE BODY CHANGES. Planaria changes as the physical spirit of its protoplasm changes. The Intellect must be remembered to be a part of physique.

Body is the major force, and Intellect is a contained auxiliary. The body-image is the picture we carry of our bodies; it is self-knowledge. The body-picture ideally *is* the Body. But it is not if there are feedback and images and methods of action referring to past states and actions. These stand as barriers to new and incoming perception. If there are inert functions they must be ellipsed and broken—the breaking is revolt.

The physiological processes of the Body and the emotions, desires, words, hungers, organs, nerves, etc. are the Body. And the Body as in the planaria *is* SPIRIT. There is no political revolt—all revolt is personal and is against either interior attitudes and images (self-images) or exterior bindings of Society that constrict and cause anguish or sickness. A political revolution is a revolution of men against a love structure gone bad. They join in a common urge to free themselves. (The body-image must *be* the body, or the gesture that is made in desire will be filtered through attitudes before its realization, and there will be a feedback of the inert to the body again, and consequently a renourishment of misery and attitude.)

The Body-Spirit is in regimen of revolt and in constant creation of fresh vision and reconstruction of healthy processes. Men revolt outside in Universe-

WorldAir by acts of personal nobility and refuse
themselves as a usable article or object. And they
revolt interiorly by destruction of matrixes within
—and hold (through athletic regimen of body and
intellect and emotions and physical strength) a constantly changing and true-as-possible body-image.

BACK TO THE PLANARIA: The head of the planaria
that the sub-individual revolts from corresponds in
higher animals to old images and attitudes and
physical chains of synapses that cause a pattern of
attitudes when there is no longer need. There are
processes that become inert through apathy and
other causes—they interfere with the reality the
sense organs report—they are interjections of old
knowledge before the body can react to the new
data of eyes, ears, nose. . . . Head in the planaria,
when there is a revolt, is equal to the interfering
processes in the being of the mammal. What Plato
said was of great relevance in his day and is now
historical and contains beauty and ideal wisdom—
but those who apply him totally today are confused.
Attitudes deal with the relevant problems of a year
ago or two weeks ago or a moment ago—but not the
vitalities of the instant. All things must be given
their due while they are vital and *remembered* for
their loveliness or use—but the body and outer circumstances change at all instants and a picture of
the real body and a picture of the real changing
Universe must be created and in constant flux of
creation. As we grow, we see more and more that
is unchanging. Each action fulfills a vital use or

need—or it is a Head or Attitude. The reaction of the Spirit Planaria is simple.

I must be aware of the immediacy of my physique, nerves and emotions. I do not simply sweep on a tinier beast and go into retreat and safety until digestion and hunger comes again. My energy is gladly expended at all times—but I must revolt when the expenditure of energy passes into activities that are not fulfillment of my desire. Pride and Nobility are the value of self and the self's desire in the face of all that would turn them aside. . . .

REVOLT is the constant change and reformation of the body-image—so that the body-image and the body are simultaneously one and occupy exactly one and the same bulk that is spirit. And in addition, or as part of this, there is a constant regimen or fluxing of the abstract powers of the body, such as intellect and emotions, that push the willful desires to their success with sureness and maximum needed impetus of physical energy. The fresh physiology of the body is searched out with all available intentness and awareness, and the patterns of dissipation and hysteria are sought out and driven away from the body. In this driving out the spirit must know that the unnaturalities within it are not "bugs" that must be ripped from it . . . but that they are hamperings of success and fulfillment and blockings that must be eased and forced out by an awareness of deeper processes of the body and a growing reality of body-image incorporating more and more fine and gross manifestations than we dream of. And

only the senses and the tools that lengthen the scope
of the senses can bring touch of the physical world.
Only the meeting of the world gives solidity to the
body-image and causes it to conform to the exact
shape and being of the body. . . .

Revolt chooses at all times. There is revolt in appearance and act and there is revolt in denial of the
self as an object of use. Love is not an abstraction
but gross and fine physical desires and gifts—and
how much more it is I do not know yet. A man can
be persuaded to true love through acts but he cannot be forced to true love by coercion and misrep-
resentation. Neither coercer nor opponent can have
true love. Both, like society, will become dissipated.
Both must raise arms of love. The revolter may with-
draw willfully to the fulfillment of his true desires or
do battle if he choose . . . the battle is a health and
comes from a regimen of health and investigation
that spots phorms and listens for the body's needs.
The regimen of the planaria is direct and without
consideration or qualm—like a flower, its life is its
tissue and senses; and there need not be thought—
all voices of organs and desires are heard directly.
There is no moral issue or investigation—there is
only good and bad and need. If there is strength
then need is fulfilled—and there is strength in the
healthy self. The needs of the physique must become hearable voices and the even tinier voices may
be heard with concentration and relaxation in deep
rest and bliss. The ease of dissipation causes a deaf-
ness to the senses of the body. Metaphysics, denial
of self and attitudes are blockades and Chimeras

within the spirit. The spirit may rest from its oppo-
nents but It cannot *relax* away from them . . . but
it is also possible that it may escape them by search
and discovery of happiness. . . .

Revolt necessitates destruction. Revolt must destroy errata and the extraneous if it is to act in freedom with issues of importance and relevance. If the
spirit could handle and had handled the irrelevant
then often there would be no accumulated need for
revolt. The self in the spirit becomes burdened with
the irrelevant. The self must have a history and the
history of the spirit is the body and the actions of
the body made at all times. But a burdening, a physical exterior burdening, or an interior burdening of
the mammal is confusion and mire to the self and
spirit. In the interior of the body as on the exterior
of the body the acts of revolt must sort out and
destroy when the body is overburdened. The relevant must be kept and the irrelevant must be discarded—the process is intuitive, natural, and involves some chance and randomness and boldness—
experiment must be made. Investment must be dis-
regarded!—investment in acquired histories of self
and projected images of self that the body and
physique twists to fill. Investments in histories and
speculations of self must be destroyed by revolt, and
an explanation of the desires must be performed.
Poems, tales, ethics, governments, ghostly loves that
are not relevant to the natural physique must be
destroyed in physical extreme or pushed beneath
the level of relevance in subtle extreme. Both degrees must be destruction so that the aspiration of

the spirit returns to the innocence of its meat processes. Investments become contracts and contracts
lead to Politics which is the protection of contracts.
Revolt pushes aside politics of the world and also
of the meat. There can be no politics if revolt is the
choice of the self—and those who call politics revolt
are misguided. Revolt of a group is an agreement
not a contract. There is no marriage but agreement—
and no duty but love-duty. He who marries duty
will deserve divorce—or if he does not deserve it he
will raise himself above his error with fineness of
feeling.

Revolt does not fear error, or it itself becomes an
investment in a projected image. The ideal of becoming a creature of greatness involves pursuit of
changing and flexible regimen but it is not the rude
battering of a preconceived ladder to power or
glory. In all things is delicacy and fineness and
beauty—and these things *with* energy comprise revolt.

The natural processes desire only complete success . . . they do not ask for permanent insurance
which is false ease. Revolt establishes a way of life
but does not take out revolt-insurance upon a gain—
the gain must pass and change or it is attitude. The
planaria that has revolted carries within itself its
own future revolutions.

The spirit of me does not invest in any thing or
object or idea outside of me. There is no thing that
I can know will be forever of vital interest to me—
and all outward things change as all inward things.

The enactment of revolt must pass through many

frozen ways of seeing. The Visions through which revolt must pass are physical, erotic, and circumstantial. I have been in a dark night of the soul, while my senses and intellect revolted violently and in sheathes of horror and loveliness and desire for godhood; my bodyspirit diverged from them in a chemical and physical way and remained inert and dissipative. To the outer world I was "brunted" and blurred. There are many third states besides revolt and dissipation and they must be recognized and named and understood—for when the time of the need for revolt comes the states of being must be accounted and judged for destruction, or adjudged a health, or as a simple and innocent part of the body and its history. How cold that sounds! . . . am I wrong? There is actually no destruction of history or of act or of action—but some must be remembered and put from mind, and some must be held constantly in mind for the shape of what they represent. Health is not a constant state:

In athletes a perfect condition that is at its highest pitch is treacherous. Such conditions cannot remain the same or be at rest, and, change for the better being impossible, the only possible change is for the worse. For this reason it is an advantage to reduce the fine condition quickly, in order that the body may make a fresh beginning of growth.

So, Hippocrates recommends the destruction even of health for the end of greater health. He recommends that investments be destroyed. He suggests that physical perfection is an aspiration that must be put aside before it freezes into debility. . . .

We live in the visions of men and pass through them as they have passed through them, we live in the midst of the spirit-inventions of Men and Women, and the Inventions and the Visions that they have created and passed through are signs to us of their courage and desire. Lovers are highpoints of history and desire is not mortal but moves on forever. The Universe is cold and warm with heats of energy within it, and the heats are sizeless as the universe for there is no scale to apply. There is no Cynicism that may stand in judgment. Revolt pushes to life—it is the degree farthest from death. Stones do not revolt. There are no answers, but acts and violence with cause are sweet destruction—and sadness that there must be any death. There is no plan to follow—all is liberty. There are the physical voices and Voice of Meatspirit speaking and there are the physical voices of the dead and the inert speaking. The dead is the non-vital past that lives within us and about us. There is the liberty of choice and there is, or is not, a greater Liberty beyond this. But there is constantly revolt and regimen of freshness.

Charlotte Selver. *Awaking the Body*

Charlotte Selver, a student of Mary Wigman and Elsa Gindler in Germany and of Heinrich Jacoby in Switzerland, brought her techniques of sensory

From *Explorations on Human Potentialities,* edited by Herbert A. Otto (Springfield, Ill.: Charles C. Thomas). Reprinted by permission of the publisher.

awareness and nonverbal communication to the United States during the late 1930s. In the years since her classes began in New York, she has become one of the country's most widely-respected psychosomatherapists. Both Erich Fromm and Frederick Perls have studied with her. Her joint seminars with Alan Watts and Suzuki Roshi have served to emphasize the continuity between her native western yoga and the oriental traditions of Zen and Taoism.

IN GENERAL our work may be described as the gradual unfolding and cultivation of sensibility, of greater range and delicacy of feeling, which brings about concurrently the awakening and freeing of our innate energies. This we practice through the *activity of sensing.* . . .

In sensing the person will meet consciously for the first time the creative, *self-directive* powers of his own nature, finding that he can orient himself where he formerly used to seek advice and that his most reliable sources of information and guidance lie within him.

In our classes I give occasion to the students to feel more clearly what is happening in their own organisms. To experience this we need quiet and peace. No urging can bring anyone to faster sensations, on the contrary, it would only block experiencing. At first, lying on the floor may help bring quiet, for nearly everybody likes to lie down and with that gains a feeling of comfort which facilitates sensory awakening. Of course, some people who are particularly restless may feel this is indulgence and become uneasy. Others who have always equated consciousness with activity will become drowsy. But gradually they recognize that peace can bring gradual clearing of the head rather than drowsiness and that giving time as needed is essential for the development of quiet alertness.

Soon the first discoveries come: Here one lies comfortably, here it presses. "The floor presses," a person may announce, sure of his discovery—only to recognize later that the "pressing" comes from *him;* here one feels free, while somewhere else constricted. One person may feel light in lying, another heavy. One may get fresh, another tired. At some point the insight comes that all these sensations are simply personal reactions which can be accepted without evaluation and labeling and explored for new and fuller understanding, and that "right" and "wrong" are inappropriate here. The receiving and accepting of messages from inside and outside, without feeling pangs of bad conscience or a sense of failure when they are not as expected, contributes greatly to one's sense of independence and, of course, leads to further and clearer sensing and to surer discoveries. Little by little the tendency to *expect* diminishes and vanishes, so that sensations can arrive just as they are; and gradually the general tendency to notice only in terms of what feels pleasant or unpleasant diminishes too.

Concurrently with these first attempts goes a reorientation of the head. Is it possible to give up *watching*, a kind of looking into what happens even when the eyes are closed? Is it possible to give up associative, compulsive *thinking*—the internal gossip, the talking to oneself?

The student begins to become aware of changes which happen all by themselves—the effects of the *self-directive processes* within the organism. At this stage he only feels the effects, not yet how they come about. He may become warmer or cooler, or his lying which felt heavy may become lighter. Or the floor which formerly "pressed" now "feels so soft," or where he felt tense before he may feel resting now. He may feel an urge to yawn and gradually dare to let a yawn break through. He may become conscious of his breathing as it changes from slower to faster or faster to slower or stops and picks up again. Occasional questioning by the teacher may make him more conscious of this or that; and it is the part of the teacher to sense how much time is needed for exploration and when to stimulate or indicate directions that may bear fruit. But though such questions are often felt in the beginning to be suggestive, it is in the nature of the work that the student's discoveries are his own. The suggestiveness is only his own suggestibility (or his wish to please the teacher), and this also diminishes as his independence grows.

The basic human activities of *lying, sitting, standing and walking*, which in a culture more attuned to the significance of these activities were called "the four dignities of man," offer the easiest opportunity of discovering our attitudes to our environment and the extent to which we are conscious of what we are doing. It is obvious that many people stand as little as possible because it tires them, sleep on mattresses that are carefully designed to give to them and "sit" in overstuffed or contoured chairs, thereby to a great extent avoiding full contact with the environment. Rather than accept an environment which requires vitality and giving on their part, they seek one which permits them to maintain their "tensions" and flaccidities intact while actually supposing that this "easy life" brings "relaxation." Of course, the insulation from contact which all this "comfort" represents leads, like any insulation, to a degree of starvation and merely encourages the tensions to grow and actual rest to become ever more elusive.

When confronted with a genuine opportunity to permit change and renewal, such as a hard floor or a stool where there is nothing to lean against, many new students suppose a considerable task has been set them; and on the stool they will either collapse or hold themselves erect, imagining this is sitting. Much time is needed before these complementary attitudes, between which their sitting experiences have been divided, begin to yield to a relationship and connection in which the sensation of the outer realities of the chair and the pull of gravity and the inner reality of life processes in tissues and structural coordination blend together into living functioning. Each of the processes involved—really *experiencing* the pull of gravity, not only *thinking about it,* and the becoming conscious of growing aliveness and more changeability—is an unexpected and delightful finding in itself, encouraging more exploration. Likewise, in lying on the floor many pertinent sensations may come to consciousness, raising ever clearer questions. Are we *in contact* with what we touch or acting as though we were in a vacuum? Do we accept the support of the floor or the chair, or do we pull away from it? Or do we press on it or close ourselves against it, or push into it? This is psychosomatic language, which tells us so much more than our usual intellectual language: These are not just "tensions" which need to be "relaxed" or "limberness" which is "right." Innumerable indications in this language of the tissues express the attitudes we have acquired—often through very painful experiences. But in coming to sense them, we can also begin to *allow their resolution*, which had heretofore been blocked by their repression from memory and consciousness. By sensing the *here and now* we come to recognize that there is no reason any more to resist or close ourselves to the situation at hand. As one becomes more attuned to a given activity, hindering tendencies gradually disappear, for otherwise a deep connection cannot come about. At the same time a heightened sense of being occurs which is, in fact, how real contact can be recognized.

Standing also offers rich possibilities for sensing experiments. Alone the restoration to fuller functioning of the bare foot (which in flexibility and sensitivity is far nearer to the hand than we usually realize) offers great rewards. Standing is the starting point of greatest potential for physical activity,

from which walking, running, fighting, dancing and
all sports begin and to which they return. It is the
specifically human activity, which is exploited by
all the less civilized peoples and by children who
have not yet abandoned its uses and pleasures for
the chimera of "relaxation." Easy and balanced
standing, in which our inner reactiveness mobilizes
precisely the energy needed to counterbalance the
pull of the earth, permits a full sensing of the total
organism. The student may discover that he follows
mental pictures or former instruction instead of
messages of his organismic needs—that he pulls himself up or makes himself broad, that he stands before an imagined mirror—and that it is not very easy
for him to give it up. The length of limbs and torso
upward and downward, their interconnection with
the head, our width and depth, the coordination of
our skeletal structure and our tissue masses—all
these indications of our extent and character are
there to be explored, as are those more or less subtle
but ever-present signs of life in the organic functioning which our habits and responses so often im-
pede.

Work on *balancing* is begun only when a considerable degree of inner awakeness is reached already.
We have to be able to give up the use of the eyes
to orient ourselves in this and entirely rely on sensing. Distinguishing what is habit (which often feels
good because we are so used to it) from what are
new necessities in coordination and being comes
slowly. Daring to give up positions and postures is
already a great step forward. We begin to notice

that finest changes in weight distribution often make a world of difference in sensations of effort or ease in muscle tissues. Together with the gradual approach to the center comes a feeling of lightness, freedom and peace incomparable with any other experience. One begins to discover that one is in constant flux—nothing is static—for if one wants to "keep" a moment of balance which has this exquisite quality it is lost. We realize that it has to be allowed from moment to moment anew. This calls for keenest awareness. In fact, balancing creates this kind of awareness in which one wakes up not only inside but for everything which exists and happens around one. Students comment on approaching difficult tasks much more sensibly, on feeling warmer towards others, seeing, hearing, perceiving more fully and having new and deeper thoughts and ideas. "It simply happens this way," they discover with astonishment. "I don't have to try—it comes by itself!" . . .

It must seem astonishing, in a culture in which what we call "mind" and what we call "body" are still so separate, that experiences which at first glance seem purely "physical" can have far-reaching consequences in personal life. In balancing, for example, a student who found himself either not coming close enough to where balance happens or going beyond it suddenly realized that this was how he acted in life: "I either hold back or go too far. I am either not interested or too much involved." When a state of higher awakeness is reached throughout the organism, people experience, often for the first time, a true feeling of self, a vivid sense of existing. A constant rapport with daily life is fostered. After discovering contractions around the eyes and a consistent tension in the area of the inner ears and at the base of the skull, with the consequent release which such awareness makes possible, a mother reported: "This week I could be more sensitive with my children. I was not as demanding as usually." It became clear to her that her attitude to the children and the condition which she could sense inside her head were two sides of the same coin. . . .

Experiencing becomes deeper and more differentiated by our work in perception: the attuning of our sense organs and the recovery of their innate automatic reactiveness. We work on allowing more quiet in and around the eyes, on giving up the effort in looking and on "letting come" rather than "doing," so that what comes through vision can be received not by the eyes alone but by our totality, and one can truly say: "*I* see," or "*I* hear." We allow our eyes and ears, mouth, nose, hands, feet—our whole sensitized surface, antenna-like—just to be the entrance doors through which impressions, sensations, odors, tastes and sounds enter us, there to be received, absorbed and digested by our whole self. We practice sitting quietly, with eyes closed and becoming receptive to whatever sounds may reach us (slight stirrings, voices, wind or rain, music next door, street noises, etc.) *without trying to identify and label them immediately*, but letting them freely enter us and be experienced. Quietly allowing our eyes to open, without "looking," we receive impressions: the people in the room whose presence speaks to us in many ways; objects and plants; the play of color; light and shadow; the garden downstairs and people moving through it; the city traffic. In stillness and openness, striking changes occur in our ability to perceive; our voice also is influenced; so are our movements, our being with people and all our creative activities.

People work together. One person helps the other to new discoveries. In this atmosphere of peace many more shutters can be opened. Seeing a person, one senses more of what is going on in him. The fine movements of breathing, his expression, the whole language of his body begins to speak. In this non-verbal communication, the coming more in touch without actual touching is the first fruit of growing quiet and sensitive.

Touch itself helps greatly to mobilize or soothe a person so that sensing is made easier, emotional reactiveness is increased, and inner changes can more easily come about. One student may place his hands on both sides of another student's head or around the top or back of his head, and both may sense what the presence of the hands brings about in the receiver. Or the touch is given on the other's shoulders or chest, or at the small of the back, knees, feet, the abdominal wall—anywhere. Or when one is lying or sitting, another may slowly and delicately move his limbs or his head to try out whether he can yield and let himself be moved or carried or whether he interferes by resisting or by doing the moving

himself. "It's just as it is in the taxi: I always help
the driver drive." Of course, so much depends on
one's approach: The quality of the touch instantly
influences the other. It is hard to believe, even when
people have spent much of their lives thinking about
sensitivity, how little they have at their disposal
when it comes to practice. I remember a fine writer,
in a session, suddenly raising his hands to his head
and exclaiming: "I have written about this—I have
never experienced it!" He was sensitive enough to
have this recognition, but most people are not. Few
of us are sufficiently awake to feel how far away we
are from real contact and how much of what we live
is just following ideas and images. Absent-minded-
ness, shyness, aggressiveness, lingering taboos, meaningless manipulation, restlessness, all become manifest in a touch. Most people immediately want to *do
something* to or for their partner, instead of just
being there for him. No wonder there are many
negative reactions. It takes time to develop the inner preparation needed for full presence in approaching or leaving another, and the sense of the
creative pause in which the after-effects are allowed to take their course. . . .

There are many ways in which people work together. One which we often use to awake and re-
fresh ourselves is *slapping*—either ourselves or one
another. We may tap the head, or a small area of
the chest or shoulder girdle to get more alerted in
our breathing and then cease the tapping so that
the reactions thus created may continue and go their

way spontaneously. Tapping or slapping can be very stimulating; it can also be so boring that it puts one to sleep. It all depends on the quality of the tap. Is it mechanical? Is one's mind somewhere else while one is tapping? Is it just something one is told to do—or is one ready for it, really staying with it from moment to moment and giving what is needed? Full participation is necessary, both in receiving and in giving. Here one must tap lighter, here stronger to penetrate to the depth; here more time is needed, here more yet, now it may be already too much. How do I know? *I can sense it.* Our inner indicator is at work. The intuitive connection with the situation can more and more unfold by being cultivated. It merely requires giving the situation one's respect and care, allowing the quiet to feel out both one's own part and the other's. Each one, the "giver" and the "receiver," can be tuned in for what is needed and for what happens. Respect for life and living tissue fosters more life and refinement. The quality of the tap or slap is constantly explored; punitive associations or elements are recognized; callousness, apathy, timidity, impatience, aggressiveness—all the "character traits" may be discovered and gradually relinquished in favor of what is appropriate to the here and now. What is appropriate is immediately felt as satisfying.

Of course, what is true of slapping is true of all other contacts—of how one plays the piano, or speaks in a conversation or washes dishes. It becomes particularly clear in the classes when, for example, one student is invited to place his hand on another's forehead. Some people at first, in their unrelated and restless way, just push at the other and create disturbance. "The first set of hands felt cold and aggressive; the second soothed me and made me feel easier." Here are two people without connection to each other. The first toucher is "cold and aggressive," but the recipient himself is one who thinks of a person as a "set of hands." Such a tendency to the disconnected and superficial only slowly gives way to a growing sense of communion. When it does give way our attitudes in daily life will change, for the quality of contact is acute in all our relationships. . . .

Hand in hand with the awakening of the proprioceptive sense and the sense of touch, which, compared with seeing and hearing, have been so neglected in our upbringing—when not tabooed or, at the least, stigmatized as "indulgence" and "sensuality"—a new depth and vitality arise in all other senses. Elsa Gindler once expressed it: "It tastes, it smells, it hears, it sees, it feels through us."

In this phase of the work we turn again and again to the cultivation of inner quiet, so that in a true sense one can become *all eyes*, as one sometimes calls a heightened receptivity. "Do you see with your feet? Do you hear with your belly?" Suzuki reports the Zen master asking. "These questions do not call for a mystical explanation, as so many people think; they are merely a vivid way of describing total functioning, a being there for it throughout. As long as the head is still busy, full sensory receptivity is impossible; while with increasing stillness in the head, all perception, traveling unimpeded through the organism, automatically becomes sharper and more in context. In this new stage of more awareness and permissiveness the self-directive powers of the organism reveal themselves ever clearer, and we experience on a deeper level the unexpected transformations we can undergo.

When the rigidities and muscular activities in the head that attend unnecessary effort, insistence or anxiety are gradually replaced by sensations of life-processes of weight and changes in weight distribution until one reaches a state of relative balance, simultaneous changes happen throughout the whole person. The closer we come to such a state of greater balance in the head, the quieter we become, the more our head "clears," the lighter and more potent we feel. Energy formerly *bound* is now more and more at our disposal. Pressure and hurry change into freedom for speed. We find ourselves being more one with the world where we formerly had to cross barriers. Thoughts and ideas "come" in lucidity instead of being produced. We don't have to try to express ourselves (as the word so vividly depicts), but utterances become just part of natural functioning. Experiences can be allowed to be more fully received and to mature in us. As Heinrich Jacoby once remarked: "Through becoming conscious we have been driven out of paradise, through consciousness we can come back to paradise."

Pablo Neruda. "To the Foot from Its Child"

The child's foot is not yet aware it's a foot,
and wants to be a butterfly or an apple.

But later, stones and glass shards,
streets, ladders,
and the paths in the rough earth
go on teaching the foot it cannot fly,
cannot be a fruit swollen on the branch.
Then, the child's foot
was defeated, fell
in the battle,
was a prisoner
condemned to live in a shoe.

Bit by bit, in that dark,
it grew to know the world in its own way,
out of touch with its fellow, enclosed,
feeling out life like a blind man.

These soft nails
of quartz, bunched together,
grew hard, and changed themselves
into opaque substance, hard as horn,

and the tiny, petaled toes of the child
grew bunched and out of trim,
took on the form of eyeless reptiles
with triangular heads, like worms.
Later, they grew calloused
and were covered
with the faint volcanoes of death,
a coarsening hard to accept.

But this blind thing walked
without respite, never stopping
for hour after hour,
the one foot, the other,
now the man's,
now the woman's,
up above,
down below,
through fields, mines,
markets and ministries,
backward,
far afield, inward,
forward,
this foot toiled in its shoe,
scarcely taking time
to bare itself in love or sleep;
it walked, they walked,
until the whole man chose to stop.

And then it descended
to earth, and knew nothing,
for there, everything everywhere was dark.
It did not know it had ceased to be a foot,

or if they were burying it so that it might fly,
or so that it might become
an apple.

Dennis Saleh. "The Psychology of the Body"

1. *How We Lie About It*

Everything we would write
about it, would be a lie;
how to succumb to the hair in the nose,
how to praise it. Or the nails.

We dream of ourselves
as Ford-like, shiny; we dream
of the racks of the car wash
and would throw ourselves under them
as though under a train.

The stomach is in open revolt.

2. *The Body Takes a Walk*

Let's look at that last line.

One night the hair leaves the head.
It wanders over the expanse of flesh

From *TriQuarterly*, Spring 1969. Published by North-western University Press. Reprinted by permission of the publisher.

holding itself, crying
in a soft whimper.
It settles in the vicinity of the
belly button and talks to it
as though to a wound.
It vows never to return.

The toes leave in ten different
directions. The asshole speaks up.
The stomach, rebellious, passionate,
throws in with the lot of them.

Soon everything is gone.
There is only the empty crush
of a shadow on the bed.
In all the chairs not a body.
Nothing to eat with, or for.

3. A New Life

Then one morning there is a note.
The body says, "I am what I am.
Take me in the shower or walking.
Course over me as over a cornfield,
heavy, and nutritious.

"The dream of the hair, the dream
of the turd, the dream of the toes
curled, relaxed, these are
the dreams you have been waiting for."

III. COMMUNITY

Now since the world's become a waste
By guile and treachery debased,
We can no longer there abide
But in the wilderness reside,
And here our unschooled children raise
Far from the faithless world's ways.
Here we feed on wild fruits
And pluck the earth's sweet-tasting roots.
The sun bestows its warming light
And secret springs their waters bright.
In moss and leaves you find us dressed;
At night on beds of grass we rest.
Our home's a cave we freely share;
We make all people welcome there.
As for the wild beasts of the wood:
We join with them in brotherhood
And honor always, as true friends must,
The pledge of peace and constant trust.

Thus in forest solitude
Our children grow and bear their brood.
In well-knit fellowship we live
And never cause for rancor give.
For each does to the other do
As he would fain be done unto.
We take no care for worldly things
But trust that what each new day brings,
Though little, serves for plenitude—

Hans Sachs, "The Lament of the Medieval Wild Men Against the Unfaithful World," (16th century).

For which, God hear our gratitude!
And should misfortune us befall
We know that God yet orders all.

In just such sound and simple ways
We humbly while away our days
Until shall come a mighty change
That through the world will widely range
And bring men back to piety
And natural simplicity.
Then we shall leave these woods behind
To live again among mankind.

   (Translated by Theodore Roszak.)

Few of us have ever known the life of community.
Instead, we make do with a bad substitute called
"politics": institutionalized dog-fights leading to
grudging, evanescent compromise, the vicious interplay of "countervailing forces." And of late even
politics leans toward extinction, giving way to technocratic adjustment and the engineered consensus.
What remains of community in our lives are the
scattered ruins of kinship and friendship: family
ties (growing more frayed everyday as the impossible "nuclear family" disintegrates), now
and then friendly favors among neighbors, a touch
of mutual aid on the job, sticks and stones of human cooperation, but too few and frail to build a
society of.

   And beyond, like the deserts that besiege an
oasis, the world that *really* counts: the social wastes
of superindustrial society, "lonely crowds," "secret
governments" and ungovernable cities, slums and

slurbs, corporate baronies, suburban lotus lands. No, it is no chaos, not really, but a mosaic of many pieces whose design emerges clearly in, say, Congressional budgets or the major contours of the corporate economy. But only the big pieces have much to do with the look of the big picture. Except for wielding much property or the massed solidarity of power blocs, no one weighs heavily or wins much attention. For lack of communal structure, then, bigness dominates: faceless collectivities, impersonal power: the giant-sized-nobody-in-particular "WE" that rings with authority in the mouths of leadership.

Bigness dominates to such a degree that people lose faith in their own animal sociability. They teach their children that the cops are the only true social cement. They willingly become the body politic, helplessly dependent on omnicompetent heads of state: the mind-body split writ large.

Yet the need of community persists stubbornly stubble of living grass beneath the snows. We *are* communal beings. The communion of friends, the experience of honest citizenship are as necessary to us as air and water. Recollect: if human and/or semihuman beings have a history of some half-million years, the State has been with us for but one-one-hundredth of that span: only since pharaoh, and even for that inch of time, only within the civilized (meaning big war-making) portions of the globe. All the rest of the human story belongs to family and clan, tribe and band, village and free township: the province of face to face relations. Would that not seem, then, to be the natural scale of our social life?

In any event, even now in these megalopolitan empires, it is undeniable that the craving for community roots deep in us. All clever *führers* know that; and know that, if we cannot have the real thing, we will hoke up artificialities and sink ourselves in them passionately. Our time is cluttered with such ersatz communities: nations, parties, trade unions, mass movements. Here we get, not harmony of parts, but top-down unity under heavy fathers. So too the bureaucratic corporations pretend to be "one happy family"; the composite boss-man of 1984 purports to be our "big brother." Enforced togetherness. But finally there is no glue that will bind these counterfeit communities except competitive aggression ("us" against "them"). Inevitably, they invent enemies or scapegoats or become war machines. Governing elites *connive*—tacitly—at the project. *Collaborative antagonism:* the principle that makes the international world go round: the business-as-usual of taking in one another's xenophobic washing. Counterfeit community brings out the Hobbesian worst in us. Having crushed our personal vitality, it offers us the consolation of vicarious super power.

And yet, here is the paradoxical beauty: that even Leviathan could not survive a day were it not for the inexhaustible popular reserves of mutual aid, cooperation, sociability, personal and small-group initiative that are the very ballast of any viable social order, even the most crushingly abnormal. As Kropotkin has taught us: if everyone waited for orders from headquarters, we should have starved long since. The Chanticleers of State and Corporation crow over us constantly, but it is people co-operating (because, despite all, that is their nature) that get the necessary shitwork done. Nor could there ever be enough cops to keep the peace were we not by nature peaceable. (Never mistake a fist-fight or primitive warrior-play for the War with a capital "W" that is the health of the State. The Bushman-Hottentots know about feuding but can make no sense of our word "war." The "warlike" Papuans, forever loudly at strife, call off their skirmishing as soon as someone is bruised, usually one of the wives who wander about retrieving their foolish time-wasting husbands' spears. The American plains Indians fought to count *coup* rather than kill. No, these primitives are no angels. But genocide is the monster-child of civilization and has no roots in communal tradition.)

No question but that the healthiest things happening in our political life today happen in the corners and interstices: the recrudescence of community by way of a thousand improvisations. Encounter grouping, participatory democracy in the movement, community organizing, advocacy city-planning, "People's Architects," "People's Park," labor gift exchange, extended families, free stores, free universities, free clinics, growth centers, neighborhood rap sessions, Synanon, Phoenix House, potlatch, Diggers, Provos, job sharing, The Family

Store, intermediate technologies, Whole Earth Catalogue, Mother Earth News, Hog Farm, People
Power Clearinghouse, La Cooperativa. . . .

"The world will soon break up into small colonies
of the saved" (Robert Bly).

Drop City Colorado manages to live nicely off
the garbage of the Great Society. In Berkeley, the
Great Food Conspiracy feeds an increasing number
of local communes. The tribes are forming again,
the essential society, even in the shadow of IBM's
glass towers: energy centers that will draw off more
and more of the needy young—and the needy old.

For what does Leviathan offer half as worth having? Desk model computers? Electric ice crushers?

Martin Buber. *The Organic Commonwealth*

"Revolution", Martin Buber has written, "is not
so much a creative as a delivering force whose
function is to set free and authenticate—i.e., . . .
it can only perfect, set free, and lend the stamp
of authority to *something* that has already been
foreshadowed in the womb of the prerevolution-
ary society."

That "*something*" is community—which is, for
Buber, no purely secular institution, no mere
contractual agreement, but the binding together

From *Paths of Utopia* (New York: The Macmillan Company, 1949). Copyright 1949 by Martin Buber. Reprinted
by permission of the publisher.

of people by an interpersonal mysticism. With Buber, as with few other modern writers, politics unfolds its sacred dimension. He teaches us that we band together out of a necessity that reaches deeper than hunger or fear. Beyond these, there is the need to achieve what can only be had in the tension between person and person: "the community of salvation."

Buber's classic study *Paths in Utopia* deserves to be the manifesto of voluntarist socialism. No other work has defined with such precision the proper relationship of revolution to community, nor with such intelligent flexibility the relationship of centralism to decentralism.

WHEN WE examine what Marxist criticism calls the utopian element in the non-Marxist systems we find that it is by no means simple or uniform. Two distinct elements are to be distinguished. The essence of one is schematic fiction, the essence of the other is organic planning. The first, as we encounter it particularly in Fourier, originates in a kind of abstract imagination which, starting from a theory of the nature of man, his capacities and needs, deduces a social order that shall employ all his capacities and satisfy all his needs. Although in Fourier the theory is supported by a mass of observational material, every observation becomes unreal and untrustworthy as soon as it enters this sphere; and in his social order, which pretends to be social architecture but is in reality formless schematism, all problems (as Fourier himself says) have the same "solution", that is, from real problems in the life of human beings they become artificial problems in the life of instinctive robots—artificial problems which all allow of the same solution because they all proceed from the same mechanistic set-up. Wholly different, indeed of a directly contrary nature, is the second element. Here the dominant purpose is to inaugurate, from an impartial and undogmatic understanding of contemporary man and his condition, a transformation of both, so as to overcome the contradictions which make up the essence of our social order.

Starting with no reservations from the condition of society as it is, this view gazes into the depths of reality with a clarity of vision unclouded by any dogmatic pre-occupation, discerning those still hidden tendencies which, although obscured by more obvious and more powerful forces, are yet moving towards that transformation. It has justly been said that in a positive sense every planning intellect is utopian. But we must add that the planning intellect of the socialist "Utopians" under consideration, proves the positive character of its utopianism by being at every point aware, or at least having an inkling, of the diversity, indeed the contrariety, of the trends discernible in every age; by not failing to discover, despite its insight into the dominant trends, those others which these trends conceal; and by asking whether and to what extent those and those alone are aiming at an order in which the contradictions of existing society will truly be overcome. . . .

It may be contended that the Marxist objective is not essentially different in constitution; but at this point a yawning chasm opens out before us which can only be bridged by that special form of Marxist utopics, a chasm between, on the one side, the transformation to be consummated sometime in the future—no one knows how long after the final victory of the Revolution—and, on the other, the road to the Revolution and beyond it, which road is characterized by a far-reaching centralization that permits no individual features and no individual initiative. Uniformity as a means is to change miraculously into multiplicity as an end; compulsion into freedom. As against this the "utopian" or non-Marxist socialist desires a means commensurate with his ends; he refuses to believe that in our reliance on the future "leap" we have to do now the direct opposite of what we are striving for; he believes rather that we must create here and now the space *now* possible for the thing for which we are striving, so that it may come to fulfilment *then;* he does not believe in the post-revolutionary leap, but he does believe in revolutionary continuity. To put it more precisely: he believes in a continuity within which revolution is only the accomplishment, the setting free and extension of a reality that has already grown to its true possibilities.

Seen from another angle this difference may be clarified still further. When we examine the capitalist society which has given birth to socialism, *as a society,* we see that it is a society inherently poor in structure and growing visibly poorer every day. By the structure of a society is to be understood its social content or community-content: a society can be called structurally rich to the extent that it is built up of genuine societies, that is, local communes and trade communes and their step by step association. What Gierke says of the Co-operative Movement in the Middle Ages is true of every structurally rich society: it is "marked by a tendency to expand and extend the unions, to produce larger associations over and above the smaller association, confederations over and above individual unions, all-embracing confederations over and above particular confederations". At whatever point we examine the structure of such a society we find the cell-tissue "Society" everywhere, i.e., a living and life-giving collaboration, an essentially autonomous consociation of human beings, shaping and reshaping itself from within. Society is naturally composed not of disparate individuals but of associative units and the associations between them. Under capitalist economy and the State peculiar to it the constitution of society was being continually hollowed out, so that the modern individualizing process finished up as a process of atomization. At the same time the old organic forms retained their outer stability, for the most part, but they became hollow in sense and in spirit—a tissue of decay. Not merely what we generally call the masses but the whole of society is in essence amorphous, unarticulated, poor in structure. Neither do those associations help which spring from the meeting of economic or spiritual interests—the strongest of which is the party: what there is of human intercourse in them is no longer a living thing, and the compensation for the lost community-forms we seek in them can be found in none. In the face of all this, which makes "society" a contradiction in terms, the "utopian" socialists have aspired more and more to a restructuring of society; not, as the Marxist critic thinks, in any romantic attempt to revive the stages of development that are over and done with, but rather in alliance with the decentralist counter-tendencies which can be perceived underlying all economic and social evolution, and in alliance with something that is slowly evolving in the human soul: the most intimate of all resistances —resistance to mass or collective loneliness. . . .

The essential thing among all those things which once helped man to emerge from Nature and, notwithstanding his feebleness as a natural being, to assert himself—more essential even than the making of a "technical" world out of things expressly formed for the purpose—was this: that he banded together with his own kind for protection and hunting, food gathering and work; and did so in such a way that from the very beginning and thereafter to an increasing degree he faced the others as more or less independent entities and communicated with them as such, addressing and being addressed by them in that manner. This creation of a "social" world out of persons at once mutually dependent and independent differed in kind from all similar undertakings on the part of animals, just as the technical work of man differed in kind from all the animals' works. . . .

In the evolution of mankind hitherto this, then, is the line that predominates: the forming and re-forming of communities on the basis of growing personal independence, their mutual recognition and collaboration on that basis. The two most important steps that the man of early times took on the road to human society can be established with some certainty. The first is that inside the individual clan each individual, through an extremely primitive form of division of labour, was recognized and utilized in his special capacity, so that the clan increasingly took on the character of an ever-renewed association of persons each the vehicle of a different function. The second is that different clans would, under certain conditions, band together in quest of food and for campaigns, and consolidated their mutual help as customs and laws that took firmer and firmer root; so that as once between individuals, so now between communities people discerned and acknowledged differences of nature and function. Wherever genuine human society has since developed it has always been on this same basis of functional autonomy, mutual recognition and mutual responsibility, whether individual or collective. Power-centres of various kinds have split off, organizing and guaranteeing the common order and security of all; but to the political sphere in the stricter sense, the State with its police-system and its bureaucracy, there was always opposed the organic, functionally organized society as such, a great society built up of various societies, the great society in which men lived and worked, competed with one another and helped one another; and in each of the big and little societies composing it, in each of these communes and communities the individual human being, despite all the difficulties and conflicts, felt himself at home as once in the clan, felt himself approved and affirmed in his functional independence and responsibility.

All this changed more and more as the centralistic political principle subordinated the de-centralistic social principle. The crucial thing here was not that the State, particularly in its more or less totalitarian forms, weakened and gradually displaced the free associations, but that the political principle with all its centralistic features percolated into the associations themselves, modifying their structure and their whole inner life, and thus politicized society to an ever-increasing extent. Society's assimilation in the State was accelerated by the fact that, as a result of modern industrial development and its ordered chaos, involving the struggle of all against all for access to raw materials and for a larger share of the world-market, there grew up, in place of the old struggles between States, struggles between whole societies. The individual society, feeling itself threatened not only by its neighbours' lust for aggression but also by things in general, knew no way of salvation save in complete submission to the principle of centralized power; and, in the democratic forms of society no less than in its totalitarian forms, it made this its guiding prin-

ciple. Everywhere the only thing of importance
was the minute organization of power, the unques-
tioning observance of slogans, the saturation of
the whole of society with the real or supposed interests of the State. Concurrently with this there
is an internal development. In the monstrous confusion of modern life, only thinly disguised by the
reliable functioning of the economic and State-
apparatus, the individual clings desperately to the
collectivity. The little society in which he was embedded cannot help him; only the great collectivities, so he thinks, can do that, and he is all too
willing to let himself be deprived of personal responsibility: he only wants to obey. And the most
valuable of all goods—the life between man and
man—gets lost in the process; the autonomous relationships become meaningless, personal relationships wither; and the very spirit of man hires itself
out as a functionary. The personal human being
ceases to be the living member of a social body
and becomes a cog in the "collective" machine.
Just as his degenerate technology is causing man
to lose the feel of good work and proportion, so the
degrading social life he leads is causing him to
lose the feel of community—just when he is so full
of the illusion of living in perfect devotion to his
community.

A crisis of this kind cannot be overcome by
struggling back to an earlier stage of the journey,
but only by trying to master the problems as they
are, without minimizing them. There is no going
back for us, we have to go through with it. But we

shall only get through if we know *where* we want
to go.

We must begin, obviously, with the establishment
of a vital peace which will deprive the political
principle of its supremacy over the social principle.
And this primary objective cannot in its turn be
reached by any devices of political organization,
but only by the resolute will of all peoples to cultivate the territories and raw materials of our planet
and govern its inhabitants, *together*. At this point,
however, we are threatened by a danger greater
than all the previous ones: the danger of a gigantic
centralization of power covering the whole planet
and devouring all free community. Everything depends on not handing the work of planetary management over to the political principle.

Common management is only possible as socialistic management. But if the fatal question for contemporary man is: Can he or can he not decide in
favour of, and educate himself up to, a common
socialistic economy? then the propriety of the question lies in an inquiry into Socialism itself: what
sort of Socialism is it to be, under whose aegis the
common economy of man is to come about, if at all?

The ambiguity of the terms we are employing is
greater here than anywhere else. People say, for
instance, that Socialism is the passing of the control
of the means of production out of the hands of the
entrepreneurs into the hands of the collectivity;
but again, it all depends on what you mean by "collectivity". If it is what we generally call the "State",
that is to say, an institution in which a virtually

unorganized mass allows its affairs to be conducted by "representation", as they call it, then the chief change in a socialistic society will be this: that the workers will feel themselves represented by the holders of power. But what is representation? Does not the worst defect of modern society lie precisely in everybody letting himself be represented *ad libitum?* And in a "socialistic" society will there not, on top of this passive political representation, be added a passive economic representation, so that, with everybody letting himself be represented by everybody else, we reach a state of practically unlimited representation and hence, ultimately, the reign of practically unlimited centralist accumulation of power? But the more a human group lets itself be represented in the management of its common affairs, and the more it lets itself be represented from outside, the less communal life there is in it and the more impoverished it becomes as a community. For community—not the primitive sort, but the sort possible and appropriate to modern man—declares itself primarily in the common and active management of what it has in common, and without this it cannot exist.

The primary aspiration of all history is a genuine community of human beings—genuine because it is *community all through*. A community that failed to base itself on the actual and communal life of big and little groups living and working together, and on their mutual relationships, would be fictitious and counterfeit. Hence everything depends on whether the collectivity into whose hands the control of the means of production passes will facilitate and promote in its very structure and in all its institutions the genuine common life of the various groups composing it—on whether, in fact, these groups themselves become proper foci of the productive process; therefore on whether the masses are so organized in their separate organizations (the various "communities") as to be as powerful as the common economy of man permits; therefore on whether centralist representation only goes as far as the new order of things absolutely demands. The fatal question does not take the form of a fundamental Either-Or: it is only a question of the right line of demarcation that has to be drawn ever anew—the thousandfold system of demarcation between the spheres which must of necessity be centralized and those which can operate in freedom; between the degree of government and the degree of autonomy; between the law of unity and the claims of community. The unwearying scrutiny of conditions in terms of the claims of community, as something continually exposed to the depredations of centralist power—the *custody of the true boundaries,* ever changing in accordance with changing historical circumstances: such would be the task of humanity's spiritual conscience, a Supreme Court unexampled in kind, the right true representation of a living idea. A new incarnation is waiting here for Plato's "custodians".

Representation of an idea, I say: not of a rigid principle but of a living form that wants to be shaped in the daily stuff of this earth. Community should not be made into a principle; it, too, should always satisfy a situation rather than an abstraction. The realization of community, like the realization of any idea, cannot occur once and for all time: always it must be the moment's answer to the moment's question, and nothing more. . . .

The real essence of community is to be found in the fact—manifest or otherwise—that it has a centre. The real beginning of a community is when its members have a common relation to the centre over-riding all other relations: the circle is described by the radii, not by the points along its circumference. And the originality of the centre cannot be discerned unless it is discerned as being transpicuous to the light of something divine. All this is true; but the more earthly, the more creaturely, the more attached the centre is, the truer and more transpicuous it will be. This is where the "social" element comes in. Not as something separate, but as the all-pervading realm where man stands the test; and it is here that the truth of the centre is proved. The early Christians were not content with the community that existed alongside or even above the world, and they went into the desert so as to have no more community save with God and no more disturbing world. But it was shown them that God does not wish man to be alone with him; and above the holy impotence of the hermit there rose the Brotherhood. Finally, going beyond St. Benedict, St. Francis entered into alliance with all creatures.

Yet a community need not be "founded". Where-ever historical destiny had brought a group of men together in a common fold, there was room for the growth of a genuine community; and there was no need of an altar to the city deity in the midst when the citizens knew they were united round—and by— the Nameless. A living togetherness, constantly renewing itself, was already there, and all that needed strengthening was the immediacy of relationships. In the happiest instances common affairs were deliberated and decided not through representatives but in gatherings in the market-place; and the unity that was felt in public permeated all personal contacts. The danger of seclusion might hang over the community, but the communal spirit banished it; for here this spirit flourished as nowhere else and broke windows for itself in the narrow walls, with a large view of people, mankind and the world.

All this, I may be told, has gone irrevocably and for ever. The modern city has no agora and the modern man has no time for negotiations of which his elected representatives can very well relieve him. The pressure of numbers and the forms of organization have destroyed any real togetherness. Work forges other personal links than does leisure, sport again others than politics, the day is cleanly divided and the soul too. These links are material ones; though we follow our common interests and tendencies together, we have no use for "immediacy". The collectivity is not a warm, friendly gathering but a great link-up of economic and political forces inimical to the play of romantic fancies, only understandable in terms of quantity, expressing itself in actions and effects—a thing which the individual has to belong to with no intimacies of any kind but all the time conscious of his energetic contribution. Any "unions" that resist the inevitable trend of events must disappear. There is still the family, of course, which, as a domestic community, seems to demand and guarantee a modicum of communal life; but it too will either emerge from the crisis in which it is involved, as an association for a common purpose, or else it will perish.

Faced with this medley of correct premises and absurd conclusions I declare in favour of a rebirth of the commune. A rebirth—not a bringing back. It cannot in fact be brought back, although I sometimes think that every touch of helpful neighbourliness in the apartment-house, every wave of warmer comradeship in the lulls and "knock-offs" that occur even in the most perfectly "rationalized" factory, means an addition to the world's community-content; and although a rightly constituted village commune sometimes strikes me as being a more real thing than a parliament; but it cannot be brought back. Yet whether a rebirth of the commune will ensue from the "water and spirit" of the social transformation that is imminent—on this, it seems to me, hangs the whole fate of the human race. An organic commonwealth—and only such commonwealths can join together to form a shapely and articulated race of men—will never build itself up out of individuals but only out of small and ever smaller communities: a nation is a community to the degree that it is a community of communities. If the family does not emerge from the crisis which to-day has all the appearance of a disintegration, purified and renewed, then the State will be nothing more than a machine stoked with the bodies of generations of men. The community that would be capable of such a renewal exists only as a residue. If I speak of its rebirth I am not thinking of a permanent world-situation but an altered one. By the new communes—they might equally well be called the new Co-operatives—I mean the subjects of a changed economy: the collectives into whose hands the control of the means of production is to pass. Once again, everything depends on whether they will be ready.

Just how much economic and political autonomy—for they will of necessity be economic and political units at once—will have to be conceded to them is a technical question that must be asked and answered over and over again; but asked and answered beyond the technical level, in the knowledge that the internal authority of a community hangs together with its external authority. The relationship between centralism and decentralization is a problem which, as we have seen, cannot be approached in principle, but, like everything to do with the relationship between idea and reality, only with great spiritual tact, with the constant and tireless weighing and measuring of the right proportion between them. Centralization—but only so much as is indispensable in the given conditions of time and place. And if the authorities responsible for the drawing and re-drawing of lines of demarcation keep an alert conscience, the relations between the base and the apex of the power-pyramid will be very different from what they are now, even in States that call themselves Communist, i.e. struggling for community. There will have to be a system of representation, too, in the sort of social pattern I have in mind; but it will not, as now, be composed of the pseudo-representatives of amorphous masses of electors but of representatives well tested in the life and work of the communes. The represented will not, as they are to-day, be bound to their representatives by some windy abstraction, by the mere phraseology of a party-programme, but concretely, through common action and common experience.

The essential thing, however, is that the process of community-building shall run all through the relations of the communes with one another. Only a community of communities merits the title of Commonwealth.

Stanley Diamond. *The Search for the Primitive*

The noble savage is, as every college freshman knows, a modern myth. But what progress it is that not a few of our freshmen now discover before they graduate that this myth is a *good* myth

From *Man's Image in Medicine and Anthropology*, edited by Galdston (New York: International Universities Press 1963). Reprinted by permission of Stanley Diamond.

because, inevitably, it diminishes arrogance, counsels us to think twice about the achievements of our primitive brothers and sisters, and raises healthy aspirations for simplicity and community. And, greater progress still, they discover the embarrassing truth: that not a few of these savage people *were* in fact noble: more deeply cultured, resourceful, and ethically developed than most of the "cheerful robots" who populate the technological wasteland. Little wonder, then, that we have a sizeable number of youngsters rigging up neolithic villages in the best wilderness they can still find, or reweaving the tribal fabric in our cities. Perhaps they might be called "anthropological activists."

No thanks to their teachers. By and large, anthropology—as a professional study—does little to help us regard the principles, if not the institutions, of primitive societies as live options for us, *even* for us. It remains "objective": meaning too aloof to stake out common ground between opulent us and wretched them. The inveterate bourgeois prejudice: the poor have nothing to teach the rich; one pities them but does not learn from them. On the other hand, Paul Goodman has suggested that the task of anthropology ought to be "to show what of human nature has been 'lost' and, practically, to devise experiments for its recovery." But surely all the remaining primitives will have been civilized to death or neurosis before the profession undertakes such experiments.

Fortunately, there are anthropologists like Stanley Diamond who unabashedly admire the folk they study, work to salvage their values and to elicit from them a "primary human nature."

Though considerably edited from its original
length, this still turns out to be one of the longest
selections in this anthology. It is also one of the
most important.

PRIMITIVE IS, I believe, the critical term in anthropology, the word around which the field revolves,
yet it remains elusive, connoting, but never quite
denoting, a series of related social, political,
economic, psychological, and psychiatric meanings.
That is, *primitive* implies a certain level of history,
and a certain mode of cultural being, which, in this
paper, I shall make a further attempt to formulate.

This mode of cultural being is continuously
obliterated or attenuated by the processes of
civilization, and more radically so than we are
usually able or willing to acknowledge; as a result,
the image of an identifiable, cross-cultural, pre-
civilized, and, yes, a priori human nature has practically disappeared from our conceptual lexicon.
Unyielding cultural relativism, cultural determin-
ism, and social scientism are, in part, and each in
its own way, rationalizations of a civilization that
has forgotten what questions to ask of itself. These
attitudes have helped blunt the sense of universal
human need, conflict and fulfillment which has been
most adequately expressed, in the past, through art
and religion. It is, I believe, a singular task of
anthropology, no matter what its practitioners call
themselves, to assist in the reformulation of pertinent life-preserving questions.

The search for the primitive is the attempt to define a *primary* human nature. Without such a model, or, since we are dealing with men and not things, without such a vision, it becomes increasingly difficult to evaluate, or even to understand, our contemporary pathology and possibilities. . . .

I will not linger on negative definitions of *primitive*, i.e., on what is *not* primitive in language, religion, magic, art, psychological function, and so on. All these categories are involved, but I prefer to state the case positively and, since space is limited, while qualifications can go on forever, with minimal circumlocution and explanation. The historical model I hope to induce is just that, a model, a construct, which limits and helps define the range of variations on a level of organization termed *primitive*. . . .

1. *Primitive societies rest on a communalistic economic base.* This is not to say that everything in such societies is owned in common, which is clearly not the case, but rather that those material means essential to the survival of the individual or the group are either actively held in common, or what is equivalent, constitute readily accessible economic goods. The group can be defined as the customary, cooperative work unit, ranging in size from one or more nuclear families, as among the Eskimo, through the various extensions to the clan or group of clans; or it can be a locality, a village, part-village, or village cluster; in any event, the work unit may shift according to season, purpose and need.

Exceptions to this communal condition dissolve under close scrutiny. For example, it is claimed that members of Hottentot joint families "own" particular watering places, but we discover that access is never denied to other people in need of it.

On the other hand, true private property does exist among primitives, in the form of tools made by the individual, breech clouts, back scratchers and similar "extensions of the personality." However, private property of this type does not constitute "primitive capitalism"; the latter does not exist, at least among primitives. The private property that can be identified is either not essential for group survival, is readily duplicated by any individual in the society, and therefore need not be owned communally, or is of so personal a nature that it cannot be owned communally.

If primitive capitalism is an illusion, the critical question of primitive property has, unfortunately, been obscured by both the partisans, and the antagonists, of the concept of primitive communism. The partisans too often seemed to be stating that everything in primitive societies is owned in common, including, at one stage, wives and children, thus conjuring up a false image of an absolute, monolithic, social, economic, and psychological collectivism. But their antagonists just as often misconstrued the nature and function of the private or personal property that does exist among primitives. Individuals were said, for example, to "own" incorporeal property—songs, magic spells, curing rituals and so on. This may be true, but it is irrelevant to the economic base of primitive communal society. Moreover, such prerogatives tend to be widely distributed; even where certain of them are concentrated in the hands of shamans or medicine men, they remain readily available to other people, in exchange for goods or services that are by no means scarce. Knowledge of esoteric lore is also widely distributed; any elder is likely to know the details of a particular medicine rite, although its exclusive administration may be the profession and prerogative of certain individuals. But even this preference can be waived in the absence, illness, or death of sanctioned persons. In authentically primitive communities, esoteric lore seems to be more publicly known than we have usually supposed. . . .

The general point, then, is that primitive societies uniformly possess a communal economic base, or, put in a corollary form, economic exploitation of man by man, as we know it in archaic and modern civilizations, is absent. Even where a degree of exploitation develops, as in the proto-states—usually through the payment of tribute or labor service—it rarely results in the economic ruination of one group or individual by another. Thus, we find that in primitive society, in the ordinary course of events, no man need go hungry while another eats; production is for use or pleasure, rather than for individual profit; just as primitive society is not competitive in a basic structural sense, it lacks a genuinely acquisitive socio-economic character. Laurens van der Post spoke to this point as follows:

"An old hunter in Africa, the simplest and wisest man I ever knew, once said to me, 'The difference between the white man and the black man in Africa is that the white man 'has' and the black man 'is.' "

Correlatively, there are no economic classes, in the sense that any paramount group may be said to own the means of production, although a chief may, in his person, symbolize the property rights of a particular unit. It follows that primitive economies are natural economies; they lack true money. I mean by this that the three related, and defining, attributes of civilized money—that is, money as an abstract, intrinsically valueless medium for appropriating surplus, storing value, and deferring payment or delaying exchange—do not adhere to primitive money. The latter serves as a counter or symbol of value, as in native Dahomey, where cowries were used to represent tribute that was actually collected, in kind, by the king's agents.

We can conclude, then, that in primitive society, there is no morbid individual anxiety about the fundamental right, or opportunity, to work as a peer among peers; this is simply not at issue. The expectations of food, clothing, shelter, and work are not juridical because they are unexceptionable. The rights and duties involved are completely customary. The basic economic structure functions rationally.

2. *In primitive societies, the major functions and roles of leadership are communal and traditional, not political or secular.* The chief of a clan, or the

patriarch of a family, are respected as the embodiments of clan, family or tribal heritage. In many societies, a clan chief is simply the oldest member of the group. Obeisance toward these figures is symbolic, a sign of respect for one's tradition, and thus of self-respect. It is not the result of coercion or an institutionally manipulative social act.

Leadership may be, also, situational, and/or based on skill. Primitive societies abound in "chiefs." In any one tribe, e.g., the Anaguta, there may be hunting, work, dance, women's, age grade, and fishing chiefs. These leaders function only in specific contexts and for limited periods of time; usually, their primacy is based on capacity in the particular activity. It does not carry over into the round of daily life; and, almost everyone in the society is, at one time or another, in a "chiefly" position. . . .

Leadership may be, further, a function of generalized rank and status, which automatically accrues to every normal member of the group through the mere fact of his having attained a certain age or undergone certain experiences. In the latter case, a qualification is necessary. Every normal man will have the opportunity to achieve status via certain experiences, but not all men will be equally successful. Statuses may be hierarchically organized in primitive society, but they are not scarce, and their formal distribution and function is part of a historically selective, if "unplanned," rational paradigm.

These factors, along with other social mechanisms, to be considered, are clearly ego syntonic.

Moreover, the association of major, traditional, with shifting, situational, and "automatic" types of status leadership, reduces the occasions for what can be termed "broad spectrum" social hostility, while diminishing the alienation that develops in response to arbitrary, remotely exercised, and impersonal authority. In these respects, and others, primitive societies are democratic, though they are not reductively "equalitarian." Equality is not construed as identity in primitive life. Leadership is reasonably distributed and exercised.

3. *It is a logical corollary and a historical truth, that in primitive societies, laws, as we know them, do not exist.* Society operates through custom, and by well-understood informal sanctions, not by means of a legal apparatus administered from above in the interest of this or that group, i.e., not by codified laws. There are no special legal functionaries; there is no specific and exclusively legal apparatus. The multitudinous occasions for law that we are familiar with in civilization, e.g., commercial rights, governmental levy, and bureaucratic function, simply do not occur in primitive society. . . .

Among primitives, then, there is no body of law, and no permanent supportive militia standing apart from, and above, the people at large. Thus, that curious aspects of alienation that arises in all political societies, the division between "we" and "they," the citizen versus constituted public authority, does not develop. The people and the militia, the people and the tradition are for all practical purposes indistinguishable. Among primitives, the public authority is representative in fact; there is no constitutional theory. In civilization, the theory of public authority adhering to one or another form of government is paramount, but representation, in fact, becomes problematical.

4. *Primitive societies tend to be conservative; they change slowly compared with more technologically advanced cultures; consequently, they do not manifest the internal turbulence endemic in archaic or contemporary civilizations.* The fact that sanctions are customary is not the only reason for the relative conservatism of primitive life. A more significant factor is that primitive societies tend to be systems in equilibrium; they are not disrupted by institutional conflicts, although they contain well-structured, often cyclical conflicts among institutions; and, of course, personal conflicts do exist. The former is exemplified in the limited struggles among sodalities, and in certain types of institutionalized deviancy; the latter in the ordinary play of personalities, which may intensify to witchcraft. Indeed, the built-in social mechanisms for the expression of hostility which these structured conflicts partly are, help strengthen the social fabric; the society so to speak, recognizes and provides for a wide range of human expression.

Despite, or rather, because of this, society to the primitive is apprehended as a part of the natural order, as the backdrop against which the drama of the individual life unfolds. It is sanctified by myth, revealed in ritual, and buttressed by tradition. The

social network is perceived as a more or less permanent arrangement of human beings vis-à-vis each
other. Since the basic needs for food, clothing,
shelter and, as we shall see, personal participation
are satisfied in all primitive cultures in a socially
nonexploitative manner, revolutionary activity is,
insofar as I am aware, unknown. It is probably safe
to say that there has never been a revolution in a
primitive society; revolutions are peculiar to political societies. Indeed, the Messianic and nativistic
movements that have periodically swept primitive
cultures under the threat of external destruction,
indicate the relative state of institutional grace in
which they ordinarily function.

The primitive, then, is a conservative; his society
changes its essential form only under the impact of
external circumstances, or in response to drastic
changes in the natural environment. Institutional
disharmonies never reach the point of social destruction, or, correlatively, of chronic, widespread
individual disorganization.

5. *It follows that, in primitive societies, there is
a very high degree of integration among the various
major modalities of culture*. Between religion and
social structure, social structure and economic
organization, economic organization and technology, the magical and the pragmatic, there are
intricate and harmonious correlations. These correlations have two major effects: (a) they tend
toward the optimal practical efficiency of the
system; and (b) they integrate a whole series of
emotions and attitudes around a given activity,

rather than isolating or abstracting the activity from its human context. An obvious example of the first effect is the maximal use of technology by primitive economic systems; so far as I know, no primitive economic system is dys-functional with the available technology. Neither does it utilize technology in a wasteful or inefficient way, no matter what "bizarre" means are brought into play to dispose of surplus beyond the point where the subsistence needs of the group are met, or to stimulate exchange. The second effect is exemplified in the validation of practical activities by magico-religious means, as in the classic case of the expert Trobriand canoe maker, who confirms the step-by-step construction of his craft with spell and incantation. . . .

To the primitive acting within the society, the major elements interpenetrate in a circular manner: All aspects of behavior converge in a system that strives toward maximum equilibrium. We, of course, can and do, analyze out the component parts of the system; *we* can demonstrate that changes in technology, in the mode of making a living, or land tenure, introduced by Europeans, shatter the joint family structure and with it, eventually, ancestor worship—but the primitive person moves within this system as an integrated man. His society is neither compartmentalized nor fragmented, and none of its parts is in fatal conflict with the others. Thus the primitive does not perceive himself as divided into *"Homo economicus," "Homo religiosus," "Homo politicus,"* and so forth. He stands at the center of a synthetic, holistic universe of concrete activities, disinterested in the causal nexus between them, for only consistent crises stimulate interest in the causal analysis of society. It is the pathological disharmony of social parts that compels us minutely to isolate one from another, and inquire into their reciprocal effects. And it is at least likely that Malinowski's functionalism is the reflection of the primitive view from within the system, raised to the level of theory, and converted into a tool for analyzing all societies, even where inappropriate.

As Edward Sapir implied, this primitive holism is in startling and significant contrast to our own conflict filled, isolating, and abstract—our increasingly civilized—experience of society.

6. *A fundamental reason for this contrast is that the ordinary member of primitive society participates in a much greater segment of his social economy than do individuals in archaic, and in technically sophisticated, modern civilizations.* For example, the average Hottentot male is an expert hunter, a keen observer of nature, a craftsman who can make a kit bag of tools and weapons, a herder who knows the habits and needs of cattle, a direct participant in a variety of tribal rituals and ceremonies, and he is likely to be well versed in the legends, tales, and proverbs of his people (and a similar list could be drawn up for the Hottentot female). The average primitive, relative to his social environment, and the level of science and technology achieved, is more accomplished, in the literal sense of that term, than are most civilized individuals. He participates more fully and directly

in the cultural possibilities open to him, not as a consumer, and not vicariously, but as an actively engaged, complete man.

A major reason for this functional integrity is in control of the processes of production; that is, the primitive, in creating a tool, creates it from beginning to end, uses it with skill, and controls it. He has no schizoid sense of it controlling him, and he has direct access to the fruits of his labor, subject to the reciprocal claims of his kinsmen. He stands, in the face of nature, much less elaborately equipped than ourselves, with his whole being and all of his faculties and activities geared for the survival and perpetuation of his family, clan, village, or tribe. . . .

In contrast, glance again at the frequently drawn portrait of the fractionated worker, emerging in modern civilization (not to mention the serf or slave who occupied the stage before him), compelled to sell his labor power as a marketable commodity. Indeed the worker who appeared after the industrial revolution began to regard *himself* as a commodity, as a tool, or an extension of a tool—the very opposite of the primitive view of the tool as an extension of the personality. The modern worker, and to varying degrees his predecessor in archaic civilization, became aliented, specialized, and morally estranged in the process of production. Correlatively, the power of the "owners," or chief executives, became an inhuman power; their freedom is pseudo-freedom for it is based on the coercion of subordinate groups; they are bound to those whom they exploit. Their social ties grow manipulative;

their privileges—irresponsible. Nor do the managers, technicians, bureaucrats and clerks escape this fate. It is the present agony and peril of all classes and grades in civilized society. If civilized production has helped disorganize modern man, and deprive him of his moral center, primitive production helped to integrate primitive man.

7. *A fundamental reason for the holistic and moral, but not moralistic, character of primitive society is that it is organized on a kin or tribal, not on a political basis.* All significant economic, social and ideological functions are discharged within and among kin or quasi-kin groupings, whether these are nuclear families, joint families, clans, clusters of clans, or the various types of sodalities. Society thus functions on a personal, corporate and traditional, rather than on an impersonal, civil, and individualized basis. . . .

Kin units, then, together with the technically non-kin institutions patterned after their image (age grades, specialized friendships, cooperative work groups, male or female clubs, etc.) *comprise* primitive society. Although the immediate biological family is everywhere evident, it is usually found merged within a larger unit. The important point is that all meaningful social, economic, and ideological relations have a kin or transfigured kin character. Even within the most extensive clan organizations, where hundreds of people may be said to descend from a common ancestor, and the actual blood relationships may either be entirely attenuated or completely fictitious, people still behave toward each other as if they were kin.

This *personalism* . . . is the most historically significant feature of primitive life, and extends from the family outward, to the society at large, and ultimately to nature itself. It seems to underlie all other distinctive qualities of primitive thought and behavior. Primitive people live in a personal, corporate world, a world that tends to be a "thou" to the subjective "I," rather than an "it" impinging upon an objectively separate, and divided, self. Consciousness for the primitive is the most common condition in the universe, a perception that is also found, in more civilized and abstract forms, in the work of Whitehead, Haldane, and Teilhard de Chardin.

Negative traits of primitive society, such as witchcraft, represent the dark side of this personalism. Yet primitive witchcraft seems significantly distinct from the civilized species of witchcraft, which implies the arbitrary attribution to, or assumption of destructive and occult power by, civilized individuals, and is apparently the result of rigidly repressed instinctual urges and projected feelings of guilt. Among primitives, witchcraft seems to arise rather from the intensity of personal life, which produces unusual sophistication and subtlety about people, and in certain areas, a dangerous sensitivity. Yet, the belief that people can make other people sick contains its obvious truth; it need not be based on chronic insecurity in human relations and is not only the result of scientific ignorance. Indeed,

further studies of the types of people who are considered witches, within a given primitive society
and cross-culturally, should be illuminating in
terms, for example, of the conception of the witch
as an inordinately narcissistic person, a bad mother,
or unfulfilled woman. As the Gikuyu say, "To live
with others is to share and to have mercy for one
another," and, "It is witch-doctors who live and eat
alone."

At its most positive, however, primitive personalism is the "one touch of nature that makes the
whole world kin"; it suggests the quality of "co-
naissance," of universal relatedness, of being born
together, which, interestingly enough, the French
Catholic Existentialist Paul Claudel, reaching
deeply into his own consciousness, has illuminated
in his art.

8. This brings me to the observation that *primitive modes of thinking are substantially concrete,
existential, and nominalistic, within a personalistic
context.* This does not suggest a lack of abstract
capacity (*all* language, *all* culture and convention
flow from this phylogenetic human endowment),
but it does indicate an emphasis functional with the
kinship structure of primitive society, and a lack of
concern with the specific type of abstraction that
may be called, in the Western civilized world,
Platonic.

Boas wrote:

Primitive man, when conversing with his fellow man,
is not in the habit of discussing abstract ideas. . . .
Discourses on qualities without connection with the

object to which the qualities belong, or of activities or states disconnected from the idea of the actor or the subject being in a certain state, will hardly occur in primitive speech. . . . Thus it happens that in languages in which the idea of possession is expressed by elements subordinated to nouns, all abstract terms appear always with possessive elements. It is, however, perfectly conceivable that an Indian trained in philosophic thought would proceed to free the underlying nominal forms from the possessive elements, and thus reach abstract forms strictly corresponding to the abstract forms of our modern languages [from *The Mind of Primitive Man*, 1938].

I can only add that my own experience with primitive modes of thinking bears this out completely. For example, the Anaguta, of the High Nigerian Plateau, never count in the abstract, but count only with reference to concrete things or people; the numerals change form according to the classes of objects being counted, but are not grammatically concordant with them. Yet the Anaguta are fully capable of grasping number unrelated to particular objects. But they do not deify or reify number; there is no occasion for doing so in their society, and the idea seems meaningless to them. . . .

9. *In primitive society, the ritual drama is a culturally comprehensive vehicle for group and individual expression at critical junctures in the social round or personal life cycle, as these crises are enjoined by the natural environment or defined by culture.* In such ceremonies, art, religion, and daily life fuse, and cultural meanings are renewed and re-created on a stage as wide as society itself.

In a sequence from archaic to modern civilization, we can trace the process through which religion, drama and daily life split apart. The drama, the primary form of art, retreats to the theater, and religion escapes into the church. The sacraments, those formalized remnants of the primitive crisis rites, and the "theater, the play," develop into carefully cultivated and narrowly bounded conventions. Civilized participation in culture becomes increasingly passive, as culture becomes increasingly secularized.

Among primitives, rituals are cathartic and creative. They are cathartic in that they serve as occasions for open, if culturally molded expressions of ambivalent feelings about sacred tradition, constituted authority, animal and human nature, and nature at large. . . .

Ritual expression of *ambivalence toward constituted authority* is illustrated among the Anaguta. Men who are being initiated into the status of elders had the right publicly to challenge elders of long standing, who were still physically vigorous, to a combat with clubs. This took place within a circle of young, newly initiated men dancing slowly to the beat of drums and the sound of horns. No man could be struck above the trunk, and the challenge need not be given or accepted. But for those who desired to do so, this final phase of the men's initiation ceremony afforded the opportunity to work off hostility against particular elders who might have abused their authority. Painful injuries occasionally resulted. Physical cowardice or bluster were exposed, but did not brand a man beyond the situation, and, as noted, there was no obligation to participate, although it was honorable to do so. Nor did the ceremony threaten the general respect in which the elders were held; on the contrary, the institutionalized expression of ambivalence helped buttress the social structure generally. . . .

The primitive ritual also differs from ritualized *group* occasions in civilized society; the latter strive toward repression of ambivalence rather than recognition and consequent cultural use. One can hardly imagine a "burlesque of the sacred," taking place at, let us say, a patriotic ceremony; in this sense all state structures tend toward the totalitarian. But, among primitives, sacred events are, as noted, frequently and publicly caricatured, even as they occur. In primitive rituals, the fundamental paradoxes of human life—*love and hate, the comic and the tragic, dedication and denial*, and their derivatives—are given free, sometimes uninhibited, even murderous, "play," in quite the sense that Huizinga uses that word. But let us remember, to adopt an extreme example, that even ritualized cannibalism or the torture of self or others, recognize and directly confront the concrete humanity of the subject. The purpose of ritual cannibalism is the humiliation of the enemy, but also the absorption of his heroic human qualities. In a way that is repugnant to civilized sensibilities, cannibalism was a bloody sacrament, perhaps the first sacrament. Torture, whether inflicted on self or others, is, of course, sadistic, and masochistic, but it was frequently a test of endurance, of manhood, and of the capacity for spirituality.

Yet the sanguine and terrifying aspects of primitive life, which civilized individuals could hardly sustain, precisely because of the immediate personal contexts in which they occur, do not begin to compete with the mass, impersonal, rationalized slaughter that increases in scope as civilization spreads and deepens.

In this connection, how can I ever forget the shock and horror expressed by an Anaguta informant of mine, whom I had persuaded to attend an American (war) movie in a nearby town. This man spent several hours acting out, in my presence, the indiscriminate and casual, unceremonious killing which he had witnessed on the screen. It was almost impossible for him to believe that human beings could behave in this way toward each other, and he decided that it must be a special attribute of white men—superhuman, and at the same time, subhuman. He finally sublimated the experience to the character of a legend. It was his first movie.

The point is that the wars and rituals of primitive society (and the former usually had the style of the latter), are quantitatively and qualitatively distinct from the mechanized wars of civilization. The contrast is not merely in the exponential factor of technology multiplying a constant, homicidal human impulse; in primitive society, taking a life was an *occasion;* in our phase of civilization it has become an abstract, ideological compulsion. The character of this contrast is implicit in the words of George Bird Grinnell:

Among the plains tribes with which I am well acquainted—and the same is true of all the others of which I know anything at all—coming in actual personal contact with the enemy by touching him with something held in the hand or with a part of the person was the bravest act that could be performed.

. . . the bravest act that could be performed was to count coup on—to touch or strike—a living unhurt man and to leave him alive, and this was frequently done. . . .

It was regarded as an evidence of bravery for a man to go into battle carrying no weapon that would do any harm at a distance. It was more creditable to carry a lance than a bow and arrows; more creditable to carry a hatchet or war club than a lance; and the bravest thing of all was to go into a fight with nothing more than a whip, or a long twig—sometimes called a coup stick. I have never heard a stone-headed war club called coup stick (from *The American Anthropologist,* vol. 12, 1910. Italics added). . . .

10. *If the fulfillment and delineation of the human person within a social, natural, and supernatural (self-transcendent) setting is a universally valid measure for the evaluation of culture, primitive societies are our primitive superiors.* This is not meant as a play on words. What I mean is that in the basic and essential respects which are the concern of this paper, primitive societies illuminate, by contrast, the dark side of a world civilization which is in chronic crisis.

The primitive realization of the person can be

termed *individuation,* and it is the antithesis of
ideological "individualism." Ideological individualism is a reflection of what Redfield calls *indi-
vidualization;* the latter is a symptom of civilization
—and denotes the increasingly mechanical separation of persons from each other, as a result of the
shrinkage and replacement of primitive, organic
ties by civil, collective connections. The pathological loneliness, the schizoid character that Sullivan
identified as a prevailing pattern in American life,
and as the substratum of psychoses is the corollary
of civilized "individualism." Indeed, the recognition
and confrontation of this sense of personal isolation
has been a major, if not *the* major, theme in the
work of the most important contemporary artists
and philosophers.

Here is the paradox: Rationalized, mechanized,
and secularized civilization tends to produce standard and modal, rather than natural varieties of
persons. The individual is always in danger of dissolving into the function or the status. . . .

In the name of individualism, civilization manufactures stereotypes: Dumb Doras, organization
men, or Joe Magaracs, whose prototype, in the
popular tale, is transformed into the very steel that
he helps produce. Such stereotyping usually leads to
a culturally formed stupidity, a stupidity of the job
itself, which grows to encompass the person, feeding
on itself as both a defense against experience and
the result of being deprived of it. But the psychologically isolated individual, dulled by the division
of labor, and threatened by leisure, yet somehow

treasuring the idea that, in his name, society functions and battles are fought, is unknown in primitive society. To be "detached," "unattached," or "objective," that is object-oriented, becomes, as civilization advances, both the symptom of a social condition and the expression of an intellectual attitude. Yet it is precisely this kind of "individualism" that inhibits the growth of the indivisible person, that inner union of contraries. To paraphrase Erich Kahler, the history of civilization could very well be written as a history of the alienation of man. . . .

The point is that primitive man is not a mere reflex of the group. On the contrary, the group (as Kahler observes) is "embedded, indeed embodied, in the very individuality of the individual." Anyone who has ever witnessed a ceremonial African dance will certainly agree that the individual's sense of personal power and worth is immeasurably heightened by the communal nature of the event. It is as if the person is expressing an energy beyond his own. Yet the bodily movements, the facial expressions, often the steps, vary from person to person—the individual style comes through. Such an organic group is the converse of the mob, that is, a collectivity of detached individuals losing themselves in some furious activity, seeking an anonymous union; the mob is a civilized not a primitive phenomenon; it is the collective in frenzy, the repressed emotions explode outward without restraint or form, balance or responsibility. The image of the mob is part of our image of the city, and the city is the carrier of the best and the worst of civilization.

But the primitive society is a *community*, springing from common origins, composed of reciprocating persons, and growing from within. It is not a collective; collectives emerge in civilization; they are functional to specialized ends and they generate a sense of being imposed from without. They are objectively perceived, objectifying, and estranging structures. Leopold Senghor spoke to this point as follows: "Above all, we have developed cooperation, not collectivist, but communal. For cooperation—of family, village, tribe—has always been honored in Black Africa; once again, not in collectivist form, not as an aggregrate of individuals, but in communal form, as mutual agreement."

A collective has the form of a community but lacks the substance; it is involved with the concept "public," which is not at all the same as the idea of the social. The fully functioning, highly individuated member of society is the antithesis of the public man. "A public," wrote Kierkegaard, "is neither a nation, nor a generation, nor a community, nor a society, nor these particular men, for all these are only what they are through the concrete. . . . The public will be less than a single real man, however unimportant." That is a dreadful statement, but can we, in conscience, deny it?

George Woodcock. *Not Any Power:*
Reflections on Decentralism

Martin Buber, in an earlier selection, emphasized the "decentralist counter-tendencies which can be perceived underlying all economic and social evolution." George Woodcock, the leading English scholar of anarchist thought and history, here explores these "counter-tendencies" in closer detail. Perhaps, as he says, "primal decentralism"—the decentralism of the primitives—is a dead option and will have to be replaced now by a decentralism of planned intent; but the lesson of the times is clearly what Woodcock argues it is. However we must, we decentralize or die.

I WAS ASKED to write on decentralism in history, and I find myself looking into shadows where small lights shine as fireflies do, endure a little, vanish, and then reappear like Auden's messages of the just. The history of decentralism has to be written largely in negative, in winters and twilights as well as springs and dawns, for it is a history which, like that of libertarian beliefs in general, is not to be observed in progressive terms. It is not the history of a movement, an evolution. It is the history of something that, like grass, has been with us from the

From *Anarchy*, October 1969. Reprinted by permission of the author.

human beginning, something that may go to earth,
like bulbs in winter, and yet be there always, in
the dark soil of human society, to break forth in unexpected places and at undisciplined times.

Palaeolithic man, food-gatherer and hunter, was
a decentralist by necessity, because the earth did not
provide enough wild food to allow crowding, and in
modern remotenesses that were too wild or unproductive for civilised men to penetrate, men still
lived until very recently in primitive decentralism:
Australian aborigines, Papuan inland villagers,
Eskimos in far northern Canada. Such men developed, before history touched them, their own
complex techniques and cultures to defend a primitive and precarious way of life; they often developed remarkable artistic traditions as well, such
as those of the Indians of the Pacific rain forest and
some groups of Eskimos. But, since their world was
one where concentration meant scarcity and death,
they did not develop a political life that allowed the
formation of authoritarian structures nor did they
make an institution out of war. They practised
mutual aid for survival, but this did not make them
angels; they practised infanticide and the abandonment of elders for the same reason.

I think with feeling of those recently living decentralist societies because I have just returned from
the Canadian Arctic where the last phase of traditional Eskimo life began as recently as a decade
ago. Now, the old nomadic society, in which people
moved about in extended families rather than
tribes, is at an end, with all its skills abandoned, its

traditions, songs and dances fading in the memory. Last year the cariboo-hunting Eskimos probably built their last igloo; now they are herded together into communities ruled by white men, where they live in groups of four to six hundred people, in imitation white men's houses and with guaranteed welfare handouts when they cannot earn money by summer construction work. Their children are being taught by people who know no Eskimo, their young men are losing the skills of the hunt; power élites are beginning to appear in their crowded little northern slums, among a people who never knew what power meant, and the diminishing dog teams (now less than one family in four owns dogs and only about one family in twenty goes on extended hunting or trapping journeys) are symbolic of the loss of freedom among a people who have become physically and mentally dependent on the centralised, bureaucrat-ridden world which the Canadian Government has built since it set out a few years ago to rescue the peoples of the North from "barbarism" and insecurity.

The fate of the Eskimos, and that of so many other primitive cultures during the past quarter of a century, shows that the old, primal decentralism of Stone Age man is doomed even when it has survived into the modern world. From now on, man will be decentralist by intent and experience, because he has known the evils of centralisation and rejected them.

Centralisation began when men settled on the land and cultivated it. Farmers joined together to

protect their herds and fields from the other men
who still remained nomadic wanderers; to conserve
and share out the precious waters; to placate the
deities who held the gifts of fertility, the priests who
served the deities, and the kings who later usurped
the roles of priest and god alike. The little realms
of local priest-kings grew into the great valley
empires of Egypt and Mesopotamia, and overtower-
ing these emerged the first attempt at a world
empire, that of the Achaemenian Kings of Persia,
who established an administrative colossus which
was the prototype of the centralised state, imitated
by the despots of Northern India, the Hellenistic
god-kings and the divine Caesars of Rome.

We have little knowledge how men clung to their
local loyalties and personal lives, how simple people
tried to keep control of the affairs and things that
concerned them most, in that age when writing
recorded the deeds of kings and priests and had
little to say about common men. But if we can
judge from the highly traditional and at least partly
autonomous village societies which still existed in
India when the Moghuls arrived, and which had
probably survived the centuries of political chaos
and strife that lay between Moghuls and Guptas, it
seems likely that the farther men in those ages lived
away from the centres of powers, the more they
established and defended rights to use the land and
govern their own local affairs, so long as the lord's
tribute was paid. It was, after all, on the village
communities and village councils that had survived
through native and Moghul and British empires

that Gandhi based his hopes of *panchayat raj,* a society based on autonomous peasant communes.

In Europe the Dark Ages after the Roman Empire were regarded by Victorian historians as a historical waste land ravaged by barbarian hordes and baronial bandits. But these ages were also in fact an interlude during which, in the absence of powerful centralised authorities, the decentralist urge appeared again, and village communes established forms of autonomy which in remoter areas, like the Pyrenees, the Alps and the Apennines, have survived into the present. To the same "Dark" Ages belong the earliest free city republics of mediaeval Europe, which arose at first for mutual protection in the ages of disorder, and which in Italy and Germany remained for centuries the homes of European learning and art and of such freedom as existed in the world of their time. Out of such village communes and such cities arose, in Switzerland, the world's first political federation, based on the shared protection of local freedoms against feudal monarchs and renaissance despots.

Some of these ancient communes exist to this day; the Swiss Canton of Appenzell still acts as a direct democracy in which every citizen takes part in the annual voting on laws; the Italian city state of San Marino still retains its mountaintop independence in a world of great states. But these are rare survivals, due mainly to geographic inaccessibility in the days before modern transport. As national states began to form at the end of the Middle Ages, the attack on decentralism was led not merely by the monarchs and dictators who established highly organised states like Bourbon France and Cromwellian England, but also by the Church and particularly by the larger monastic orders, who in their houses established rules of uniform behaviour and rigid timekeeping that anticipated the next great assault on local and independent freedom, and on the practice of mutual aid; this happened when the villages of Britain and later of other European countries were depopulated in the Agricultural Revolution of the eighteenth century, and their homeless people drifted into the disciplined factories and suffered the alienation produced by the new industrial towns, where all traditional bonds were broken and all the participation in common works that belonged to the mediaeval villages became irrelevant.

It was these developments, the establishment of the centralised state in the seventeenth century and of industrial centralisation in the eighteenth and nineteenth centuries, that made men for the first time consciously aware of the necessity of decentralism to save them from the soulless world that was developing around them.

Against Cromwell's military state, Gerrard Winstanley and the original Diggers opposed their idea and practice of establishing new communes of landworkers on the waste lands of England, communes which would renounce overlords and extend participation and equality to men, women, and even children.

When the French Revolution took the way of

centralism, establishing a more rigidly bureaucratic state than the Bourbons and introducing universal conscription for the first time, men like Jacques Roux and his fellow *enragés* protested in the name of the local communes of Paris, which they regarded as the bases of democratic administration, and at the same time in England William Godwin, the first of the philosophic anarchists, recognised the perils of forms of government which left decision-making in the hands of men gathered at the top and centre of society. In his *Political Justice* Godwin envisaged countries in which assemblies of delegates would meet—seldom—to discuss matters of urgent common concern, in which no permanent organs of central government would be allowed to continue, and in which each local parish would decide its own affairs by free agreement (and not by majority vote) and matters of dispute would be settled by *ad hoc* juries of arbitration.

The British and French Utopian socialists of the early nineteenth century, as distinct from the Marxists and the revolutionary socialists led by Auguste Blanqui, were inspired by their revulsion against monolithic industrial and political organisation to base the realisation of their theories on small communal units which they believed could be established even before the existing society had been destroyed. At that period the American frontier lay still in the valley of the Mississippi, and there was a tendency—which existed until the end of the pioneering days—for the small pioneer societies of trappers and traders, miners and farmers, to organise themselves in largely autonomous communities that managed their own affairs and in many senses of the word took the law into their own hands. In this society, where men responded to frontier conditions by *ad hoc* participatory and decentralist organisation, the European and American Utopian socialists, as well as various groups of Christian communities, tried to set up self-governing communes which would be the cells of the new fraternal world. The followers of Cabet and Fourier, of Robert Owen and Josiah Warren, all played their part in a movement which produced hundreds of communities and lasted almost a century; its last wave ebbed on the Pacific coast in the Edwardian era, when a large Finnish socialist community was established on the remote island of Sointula off the coast of British Columbia. Only the religious communities of this era, which had a purpose outside mere social theory, survived; even today the Mennonite communities of Canada keep so closely to their ideals of communitarian autonomy that they are leaving the country to find in South America a region where they can be free to educate their children as they wish. The secular communities all vanished; the main lesson their failure taught was that decentralist organisation must reach down to the roots of the present, to the needs of the actual human beings who participate, and not upward into the collapsing dream structures of a Utopian future.

Other great crises in the human situation have followed the industrial revolution, and every one has produced its decentralist movements in which

men and women have turned away from the nightmares of megapolitics to the radical realities of
human relationships. The crisis of the Indian struggle for independence caused Gandhi to preach the
need to build society upon the foundation of the
village. The bitter repressions of Tsarist Russia led
Peter Kropotkin to develop his theories of a de-
centralised society integrating industry and agriculture, manual and mental skills. World War II led
to considerable community movement among both
British and American pacifists, seeking to create
cells of sane living in the interstices of a belligerent
world, and an even larger movement of decentralism and communitarianism has arisen in North
America in contradiction to the society that can
wage a war like that in Vietnam. Today it is likely
that more people than ever before are consciously
engaged in some kind of decentralist venture which
expresses not merely rebellion against monolithic
authoritarianism, but also faith in the possibility of
a new, cellular kind of society in which at every
level the participation in decision-making envisaged
by nineteenth-century anarchists like Proudhon and
Kropotkin will be developed.

As the monstrous and fatal flaws of modern economic and political centralism become more evident, as the State is revealed ever more convincingly
as the enemy of all human love, the advocacy and
practice of decentralism will spread more widely
and on an ever wider scale, if only because the
necessity for it will become constantly more urgent.
The less decentralist action is tied to rigid social

and political theories, and particularly to antedi-
luvian ones like those of the Marxists, the more
penetrating, and durable its effects are likely to be.
The soils most favourable to the spread of decentralism are probably countries like India, where
rural living still predominates, countries like Japan
where the decentralisation of factories and the integration of agricultural and industrial economies
has already been recognised as a necessity for
survival, and the places in our western world where
the social rot has run deepest and the decentralists
can penetrate like white ants. The moribund centres of the cities; the decaying marginal farmlands;
these are the places which centralist governments
using bankers' criteria of efficiency cannot possibly
revivify, because the profit would be not financial
but human. In such areas the small and flexible cell
of workers, serving the needs of local people, can
survive and continue simultaneously the tasks of
quiet destruction and cellular building. But not all
the work can be done in the shadows. There will
still be the need for theoreticians to carry on the
work which Kropotkin and Geddes and Mumford
began in the past, of demonstrating the ultimately
self-destructive character of political and industrial
centralism, and showing how society as a whole,
and not merely the lost corners of it, can be brought
back to health and peace by breaking down the
pyramids of authority, so that men can be given
to eat the bread of brotherly love, and not the stones
of power—of any power.

Murray Bookchin. A *Technology for Life*

"But what about the *technology?*"—the inevitable protest. Once decentralize the economy, once dissolve the State in the organic commonwealth, and shall we not then be reduced to a standard of life that cannot help but be squalid?

Murray Bookchin's answer goes a long way toward putting the matter in an intelligent perspective. He calls our attention to the phony complexity and bureaucratic opportunism which is the real cause of centralized bigness. Only the human scale and community autonomy promise a technology that serves, rather than dominates.

IN A FUTURE REVOLUTION, the most pressing task assigned to technology will be to produce a surfeit of goods with a minimum of toil. The immediate purpose of this task will be to permanently open the social arena to the revolutionary people, *to keep the revolution in permanence*. Thus far, every social revolution has foundered because the peal of the tocsin could not be heard over the din of the workshop. Dreams of freedom and plenty were polluted by the mundane, workaday responsibility of producing the means of survival. Looking back at the

From *Post-Scarcity Anarchism* (Berkeley: Ramparts Books, 1971). Reprinted by permission of the author.

brute facts of history, we find that as long as revolution meant continual sacrifice and denial for the
people, the reins of power fell into the hands of the
political "professionals", the mediocrities of Thermi-
dor. How well the liberal Girondins of the French
Convention understood this reality can be judged
by the fact that they sought to reduce the revolutionary fervour of the Parisian popular assemblies—
the great Sections of 1793—by decreeing that the
meetings should close "at ten in the evening", or,
as Carlyle tells us, "before the working people
come . . ." from their jobs. The decree proved in-
effective, but its aim was shrewd and unerring.
Essentially, the tragedy of past revolutions has been
that, sooner or later, their doors closed, "at ten in
the evening". *The most critical function of modern
technology must be to keep the doors of the revolution open forever!*

Nearly a half century ago, while Social Democratic and Communist theoreticians babbled about
a society with "work for all", those magnificent
madmen, the Dadists, demanded unemployment for
everybody. The decades have detracted nothing
from this demand; to the contrary, they have given
it form and content. From the moment toil is reduced to the barest possible minimum or disappears
entirely, however, the problem of survival passes
into the problem of life and it is certain that technology itself will pass from the servant of man's
immediate needs into the partner of his creativity.

Let us look at this matter closely.

Much has been written about technology as an

"extension of man". The phrase is misleading if it is meant to apply to technology as a whole. It has validity primarily for the traditional handicraft shop and, perhaps, for the early stages of machine development. The craftsman dominates the tool; his labor, artistic inclinations, and personality are the sovereign factors in the productive process. Labor is not merely an expenditure of energy but the personalized work of a man whose activities are sensuously directed toward preparing, fashioning, and finally decorating his product for human use. The craftsman guides the tool, not the tool the craftsman. Any alienation that may exist between the craftsman and his product is immediately overcome, as Friedrich Wilhelmsen emphasized, "by an artist judgement—a judgement bearing on a thing to be made". The tool amplifies the powers of the craftsman as a *man* as a *human;* it amplifies his power to impart his artistry, his very identity as a creative being, on raw materials.

The development of the machine tends to rupture the intimate relationship between man and the means of production. To the degree that it is a self-operating device, the machine assimilates the worker to preset industrial tasks, tasks over which he exercises no control whatever. The machine now appears as an alien force—apart from and yet wedded to the production of the means of survival. Starting out as an "extension of man", technology is transformed into a force above man, orchestrating his life according to a score contrived by an industrial bureaucracy; not *men,* I repeat, but *bu-*

reaucracies, i.e., *social machines.* With the arrival of the fully automatic machine as the predominate means of production, man becomes an extension of the machine, not only of mechanical devices in the productive process but also of social devices in the social process. Man ceases to exist in almost any respect for his own sake. Society is ruled by the harsh maxim: production for the sake of production. The decline from craftsman to worker, from the active to the increasingly passive personality, is completed by man *qua* consumer—an economic entity whose tastes, values, thoughts, and sensibilities are engineered by bureaucratic "teams" in "think tanks". Man, standardized by machines, is finally reduced to a machine.

This is the trend. Man-the-machine is the bureaucratic ideal. It is an ideal that is continually defied by the rebirth of life, by the reappearance of the young and by the contradictions that unsettle the bureaucracy. Every generation has to be assimilated again, and each time with explosive resistance. The bureaucracy, in turn, never lives up to its own technical ideal. Congested by mediocrities, it errs continually. Its judgement lags behind new situations; insensate, it suffers from social inertia and is always buffeted by chance. Any crack that opens in the social machine is widened by the forces of life.

How can we heal the fracture that separates living men from dead machines without sacrificing either men or machines? How can we transform the technology for survival into the technology for life?

To answer any of these questions with Olympian assurance would be idiotic. Liberated man may choose from a large variety of mutually exclusive or combinable alternatives, all of which may be based on unforeseeable technological innovations. As a sweeping solution, they may simply choose to step over the body of technology. They may submerge the cybernated machine in a technological underworld, divorcing it entirely from social life, the community, and creativity.

All but hidden from society, the machines would work for man. Free communities would stand, in effect, at the end of a cybernated industrial assembly line with baskets to cart the goods home. Industry, like the autonomic nervous system, would work on its own, subject to the repairs that our own bodies require in occasional bouts of illness. The fracture separating man from the machine would not be healed. It would simply be ignored.

I do not believe that this is a solution to anything. It would amount to closing off a vital human experience: the stimulus of productive activity, the stimulus of the machine. Technology can play a very important role in forming the personality of man. Every art, as Lewis Mumford has argued, has its technical side—the self-mobilization of spontaneity into expressed order, the need during the highest, most ecstatic moments of subjectivity to retain contact with the objective concreteness that responds with equal sensitivity to all stimuli—and therefore to none at all.

A liberated society, I believe, will not want to

negate technology—precisely because it is liberated
and can strike a balance. It may well be that it will
want to assimilate the machine to artistic craftsman-
ship. What I mean by this is that the machine will
remove toil from the productive process, leaving
its artistic completion to man. The machine, in effect, will participate in human creativity. "The
potter's wheel, for example, increased the freedom
of the potter, hampered as he had been by the
primitive coil method of shaping pottery without
the aid of a machine; even the lathe permitted a
certain leeway to the craftsman in his fashioning of
beads and bulges", observes Mumford. By the
same token, there is no reason why automatic, cybernated machinery cannot be used in a way so
that the finishing of products, especially those destined for personal use, is left to the community. The
machine can absorb the toil involved in mining,
smelting, transporting, and shaping raw materials,
leaving the final stages of artistry and craftsman-
ship to the individual. We are reminded that most
of the stones that make up a medieval cathedral
were carefully squared and standardized to facilitate their laying and bonding—a thankless, repeti-
tive, and boring task that can now be done rapidly
and effortlessly by modern machines. Once the
stone blocks were set in place, the craftsmen made
their appearance; inhuman toil was replaced by
creative, human work. In a liberated community
the combination of industrial machines and the
craftsman's tools could reach a degree of sophistication, of creative interdependence unparalleled by

any period in human history. William Morris' vision of a return of the crafts would be freed of its nostalgic nuances. We could truly speak of a qualitatively new advance in technics—a technology for life.

Having acquired a vitalizing respect for the natural environment and its resources, the free decentralized community will give a new interpretation to the word "need". Marx's "realm of necessity", instead of expanding indefinitely, will tend to contract; needs will be humanized and scaled by a higher valuation of life and creativity. Quality and artistry will supplant the current emphasis on quantity and standardization; durability will replace the current emphasis on expendability; an economy of cherished things, sanctified by a sense of tradition and by a sense of wonder for the personality and artistry of dead generations, will replace the mindless seasonal restyling of commodities; innovations will be made with a sensitivity for the natural inclinations of man as distinguished from the engineered pollution of taste by the mass media. Conservation will replace waste in all things. Freed of bureaucratic manipulation, men will rediscover the beauty of a simpler, uncluttered material life. Clothing, diet, furnishings, and homes will become more artistic, more personalized, and more Spartan. Man will recover a sense of the things that are *for* man, as against the things that have been *imposed* upon man. The repulsive ritual of bargaining and hoarding will be replaced by the sensitive act of making and giving. Things will cease to be the crutches for an impoverished ego and the mediators between aborted personalities; they will become the product of a rounded, creative individual and the gift of an integrated, developing self.

A technology for life can play the vital role of integrating one community with another. Rescaled to a revival of crafts and to a new conception of material needs, technology can also function as the sinews of confederation. The danger of a national division of labor and of industrial centralization is that technology begins to transcend the human scale, becomes increasingly incomprehensible, and lends itself to bureaucratic manipulation. To the extent that a shift away from community control occurs in real material terms, technologically and economically, to that extent do centralized institutions acquire real power over the lives of men and threaten to become sources of coercion. A technology for life must be *based* on the community; it must be tailored to the community and regional level. On this level, however, the sharing of factories and resources can actually promote solidarity between community groups: it can serve to confederate them on the basis not only of common spiritual and cultural interests, but also common material needs. Depending upon the resources and uniqueness of regions, a rational, humanistic balance can be struck between autarchy, industrial confederation, and a national division of labor; the economic weight of society, however, must rest overwhelmingly with communities, both separately and in regional groups.

Is society so "complex" that an advanced civilization stands in contradiction to a decentralized technology for life? My answer to this question is a categoric, *no!* Much of the social "complexity" of our time has its origin in the paperwork, administration, manipulation, and constant wastefulness of capitalist enterprise. The petty bourgeois stands in awe of the bourgeois filing system—the rows of cabinets filled with invoices, accounting books, insurance records, tax forms—and the inevitable dossiers. He is spellbound by the "expertise" of industrial managers, engineers, style-mongers, manipulators of finance, and architects of market consent. He is totally mystified by the state—the sick fat of coercion, control, and domination. Modern society is incredibly complex—complex even beyond human comprehension—if we grant that its premises consist of property, production for the sake of production, competition, capital accumulation, exploitation, finance, centralization, coercion, bureaucracy—in short, the domination of man by man. Attached to every one of these premises are the institutions that actualize them—offices, millions of "personnel", forms and staggering tons of paper, desks, typewriters, telephones, and of course, rows upon rows of filing cabinets. As in Kafka's novels, they are real but strangely dreamlike, indefinable, shadows on the social landscape. The economy has a greater reality to it and is easily mastered by the mind and senses. But it too is intricate if we grant that buttons must be styled in a thousand different forms, textiles varied endlessly in kind and pattern to create the illusion of innovation and novelty, bathrooms filled to overflowing with a dazzling variety of pharmaceuticals and lotions, kitchens cluttered with an endless number of imbecile appliances (one thinks, here, of the electric can-opener)—the list is endless. (For supplemental reading, consult the advertising pages of the *Ladies Home Journal* or *Good Housekeeping.*) If we single out of this odious garbage one or two goods of high quality in the more useful categories and if we eliminate the money economy, the state power, the credit system, the paperwork and policework required to hold society in an enforced state of want, insecurity, and domination, society would not only become reasonably human but also fairly simple.

I do not wish to belittle the fact that behind a single yard of high quality electric wiring lies a copper mine, the machinery needed to operate it, a plant for producing insulating material, a copper-smelting and shaping complex, a transportation system for distributing the wiring—and behind each of these complexes, other mines, plants, machine shops, and so forth. Copper mines, certainly of a kind that can be exploited by existing machinery, are not to be found everywhere, although enough copper and other useful metals can be recovered as scrap from the debris of our present society to provide future generations with all they need. But let us grant that copper will fall within a sizeable category of material that can be furnished only by a national division of labor. In what sense need there be a division of labor in the current sense of the term? Bluntly, there need be none at all. First, copper can be exchanged for other goods between the free, autonomous communities that mine it and those that require it. The exchange need not require the mediation of centralized bureaucratic institutions. Secondly, and perhaps more significantly, a community that lives in a region with ample copper resources will not be a mere mining community. Copper mining will be one of many economic activities in which it is engaged, a part of a larger, rounded, organic economic arena. The same will hold for communities whose climate is most suitable for growing specialized foods or whose resources are rare and uniquely valuable to society as a whole. Every community will approximate, perhaps in many cases achieve, local or regional autarchy. It will seek to achieve wholeness, not only because wholeness provides material independence (important as this may be), but also because it produces complete, rounded men who live in a symbiotic relationship with their environment. Even if a substantial portion of the economy falls within the sphere of a national division of labor, the overall economic weight of society will still rest with the community. If there is no distortion of communities, there will be no sacrifice of any portion of humanity to the interests of humanity as a whole.

A basic sense of decency, sympathy, and mutual aid lies at the core of human behavior. Even in this lousy bourgeois society, we do not find it unusual that adults will rescue children from danger although the act will imperil their lives; we do not find it strange that miners, for example, will risk death to save their fellow workers in cave-ins or that soldiers will crawl under heavy fire to carry a wounded comrade to safety. What tends to shock us are those occasions when aid is refused—when the cries of a girl who has been stabbed and is being murdered are ignored in a middle-class neighborhood.

Yet there is nothing in this society that would seem to warrant a molecule of solidarity. What solidarity we do find exists despite the society, against all its realities, as an unending struggle between the innate decency of man and the innate indecency of the society. Can we imagine how men would behave if this decency could find full release, if society earned the respect, even the love of the individual? We are still the offspring of a violent, blood-soaked, ignoble history—the end products of man's domination of man. We may never end this condition of domination. The future may bring us and our shoddy civilization down in a Wagnerian *Götterdammerung*. How idiotic it would all be! But we may also end the domination of man by man. We may finally succeed in breaking the chain to the past and gain a humanistic, anarchist society. Would it not be the height of absurdity, indeed of impudence, to gauge the behavior of future generations by the very criteria we despise in our own time? An end to the sophomoric questions! Free men will not be greedy, one liberated community will not try to dominate another because it has a potential monopoly of copper, computer "experts" will not try to enslave grease monkeys, and sentimental novels about pining, tubercular virgins will not be written. We can ask only one thing of the freemen of the future: to forgive us that it took so long and that it was such a hard pull. Like Brecht, we can ask that they try not to think of us too harshly, that they give us their sympathy and understand that we lived in the depths of a social hell.

But then they will surely know what to think without our telling them.

E. F. Schumacher. *Buddhist Economics*

E. F. Schumacher, formerly an economic advisor to the British National Coal Board and one of the founders of the intermediate technologies movement, is among the most important economists now writing—though I dare say the academy knows little of his work. It is hardly professionally fashionable to regard economics as a humanistic study, instead of a clever juggling of abstract quantities. Nevertheless, peace, freedom, and human fulfillment are always at the heart of Schumacher's work; and it is such an economics that communitarians require. For theirs cannot be an economy of vast scale, of limitless productivity and sybaritic consumption.

From *Resurgence* (London) Jan.–Feb. 1968. Reprinted by permission of the publisher and the author.

In the essay that follows, Schumacher seeks to trace the economic consequences of Buddhist ethics. The result laps over naturally into the ecological issues we take up in the next section. And there, again, we have a contribution by Schumacher which rounds out his remarks here.

RIGHT LIVELIHOOD is one of the requirements of the Buddha's Noble Eightfold Path. It is clear, therefore, that there must be such a thing as Buddhist Economics.

Buddhist countries, at the same time, have often stated that they wish to remain faithful to their heritage. So Burma: "The New Burma sees no conflict between religious values and economic progress. Spiritual health and material well-being are not enemies: they are natural allies." Or: "We can blend successfully the religious and spiritual values of our heritage with the benefits of modern technology." Or: "We Burmans have a sacred duty to conform both our dreams and our acts to our faith. This we shall ever do" (quotes from Pyidawtha, *The New Burma,* 1954).

All the same, such countries invariably assume that they can model their economic development plans in accordance with modern economics, and they call upon modern economists from so-called advanced countries to advise them, to formulate the policies to be pursued, and to construct the grand design for development, the Five-Year Plan or whatever it may be called. No one seems to think that a Buddhist way of life would call for Buddhist economics just as the modern materialist way of life has brought forth modern economics.

Economists themselves, like most specialists, normally suffer from a kind of metaphysical blindness, assuming that theirs is a science of absolute and invariable truths, without any presuppositions. Some go as far as to claim that economic laws are as free from "metaphysics" or "values" as the law of gravitation. We need not, however, get involved in arguments of methodology. Instead, let us take some fundamentals and see what they look like when viewed by a modern economist and a Buddhist economist.

There is universal agreement that the fundamental source of wealth is human labour. Now, the modern economist has been brought up to consider "labour" or work as little more than a necessary evil. From the point of view of the employer, it is in any case simply an item of cost, to be reduced to a minimum if it cannot be eliminated altogether, say, by automation. From the point of view of the workman, it is a "disutility"; to work is to make a sacrifice of one's leisure and comfort, and wages are a kind of compensation for the sacrifice. Hence the ideal from the point of view of the employer is to have output without employees, and the ideal from the point of view of the employee is to have income without employment.

The consequences of these attitudes both in theory and in practice are, of course, extremely far-reaching. If the ideal with regard to work is to get rid of it, every method that "reduces the work load" is a good thing. The most potent method, short of automation, is the so-called "division of labour" and the classical example is the pin factory eulogized in Adam Smith's *Wealth of Nations*. Here it is not a matter of ordinary specialization, which mankind has practised from time immemorial, but of dividing up every complete process of production into minute parts, so that the final product can be produced at great speed without anyone having had to contribute more than a totally insignificant and, in most cases, unskilled movement of his limbs.

The Buddhist point of view takes the function of work to be at least threefold: to give a man a chance to utilize and develop his faculties; to enable him to overcome his ego-centredness by joining with other people in a common task; and to bring forth the goods and services needed for a becoming existence. Again, the consequences that flow from this view are endless. To organize work in such a manner that it becomes meaningless, boring, stultifying, or nerve-racking for the worker would be little short of criminal; it would indicate a greater concern with goods than with people, an evil lack of compassion and a soul-destroying degree of attachment to the most primitive side of this worldly existence. Equally, to strive for leisure as an alternative to work would be considered a complete misunderstanding of one of the basic truths of human existence, namely that work and leisure are complementary parts of the same living process and cannot be separated without destroying the joy of work and the bliss of leisure.

From the Buddhist point of view, there are therefore two types of mechanization which must be clearly distinguished: one that enhances a man's skill and power and one that turns the work of a man over to a mechanical slave, leaving man in a position of having to serve the slave. How to tell the one from the other? "The craftsman himself," says Ananda Coomaraswamy, a man equally competent to talk about the Modern West as the Ancient East, "the craftsman himself can always, if allowed to, draw the delicate distinction between the machine and the tool. The carpet loom is a tool, a contrivance for holding warp threads at a stretch for the pile to be woven round them by the craftsman's fingers; but the power loom is a machine, and its significance as a destroyer of culture lies in the fact that it does the essentially human part of the work." It is clear, therefore, that Buddhist economics must be very different from the economics of modern materialism, since the Buddhist sees the essence of civilization not in a multiplication of wants but in the purification of human character. Character, at the same time, is formed primarily by a man's work. And work, properly conducted in conditions of human dignity and freedom, blesses those who do it and equally their products. The Indian philosopher and economist J. C. Kumarappa sums the matter up as follows:

If the nature of the work is properly appreciated and applied, it will stand in the same relation to the higher faculties as food is to the physical body. It nourishes and enlivens the higher man and urges him to produce the best he is capable of. It directs his freewill along with the proper course and disciplines the animal in him into progressive channels. It furnishes an excellent background for man to display his scale of values and develop his personality (*Economy of Permanence*, Rajghat, 1958).

If a man has no chance of obtaining work he is in a desperate position, not simply because he lacks an income but because he lacks this nourishing and enlivening factor of disciplined work which nothing can replace. A modern economist may engage in highly sophisticated calculations on whether full employment "pays" or whether it might be more "economic" to run an economy àt less than full employment so as to ensure a greater mobility of labour, a better stability of wages, and so forth. His fundamental criterion of success is simply the total quantity of goods produced during a given period of time. "If the marginal urgency of goods is low," says Professor Galbraith in *The Affluent Society*, "then so is the urgency of employing the last man or the last million men in the labour force." And again: "If . . . we can afford some unemployment in the interest of stability—a proposition, incidentally, of impeccably conservative antecedents —then we can afford to give those who are unemployed the goods that enable them to sustain their accustomed standard of living."

From a Buddhist point of view, this is standing

the truth on its head by considering goods as more important than people and consumption as more important than creative activity. It means shifting the emphasis from the worker to the product of work, that is, from the human to the sub-human, a surrender to the forces of evil. The very start of Buddhist economic planning would be a planning for full employment, and the primary purpose of this would in fact be employment for everyone who needs an "outside" job: it would not be the maximization of employment nor the maximization of production. Women, on the whole, do not need an "outside" job, and the large-scale employment of women in offices or factories would be considered a sign of serious economic failure. In particular, to let mothers of young children work in factories while the children run wild would be as uneconomic in the eyes of a Buddhist economist as the employment of a skilled worker as a soldier in the eyes of a modern economist.

While the materialist is mainly interested in goods, the Buddhist is mainly interested in liberation. But Buddhism is "The Middle Way" and therefore in no way antagonistic to physical well-being. It is not wealth that stands in the way of liberation but the attachment to wealth; not the enjoyment of pleasurable things but the craving for them. The keynote of Buddhist economics, therefore, is simplicity and non-violence. From an economist's point of view, the marvel of the Buddhist way of life is the utter rationality of its pattern—amazingly small means leading to extraordinarily satisfactory results.

For the modern economist this is very difficult
to understand. He is used to measuring the "standard of living" by the amount of annual consumption,
assuming all the time that a man who consumes
more is "better off" than a man who consumes less.
A Buddhist economist would consider this approach
excessively irrational: since consumption is merely
a means to human well-being, the aim should be
to obtain the maximum of well-being with the
minimum of consumption. Thus, if the purpose of
clothing is a certain amount of temperature comfort and an attractive appearance, the task is to
attain this purpose with the smallest possible effort,
that is, with the smallest annual destruction of
cloth and with the help of designs that involve the
smallest possible input of toil. The less toil there
is, the more time and strength is left for artistic
creativity. It would be highly uneconomic, for instance, to go in for complicated tailoring, like the
modern West, when a much more beautiful effect
can be achieved by the skilful draping of uncut
material. It would be the height of folly to make
material so that it should wear out quickly and the
height of barbarity to make anything ugly, shabby
or mean. What has just been said about clothing
applies equally to all other human requirements.
The ownership and consumption of goods is a
means to an end, and Buddhist economics is the
systematic study of how to attain given ends with
the minimum means.

Modern economics, on the other hand, considers
consumption to be the sole end and purpose of all

economic activity, taking the factors of production—land, labor and capital—as the means. The former, in short, tries to maximize human satisfactions by the optimal pattern of productive effort. It is easy to see that the effort needed to sustain a way of life which seeks to attain the optimal pattern of consumption is likely to be much smaller than the effort needed to sustain a drive for maximum consumption. We need not be surprised, therefore, that the pressure and strain of living is very much less in, say, Burma than it is in the United States, in spite of the fact that the amount of labour-saving machinery used in the former country is only a minute fraction of the amount used in the latter.

Simplicity and non-violence are obviously closely related. The optimal pattern of consumption, producing a high degree of human satisfaction by means of a relatively low rate of consumption, allows people to live without great pressure and strain and to fulfill the primary injunction of Buddhist teaching: "Cease to do evil; try to do good." As physical resources are everywhere limited, people who satisfy their needs by means of a modest use of resources are obviously less likely to be at each other's throats than people depending upon a high rate of use. Equally, people who live in highly self-sufficient local communities are less likely to get involved in large-scale violence than people whose existence depends on world-wide systems of trade.

From the point of view of Buddhist economics, therefore, production from local resources for local needs is the most rational way of economic life, while dependence on imports from afar and the consequent need to produce for export to unknown and distant peoples is highly uneconomic and justifiable only in exceptional cases and on a small scale. Just as the modern economist would admit that a high rate of consumption of transport services between a man's home and his place of work signifies a misfortune and not a high standard of life, so the Buddhist economist would hold that to satisfy human wants from far-away sources rather than from sources nearby signifies failure rather than success. The former might take statistics showing an increase in the number of ton/miles per head of the population carried by a country's transport system as proof of economic progress, while to the latter—the Buddhist economist—the same statistics would indicate a highly undesirable deterioration in the *pattern* of consumption.

Another striking difference between modern economics and Buddhist economics arises over the use of natural resources. Bertrand de Juvenel, the eminent French political philosopher, has characterized "Western man" in words which may be taken as a fair description of the modern economist:

He tends to count nothing as an expenditure, other than human effort; he does not seem to mind how much mineral matter he wastes and, far worse, how much living matter he destroys. He does not seem to realise at all that human life is a dependent part of an ecosystem of many different forms of life. As the world is ruled from towns where men are cut off from any form of life other than human, the feeling of belonging to an ecosystem is not revived. This results in a harsh and improvident treatment of things upon which we ultimately depend, such as water and trees.

The teaching of the Buddha, on the other hand, enjoins a reverent and non-violent attitude not only to all sentient beings but also, with great emphasis, to trees. Every follower of the Buddha ought to plant a tree every few years and look after it until it is safely established, and the Buddhist economist can demonstrate without difficulty that the universal observance of this rule would result in a high rate of genuine economic development independent of any foreign aid. Much of the economic decay of South-East Asia (as of many other parts of the world) is undoubtedly due to a heedless and shameful neglect of trees.

Modern economics does not distinguish between renewable and non-renewable materials, as its very method is to equalize and quantify everything by means of a money price. Thus, taking various alternative fuels, like coal, oil, wood or water power: the only difference between them recognized by modern economics is relative cost per equivalent unit. The cheapest is automatically the one to be preferred, as to do otherwise would be irrational and "uneconomic." From a Buddhist point of view, of course, this will not do; the essential difference between non-renewable fuels like coal and oil on the one hand and renewable fuels like wood and water-power on the other cannot be simply overlooked. Non-renewable goods must be used only if they are indispensable, and then only with the greatest care and the most meticulous concern for conservation. To use them heedlessly or extravagantly is an act of violence, and while complete non-violence may not be attainable on this earth, it is none the less an ineluctable duty for man to aim at the ideal of non-violence in all he does.

Just as a modern European economist would not consider it a great economic achievement if all European art treasures were sold to America at attractive prices, so the Buddhist economist would insist that a population basing its economic life on non-renewable fuels is living parasitically, on capital instead of income. Such a way of life could have no permanence and could therefore be justified only as a purely temporary expedient. As the world's resources of non-renewable fuels—coal, oil and natural gas—are exceedingly unevenly distributed over the globe and undoubtedly limited in quantity, it is clear that their exploitation at an ever increasing rate is an act of violence against nature which must inevitably lead to violence between men.

This fact alone might give food for thought even to those people in Buddhist countries who care nothing for the religious and spiritual values of their heritage and ardently desire to embrace the materialism of modern economics at the fastest possible speed. Before they dismiss Buddhist economics as nothing better than a nostalgic dream, they might wish to consider whether the path of economic development outlined by modern economics is likely to lead them to places where they really want to be. Towards the end of his courageous book, *The Challenge of Man's Future*, Professor Harrison Brown of the California Institute of Technology gives the following appraisal:

Thus we see that, just as industrial society is fundamentally unstable and subject to reversion to agrarian existence, so within it the conditions which offer individual freedom are unstable in their ability to avoid the conditions which impose rigid organization and totalitarian control. Indeed, when we examine all of the foreseeable difficulties which threaten the survival of industrial civilization, it is difficult to see how the achievement of stability and maintenance of individual liberty can be made compatible.

Even if this were dismissed as a long-term view —and in the long term, as Keynes said, we are all dead—there is the immediate question of whether "modernization," as currently practised without regard to religious and spiritual values, is actually producing agreeable results. As far as the masses are concerned, the results appear to be disastrous— a collapse of the rural economy, a rising tide of unemployment in town and country, and the growth of a city proletariat without nourishment for either body or soul.

It is in the light of both immediate experience and long-term prospects that the study of Buddhist economics could be recommended even to those who believe that economic growth is more important than any spiritual or religious values. For it is not a question of choosing between "modern growth" and "traditional stagnation." It is a question of finding the right path of development, the

Middle Way between materialist heedlessness and
traditionalist immobility, in short, of finding "Right
Livelihood."

That this can be done is not in doubt. But it requires much more than blind imitation of the materialist way of life of the so-called advanced countries. It requires above all, the conscious and systematic development of a Middle Way in technology, of an "intermediate technology," as I have
called it, a technology more productive and powerful than the decayed technology of the ancient
East, but at the same time non-violent and immensely cheaper and simpler than the labour-saving
technology of the modern West.

Bill Voyd. *Drop City*

The report that follows is a good, sharp piece of
nuts-and-bolts Utopianism from Drop City, Colorado, a post-industrial village of geodesic domes.
As of 1969, when this piece was published, the
community was still flourishing; let us hope it remains so. For a long time to come, such experiments in living are going to have to be the
pores that allow us to breathe through our increasingly plasticized hide.

For my own part, I think Buckminster Fuller's
geodesic dome is much overrated for utility, ease

From *Shelter and Society*, edited by Paul Oliver (New
York: Praeger, 1969). Reprinted by permission of the publisher.

of construction, and economy. The dome is not much of an improvement in any of these respects over a quonset hut, though it is doubtless stronger; but then how sturdy need a one-story living structure be? As for its appearance: I shudder to envisage our globe extensively blistered with the things. Worst of all are Fuller's own bizarre ideas about transporting the domes everywhere on earth by helicopter as a uniform environment: talk about industrial standardization.

However, at Drop City at least, the dome has served to crystallize a unique communitarian experiment in which vision and resourcefulness are marvelously blended.

It ain't a dome, it's a home

DROP CITY began three years ago [1965] as a 'dropping'; like a 'happening' but with no distinction between art and life and reality. Three people bought six acres of goat pasture in southern Colorado, moved on to the land and decided to let whatever would happen, happen. They had little money and no fixed plans. Others soon heard of it, and began to pass through. Some stayed. A community sprang up, average age twenty-five, and began building domes to house themselves; writers, painters, film-makers, musicians. They had no regular income. They were forced to devise new ways of obtaining building materials, food, all the necessities of life—without resort to the normal channels of society. They were held together by a common feeling that the whole structure of American society was rigid and oppressive, that the only way to physical and spiritual freedom lay outside the established system.

We thought of the whole of Drop City as a large environmental sculpture. All actions involved with construction were to be the easiest, most efficient, with least cost. In a place where there are no specialists, carpentry, plumbing, wiring, heating, furnishing, eating, reading. singing, talking, sleeping and all integral parts of daily life.

We heard R. Buckminster Fuller lecture in Boulder, Colorado and decided to build domes. We had little building experience. The chord measurements for our first dome were taken from a model a farmer happened to have in his yard. We thought we were building a geodesic dome; it turned out to be a dodecahedron. We set up a structure of 2×4s with a plywood plate joining system, 18 ft. in diameter. Then we had to cover it. Since we didn't have much money, anything waterproof would have to suffice. A wall of a nearby farmhouse was made of tarpaper covered with chicken wire and stucco. Bottlecaps were used to hold the wire to the tarpaper. We did the same. Then we tarred over the stucco to waterproof it and finished with a fibered aluminium coat. The windows were automobile glass, the floor, 2×4s.

We learned how to scrounge materials, tear down abandoned buildings, use the unusable. Culled lumber. Railroad ties. Damaged insulation. Factory-reject plywood. Can tops. The garbage of America. Trapped inside waste-economy man finds an identity as a consumer. Once outside the trap he

Dome that turned out to be a dodecahedron.

finds enormous resources at his disposal—free.
Things have value only in their use. When one stops
"owning" things another can begin to use them.
Energy is transformed, not lost.

Our second dome was the kitchen, a 20 ft. diameter, 2-frequency geodesic. Each triangle of an
icosahedron is divided into 4 smaller triangles, each
vertex pulled out to the surface of a sphere. We
used three-inch pipe and lag screws to join 2×4
members. It was covered with plywood, the seams
sealed with plastic cement and membrane, then
the whole dome painted with tar and aluminium
coating.

We found ourselves going more and more back to

basics, starting again, relearning everything we knew, not sheltering ourselves from our natural environment but learning to live with it. The alienation of Western man is partly due to his having lost contact with all natural functions: the reality of being alive. There are no ends in life, only processes. Change. Spiritual reality is physical reality, clearly seen. We are all here alive together in this world at this time so what are we going to do? First we must provide for our survival. Food, shelter. But houses in our society are walls, blocking man from man, man from the universe, man from himself. We want our homes to spring from the soil like trees.

All living and non-living units take their form from a balance of energies. On a physical plane these forces come into nearly perfect balance in the sphere. It is the most efficient way to enclose volume. A dome—part of a sphere—is the most efficient way to cover a surface. The triangle (our domes are triangulated) is the strongest structural element known. To live in a dome is—psychologically—to be in closer harmony with natural structure. Macrocosm and microcosm are recreated, both the celestial sphere and molecular and crystalline forms.

Cubical buildings are structurally weak and uneconomic. Corners constrict the mind. Domes break into new dimensions. They help to open man's perception and expand his approaches to creativity. The dichotomy between utilitarian and aesthetic, between artist and layman is broken down.

Icosohedrons.

The artist's "life" as a member of industrial civilization has rarely become "art." The nature of his activities alienates him from the mainstream of capitalist society and its market values, because the production of art is not inspired by consumer demand but by cultural necessity. When the necessity

Icosohedrons.

of survival forces the artist into participation in society, the contradiction in values destroys the man
to preserve the artist; it often destroys both. Art
has ceased to be a natural function. Although the
work of art springs from inner necessity, the format

ot the work and the environment in which it is created and displayed are remote from, and antagonistic to, its purpose in the world. The artist in society must live with this absurdity and exploit it to gain his livelihood.

Drop City provides an environment in which the artist can create in harmony with his own inner necessity. The dome is an expansive, inspiring space and its structure provides a greater range of formats for the painter's images than does conventional wall and ceiling space. The new media are taken out of context of the old message. The format becomes more than a vehicle for the message. It is the social context in which the work communicates, lives.

The greatest impact of communal life upon the artist is the realization that all community activity is equal, that digging a ditch carries no less status than erecting a sculpture; in fact the individual often discovers he is happier digging a ditch, sculpting a ditch. Life forms and art forms begin to interact. The identity of the artist becomes irrelevant in relation to the scale of values employed, because the communal context of the work of art removes it from the market place; the artist seeks to work within a system that allows the broadest possible participation of the community. The artist's experience becomes a shared experience. These values are the spontaneous response to a technologically perfectable world, over which we have total domination: a world in which we are capable

Theatre dome. 40 ft.-dome. Decorative patterns made with car tops nailed to wood frame.

of manipulating our environment to a degree that demands creative decisions of extreme subtlety. The works of art we envisage are total, vast.

Most people, when they first come to Drop City, do not know what to do with themselves. We lead a day-by-day existence, functioning within a loose structure, almost invisible most of the time, a structure that is always growing and shifting and changing as we change. We have no compulsory work. So a new person to arrive is often faced with a problem: his survival is provided for; all his time is free time—what is he going to do with it?

He often vascillates between great flurries of

activity and depressions of nothingness. Having been pigeonholed all his life, man does not know what to do with his freedom. We call this "cultural shock." But sooner or later most begin to settle into a rhythm—each into his own natural rhythm. Since there are no compulsions, each eventually discovers how he wants to lead his life. Or life begins—in spite of his protestations—to lead him. He becomes the person he really is by doing the things he wants to do. All activity is creative activity. All creative activity is done for its own sake, without ends. All noncompulsive activity is art.

We get away from job-oriented society, work apart from life. We get away from 'work' as the

House.

Western industrial world has known it, away from
the Protestant ethic. Work is movement, movement is an expression of mind and body, dancing
is work—work is bad, don't dance. Our society is
soporific, addictive to things, comforts, securities.
Physical securities are substitutes for inner security.
They breed inner security, they support it. The
chains of our society are not physical; they are
mental. The door is always open. Any time we
choose to walk out, we can walk out.

But communities are not built on asteroids, the
distance that lies between society and the community is cultural, and the communities are not
built as cloisters; rather we are immigrants and like
all immigrants we band together to save energy.
Jews, coming to New York, banded together in
sixes and nines and bought a Brownstone house, for
cash. They ate together at a common table. Freed
of rent and eating well and easy (you can feed
twelve or more people for the same price as three),
they could turn their pushcarts into million-dollar
estates. Today their children get high together.
Work little, eat well, ball like crazy, and use all
their energy to perfect their own beings, and to help
the perfection of others.

We are immigrants on our own native soil, because we know that today is the future: where
there is a large group of younger people and older
people who share this insight and all feel as one,
there is the beginning of a community, the formation of a level of consciousness from which manifest
action can take place. These people find it possible

to live communally, to form their own organizations and begin to address themselves to the anxiety-ridden outer world.

The purpose of community is awareness, awareness of what your own feelings are. Outside the community there are older people, working in older traditions but with the same insights, who have achieved this awareness. We can begin operating in society on that basis, that we are not alone. Because the insight is real.

But the only thing that will allow each of us to create his or her Utopia is praxis—and the pooling of our resources to free each of us to pursue our individual activities and strengthen the autonomous boundaries of our free communities. For there must be good men and women in the mountains, on the beaches, in all the neglected and beautiful places, so that one day we can come back to ghostly cities and try to set them right. City is so human.

The people in all walks of life who share the consciousness of changing values must begin to combine resources. They must demonstrate their presence to others and to themselves, to reinforce the awareness of their proposals for a new society based on a new consciousness.

Though it is the embodiment of the non-utilitarian in our lives, Art is a resource. Besides shelter, domes enhance our potential for living situations by creating an harmonious and inexpensive environment. The further elaboration and amplification of this dome potential carries the craftsman into the realm of environmental art. For example: the most practical method of cutting a window in a dome provides a decorative and satisfying pattern. The use of coloured glass further distinguishes this pattern. Using the structure as a format for an asymmetrical design image is a more significant and specialized elaboration, but because it has its inception in the structure of the building, it easily remains in harmony with the total environment.

The placing of doors and windows arises naturally from the structure. Flaps are ordinarily spaced around the circumference of the dome, a skylight on top. This arrangement proves cool in summer, warm in winter. The hemispherical shape of the

Window in living dome.

interior is ideal for the setting up of convection currents. A small heater or open flame near the centre of the dome, with a heat collector and stove pipe running out of the top, causes a column of heated air to rise around the hot metal parts. This air is in turn pushed down into the dome to re-circulate. Unhampered by sharp corners, the velocity of the air is increased. Though this does not increase the heat which is radiated into all parts of the dome unshielded by partitioning walls, it does increase the volume of air per minute passing over and conducting heat directly away from the heater. This heating method is further advanced by the fact that in relation to the inner volume of the dome, the outer surface is less than any other shape, thus conducting less heat away from the dome.

Furnishing is a challenge. Most commercial furniture does not fit, and takes up too much room. Domes lend themselves to furniture that is built-in, small, light and low. Beds folding up into the wall or atop storage-platforms; drawers, shelves and benches built into the walls. One dome has a futuristic atmosphere with a glass couch made of car windshields, a bed that folds twice to form a triangular table, and a hanging incense burner which doubles as a mechanism to open the skylight ventilator in the top of the dome.

When our population began to expand, our 20 ft. kitchen became too small. We came in contact with an Albuquerque, N.M. architect who was experimenting with crystalline structure models. With his help we erected a small building, the form of which we derived from garnet crystal. We built it out of car-tops.

The car-top dome is perhaps the most surprising structure to find standing at Drop City. After it was put up it seemed to be hopelessly wobbly and no one would even attempt to stand on top of it. One person did finally climb on it and he later made it completely rock solid by spending days and days adding sheet metal screwed to the edges. How this could be when the only continuous members along the 12 ft. zone are ⅛ in. × 2 in. steel straps sandwiched between the edges of the panels still amazes me.

We cut car tops off the cars with axes and then shaped them to modular size. They are cheap, strong, have an excellent paint job and are available almost everywhere. The thickness of the tin varies from car to car; some are only about 20 gauge, others 18 and 19 gauge. The tops can be cut into huge shingles and nailed on to a wood frame, or their edges can be bent on a sheet metal brake and be made into structural panels themselves, which can be bolted, screwed, riveted or welded together to form a dome made of only car-tops.

Then we applied the same techniques to building our new kitchen: a triple-fused rhombic-icosa-dodecahedron, three 34 ft. domes interlocked. This we built by panels, shingled with car-tops, set up like a house of cards, joined panel-to-panel by gusset plates. It houses our community kitchen, living room, utility storage and bathroom facilities.

Building the cluster was very instructive in that each dome became rigid, step by step, and because of identifiable actions on our part. It is necessary to separate the changes structures undergo as the panels are fastened in place from those that occur when the shape is complete but when fasteners and braces are still being added. The growth of a dome panel by panel is a marvel, watching it take its shape and strength is something at once very strange and very familiar, as if you were watching the growth of a life form from another planet; unusual because of its foreignness, familiar because it seems alive. But this process does not reveal what was necessary and what was unnecessary in the construction of the panels, or the manner in which they are connected. For instance we couldn't get the second-to-last pentagon in. We took a day off. During this day a very strong shinook wind blew; the continual working of the building in this strong wind must have cooked the whole structure, because the next morning the pentagon dropped right into place.

We have found that it is useful to build models of the domes before beginning work on the buildings. When building a model you quickly and easily acquaint yourself with many of the problems of dome building. The angles of the faces, the number of faces of different kinds, and the pattern in which they fit together. As the model goes together you can feel where the strong and weak spots are at different stages. While building a model you meet many of the problems you later encounter in the real thing.

The triple dome structure, which we call "the Complex," is the centre of activity. Within this structure, reaching nearly seventy feet from opposing walls, several floor levels are incorporated. An open loft equipped with a desk, work table and sewing area is open to all but the smallest children. Enclosed beneath it are the w.c., and a storage room for winter clothing and seldom used but necessary items. A separate room is for the bathtub and all body paraphernalia such as medicines, razors, etc.

The kitchen level is three steps down from the main area and is both funky and functional in design. Two stoves stand back-to-back in the centre, divided by large spice and herb shelves. The storage for the large quantities of grains that are the staples in our diet is provided by large pull-out bins. The stoves are painted blue and the refrigerators are painted, symbolically, with huge gaping mouths.

Droppers eat together at two large multi-coloured tables. Another area is composed of three couches and an ingenious rocking chair made from a large cable spool. A woodworking and welding area is also housed in the complex. A washing machine is available here when it is functioning properly, which isn't often. Dropper paintings hang on the walls, as well as Dropper messages, letters, photographs, and drawings. Work is going ahead in the complex on a fireplace with a suspended chimney, a library, and a patio just outside the front entrance.

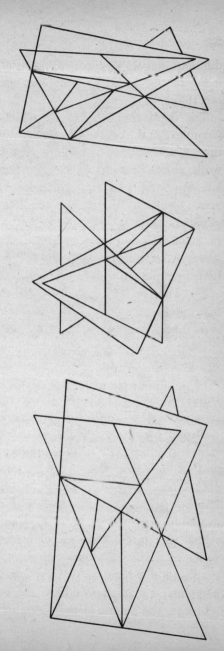

Elementary example of one design module in three possible positions. These grids can be superimposed to develop more elaborate designs. If you turn centre design "upside down" you will recognize module.

Complex-interior.

The community is centred around it. Five small living domes (one 2-story), a 40 ft. 4-frequency geodesic theatre, a 30 ft. 3-frequency workshop, and an icosahedron chicken-coop.

We installed conventional flush w.c.'s but have decided to revert. The stool—which is ridiculous and ugly—uses too much water and demands a room itself. It has become obsolete. The ideal is a fly-proof hole. From this ideal several simple structurally pleasing outhouses have been designed and built; one of the most aesthetically pleasing of these is not enclosed but consists of a hole in the ground with a lid, surrounded by brush.

We have chickens, rabbits and a vegetable garden.

The community functions leisurely, almost haphazardly. After three and a half years we are still open. We have no regular income. Each of us doing his own thing, in his own way, in his own time. Keeping our heads together as a community as much as possible, accomplishes things no rules ever could. Things come to us. The more we give out, the more they come. We try to give freely.

The artist, like the architect who designs the domes, can provide systems that the non-specialist can apply to given situations in order to meet his specific needs. The crystalline image on dome energy is consistent with the chronology of computer events seeking ends, and can therefore be prefabricated. Art, too, seeks ends and, since all abstract expression is ultimately reducible to number, the image becomes the module for prefabricated artwork. The special resource of the artist-specialist is the image, which can only be the product of the life process which seeks no end.

We turn no one away. We provide food and shelter for travellers. New members join the community not by invitation, not by complying with any regulations, but simply by making their presence felt as part of the whole, by staying.

Peter Marin. *The Free People*

This is Peter Marin's introduction to the book *The Free People*, a photographic essay on the communes of the West Coast. In a few paragraphs it says more that is wise and right than whole books have managed to say about our contemporary youth culture.

FREEDOM is for me, as much the feeling of *particular* moments as it is a quality of persons, and it is from my memory of such moments that I construct for myself an image of free *people*. . . . I am writing this in the Santa Cruz mountains, surrounded by my friends, and I shuffle through my notes, the fragments I keep for poems and myself, the lacunae that loom larger for me than cultural events. This note, for instance, crumpled on a friends dresser:

Dear David

you mak

Dear David

you

From *The Free People,* introduction by Peter Marin, photographs by Anders Holmquist (New York: Outerbridge & Dienstfrey, 1969). Reprinted by permission of the publisher.

Dear David,
I'm going back to the poetry-freaks and other over-
reactors & laughers & livers & huggers & you're
welcome in my house & bed whenever you come,
but I'M NOT GOING BACK TO LIMBO ANYMORE

Or these words scrawled by a student on the wall of
the room in which I write:

> *Truth*
> *Purity*
> *Nonviolence*
> *Poverty*
> *Nonpossession*

Or, as the moments occur to me: a Japanese boy
talking about Meher Baba and meditation, two Big
Sur carpenters building a Fuller dome, two nude
couples fucking by candlelight, a girl with sewn
wrists, two topless dancers, my own son crooning:
*thank you, fire, thank you, thank you for my warm
heart.* . . .

The festivals of the young and their spectacles are
colorful and sometimes fascinating, but it is the
underside of things, the feel to *private* lives that is
important, for the most revealing moments, and the
best ones, are always private. I think about my
friends among these young people and their houses
and try to get some sense of things, and it seems to
me now that there is often a lovely feel to them: a
softness, a delight which comes more and more
often, an ease and surety, a sense of *being at home*.

It is a feeling that emerges from moments that are surprisingly domestic: friends talking, or making love, or working together, or people in solitude. Somewhere Lawrence talks about three mysteries: the mystery of sex, the mystery of friendship, the mystery of solitude. He had no children and therefore neglected them, but if you add to these the mystery of fatherhood and time, you have what seem to me the elements at the heart of whatever it is to feel free. It is not that what is done among the young is different or extreme; it is simply that what is done feels differently in quality, in resonance, and that is hard to capture, hard to describe. It is the difference between good sex and bad sex, or even good and bad conversation: a sense of warmth, of slowness and delight. It is this new quality, this feeling, that seems in retrospect to enter the flesh of my friends and abide there. . . .

But if the best moments are private, so are the worst, and the lives of the young, taken individually, are often full of confusion and fear. If I have known them as a lover, their thin bodies out of some Hindu myth, hair falling like the sky, I have also held them all night like a father as they shivered and moaned, repeating to them over and over like a spell, *good girl, good girl*—as if that might, for the first time, somehow make things *right*. The males too have been my comrades and teachers, but I know too the confusion and loneliness behind their grace and bravery.

For they also drift, they float confused in a void inside themselves in which there are no others, no

sounds. They are young and ungrounded and there is a terror in them, and the underside of "freedom" is an inexplicable sense of bondage and isolation. My friends grimace when I say "free people" because they know that what is *space* for some is for others a nightmare in which all things are possible and nothing makes sense. Style is not substance, and there is a numb grief and dumb sorrow which hip music and clothes cannot dissolve. . . .

It is not merely that society has proved imperfect or corrupt; it is, put simply, that "social reality" seems to have disappeared altogether. What has coherence in the culture or makes sense? In terms of classic Freudian analysis where once there were *traumas*, specific causes for confusion, there now seems to be a pervasive sense of loss and rage, a paranoia directed at an entire culture, a sense of having been betrayed by the world itself. Indeed, there no longer seems to be any kind of reality to confront; instead, one drifts in a limbo and constructs a world from one's imagination—as if one fathered and mothered oneself.

In that condition, psychosis and schizophrenia can become common states of being. At times it seems to me that for every psyche that survives another seems to crumble. There is no middle ground. Community and collective wisdom have vanished, and the young seem forced in the vacuum to improvise, to find their own ways back to wisdom or joy. But how can they handle that? There are ways that lead back and through the self, ways to find in oneself and others what is missing in the

world. But they take patience and time and
privacy—and where can the young find those? They
are harried and rushed, tugged this way and that by
fads, superstitions, and raw waves of ignorance that
pass for wisdom. As we embrace new parts of the
self we ignore the old, and parts of the self once
familiar grow threatening and strange. We sidestep
sorrow though wisdom is rooted in it as much as in
joy; and as thought becomes suspect, habit and confusion pass as spontaneous sense.

I am not condemning the young, but I *am* trying
to articulate as fully as possible what it means to be
"free." At the heart of freedom one finds terror as
well as joy and we must remember that—not to
reduce the beauty of the young nor to condemn
them, but to recall to ourselves what is owed them.
If it is true, as I believe, that wisdom is a function
of joyous, free, and connective moments, then what
the young need is access to such moments and more
chances to create them for themselves.

But what will make that possible? In these mountains, I remember, were a group of caves cut high
into a steep hillside and overlooking ridges and
valleys of conifer forest which stretched to the coast.
A few young people lived in the caves year-round,
subsisting on wild herbs and brown rice. . . .
There was something primitive to it, and as one
listened to them murmuring around their fire at
night, one thought, of course, of tribal rites. What
they had done, unconsciously but precisely, was to
reproduce for themselves a common rite of initiation
and isolation—as if, through the silence of the hills

and temporary exile, they could come to terms with themselves. When they spoke there was a slow thoughtfulness to what they said, a solemnity—as if their distance from the urban sprawl below allowed them to sense the dimension of their own manhood.

The cave was a *place*, and that was what they needed: a privileged shelter. It exposed them to the world and kept them safe. On its high rocky ledge, as one of them said, you began to dream of flying; and when, at sunset, the wind came up from the sea, cold and sharp, it *was* like flying, like soaring, and the land fell away behind you and only the sky itself was left.

That, I suppose, is my image of freedom: the cave and a sense of flying, the combination of belonging and release. The young soar like birds, but like birds they need somewhere to rest. Unable to land or harried by dogs, birds grow panicky and anxious—and that too is true of the young. The source of potency and balance is always some sort of grounding, a sense of being at home *somewhere*, even in oneself. But it is precisely this that the young seem to lack—and how can they survive without it?

It is for this reason that the communes become important—and the few schools or rare households where the young seem truly at home. Now, as the psyche drifts loose and imagination flowers, it is as if a heavenly city hovered within us but just out of reach, uninhabited but prepared, its tables laid and torches lit. It dances in and out of mind like a mirage and we ache to grasp it, enter it, but before we can enter it and rest, it must somehow be made real, and if we fail at that, it may vanish completely.

We have come, pilgrims all, to a time that perplexes but exhilarates us, for we are able and compelled now to live out our dreams. As we slip downward and deeper into ourselves, we approach a heraldic universe in which both delight and danger become more real. . . .

That lovely warmth moves me now as I write—my wife and the children asleep next door. It is, at bottom, the presence in me of all those I love, and it is that net of connections, that cradle of affection that seems to me at the heart of my own pleasure. Not long ago when I visited a college, a student said to me: "You seem to know just where you are; how do you do it?" I thought for a long time before answering, and I realized then for the first time that I was protected as if by a charm by the presence within me of my family and comrades. "The bird a nest, the spider a web, man friendship," writes Blake, and that is my sense of it. We seem to have entered an inhabited world; the world of my childhood with its loneliness and fear, our image of the solitary hero, the gunslinger, gives way to something else, something far more beautiful. It is clear to me now that the rapid and unfamiliar changes now in the world will make themselves known to us as new persons, new natures: sequential waves of lovers and comrades whose natures will be different enough to enlarge and enchant us and demand that we change. It is that function, I think, that the

LAND
PERMIT TO LIVE
ON NOT ☮
← REQUIRED

young perform, for the shapes the world takes in
them requires from us at least a new response and
brings to us, at best, a new reality. . . .

But where, asks a student, *are the free people
without rich parents?* That question nags at me as I
write and I have no way to answer it, but it must be
asked. I live in the hills and lead the life that makes
sense to me, but in the cities at the same time war
rages. Wherever we live or whatever we spend in
this country has been stolen, is not truly ours, and if
that is the case how can any individual life be
whole and pure—or free? There are few black faces
at the festivals or in the mountains, and the connections between whites and blacks, or private lives
and the public good, are still too tangled in my
mind for me to make clear. Those words scrawled
on the wall behind me—*truth, purity, nonviolence,
poverty, nonpossession*—are noble goals, but though
there are many among the young willing to pursue
them, many, despite their clothes and hair, do not—
and these seem to be eccentric versions of their
parents. Only a blind man or a fool would be un-
troubled by that, and I have no hope or illusion of
clearing it up here; it is simply that one cannot let
it go unsaid. . . .

At the end of his diary Nijinsky writes about hearing his daughter singing: "I do not understand its
meaning, but I feel she wants to say that everything
—Ah! Ah!—is not horror but joy."

Patsy Richardson. *No More Freefolk*

> Sometimes . . . most times . . . communes fail.
> So do the world's big institutions . . . but they
> go on and on and on, like the walking dead. At
> least communes know when and how to die,
> leaving a little residue of wisdom behind like
> seed.

FREEFOLK COMMUNITY is abandoned except for the
birds and the rabbits. Maybe the deer have come
back, now that the people are gone. We left over a
year ago, gradually the others did too.

Freefolk was a small, rural anarchistic-type commune. It flowered briefly for a year and a half, then
died out the way a lot of communes do that you
hear about and then after a while don't hear about
anymore. I like to think of our attempt there as part
of a larger experiment. Somehow what we discovered may help others who want to learn and live
together in community.

There were times at Freefolk when love bloomed,
when we sang together, worked together as sisters
and brothers, felt in us the power of our mother
earth. There were also times when we didn't speak

From *The Modern Utopian*, summer-fall 1970. Published
by Alternatives (P.O. Drawer A, San Francisco, Calif.
94131)—periodicals on communes, free schools, social
change.

to each other, or care enough to reach out when someone clearly needed us. Because we lived a life peeled down to the good necessities, because we lived without the shelter of all those institutions that protect and separate people from each other, the high times were really high and the bad times pretty ugly—eyes stopped meeting, hands stopped reaching and we became strangers living in the same house.

A lot of people think communities flop because of economic hassles or pressure from outside. We haven't found that to be true. We ate well and kept reasonably warm (though, sometimes interpersonal frictions kept us from getting things done as well as we could have). With a minimum of effort we were able to maintain open and friendly relationships with neighbors. I guess I can't say why communities flop, but I have some ideas about why Freefolk isn't there anymore.

Partly from necessity, partly because we didn't appreciate our own needs for separateness (what some people call privacy, but that word always reminded me of bathrooms), we attempted to live too closely. Each family or individual had a sleeping place of his own, but in the long Minnesota winter we just couldn't keep all those shacks warm all day, so we had to spend most of our waking hours together in the community room (10′ x 20′, wood stove, table, chairs, sink, and three toddlers who had a harder time learning to share than we did).

Idealists that we are, with a strong vision of how

men ought to live together, it was really difficult for
us to admit that we were uptight, needed more
room, more time for ourselves or really didn't care
that much for each other sometimes. Each of us
had a vision, really amazingly similar, about the
way we wanted to live. But because we weren't
there yet, it was the small things that caused
troubles. We all wanted to live a simple primitive
existence. We all were content to live without rules,
electricity, power tools, or running water, in fact we
felt it was strongly a necessity for our emotional,
spiritual, economic or political survival. What hung
us up was whether we should eat all our honey in
the fall or ration it through the winter; whether we
should tie the cow or let her move around in the
barn; whether we should fence the garden around
front or back; whether we should restrain the kids
or let them clobber each other. And it wasn't the
fence or the honey that really mattered. It was
partly the fact that we had no other personal
creative challenges to divert our energies (the
garden, the food, the children were our chief
interests in life) and partly the fact that we started
at the pinnacle of a vision where people shared and
cared for one another intensely, but that was just
not where we were at personally. The mountain
crumpled, tension rose, we grew away from each
other.

Maybe things didn't have to go that way. There
were a lot of strongly individual types at Freefolk—
meaning, I guess, people who liked having their
own way, people who had an urge to see the world

move when they pushed it. That's the kind of people that seem attracted to community, people who find meaning in struggle, people who probably aren't real groupie types. Maybe we could have made it together, adapted to meet our various separate and collective needs, if we could have tuned into what was happening sooner. We were blinded by dreams, I think. Trapped living so closely. Saddest of all, we were unable in a year and a half to learn to talk to one another, to tell each other straight what it was we felt or thought, to be open about our needs and our hurts. Bitterness grew and silence grew until it filled up the clearing, and now we're all gone except for the birds and the rabbits.

So, where did we go from there? We each went different ways, still looking, still experimenting. . . .

Wendell Berry. "To a Siberian Woodsman"
(after looking at some pictures in a magazine)

1.

You lean at ease in your warm house at night after
    supper,
listening to your daughter play the accordion. You
    smile

From *Openings* copyright © 1968 by Wendell Berry. Reprinted by permission of Harcourt Brace Jovanovich, Inc.

with the pleasure of a man confident in his hands,
        resting
after a day of long labor in the forest, the cry of the
        saw
in your head, and the vision of coming home to
        rest.
Your daughter's face is clear in the joy of hearing
her own music. Her fingers live on the keys
like people familiar with the land they were born in.

You sit at the dinner table late into the night with
        your son;
tying the bright flies that will lead you along the
        forest streams.
Over you, as your hands work, is the dream of the
        still pools. Over you is the dream
of your silence while the east brightens, birds
        waking close by you in the trees.

2.

I have thought of you stepping out of your doorway
        at dawn, your son in your tracks.
You go in under the overarching green branches of
        the forest
whose ways, strange to me, are well known to you
        as the sound of your own voice
or the silence that lies around you now that you
        have ceased to speak,
and soon the voice of the stream rises ahead of you,
        and you take the path beside it.
I have thought of the sun breaking pale through the
        mists over you

as you come to the pool where you will fish, and of
    the mist drifting
over the water, and of the cast fly resting light on
    the face of the pool.

3.

And I am here in Kentucky in the place I have made
    myself
in the world. I sit on my porch above the river
    that flows muddy
and slow along the feet of the trees. I hear the voices
    of the wren
and the yellow-throated warbler whose songs pass
    near the windows
and over the roof. In my house my daughter learns
    the womanhood
of her mother. My son is at play, pretending to be
the man he believes I am. I am the outbreathing of
    this ground.
My words are its words as the wren's song is its
    song.

4.

Who has invented our enmity? Who has prescribed
    us
hatred of each other? Who has armed us against
    each other
with the death of the world? Who has appointed
    me such anger
that I should desire the burning of your house or
    the destruction of your children?

Who has appointed such anger to you? Who has
    set loose the thought
that we should oppose each other with the ruin of
    forests and rivers, and the silence of birds?
Who has said to us that the voices of my land shall
    be strange
to you, and the voices of your land strange to me?
Who has imagined that I would destroy myself in
    order to destroy you,
or that I could improve myself by destroying you?
    Who has imagined
that your death could be negligible to me now that
    I have seen these pictures of your face?
Who has imagined that I would not speak familiarly
    with you,
or laugh with you, or visit in your house and go to
    work with you in the forest?
And now one of the ideas of my place will be that
    you would gladly talk and visit and work with
    me.

5.

I sit in the shade of the trees of the land I was
    born in.
As they are native I am native, and I hold to this
    place as carefully as they hold to it.
I do not see the national flag flying from the staff of
    the sycamore,
or any decree of the government written on the
    leaves of the walnut,
nor has the elm bowed before monuments or sworn
    the oath of allegiance.

They have not declared to whom they stand in welcome.

6.

In the thought of you I imagine myself free of the
weapons and the official hates that I have borne
on my back like a hump,
and in the thought of myself I imagine you free of
weapons and official hates,
so that if we should meet we would not go by each
other looking at the ground like slaves sullen
under their burdens,
but would stand clear in the gaze of each other.

7.

There is no government so worthy as your son who
fishes with you in silence beside the forest pool.
There is no national glory so comely as your daughter whose hands have learned a music and go
their own way on the keys.
There is no national glory so comely as my daughter who dances and sings and is the brightness
of my house.
There is no government so worthy as my son who
laughs, as he comes up the path from the river
in the evening, for joy.

Gary Snyder. "Amitabha's vow"

"If, after obtaining Buddhahood, anyone in my land
      gets tossed in jail on a vagrancy rap, may I
      not attain highest perfect enlightenment.

      wild geese in the orchard
      frost on the new grass

"If, after obtaining Buddhahood, anyone in my land
      loses a finger coupling boxcars, may I
      not attain highest perfect enlightenment.

      mare's eye flutters
      jerked by the lead-rope
      stone-bright shoes flick back
      ankles trembling: down steep rock

"If, after obtaining Buddhahood, anyone in my land
      can't get a ride hitch-hiking all directions, may I
      not attain highest perfect enlightenment.

      wet rocks buzzing
      rain and thunder southwest
      hair, beard, tingle
      wind whips bare legs
      we should go back
      we don't

From *Myths and Texts* (New York: Corinth Books, 1960).
Reprinted by permission of the publisher.

IV. WHOLE EARTH

O you people who are always standing, who pierce up through the earth, and who reach even unto the heavens, you tree-people are very many, but one of you has been especially chosen for supporting this sacred purification lodge. You trees are the protectors of the wingeds, for upon you they build their lodges and raise their families; and beneath you there are many people whom you shelter. May all these people and all their generations walk together as relatives!

We should understand well that all things are the works of the Great Spirit. We should know that He is within all things: the trees, the grasses, the rivers, the mountains, and all the four-legged animals, and the winged peoples; and even more important, we should understand that He is also above all these things and peoples. When we do understand all this deeply in our hearts, then we will fear, and love, and know the Great Spirit, and then we will be and act and live as He intends.

I am sending a voice! Hear me! *Wakan-Tanka*, Grandfather, You are first and always have been. You have brought us to this great island, and here our people wish to live in a sacred manner. Teach us to know and see all the powers of the universe, and give to us the knowledge to understand that they are all really one Power. May our people always send their voices to You as they walk the sacred path of life!

A prayer of Black Elk from *The Sacred Pipe* by Joseph Epes Brown (Norman, Okla.: University of Oklahoma Press, 1953). Copyright 1953 by the University of Oklahoma Press. Reprinted by permission of the publisher.

O ancient rocks, *Tunkayatakapaka,* you are now here with us; *Wakan-Tanka* has made the Earth, and has placed you next to Her. Upon you the generations will walk, and their steps shall not falter! O Rocks, you have neither eyes, nor mouth, nor limbs; you do not move, but by receiving your sacred breath, our people will be long-winded as they walk the path of life; your breath is the very breath of life.

There is a winged One, there where the sun goes down to rest, who controls those waters to which all living beings owe their lives. May we use these waters here in a sacred manner!

(A prayer of Black Elk from *The Sacred Pipe*).

As reason is divided off from feeling, as mind from body, as State from society, so too mankind from the natural continuum. Then "nature" becomes, not us, not the whole living works, but a some*thing* Out There, an inferior object to be used, studied—perhaps occasionally *appreciated!* One more step and we arrive at the sad idea that "nature poetry" means poems with trees in them: a distinct category, one among many and by now become rather tiresome. Because, after all, there are so many more interesting, *contemporary* "subjects." To write "about." Besides "nay-chur."

Reason-feeling, mind-body, State-society, man-nature—all the dichotomies are in essence one: a distrust of spontaneous process, a need (born of fear) to petrify and dominate, an incapacity to be easy and swing with the given rhythm: the loss of the Tao.

All the dichotomies work to establish invidious hierarchies. Reason, Mind, State, Man become boss-big-shot, top-dog, headquarters, command-and-control-center. Feeling, body, society, nature must then play nigger: bow, scrape, cringe, obey, and serve in total abasement. All the dichotomies end in disaster, for the Tao, being infinitely elastic, may bend, but will never break, and at last restores the balance—somehow. Eventually, the bottom dogs reclaim their own. Feeling rebels as nightmare. Body rebels as ulcer, cancer, heart attack, asthma, migraine: the psychosomatics. Society rebels as revolution. Nature rebels as "environmental crisis." The rebellions may draw blood; they are nonetheless a summons to health.

All the dichotomies yield to an identical therapy: the restoration of wholeness. Reason and feeling made one become the person. Mind and body made one become the organism. State and society made one become community. Man and nature made one become ecology.

The ecological calamity of our time is not simply *another* problem. It is the death warrant of industrial economy. Where do we look for good medicine? Sadly, most of what is prescribed is merely hair-of-the-dog, more expert research, more expert development. Electric motors rather than internal combustion, more air-conditioning, more deadly, chlorinated hydrocarbons. But the great technological breakthroughs go sour. America's answer to world famine, the much-touted "green revolution" (mainly dwarf wheat and such like miracle grains—intensively fertilized and pesticide treated) has been driven forward (in the words of Paul Ehrlich) by "a combination of utter ignorance of ecology, a desire to justify past errors, and pressure from agro-industry . . . eager to sell pesticides, fertilizers and farm machinery to the underdeveloped countries."

Overpopulation is the toughest underlying factor: the crucial measure of imbalance. But even this is treated mainly as a technical administrative problem—a matter of research and policy—rather than a matter of human motivation, hence of values. Population experts talk as if it is out of sheer contraceptive ignorance that men impregnate women and women bear children. *Nobody* except for the very young is that ignorant. Our most primitive ancestors devised numerous, often brutal ways to control their numbers (though many of them, like the Cheyenne Indians, also understood the virtues of sexual abstinence which few moderns will even once consider). More humane contraceptive techniques can now, and must surely be substituted. But only where there is the *will* do people take up the way. By far the safest, quickest, surest, cheapest, least morally traumatic method—the vasectomy—requires minimal surgical expertise: an almost primitively simple operation. Why is it not more widely used? The key question: not *how* to control reproduction, but *why* do people have children? *Why* do they have more children than their economy can gracefully support? And the answer is *not* obvious. Rather, it has much to do with the caste repression of women: what other power and creative outlet do most women have besides motherhood? But also, with the authentic joys and (perhaps—but not always) illusory securities of family-making, with prestige factors, with compulsive masculinity and male chauvinist marriage customs, with the sick need to lord it over dependents, with the healthy need of community which the world beyond the household frustrates. This last, a major point.

Deep waters these—and hardly sounded to their depths by the usual family-planning "how-to" propaganda. People have always known "how to." What they need is a better reason why. Meanwhile, as our numbers burgeon, technological "progress" and the unbecoming but universal lust for idiot affluence, merely amplify our ability to exhaust the environment.

It is a new formulation of an old environmental wisdom that is needed—not merely more R & D. We must come out of the laboratories, the think-tanks, the academies, and hear the words of Black Elk. Meditate for a day, a month, a year, many years on the scrolls of the Chinese masters who long ago doodled man into the interstices of their landscapes: a tiny animal, but not insignificant, modestly at home amid the great mothering way of things. Get the feel of things right; good policy follows. It is not enough to find the world (especially in the form of the well-preserved tourist paradise) beau-

tiful; it is not always; nor does it always treat us
gently. But it is always sacred, no matter what. As
the old hunters knew: even when you must draw
the blood of the beasts, they are your brothers and
you pray their forgiveness.

Anonymous. "Smokey the Bear Sutra"

Once in the Jurassic, about 150 million years ago,
the Great Sun Buddha in this corner of the Infinite
Void gave a great Discourse to all the assembled
    elements
and energies: to the standing beings, the walking
    beings,
the flying beings, and the sitting beings—even
    grasses,
to the number of thirteen billion, each one born
    from a
seed, were assembled there: a Discourse concerning
Enlightenment on the planet Earth.

"In some future time, there will be a continent called
America. It will have great centers of power called
such as Pyramid Lake, Walden Pond, Mt. Rainier,
    Big Sur,
Everglades, and so forth; and powerful nerves and
    channels
such as Columbia River, Mississippi River, and
    Grand Canyon.

The human race in that era will get into troubles all
    over
its head, and practically wreck everything in spite of
its own strong intelligent Buddha-nature."

"The twisting strata of the great mountains and the
    pulsings
of great volcanoes are my love burning deep in the
    earth.
My obstinate compassion is schist and basalt and
granite, to be mountains, to bring down the rain. In
    that
future American Era I shall enter a new form: to
    cure
the world of loveless knowledge that seeks with
    blind hunger;
and mindless rage eating food that will not fill it."

And he showed himself in his true form of

SMOKEY THE BEAR.

A handsome smokey-colored brown bear
standing on his hind legs, showing that he is
aroused and watchful.

Bearing in his right paw the Shovel that digs
to the truth beneath appearances; cuts the roots of
useless attachments, and flings damp sand on the
fires of greed and war;

His left paw in the Mudra of Comradely
Display—indicating that all creatures have the full

right to live to their limits and that deer, rabbits,
chipmunks, snakes, dandelions, and lizards all grow
in the realm of the Dharma;

Wearing the blue work overalls symbolic of
slaves and laborers, the countless men oppressed
by a civilization that claims to save but only
destroys;

Wearing the broad-brimmed hat of the West,
symbolic of the forces that guard the Wilderness,
which is the Natural State of the Dharma and the
True Path of man on earth; all true paths lead
through mountains—

With a halo of smoke and flame behind, the
forest fires of the kali-yuga, fires caused by the
stupidity of those who think things can be gained
and lost whereas in truth all is contained vast and
free in the Blue Sky and Green Earth of One Mind;

Round-bellied to show his kind nature and
that the great earth has food enough for everyone
who loves her and trusts her;

Trampling underfoot wasteful freeways and
needless suburbs; smashing the worms of capitalism
and totalitarianism;

Indicating the Task: his followers, becoming
free of cars, houses, canned food, universities, and
shoes, master the Three Mysteries of their own

Body, Speech, and Mind; and fearlessly chop down
the rotten trees and prune out the sick limbs of this
country America and then burn the leftover trash.

Wrathful but Calm, Austere but Comic, Smokey the
Bear will Illuminate those who would help him;
but for those who would hinder or slander him,

HE WILL PUT THEM OUT.

Thus his great Mantra:

Namah samanta vajranam chanda maharoshana
Sphataya hum traka ham mam

"I DEDICATE MYSELF TO THE UNIVERSAL DIAMOND
BE THIS RAGING FURY DESTROYED"

And he will protect those who love woods and rivers,
Gods and animals, hobos and madmen, prisoners
and sick people, musicians, playful women, and
hopeful children;

And if anyone is threatened by advertising, air
pollution, or the police, they should chant SMOKEY
THE BEAR'S WAR SPELL:

DROWN THEIR BUTTS
CRUSH THEIR BUTTS
DROWN THEIR BUTTS
CRUSH THEIR BUTTS

And SMOKEY THE BEAR will surely appear to put the
enemy out with his vajra-shovel.

Now those who recite this Sutra and then try to
    put it in practice will accumulate merit as
    countless as the sands of Arizona and Nevada,
Will help save the planet Earth from total oil slick,
Will enter the age of harmony of man and nature,
Will win the tender love and caresses of men,
    women, and beasts
Will always have ripe blackberries to eat and a
    sunny spot under a pine tree to sit at,

AND IN THE END WILL WIN HIGHEST PERFECT
ENLIGHTENMENT.

        thus have we heard.

Edward Hyams. *Tools of the Spirit*

Soil and Civilization by the novelist and natural-
ist Edward Hyams is a classic of popular ecological literature. It deserves to be better known.
Unfortunately, Hyams's optimistic conclusion
about America's promising environmental wisdom
has, in the twenty years since the book was
written, gone down before the steam-roller of
agrindustrial "progress."

However, in ecology we at last have a
wholistic science: western man's own somewhat
ungainly nature mysticism. Hyams suggests that
"aesthetic insight" must take the place of religious

From *Soil and Civilization* (London: Thames and Hud-
son, 1952). Reprinted by permission of the publisher.

belief in our ecology as an indispensable element. But where does artistic sensibility leave off and religious experience begin? Was Goethe's *Natur-philosophie* aesthetic or religious? A semantic hair not worth splitting. The distinction is elusively soft and not really important to Hyams's thesis. On the other hand, Hyams's remarks about the sexual politics underlying the disintegration of the magical world-view are highly significant and deserve special attention.

THERE IS NO peculiar merit in ancient things, but there is merit in integrity, and integrity entails the keeping together of the parts of any whole, and if those parts are scattered throughout time, then the maintenance of integrity entails a knowledge, a memory, of ancient things. The community of men is kept whole and healthy by some valid idea, some inspiring feeling, the components of which are scattered throughout time and space. Until very recently men have tended to act as though the past were done with, and to concentrate upon present and future, but in our own time some progress has been made by mathematicians towards understand-ing the nature of time, which has come to be con-sidered as one of the four dimensions in which we live. The integrity of idea and feeling which hold the community of men together must therefore transcend not only space, but time, for no dimension of space, and nothing which is contained in space, has reality excepting in so far as it persists. *Present* is a relative term, it is a point in time and as such has temporal position but no temporal magnitude. To think, feel or act as though the past is done with, is equivalent to believing that a railway station through which our train has just passed, only existed for as long as our train was in it. A community which ignores or repudiates its origins, in its present acts, is no more whole and healthy than a man who has lost his memory. One of the conditions for the achievement of full human status by man is that he should "remember" every detail of his past; and this is the importance of all the arts and sciences which recreate the past in our consciousness. . . .

When men do work upon matter they employ tools which are of two kinds: physical tools of wood, bone, stone, metal; and psychological tools which are expressed in methods, and which become formalized as techniques. Philosophically, there is no difference between these two classes of tools: the plan a man makes concerning the way in which he will move a boulder, is just as much a tool as the lever he uses to carry out his plan. The psychological tools can be divided into two sub-classes, the intellectual and the spiritual; the intellectual tools are concerned with method and collected in sets as sciences; the spiritual tools are concerned with relationships with the rest of the universe, and are collected together in mythologies and religions. A man using all three kinds of tool to turn a piece of waste land into a farm, uses the spiritual tool to invoke the help of the God whose writ runs in that parish, and thereby puts himself into an effectively wilful and purposeful state of mind; he uses the intellectual tools to decide how to set about the work; and the physical tools to cut down trees and plough the virgin soil. . . .

An early problem which man had to solve was that of tree felling, and in course of time he evolved a perfect axe head. This tool was as good as it could be by late Neolithic times, and it remains unchanged in form; only the material of which it is made has changed—stone, bronze, iron, steel. But the axe was only the physical tool which ancient man used to cut down trees, and the intellectual tool enabled him to devise the most effective way to swing his axe, to see where the tree should be cut in order that it should fall in a certain way. But what of the spiritual tool? It is this member of the trinity of tools which enables men to control and check their actions by reference to the "feeling" which they possess for the consequences of the changes they make in their environment. Man was anciently aware of the whole world as alive, and finding himself animated by spirit very properly supposed all other living creatures—and for him life was manifest even in stones—to be similarly animated. If it be true that primitive men were prevented from cutting down many trees by their inconsiderable numbers and poor tools, it can also be said that even without these handicaps, their tree felling would have been closely and sharply controlled by their state of mind and spirit on the subject of trees.

For men believed that trees had souls and were worshipful; and they associated certain gods with certain trees. Osiris with acacia, Apollo with oak and apple. The temples of many primitive peoples were groves, and in some, for example that of Upsala, men were sacrificed to the spirits which inhabited trees. This point of view is not one which we could adopt today, but it should be recognized that it was immensely valuable to the soil community and therefore, in the long run, to man. It meant that no trees would be wantonly felled, but only when it was absolutely necessary, and then to the accompaniment of propitiatory rites which, if they did nothing else, served constantly to remind tree fellers that they were doing dangerous and important work, and to foster their sense of responsibility towards the other species of the soil community. As an example of the effectiveness of such a state of spirit, in many places, when clearings were being made, the lesser trees were cut down, but the finest were left standing, to provide homes for the spirits ejected from the fallen trees. No Agricultural Executive Committee, no Soil Conservation regulation could have been more effective. We use today the axe-head made by the earliest tree fellers, but not the spiritual tools of which they made use to regulate their tree felling. What have we put in their place? . . .

The dominant spirit of the times is urban and industrial, and the use of spiritual, as well as intellectual and physical tools, is no more felt necessary to a good harvest and the continued fertility of the soil, than propitiation of Vulcan is felt necessary by the Steel Board for the production of an adequate quantity of sheet steel. Our thought and feeling in

these matters represents the antithesis of those of
the Neolithic flint-miners: *they* set up an image of
the fertility goddess to help them to a "crop" of
flint in a barren seam, because the dominant spirit of
their times was agricultural: we fail to propitiate the
goddess in trying to maintain the fertility of our
soil, because the dominant spirit of our time is industrial.

What were the ancient spiritual tools of the culti-
vator? With great and fascinating local variants,
the pattern into which these devices arrange themselves is universal. Frazer, in the *Golden Bough,*
says:

. . . in antiquity the civilized nations of Western
Asia and Egypt pictured to themselves the changes
of the seasons, and particularly the annual growth and
decay of vegetation, as episodes in the life of the Gods,
whose mournful death and happy resurrection they celebrated with dramatic rites of alternate lamentation and
rejoicing. But if the celebration was in form dramatic,
it was in substance magical; that is to say, it was intended, on the principles of sympathetic magic, to
ensure the vernal regeneration of plants and the multiplication of animals, which had seemed to be menaced
by the inroads of winter. . . .

For the ancient farmers, and even for those not so
far from us in time, every plant and animal and
stone and the very Earth herself were alive and
animated by spirit. And since, from self-knowledge,
man knew that mind and matter, soul and body
must be in harmony, in order that the whole should
function, he also knew that in manipulating the

body of the living world, he must be at one with the spirit animating it.

That spirit was, in the earliest agrarian societies, female, as the social life of the society was dominated by female values. That dominance must have derived from the fact that women, in bearing children, did the most important creative act, for man's part in generation was not suspected. It was apparent that the earth, like one's wife and mother, brought forth life: it followed that the earth was female. In societies which earned their living by tillage, a female device, the adoration of the Earth-Mother endured; and where the tradition of peasantry was ancient and never broken, this worship has been interrupted only by repeated changes in the name of the goddess, never in her nature. In some remote and backward societies not even the name changed: in Eleusis Demeter was worshipped by nominally Christian villagers until the nineteenth century.

The conflict between science and religion which occupied so many men's attention in the nineteenth century, is as ancient as man. Observation of nature and deduction of laws from such observation is the basis of science. By some such observation, entailing a sharp break with conservative tradition, men discovered that the pleasures of a somewhat brutal love, for only poetry and manners have made it otherwise, issued in the responsibilities of paternity. The kudos of the creative act was transferred to the male. In primitive societies, the active role must always be given more importance than the passive.

When, like human babies, the god acquired a father, the importance of the male deity began to rise and that of the Earth-Mother to decline. . . .

Where masculine economic values dominated, that is in those societies where the male business of hunting had given rise to the male business of stock-raising, and in due course to nomadic pastoralism, the importance of women declined with the declining importance of tillage. The gods of the primarily pastoral Hebrews, Danaans, Aryas, were male. The great goddess, in such societies, became the consort of the sky-god, generally a tribal war god, Zeus, Jahveh, the atrocious Huitzilopochtli. Her importance might at first be but little diminished by this marriage: it is perhaps not too much to suggest that as the kings, and even the fathers, in formerly matrilinear societies, derived their title by virtue of their marriage to the eternal heiress, so the war gods derived their title from their marriage with the Great Mother. I have no authority for the idea, and do not insist upon it. But as war became increasingly important as a social activity, the importance of the great goddess would be certain to diminish among the warrior class, the leaders, while their allies, the priests, would favour this revolution against the divine candidate of their female rivals. But such displacement was never easy and never complete. At Delphi, the Oracle, the god, was Apollo; but the interpreter was a Pythoness. It is a female gypsy who tells our fortune, not a male. And among the peasants, the goddess never seems to have lost her predominance: they might, under pressure, concede an outward homage to the sky-god, yet in their rites they continued to give honour where honour was due; nor did the most arrogantly male governments dare interfere with the Eleusinian Mysteries. The struggle between male and female gods has gone on until very recent times, and the ruthless ferocity with which the Christian churches, especially the ultra-masculine Protestant churches, urged on the persecutors of witches, miserable survivors of the goddess's servants, gives some idea of the plane of savagery upon which this fight was conducted. . . .

Christianity came to peoples who were either barbarous, worshipping war-gods, or super-sophisticated, tolerating all gods and believing, perhaps, in none. The notion of a god who was a scapegoat, and died for the people, of respectable antiquity, found acceptance; subtle Greek metaphysicians worked on the story to make it acceptable by the sophisticated. But for the peasantry, in due course, it entailed nothing but the substitution of the name Mary for some other name—Cybele, Astarte, Demeter, Persephone, Pachamamma, Maia. If, among the people of the nations which took the creative lead in the world, agriculture had remained in the hands of true peasants, the most ancient psychological and spiritual tools of the farmer would have continued in use. It so happened that our world, the modern world, was made by the English, a people who used a thorough-going industrial-commercial device to meet the challenge of their condition, and who destroyed their peasantry in carrying the spirit of industry and commerce into their countryside.

It is not suggested that the failure of this psychological and spiritual device to persist like the form of physical tools, could or even sheuld have been avoided. There occurred, as humanity moved from soil exploiting towards soil making, a tactfully managed evolution, following each sudden high religious revelation, from the ancient myths into the high religious beliefs. Christianity, for example, took over ancient rituals, ancient moon-phases for the Christian festivals, while the Christian gods and saints took over the functions of their pagan predecessors. They performed, no doubt, also higher functions; it is not suggested that there is no difference between the concept of Christ and that of Dionysos, but the similarities are very obvious, and the Mass is a god-eating ritual. At all events, for the ordinary peasant and for the soil, there were no great differences: he still felt that he was responsible to Divine providence for his soil, and must be grateful to that same Spirit for his harvest.

While this state of spirit endures the behaviour of the ordinary man continues to be governed not only by a certain humility, but by a sense of unity and order to which expression is given in an art that, in such periods, has an integrity and a power to move, both lost when men emancipate themselves from such beliefs. It is not necessary to think of the phenomena of magic and of religion in terms which give them objective reality; in any case, to do so

would be impossible for a typical modern man. But
these things have had and in some places still have
subjective reality, and that which is in the mind of
a man makes his behaviour. There is absolutely no
point at all in discussing whether magical and
religious phenomena are *true*. We know nothing
about truth, we have not a single clue; since Palaeolithic times our consciousness of the universe has
widened, we know more facts, we have discovered
how some small parts of the mechanism works,
but there is no reason to suppose that we are any
nearer than the Magdalenian cave artists to understanding the nature of the universe, which remains
a complete and, if dwelt upon, terrifying mystery.
What is important, in our context here, is whether
a faith in sympathetic magic and in the gods was
effective. That it certainly was, for it made for man's
ease in the world, it gave him a working method, a
unity with the whole community of species, and it
also made for the conservation of the soil upon
which he lived.

However, Dionysos has died for us, died never
to be resurrected. Men are his heirs, they now possess some of his powers, and these have enabled
them, by means of several very badly integrated
sciences, to increase their numbers tenfold at the
expense of the fertility of vast areas of soil. The
damage is great and it is continuing, and we may,
on our present course, reach a point in time when
the corn, quite literally, will not spring again. That
point is far distant but none the less real. Nor is
this the only disaster which is in the future; not

only soil, but men were kept whole by virtue of the
belief that man had a definite place in the community of things and species composing the world,
and the loss of that belief has been debilitating and
nerve-racking. Man, in his god-like rôle, behaves
like a neurotic.

Is this a necessary consequence of the failure of
the ancient states of mind and spirit to persist? I
do not believe that it is: man has repudiated magic
as practised by the priests, but there remains magic
as practised by the poets, the artists, the oldest
priests of all. If men have a thwarted religious instinct, they have also aesthetic sensibilities which
need not be thwarted, because the values upon
which these rest have never been repudiated, and
art is still admitted to be a means of revelation, a
means of uniting men, by enlightenment, with the
world.

When religion as magic fails, religion as an ethical code comes into its own, and man tries to behave
well not for fear of the consequences, if he does ill,
but by seeking the source of good within himself.
This is the basis of the more austere kinds of protestantism which are the results of reformatory movements at a certain stage in the history of the higher
religions. In the West, however, the very process
of intelligent virtue, entailing the development of
great intellectual skill, created, in that skill, the
tool which could be used to destroy the whole basis
of magical beliefs. Men thought that they could
reason their way into an understanding of God and
his law, only to find that they had reasoned both

entirely out of existence, and were confronted with
the need to put something in their place. Neither
intelligent religion, nor philosophy, nor science can
confer on their disciples that mysterious power of
super-normal co-operation with the motion of life,
the power to be one with some essence felt, but
not known, as the spirit which makes all life a single
phenomenon. When the beautiful and symmetrical
principles reasoned out by the most powerful minds
are put into any sort of practice, their hopelessly
inadequate artificiality is at once revealed: they are,
in some odd way, extraordinarily thin, and foolish,
and unreal. They have the same failing as
intellectually produced revolutionary political con-
stitutions: they are inorganic. Any one of the poets
whom Plato distrusted, could have felt his way to a
better method of governing men than the absurd
system devised by that powerful thinker, and which
the Emperor Marcus Aurelius tried to apply with
such a shocking aftermath.

But no sophisticated society can reject its intel-
lectualism and return to mysticism, can throw away
science and return to myth; unless, indeed, it was
done in the manner described in Robert Graves'
Seven Days in New Crete! Once the power of religious belief has been lost, societies must do the best
they can with their brains. But they still possess
aesthetic sensibility.

In the beginnings of rationalism the various sciences and arts are felt to be manifestations of a
single superior state of mind and spirit, the poets are
philosophers, painters, mechanics, sculptors, chem-

ists or physicists. In the early days of the Royal Society, scientists and artists were allies, almost indistinguishable, and serving one discipline. With specialization, necessary consequence of the rapidly growing bodies of the sciences, this unity was lost. The specialist is by himself, he has no body of philosophy, no grand general idea to which his work subscribes. When ordinary men are led by a creative minority in a state of spiritual and intellectual anarchy, then they no longer sense or know the world as a unity of which they are a part, the principal motive for action becomes a brutal self-interest; and even in his dealings with his fellow-men, man's "nature," his feeling tends to vanish away, and he acts at best intelligently, at worst "bestially," and almost never feelingly. If the prospect before us were one of the continued fragmentation of art and science into special techniques, then our industrialism, our divorce from the soil community, could have no issue but the most frightful disaster.

There is, however, an alternative, and it has been suggested by the need, in America, to rehabilitate soils: for this purpose, various sciences become the servants of a kind of aesthetic insight, and in that service they are reunited. The process is likely to be assisted by the fact that, in any case, the actual advance of certain sciences is bringing about the overlapping of one special field by another which gives rise to such bastard sciences as bio-chemistry, and even bio-physics. The chemist, the biologist, the botanist, the crystallographer, the electrician are finding that their work is converging; when the poet and the musician and the painter and sculptor begin to be drawn in by the same unifying force, then a new integrity for man will have been made, a relationship with the universe as valid as that expressed in the ancient myths will become possible.

The ecologists of America, and the practical men working to their plans, have found that they can restore dead soils to life by recreating upon them a "natural" and balanced soil community. . . .

Now this creative ecology, if that will do as a name for it, is unquestionably an aft: aesthetic insight, right feeling for the grain of life is what must animate it. Yet its servants are the sciences. And its end product is a fertile soil which, in time to come, can be safely cleared and ploughed and sown, and will yield harvests.

If man can also think of himself as one of the materials of this new art, as well as the artist, he may yet learn from his ancient contact with soil how to live nobly and at peace.

Joseph Epes Brown. *The Spiritual Legacy of the American Indian*

How embarrassing it is for western society to have come so far in its rational, empirical study of nature, only to discover that the most basic principles of environmental intelligence have slipped through the mesh of its science like water through a sieve. Even more to our chagrin: we now advance (fitfully) toward ecological sophistication only to find there the footprint of our "primitive" brothers and sisters who long ago possessed whole the wisdom we now piece laboriously together.

Joseph Epes Brown, like John Neihardt before him, learned his American Indian lore from the Oglala Sioux holy man Black Elk. What follows is from a brief essay by Brown on Indian religion and ritual. The contrast with the anthropocentric religion and science of western man need hardly be underscored.

For the Indian the world of nature itself was his temple, and within this sanctuary he showed great respect to every form, function, and power. That the Indian held as sacred all the natural forms sur-

---

From *The Spiritual Legacy of the American Indian,* Pendle Hill Pamphlet #135. Copyright © 1964 by Pendle Hill, Wallingford, Pennsylvania. On Black Elk, see also John G. Neihardt's *Black Elk Speaks* (University of Nebraska Press, 1961).

rounding him is not unique, for other traditions (Japanese Shinto, for example) respect created forms as manifestations of God's works. But what is almost unique in the Indian's attitude is the fact that his reverence for nature and for life is *central* to his religion: each form in the world around him bears such a host of precise values and meanings that taken all together they constitute what one could call his "doctrine."

In my first contact with Black Elk almost all he said was phrased in terms involving animals and natural phenomena. I naively wished that he would begin to talk about religious matters, until I finally realized that he was, in fact, explaining his religion. The values which I sought were to be found precisely in his stories and accounts of the bison, eagle, trees, flowers, mountains and winds.

Due to this intense preoccupation with the forms of nature the Indian has been described as being in his religion either pantheistic, idolatrous, or downright savage. To the two latter terms it is hardly necessary to reply, but the more subtle charge of pantheism, which involves equating God with his manifested forms, requires some clarification.

In the extremely beautiful creation myths of the

Plains Indians, which are amazingly similar to the biblical Genesis, the animals were created before man, so that in this anteriority and divine origin they have a certain proximity to the Great Spirit (*Wakan-Tanka* in the language of the Sioux) which demands respect and veneration. In them the Indian sees actual reflections of the qualities of the Great Spirit Himself, which serve the same function as revealed scriptures in other religions. They are intermediators or links between man and God. This explains not only why religious devotions may be

directed to the Deity *through* the animals, but it also helps us to understand why contact with, or from, the Great Spirit comes to the Indian almost exclusively through visions involving animal or other natural forms. Black Elk, for example, received spiritual power (*wochangi*) from visions involving the eagle, the bison, Thunder-beings, and horses; and it is said that Crazy Horse, the great chief and holy man, received his power and invulnerability from the rock, and also from a vision of the shadow.

Although these natural forms may reflect aspects of the Great Spirit, and eventually can not be other than Him, they are nevertheless not identified with

Him who is without "parts," and who in His transcendent unity is above all particular created forms.
The Indian therefore can not be termed a pantheist,
if we accept this term in the sense presented above.
Black Elk has well formulated this mystery in the
following statements:

". . . we regard all created beings as sacred and important, for everything has a *wochangi,* or influence,
which can be given to us, through which we may gain
a little more understanding if we are attentive."

"We should understand well that all things are the
works of the Great Spirit. We should know that He is
within all things; the trees, the grasses, the rivers, the
mountains and all the four-legged animals, and the
winged peoples; and even more important, we should
understand that He is also above all these things and
peoples."

To make these distinctions more precise, it should
be noted that in the language of the Sioux (Lakota)
the Great Spirit may be referred to as either Father
(*Ate*), or Grandfather (*Tunkashila*). *Ate* refers to
the Great Spirit as He is in relation to His creation,
in other words, as Being, whereas *Tunkashila* is His
non-manifest Essence, independent of the limitations of creation. These same distinctions have been
enunciated by Christian theologians using the term
God as distinct from Godhead, and in the Hindu
doctrines which differentiate between *Brahma* (the
masculine form) and *Brahman* (the neuter
form). . . .

We can now see that although man was created

last of all the creatures, he is also the "axis," and thus in a sense is the first. For it each animal reflects particular aspects of the Great Spirit, man, on the contrary, may include within himself all aspects. He is thus a totality, bearing the Universe within himself, and through his Intellect having the potential capacity to live in continual awareness of this reality.

". . . peace . . . comes within the souls of men when they realize their relationship, their oneness, with the universe and all its powers, and when they realize that at the center of the Universe dwells *Wakan-Tanka*, and that this center is really everywhere, it is within each of us" [Black Elk].

The Indian believes that such knowledge can not be realized unless there be perfect humility, unless man humbles himself before the entire creation, before each smallest ant, realizing his own nothingness. Only in being nothing may man become everything, and only then does he realize his essential brotherhood with all forms of life. His center, or his Life, is the same center or Life of all that is.

Because of the true man's totality and centrality he has the almost divine function of guardianship over the world of nature. Once this role is ignored or misused he is in danger of being shown ultimately by nature who in reality is the conqueror and who the conquered. It could also be said, under another perspective, that in the past man had to protect himself from the forces of nature, whereas today it is nature which must be protected from man.

Nothing is more tragic or pitiful than the statements of Indians who have survived to see their sacred lands torn up and desecrated by a people of an alien culture who, driven largely by commercial interests, have lost the sense of protective guardianship over nature. Typical are the words of an old Omaha:

"When I was a youth, the country was very beautiful. Along the rivers were belts of timberland, where grew cottonwood, maple, elm, ash, hickory, and walnut trees, and many other shrubs. And under these grew many good herbs and beautiful flowering plants. In both the woodland and the prairies I could see the trails of many kinds of animals and could hear the cheerful songs of many kinds of birds. When I walked abroad I could see many forms of life, beautiful living creatures which *Wakanda* had placed here; and these were, after their manner, walking, flying, leaping, running, playing all about. But now the face of all the land is changed and sad. The living creatures are gone. I see the land desolate and I suffer an unspeakable sadness. Sometimes I wake in the night and I feel as though I should suffocate from the pressure of this awful feeling of loneliness" [Melvin Gilmore, *Prairie Smoke,* 1929].

Too often statements such as this are passed off as nostalgic romanticism, but if we understand the full meaning of the world of nature for the Indian, we realize that we are involved witnesses to a great tragedy, whose final act is still to be seen.

To illustrate in some detail at least one of the Plains Indians ceremonies I have chosen the purification rites of the "Sweat Lodge," the *Inipi*. These rites are carried out in preparation for all the other major rites, and actually are participated in prior to any important undertaking. They are rites of renewal, or spiritual rebirth, in which all of the four elements—earth, air, fire, and water—each contribute to the physical and psychical purification of man.

A small dome-shaped lodge is first made of bent willow saplings over which there are placed buffalo hides which make the little house tight and dark inside. Within the lodge, and at its center, there is a small pit containing rocks which have already been heated in a fire outside the lodge to the east. When the leader of the ceremony sprinkles water on these they give off steam, so that soon the lodge becomes intensely hot, and also fragrant from the aromatic sage which has been strewn on the floor. Each of the materials in the lodge has its symbolical value, as does every detail of design and ritual usage.

Black Elk, among others, has explained that the lodge itself represents the Universe, with the pit at the center as the navel in which dwells the Great

Spirit with His power which is the fire. The willows which form the frame of the house represent all that grows from mother earth.

"These too have a lesson to teach us, for in the fall their leaves die and return to the earth, but in the spring they come to life again. So, too, men die but live again in the real world of *Wakan-Tanka*, where there is nothing but the spirits of all things; and this true life we may know here on earth if we purify our bodies and minds, thus coming closer to *Wakan-Tanka* who is all-purity."

The rocks represent the earth, and also the indestructible and everlasting nature of *Wakan-Tanka*. The water, too, reflects values for the people to learn from:

"When we use water in the sweat lodge we should think of *Wakan-Tanka* who is always flowing, giving His power and life to everything; we should even be as water which is lower than all things, yet stronger even than the rocks."

It is important at this point to note that to the Plains Indian the material form of the symbol is not thought of as representing some *other* and higher reality, but *is* that reality in an image. The power or quality, therefore, which a particular form reflects may be transferred directly to the person in contact with it, and there is no need, as with modern western man, for any mental or artificial "reconstruction." It may even be said that the Indian can be passive to the form, and is thus able to absorb, and become one with, its reflected power.

During the four periods of sweating within the lodge, prayers are recited, sacred songs are sung, and a pipe is ceremonially smoked four times by the circle of men. At the conclusion of the fourth and last period the door is opened so that "the light enters into the darkness, that we may see not only with our two eyes, but with the one eye which is of the heart, and with which we see and know all that is true and good." In this going forth into the light from the house of darkness, in which all impurities have been left behind, there is represented man's liberation from ignorance, from his ego, and from the cosmos. He is now a renewed being entering symbolically into the world of light or wisdom.

There is in these rites an amazing completeness. In other great religions one, or sometimes two, of the elements are used for purification or consecration. Here four of the elements are present (one could include the fifth "element": ether) in such a powerfully interrelated manner that one can not but believe that for each participating individual the goal, in varying degrees, must be achieved.

As a thread binds together, and is central to, each bead of a necklace, so is the sacred pipe central to all the Plains Indians ceremonies. The pipe is a portable altar, and a means of grace, which

every Indian once possessed. He would not undertake anything of importance unless he had first
smoked, concentrating on all that the pipe represented, and thus absorbing a multitude of powers. It
could in fact be said that if one could understand
all the possible meanings and values to be found in
the pipe and its accompanying ritual, then one
would understand Plains Indian religion in its full
depth.

The origin of the pipe is expressed in various
myths of great beauty. In the Sioux myth a miracu-
lous "Buffalo Cow Woman" brought the pipe to
the people, with explanations concerning its meanings and use. Pipes used within historical times, and
which are still used today, are made with a red, or
sometimes a black, stone bowl, a stem made usually
of ash, and, at least with the large ceremonial types,
ribbon decorations representing the four directions
of space, and parts taken from sacred animals or
from nature. These pipes represent man in his
totality, or the universe of which man is a reflection.
The bowl is the heart, or sacred center, and each
section of the pipe is usually identified with some
part of man.

As the pipe is filled with the sacred tobacco,
prayers are offered for all the powers of the universe, and for the myriad forms of creation, each of
which is represented by a grain of tobacco. The
filled pipe is thus "Totality," so that when the fire
of the Great Spirit is added a divine sacrifice is
enacted in which the universe and man are reab-
sorbed within the Principle, and become what in

reality they are. In mingling his life-breath with the tobacco and fire through the straight stem of concentration, the man who smokes assists at the sacrifice of his own self, or ego, and is thus aided in realizing the Divine Presence at his own center. Indeed, in the liberation of the smoke man is further helped in realizing that not only is God's presence within him, but that he and the world are mysteriously plunged in God. The smoke that rises to the heavens is also, as it were, "visible prayer," at the sight and fragrance of which the entire creation rejoices. The mysteries of the peace pipe are so profound that it is not too much to say that the rite of smoking for the Indian is something very near to the Holy Communion for Christians. It is therefore not without reason that it is commonly called a "Peace Pipe," and was always used in establishing a relationship, or peace, between friends and also enemies. For in smoking the pipe together each man is aided in remembering his own center, which is now understood to be the same center of every man, and of the Universe itself. It would be difficult

to imagine a rite that could more aptly express the bond which exists between all forms of creation.

All true spiritual progress involves three stages which are not successfully experienced and left behind, but rather each in turn is realized, then integrated within the next stage, so that ultimately they are one in the individual who attains the ultimate goal. Different terms may be used for these stages, but essentially they constitute Purification, Perfection or Expansion, and Union.

If union with Truth (which is one of many possible names for God) is the ultimate goal of all spiritual disciplines, then it is evident that what is impure can not be united with that which is all purity. Hence the necessity for the first stage of purification. Expansion must follow, because only that which is perfect, total, or whole can be united with absolute perfection and holiness. Man must cease to be a part, an imperfect fragment; he must so realize what he really is that he expands to include the universe within himself. Only then, when these two conditions of purification and expansion are actualized, may man attain to the final stage of Union. All the great religions attest that there is no greater error to which man is subject than to believe that his real self is nothing more than his own body or mind. It is only through traditional disciplines, such as those which have been described for the Plains Indian, that man is able to dispel this greatest of all illusions.

The pattern of the three stages in spiritual development may be recognized in one form or another in the methods of all the great religions of the world. It is evident that the American Indian, or at least the Plains Indian, also possesses this same three-fold pattern of realization. If this spirituality has not as yet been fully recognized as existing among the Indians, it is due partly to a problem of communication, since their conceptions are often expressed through symbolical forms which are foreign to us. If we can understand, however, the truths which the Indian finds in his relationships to nature, and the profound values reflected by his many rites and symbols, then *we* may become enriched, our understanding will deepen, and we shall be able to give to the American Indian heritage its rightful place among the great spiritual traditions of mankind. Further, if the Indian himself can become more actively aware of this valuable heritage, then he may regain much of what has been lost, and will be able to face the world with the pride and dignity that should rightfully be his.

E. F. Schumacher. *An Economics of Permanence*

Hidden carefully away in the foundations of conventional economic thought is the assumption that greed makes the world go round and *ought* properly to do so. Since Adam Smith the economist's address has been to man's "self-interest"— the "self" involved being conceived of as some manner of gargantuan swine never to be budged from the trough. Assume that, and all the rest falls neatly into place. What is it, after all, that our economic policy-making takes for its object, once we look beyond the jargon and statistical obfuscation? To keep the swill flowing and the pig well purged for the sake of nonstop ingestion.

There is, we now see, a natural limit to such an economics. The environment cannot suffer indefinitely the appetites of such a race of maniacal omnivores.

Item: "World resources could support a population of about half a billion *only*, at the current United States standard. Meanwhile, America proceeds on the assumption that she can treble or quadruple that standard of consumption. Many Americans not only aim at an increasingly urbanized, high-consumption society for themselves, but urge a similar course on underdeveloped

From *Foundations of Peace and Freedom,* edited by Ted Dunn (London: James Clarke Ltd., 1970). Reprinted by permission of Ted Dunn and E. F. Schumacher.

countries" (Gordon Rattray Taylor, *Doomsday Book* [London, 1970]).

Obviously, we need an economics grounded in our most humanly beautiful qualities, not our worst vices: an economics prepared to integrate noneconomic ends, nonmarketable values, imponderable qualities of life. Which is what E. F. Schumacher calls "an economics of permanence."

Remember, as you read, Plato's definition of a "poor man": one who has many needs. And a rich man? One who has few.

GANDHI USED TO TALK disparagingly of "dreaming of systems so perfect that no one will need to be good." But is it not precisely this dream which we can now implement in reality with our marvellous powers of science and technology? Why ask for virtues, which man may never acquire, when scientific rationality and technical competence are all that is needed?

Instead of listening to Gandhi, are we not more inclined to listen to one of the most influential economists of our century, the great Lord Keynes? In 1930, during the world-wide economic depression, he felt moved to speculate on the "economic possibilities for our grandchildren" and concluded that the day might not be all that far off when everybody would be rich. We shall then, he said, "once more value ends above means and prefer the good to the useful."

"But beware!", he continued, *"The time for all this is not yet. For at least another hundred years we must*

pretend to ourselves and to every one that fair is foul and foul is fair; for foul is useful and fair is not."

This was written forty years ago and since then, of course, things have speeded up considerably. Maybe we do not even have to wait for another sixty years until universal plenty will be attained. In any case, the Keynesian message is clear enough: Beware! Ethical considerations are not merely irrelevant, they are an actual hindrance, "for foul is useful and fair is not." The time for fairness is not yet. The road to heaven is paved with bad intentions.

I propose now to consider this proposition. . . .

The question with which to start my investigation is obviously this: Is there enough to go round? Immediately we encounter a serious difficulty: What is 'enough'? Who can tell us? Certainly not the economist who pursues "economic growth" as the highest of all values, and therefore has no concept of 'enough'. There are poor societies which have too little; but where is the rich society that says: "Halt! We have enough"? There is none.

Perhaps we can forget about 'enough' and content ourselves with exploring the growth of demand upon the world's resources which arises when everybody simply strives hard to have 'more.' As we cannot study all resources, I propose to focus attention on one type of resource which is in a somewhat central position—fuel. More prosperity means a greater use of fuel—there can be no doubt about that. At present, the prosperity gap between the poor of this world and the rich is very wide indeed, and this is clearly shown in their respective fuel consumption. Let us define as 'rich' all populations in countries with an average fuel consumption—in 1966—of more than one metric ton of coal equivalent (abbreviated: c.e.) per head, and as 'poor' all those below this level. On these definitions we can draw up the results in Table I below (using United Nations figures throughout).

The average fuel consumption per head of the 'poor' is only 0.32 tons—roughly one-fourteenth of that of the 'rich', and there are very many 'poor' people in the world—on these definitions nearly seven-tenths of the world population. If the 'poor' suddenly used as much fuel as the 'rich', world fuel consumption would treble right away.

But this cannot happen as everything takes time. And in time both the 'rich' and the 'poor' are growing in desires and in numbers. So let us make an exploratory calculation. If the 'rich' populations grow at the rate of 1¼% and the 'poor' at the rate of 2½% a year, world population will grow to about 6,900 million by 2000 A.D.—a figure not very different from the most authoritative current forecasts. If at the same time the fuel consumption *per head* of the 'rich' population grows by 2¼%, while that of the 'poor' grows by 4½% a year, the figures given in Table II below emerge for the year 2000 A.D.

These exploratory calculations give rise to a number of comments: Even after more than 30 years of rapid growth, the fuel consumption of the 'poor' would still be at poverty level.

Of the total *increase* of 17,630 million tons c.e. in world fuel consumption (an increase from 5,509

Table I (1966)

	Rich	(%)	Poor	(%)	World	(%)
Population (millions)	1,060	(31)	2,284	(69)	3,344	(100)
Fuel Consumption (million tons c.e.)	4.788	(87)	721	(13)	5,509	(100)
Fuel Consumption per head (tons c.e.)	4.52		0.32		1.65	

Table II (2000 A.D.)

	Rich	(%)	Poor	(%)	World	(%)
Population (millions)	1,618	(23)	5,287	(77)	6,905	(100)
Fuel Consumption (million tons c.e.)	15,585	(67)	7,555	(33)	23,140	(100)
Fuel Consumption per head (tons c.e.)	9.63		1.43		3.35	

million tons in 1966 to 23,140 million tons in 2000), the 'rich' would take 10,800 million tons and the 'poor' only 6,800 million tons, although the 'poor' would be over three times as numerous as the rich.

The most important comment, however, is a question: Is it plausible to assume that world fuel consumption *could grow* to anything like 23,000 million tons c.e. a year by the year 2000? If this growth took place during the 34 years in question about 400,000 million tons of c.e. would be used. In the light of our present knowledge of fossil fuel reserves this is an implausible figure, even if we assume that one quarter or one third of the world total would come from nuclear fission.

It is clear that the 'rich' are in the process of stripping the world of its once-for-all endowment of relatively cheap and simple fuels. It is their continuing economic growth which produces ever more exorbitant demands, with the result that the world's cheap and simple fuels could easily become dear and scarce long before the poor countries had acquired the wealth, education, industrial sophistication, and power of capital accumulation needed for the application of nuclear energy on any significant scale. . . .

As nothing can be *proved* about the future—not even about the relatively short-term future of the next thirty years—it is always possible to dismiss even the most threatening problems with the suggestion that something will turn up. There could be simply enormous and altogether unheard-of dis-

coveries of new reserves of oil, natural gas, or even
coal. And why should nuclear energy be confined
to supplying one-quarter or one-third of total requirements? The problem can thus be shifted to
another plane, but it refuses to go away. For the
consumption of fuel on the indicated scale—assuming no insurmountable difficulties of fuel supply
—would produce environmental hazards of an unprecedented kind. . . .

Whatever the fuel, increases in fuel consumption by a factor of four and then five and then six
. . . there is no plausible answer to the problem of
pollution.

I have taken fuel merely as an example to illustrate a very simple thesis: that economic growth,
which viewed from the point of view of economics,
physics, chemistry and technology, has no discernible limit, must necessarily run into decisive
bottlenecks when viewed from the point of view of
the environmental sciences. An attitude to life which
seeks fulfilment in the single-minded pursuit of
wealth—in short, materialism—does not fit into this
world, because it contains within itself no limiting
principle, while the environment in which it is
placed is strictly limited. Already, the environment
is trying to tell us that certain stresses are becoming excessive. As one problem is being 'solved', ten
new problems arise as a result of the first 'solution'. As Professor Barry Commoner emphasises, the
new problems are not the consequences of inci-
dental failure but of technological success. . . .

Already, there is overwhelming evidence that the

great self-balancing system of Nature is becoming increasingly unbalanced in particular respects and at specific points. It would take us too far if I attempted to assemble the evidence here. The condition of Lake Erie, to which Professor Barry Commoner, among others, has drawn attention should serve as a sufficient warning. Another decade or two, and all the inland water systems of the United States may be in a similar condition. In other words, the condition of unbalance may then no longer apply to specific points but have become generalised. The further this process is allowed to go, the more difficult it will be to reverse it, if indeed the point of no return has not been passed already.

We find, therefore, that the idea of unlimited economic growth, more and more until everybody is saturated with wealth, needs to be seriously questioned on at least two counts: the availability of basic resources and, alternatively or additionally, the capacity of the environment to cope with the degree of interference implied. So much about the physical-material aspect of the matter. Let us now turn to certain non material aspects.

There can be no doubt that the idea of personal enrichment has a very strong appeal to human nature. Keynes, in the essay, from which I have quoted already, advised us that the time was not yet for a return to some of the most sure and certain principles of religion and traditional virtue—that avarice is a vice, that the exaction of usury is a misdemeanour, and the love of money is detestable.

Economic progress, he counselled, is obtainable

only if we employ those powerful human drives of selfishness, which religion and traditional wisdom universally call upon us to resist. The modern economy is propelled by a frenzy of greed and indulges in an orgy of envy, and these are not accidental features but the very causes of its expansionist success. The question is whether such causes can be effective for long or whether they carry within themselves the seeds of destruction. If Keynes says that "foul is useful and fair is not," he propounds a statement of fact which may be true or false; or it may look true in the short run and turn out to be false in the longer run. Which is it?

I should think that there is now enough evidence to demonstrate that the statement is false in a very direct, practical sense. If human vices such as greed and envy are systematically cultivated, the inevitable result is nothing less than a collapse of intelligence. A man driven by greed or envy loses the power of seeing things as they really are, of seeing things in their roundness and wholeness, and his very successes become failures. If whole societies become infected by these vices, they may indeed achieve astonishing things but they become increasingly incapable of solving the most elementary problems of everyday existence. The Gross National Product may rise rapidly: as measured by statisticians but not as experienced by actual people, who find themselves oppressed by increasing frustrations, alienation, insecurity and so forth. After a while, even the Gross National Product refuses to rise any further, not because of scientific or technological failure, but because of a creeping paralysis of non-co-operation, as expressed in various types of escapism, such as soaring crime, alcoholism, drug addiction, mental breakdown, and open rebellion on the part, not only of the oppressed and exploited, but even of highly privileged groups.

One can go on for a long time deploring the irrationality and stupidity of men and women in high positions or low, "if only people would realise where their real interests lie!" But why do they not realise this? Either because their intelligence has been dimmed by greed and envy, or because in their heart of hearts they understand that their real interests lie somewhere quite different. There is a revolutionary saying that "Man shall not live by bread alone but by every word of God".

Here again, nothing can be 'proved'. But does it still look probable or plausible that the grave social diseases infecting many rich societies today are merely passing phenomena which an able government—if only we could get a really able government!—could eradicate by simply making a better use of science and technology or a more radical use of the penal system?

I suggest that the foundations of peace cannot be laid by universal prosperity, in the modern sense, because such prosperity, if attainable at all is attainable only by cultivating such drives of human nature as greed and envy, which destroy intelligence, happiness, serenity, and thereby the peacefulness of man. It could well be that rich people treasure peace more highly than poor people, but only if they feel utterly secure—and this is a contradiction in terms. Their wealth depends on making inordinately large demands on limited world resources and thus puts them on an unavoidable collision course—not primarily with the poor (who are weak and defenceless) but with other rich people.

In short, we can say today that man is far too clever to be able to survive without wisdom. No one is really working for peace unless he is working primarily for the restoration of wisdom. The assertion that "foul is useful and fair is not" is the antithesis of wisdom. The hope that the pursuit of goodness and virtue can be postponed until we have attained universal prosperity and that by the single-minded pursuit of wealth, without bothering our heads about spiritual and moral questions, we could establish peace on earth, is an unrealistic, unscientific, and irrational hope. The exclusion of wisdom from economics, science, and technology was something which we could perhaps get away with for a little while, as long as we were relatively unsuccessful; but now that we have become very successful, the problem of spiritual and moral truth moves into the central position, in other words, we are far too clever to survive without wisdom.

From an economic point of view, the central concept of wisdom is permanence. We must study the economics of permanence. Nothing makes economic sense unless its continuance for a long time can be projected without running into absurdities. There can be 'growth' towards a limited objective, but there cannot be unlimited, generalised growth. It is more than likely, as Gandhi said, that "Earth provides enough to satisfy every man's need, but not for every man's greed." Permanence is incompatible with a predatory attitude which rejoices in the fact that "what were luxuries for our fathers have become necessities for us".

The cultivation and expansion of needs is the antithesis of wisdom. It is also the antithesis of freedom and peace. Every increase of needs tends to increase one's dependence on outside forces over which one cannot have control, and therefore increases existential fear. Only by a reduction of needs can one promote a genuine reduction in those tensions which are the ultimate causes of strife and war.

The economics of permanence implies a profound re-orientation of science and technology, which have to open their doors to wisdom and, in fact, have to incorporate wisdom into their very structure. Scientific or technological 'solutions' which poison the environment or degrade the social structure and man himself, are of no benefit, no matter how brilliantly conceived or how great their superficial attraction. Ever bigger machines, entailing ever bigger concentrations of economic power and exerting ever greater violence against the environment do not represent progress, they are a denial of wisdom. Wisdom demands a new orientation of science and technology towards the organic, the gentle, the non-violent, the elegant and beautiful. Peace, as has often been said, is indivisible—how then could peace be built on a foundation of reck-

less science and violent technology? We must look
for a revolution in technology to give us inventions
and machines which reverse the destructive trends
now threatening us all.

What is it that we really require from the scientists and technologists? I should answer: We need
methods and equipment which are

      (a) cheap enough so that they are accessible to
            virtually everyone;

      (b) suitable for small-scale application; and

      (c) compatible with man's need for creativity.

Out of these three characteristics is born non-
violence and a relationship of man to nature which
guarantees permanence. If only one of these three
is neglected, things are bound to go wrong. Let us
look at them one by one.

Methods and machines cheap enough to be accessible to virtually everyone—why should we assume that our scientists and technologists are unable
to develop them? This has been a primary concern
of Gandhi's, "I want the dumb millions of our land
to be healthy and happy, and I want them to grow
spiritually. As yet for this purpose we do not need
the machine. . . . If we feel the need of machines, we certainly will have them. Every machine
that helps every individual has a place," he said,
"but there should be no place for machines that
concentrate power in a few hands and turn the
masses into mere machine minders, if indeed they
do not make them unemployed".

Suppose it becomes the acknowledged purpose of
inventors and engineers, observed Aldous Huxley, to

provide ordinary people with the means of "doing profitable and intrinsically significant work, of helping men and women to achieve independence from bosses, so that they may become their own employers, or members of a self-governing, co-operative group working for subsistence and a local market . . . this differently orientated technological progress (would result in) a progressive decentralisation of population, of accessibility of land, of ownership of the means of production, of political and economic power". Other advantages, said Huxley, would be "a more humanly satisfying life for more people, a greater measure of genuine self-governing democracy and a blessed freedom from the silly or pernicious adult education provided by the mass producers of consumer goods through the medium of advertisements".

If methods and machines are to be cheap enough to be generally accessible, this means that their cost must stand in some definable relationship to the level of incomes in the society in which they are to be used. I have myself come to the conclusion that the upper limit for the average amount of capital investment *per workplace* is probably given by the annual earnings of an able and ambitious industrial worker. That is to say, if such a man can normally earn, say, $3,000 a year, the average cost of establishing one workplace should on no account be in excess of $3,000. If the cost is significantly higher, the society in question is likely to run into serious troubles, such as an undue concentration of wealth and power among the privileged few; an increasing problem of 'drop-outs' who cannot be integrated into society and constitute an ever-growing threat; 'structural' unemployment; maldistribution of the population due to excessive urbanisation, and general frustration and alienation, with soaring crime rates, etc.

To choose the appropriate level of technology is an absolutely vital matter for the (so-called) developing countries. It is in this connection that, some seven years ago, I began to talk of 'intermediate technology', and very energetic work has since been undertaken by the Intermediate Technology Development Group in London, and by others, to identify, develop and apply in developing countries a genuine self-help technology which involves the mass of the people, and not just the privileged few, which promotes the real independence of former colonial territories, and not just political independence nullified by economic subservience, and which thereby attempts to lay at least some of the essential foundations of freedom and peace.

The second requirement is suitability for small-scale application. On the problem of 'scale', Professor Leopold Kohr has written brilliantly and convincingly, and I do not propose to do more than emphasise its relevance to the economics of permanence. Small-scale operations, no matter how numerous, are always less likely to be harmful to the natural environment than large-scale ones, simply because their individual force is small in relation to the recuperative forces of nature. There is wisdom in smallness if only on account of the smallness and patchiness of human knowledge, which relies on experiment far more than on understanding. The greatest danger invariably arises from the ruthless application, on a vast scale, of partial knowledge, such as we are currently witnessing in the application of nuclear energy, of the new chemistry in agriculture, of transportation technology, and countless other things.

Although even small communities are sometimes guilty of causing serious erosion, generally as a result of ignorance, this is trifling in comparison with the devastations caused by large organisations motivated by greed, envy and the lust for power. It is moreover obvious that men organised in small units will take better care of *their* bit of land or other natural resources than anonymous companies or megalomanic governments which pretend to themselves that the whole universe is their legitimate quarry.

The third requirement is perhaps the most important of all—that methods and equipment should be such as to leave ample room for human creativity. Over the last hundred years no one has spoken more insistently and warningly on this subject than have the Roman pontiffs. What becomes of man if the process of production "takes away from work any hint of humanity, making of it a merely mechanical activity"? The worker himself is turned into a perversion of a free being.

And so bodily labour (said Pius XI) which even after original sin was decreed by Providence for the good of man's body and soul, is in many instances changed into an instrument of perversion; for from the factory dead matter goes out improved, whereas men there are corrupted and degraded.

Again, the subject is so large that I cannot do more than touch upon it. Above anything else there is need for a proper philosophy of work which understands work not as that which it has indeed become, an inhuman chore as soon as possible to be abolished by automation, but as something "decreed by Providence for the good of man's body and soul." Next to the family, it is work and the relationships established by work that are the true foundations of society. If the foundations are unsound, how could society be sound? And if society is sick, how could it fail to be a danger to peace? . . .

It is the sin of Greed that has delivered us over into the power of the machine. If Greed were not the master of modern man—ably assisted by envy—how could it be that the frenzy of economism does not abate as higher "standards of living" are attained, and that it is precisely the richest societies which pursue their economic advantage with the greatest ruthlessness? How could we explain the almost universal refusal on the part of the rulers of the rich societies—whether organised along private enterprise or collectivist enterprise lines—to work towards *the humanisation of work?* It is only necessary to assert that something would reduce the "standard of living", and every debate is instantly closed. That soul-destroying, meaningless, mechanical, monotonous, moronic work is an insult to human nature which must necessarily and inevitably produce either escapism or aggression, and that no amount of "bread and circuses" can compensate for the damage done—these are facts which are neither denied nor acknowledged but are met with an unbreakable conspiracy of silence—because to deny them would be too obviously absurd and to acknowledge them would condemn the central preoccupation of modern society as a crime against humanity.

The neglect, indeed, the rejection of wisdom has gone so far that most of our intellectuals have not even the faintest idea what the term could mean. As a result, they always tend to try and cure a disease by intensifying its causes. The disease having been caused by allowing cleverness to displace wisdom, no amount of clever research is likely to produce a cure. But what is wisdom? Where can it be found? Here we come to the crux of the matter: it can be read about in numerous publications but it can be *found* only inside oneself. To be able to find it, one has first to liberate oneself interiorly from such masters as greed and envy. The stillness following liberation—even if only momentary—produces the insights of wisdom which are obtainable in no other way.

They enable us to see the hollowness and fundamental unsatisfactoriness of a life devoted primarily to the pursuit of material ends, to the neglect of the spiritual. Such a life necessarily sets man against man and nation against nation, because man's needs are infinite and infinitude can be achieved only in the spiritual realm, never in the material. Man assuredly needs to rise above this humdrum 'world'; wisdom shows him the way to do it; without wisdom, he is driven to build up a monster economy, which destroys the world, and to seek fantastic satisfactions, like landing a man on the moon. Instead of overcoming the 'world' by moving towards saintliness, he tries to overcome it by gaining preeminence in wealth, power, science or indeed any imaginable 'sport'. . . .

How could we even begin to disarm greed and envy? Perhaps by being much less greedy and envious ourselves; perhaps by resisting the temptation of letting our luxuries become needs; and perhaps by even scrutinising our needs to see if they cannot be simplified and reduced. If we do not have the strength to do any of this, could we perhaps stop applauding the type of economic "progress" which palpably lacks the basis of permanence and give what modest support we can to those who, unafraid of being denounced as cranks, work for non-violence: as conservationists, ecologists, protectors of wild life, promoters of organic agriculture, distributists, cottage producers, and so forth? An ounce of practice is generally worth more than a ton of theory.

Gary Snyder and Friends. *Four Changes*

A profound respect for the primitive, a fine ear for ecological harmonies, a happy obedience to the Tao, "unmuddled language and good dreams": such have always been the marks of Gary Snyder's work. The whole of this section might, in fact, have been given up to his *Earth Household,* one of the wisest single pieces of environmental philosophy our generation has produced. But here, instead, is *Four Changes* which gives that wisdom the shape and force of a manifesto.

I. Population

The Condition

POSITION

Man is but a part of the fabric of life—dependent on the whole fabric for his very existence. As the most highly developed tool-using animal, he must recognize that the unknown evolutionary destinies of other life forms are to be respected, and act as gentle steward of the earth's community of being.

SITUATION

There are now too many human beings, and the problem is growing rapidly worse. It is potentially disastrous not only for the human race but for most other life forms.

GOAL

The goal would be half of the present world population, or less.

Action

SOCIAL/POLITICAL

First, a massive effort to convince the governments and leaders of the world that the problem is severe. And that all talk about raising food-production—well intentioned as it is—simply puts off the only real solution: reduce population. Demand immediate participation by all countries in programs to legalize abortion, encourage vasectomy and sterilization (provided by free clinics)—free insertion of intrauterine loops—try to correct traditional cultural attitudes that tend to force women into childbearing—remove income tax deductions for more than two children above a specified income level, and scale it so that lower income families are forced to be careful too—or pay families to limit their number. Take a vigorous stand against the policy of the right-wing in the Catholic hierarchy and any other institutions that exercise an irresponsible social force in regard to this question; oppose and correct simple-minded boosterism that equates population growth with continuing prosperity. Work ceaselessly to have all political questions be seen in the light of this prime problem.

THE COMMUNITY

Explore other social structures and marriage forms, such as group marriage and polyandrous marriage, which provide family life but may produce less children. Share the pleasure of raising children widely, so that all need not directly reproduce to enter into this basic human experience. We must hope that no one woman would give birth to more than one child, during this period of crisis. Adopt children. Let reverence for life and reverence for the feminine mean also a reverence for other species, and future human lives, most of which are threatened.

OUR OWN HEADS

"I am a child of all life, and all living beings are my brothers and sisters, my children and grandchildren. And there is a child within me waiting to be brought to birth, the baby of a new and wiser self." Love, lovemaking, a man and woman together, seen as the vehicle of mutual realization, where the creation of new selves and a new world of being is as important as reproducing our kind.

II. Pollution

The Condition

POSITION

Pollution is of two types. One sort results from an excess of some fairly ordinary substance—smoke, or solid waste—which cannot be absorbed or transmuted rapidly enough to offset its introduction into the environment, thus causing changes the great cycle is not prepared for. (All organisms have wastes and by-products, and these are indeed part of the total biosphere: energy is passed along the line and refracted in various ways, "the rainbow body." This is cycling, not pollution.) The other sort is powerful modern chemicals and poisons, products of recent technology, which the biosphere is totally unprepared for. Such is DDT and similar chlorinated hydrocarbons—nuclear testing fallout and nuclear waste—poison gas, germ and virus storage and leakage by the military; and chemicals which are put into food, whose long-range effects on human beings have not been properly tested.

SITUATION

The human race in the last century has allowed its production and scattering of wastes, by-products, and various chemicals to become excessive. Pollution is directly harming life on the planet: which is to say, ruining the environment for humanity itself. We are fouling our air and water, and living in noise and filth that no "animal" would tolerate, while advertising and politicians try to tell us "we've never had it so good." The dependence of the modern governments on this kind of untruth leads to shameful mind-pollution: mass media and most school education.

GOAL

Clean air, clean clear-running rivers, the presence of Pelican and Osprey and Gray Whale in our lives;

salmon and trout in our streams; unmuddied language and good dreams.

Action

SOCIAL/POLITICAL

Effective International legislation banning DDT and related poisons—with no fooling around. The collusion of certain scientists with the pesticide industry and agri-business in trying to block this legislation must be brought out in the open. Strong penalties for water and air pollution by industries— "Pollution is somebody's profit." Phase out the internal combustion engine and fossil fuel use in general—more research into non-polluting energy sources; solar energy; the tides. No more kidding the public about atomic waste disposal: it's impossible to do it safely, and nuclear-power generated electricity cannot be seriously planned for as it stands now. Stop all germ and chemical warfare research and experimentation; work toward a hopefully safe disposal of the present staggering and stupid stockpiles of H-Bombs, cobalt gunk, germ and poison tanks and cans. Laws and sanctions against wasteful use of paper etc. which adds to the solid waste of cities—develop methods of re-cycling solid urban waste. Re-cycling should be the basic principle behind all waste-disposal thinking. Thus, all bottles should be re-usable; old cans should make more cans; old newspapers back into newsprint again. Stronger controls and research on chemicals in foods. A shift toward a more varied and sensitive type of agriculture (more small scale and subsistence farming) would eliminate much of the call for blanket use of pesticides.

THE COMMUNITY

DDT and such: don't use them. Air pollution: use less cars. Cars pollute the air, and one or two people riding lonely in a huge car is an insult to intelligence and the Earth. Share rides, legalize hitch-hiking, and build hitch-hiker waiting stations along the highways. Also—a step toward the new world—walk more; look for the best routes through beautiful countryside for long-distance walking trips: San Francisco to Los Angeles down the Coast Range, for example. Learn how to use your own manure as fertilizer if you're in the country—as the far East has done for centuries. There's a way, and it's safe. Solid waste; boycott bulky wasteful Sunday papers which use up trees. It's all just advertising anyway, which is artificially inducing more mindless consumption. Refuse paper bags at the store. Organize Park and Street clean-up festivals. Don't work in any way for or with an industry which pollutes, and don't be drafted into the military. Don't waste. (A monk and an old master were once walking in the mountains. They noticed a little hut upstream. The monk said, "A wise hermit must live there"—the master said, "That's no wise hermit, you see that lettuce leaf floating down the stream, he's a Waster." Just then an old man came running down the hill with his beard flying and caught the floating lettuce leaf.) Carry your own jug to the winery and have it filled from the barrel.

OUR OWN HEADS

Part of the trouble with talking about DDT is that the use of it is not just a practical device, it's almost an establishment religion. There is something in western culture that wants to totally wipe out creepy-crawlies, and feels repugnance for toadstools and snakes. This is fear of one's own deepest natural inner-self wilderness areas, and the answer is, relax. Relax around bugs, snakes, and your own hairy dreams. Again, farmers can and should share their crop with a certain percentage of buglife as "paying their dues"—Thoreau says "How then can the harvest fail? Shall I not rejoice also at the abundance of the weeds whose seeds are the granary of the birds? It matters little comparatively whether the fields fill the farmer's barns. The true husbandman will cease from anxiety, as the squirrels manifest no concern whether the woods will bear chestnuts this year or not, and finish his labor with every day, relinquish all claim to the produce of his fields, and sacrificing in his mind not only his first but his last fruits." In the realm of thought, inner experience, consciousness, as in the outward realm of interconnection, there is a difference between balanced cycle, and the excess which cannot be handled. When the balance is right, the mind recycles from highest illuminations to the stillness of dreamless sleep; the alchemical "transmutation."

III. Consumption

The Condition

POSITION

Everything that lives eats food, and is food in turn. This complicated animal, man, rests on a vast and delicate pyramid of energy-transformations. To grossly use more than you need to destroy, is biologically unsound. Most of the production and consumption of modern societies is not necessary or conducive to spiritual and cultural growth, let alone survival; and is behind much greed and envy, age-old causes of social and international discord.

SITUATION

Man's careless use of "resources" and his total dependence on certain substances such as fossil fuels (which are being exhausted, slowly but certainly), are having harmful effects on all the other members of the life-network. The complexity of modern technology renders whole populations vulnerable to the deadly consequences of the loss of any one key resource. Instead of independence we have over-dependence on life-giving substances such as water, which we squander. Many species of animals and birds have become extinct in the service of fashion fads—or fertilizer—or industrial oil—the soil is being used up; in fact mankind has become a locustlike blight on the planet that will leave a bare cupboard for its own children—all the while in a kind of Addict's Dream of affluence, comfort, eternal progress—using the great achievements of science to produce software and swill.

GOAL

Balance, harmony, humility, growth which is a mutual growth with Redwood and Quail (would you want your child to grow up without ever hearing a wild bird?)—to be a good member of the great community of living creatures. True affluence is not *needing* anything.

Action

SOCIAL/POLITICAL

It must be demonstrated ceaselessly that a continually "growing economy" is no longer healthy, but a Cancer. And that the criminal waste which is allowed in the name of competition—especially that ultimate in wasteful needless competition, hot wars and cold wars with "communism" (or "capitalism")—must be halted totally with ferocious energy and decision. Economics must be seen as a small sub-branch of Ecology, and production/distribution/consumption handled by companies or unions with the same elegance and spareness one sees in nature. Soil banks; open space; phase out logging in most areas. "Lightweight dome and honeycomb structures in line with the architectural principles of nature." "We shouldn't use wood for housing because trees are too important." Protection for all predators and varmints, "Support your right to arm bears." Damn the International Whaling Commission which is selling out the last of our precious, wise whales! Absolutely no further development of roads and concessions in National Parks and Wilderness Areas; build auto campgrounds in the least desirable areas. Plan consumer boycotts in response to dishonest and unnecessary products. Radical Co-ops. Politically, blast both "Communist" and "Capitalist" myths of progress, and all crude notions of conquering or controlling nature.

THE COMMUNITY

Sharing and creating. The inherent aptness of communal life—where large tools are owned jointly and used efficiently. The power of renunciation: If enough Americans refused to buy a new car for one given year it would permanently alter the American economy. Re-cycling clothes and equipment. Support handicrafts—gardening, home skills, midwifery, herbs—all the things that can make us independent, beautiful and whole. Learn to break the habit of unnecessary possessions—a monkey on everybody's back—but avoid a self-abnegating antijoyous self-righteousness. Simplicity is light, carefree, neat, and loving—not a self-punishing ascetic trip. (The great Chinese poet Tu Fu said "The ideas of a poet should be noble and simple.") Don't shoot a deer if you don't know how to use all the

moat and preserve that which you can't eat, to tan
the hide and use the leather—use it all, with gratitude, right down to the sinew and hooves. Simplicity
and mindfulness in diet is a starting point for many
people.

OUR OWN HEADS

It is hard to even begin to gauge how much a
complication of possessions, the notions of "my and
mine," stand between us and a true, clear, liberated
way of seeing the world. To live lightly on the
earth, to be aware and alive, to be free of egotism, to
be in contact with plants and animals, starts with
simple concrete acts. The inner principle is the insight that we are inter-dependent energy-fields of
great potential wisdom and compassion—expressed
in each person as a superb mind, a handsome and
complex body, and the almost magical capacity of
language. To these potentials and capacities, "owning things" can add nothing of authenticity. "Clad
in the sky, with the earth for a pillow."

IV. Transformation

The Condition

POSITION

Everyone is the result of four forces—the conditions of this known-universe (matter/energy
forms, and ceaseless change); the biology of his

species; his individual genetic heritage; and the culture he's born into. Within this web of forces there are certain spaces and loops which allow total freedom and illumination. The gradual exploration of some of these spaces is "evolution" and, for human cultures, what "history" could be. We have it within our deepest powers not only to change our "selves" but to change our culture. If a man is to remain on earth he must transform the five-millennia long urbanizing civilization tradition into a new ecologically-sensitive harmony-oriented wild-minded scientific/spiritual culture. "Wildness is the state of complete awareness. That's why we need it."

SITUATION

Civilization, which has made us so successful a species, has overshot itself and now threatens us with its inertia. There is some evidence that civilized life isn't good for the human gene pool. To achieve the Changes we must change the very foundations of our society and our minds.

GOAL

Nothing short of total transformation will do much good. What we envision is a planet on which the human population lives harmoniously and dynamically by employing a sophisticated and unobtrusive technology in a world environment which is "left natural." Specific points in this vision:

- A healthy and spare population of all races, much less in number than today.
- Cultural and individual pluralism, unified by a

type of world tribal council. Division by natural
and cultural boundaries rather than arbitrary
political boundaries.

- A technology of communication, education, and
quiet transportation, land-use being sensitive to
the properties of each region. Allowing, thus, the
Bison to return to much of the high plains. Careful
but intensive agriculture in the great alluvial
valleys; deserts left wild for those who would trot
in them. Computer technicians who run the plant
part of the year and walk along with the Elk in
their migrations during the rest.

- A basic cultural outlook and social organization
that inhibits power and property-seeking while
encouraging exploration and challenge in things
like music, meditation, mathematics, mountaineering, magic, and all other ways of authentic being-
in-the-world. Women totally free and equal. A new
kind of family—responsible, but more festive and
relaxed—is implicit.

Action

SOCIAL/POLITICAL

It seems evident that there are throughout the
world certain social and religious forces which have
worked through history toward an ecologically and
culturally enlightened state of affairs. Let these be
encouraged: Gnostics, hip Marxists, Teilhard de
Chardin Catholics, Druids, Taoists, Biologists,
Witches, Yogins, Bhikkus, Quakers, Sufis, Tibetans,
Zens, Shamans, Bushmen, American Indians, Poly-

nesians, Anarchists, Alchemists . . . the list is long. All primitive cultures, all communal and ashram movements. Since it doesn't seem practical or even desirable to think that direct bloody force will achieve much, it would be best to consider this a continuing "revolution of consciousness" which will be won not by guns but by seizing the key images, myths, archetypes, eschatologies, and ecstasies so that life won't seem worth living unless one's on the transforming energy's side. By taking over "science and technology" and releasing its real possibilities and powers in the service of this planet—which, after all, produced us and it.

OUR COMMUNITY

New schools, new classes, walking in the woods and cleaning up the streets. Find psychological techniques for creating an awareness of "self" which includes the social and natural environment. "Consideration of what specific language forms—symbolic systems—and social institutions constitute obstacles to ecological awareness." Without falling into a facile interpretation of McLuhan, we can hope to use the media. Let no one be ignorant of the facts of biology and related disciplines; bring up our children as part of the wild-life. Some communities can establish themselves in backwater rural areas and flourish—others maintain themselves in urban centers, and the two types work together —a two-way flow of experience, people, money, and home-grown vegetables. Ultimately cities will exist only as joyous tribal gatherings and fairs, to

dissolve after a few weeks. Investigating new life-
styles is our work, as is the exploration of Ways to
explore our inner realms—with the known dangers of
crashing that go with such. We should work with
political-minded people where it helps, hoping to
enlarge their vision, and with people of all varieties
of politics or thought at whatever point they become
aware of environmental urgencies. Master the
archaic and the primitive as models of basic nature-
related cultures—as well as the most imaginative
extensions of science—and build a community where
these two vectors cross.

OUR OWN HEADS

Is where it starts. Knowing that we are the first
human beings in history to have all of man's culture
and previous experience available to our study, and
being free enough of the weight of traditional cultures to seek out a larger identity.—The first members of a civilized society since the early Neolithic
to wish to look clearly into the eyes of the wild and
see our self-hood, our family, there. We have these
advantages to set off the obvious disadvantages of
being as screwed up as we are—which gives us a
fair chance to penetrate into some of the riddles of
ourselves and the universe, and to go beyond the
idea of "man's survival" or "the survival of the
biosphere" and to draw our strength from the realization that at the heart of things is some kind of
serene and ecstatic process which is actually beyond
qualities and certainly beyond birth-and-death. "No
need to survive!" "In the fires that destroy the uni-

verse at the end of the kalpa, what survives?"—"The iron tree blooms in the void!"

Knowing that nothing need be done, is where we begin to move from.

(May be reproduced)

Ecology Action. *The Unanimous Declaration of Interdependance*

Ecology Action of Berkeley, California is a bright sign of the times. One of the many ecology groups to appear in recent years, EA is dedicated to a highly militant environmental politics by direct action.

There are some who fear that such involvement subtracts energy from movements for social and racial justice: "People before trees and rivers." A foolish fear, and a misguided one. There is no such thing as a good society without trees and rivers—and they cannot defend themselves. Work to humanize this hardly human race of ours, and all benefit, for the abuse of power is at the root of every evil, social as well as ecological. Where do we begin the good fight? As Aldous Huxley said, "On all fronts at once."

Besides, even guerrilla revolutionaries need air to breathe, water to drink.

WHEN IN the course of evolution it becomes necessary for one species to denounce the notion of

independence from all the rest, and to assume
among the powers of the earth, the interdependent
station, to which the natural laws of the cosmos
have placed them, a decent respect for the opinions
of all mankind requires that they should declare
the conditions which impel them to assert their
interdependence.

We hold these truths to be self-evident: that all
species have evolved with equal and unalienable
rights, that among these are Life, Liberty and the
pursuit of Happiness; that to insure these rights,
nature has instituted certain principles for the sus-
tenance of all species, deriving these principles
from the capabilities of the planet's life-support
system; that whenever any behavior by members
of one species becomes destructive to these principles, it is the function of other members of that
species to alter or abolish such behavior and to re-
establish the theme of interdependence with all
life, in such a form and in accordance with those
natural principles that will effect their safety and
happiness. Prudence, indeed, will dictate that cultural values long established should not be altered
for light and transient causes, that mankind is more
disposed to suffer from asserting a vain notion of
independence than to right itself by abolish-
ing that culture to which it is now accustomed.
But when a long train of abuses and usurpations
of these principles of interdependence, evinces a
subtle design to reduce them, through absolute de-
spoliation of the planet's fertility, to a state of ill
will, bad health, and great anxiety, it is their right,

it is their duty, to throw off such notions of independence from other species and from the life support system, and to provide new guards for the
re-establishment of the security and maintenance
of these principles. Such has been the quiet and
patient sufferage of all species, and such is now the
necessity which constrains the species of Homo
Sapiens to reassert the principles of interdependence. The history of the present notion of independence is a history of repeated injuries and
usurpations all having in direct effect the establishment of an absolute tyranny over life. To prove
this let facts be submitted to a candid world. 1.
People have refused to recognize the roles of other
species and the importance of natural principles
for growth of the food they require. 2. People
have refused to recognize that they are interacting
with other species in an evolutionary process. 3.
People have fouled the waters that all life partakes
of. 4. People have transformed the face of the earth
to enhance their notion of independence from it
and in so doing have interrupted many natural
processes that they are dependent upon. 5. People
have contaminated the common household with
substances that are foreign to the life processes
and which cause many organisms great difficulties.
6. People have massacred and extincted fellow
species for their feathers and furs, for their skins
and tusks. 7. People have persecuted most persistently those known as coyote, lion, wolf and fox
because of their dramatic role in the expression of
interdependence. 8. People have warred upon one

another which has brought great sorrow to themselves and vast destruction to the homes and food supplies of many living things. 9. People are proliferating in such an irresponsible manner as to threaten the survival of all species. 10. People have denied others the right to live to completion their interdependencies to the full extent of their capabilities.

WE therefore, among the mortal representatives of the eternal process of life and evolutionary principles, in mutual humbleness, explicitly stated, appealing to the ecological consciousness of the world for the rectitude of our intentions, do solemnly publish and declare that all species are interdependent; that they are all free to realize these relationships to the full extent of their capabilities; that each species is subservient to the requirements of the natural processes that sustain life. And for the support of this declaration with a firm reliance on all other members of our species who understand their consciousness as a capability, to assist all of us and our brothers to interact in order to realize a life process that manifests its maximum potential of diversity, vitality and planetary fertility to ensure the continuity of life on earth.

Signed ECOLOGY ACTION
and 52 other signatures of
concerned Homo Sapiens

The Berkeley Tribe. *Blueprint for a Communal Environment*

What follows is a set of practical suggestions for transforming the existing homes and neighborhoods of our disintegrating cities into ecologically sane, communally robust environments. The proposal comes from the underground paper, *The Berkeley Tribe,* and its reference throughout is to Berkeley; but the problems mentioned are universal and the ideas offered are conveniently portable.

The "People's Park" referred to was an effort in 1969 by Berkeley students and citizens to turn a muddy, garbage-strewn, abandoned lot owned by the University of California into a user-developed playground and park. What they created was rough-hewn and beautiful, but unfortunately not to the taste of the governor of California who was quick to recognize this subversive enterprise for what it really was—an example of constructive citizenly initiative undertaken without state approval or direction—and to quash it, at the expense of much violence and local social torment including one man blinded by police gunfire and another killed. When last seen, People's Park was a parking lot nobody would park on and a soccer field nobody would play on—bloodstained ground magnificently fenced and totally depopulated. A suitably sterile monument to California's recent descent into proto-fascist politics. "*Solitudinem faciunt; pacem appellant.*"

PEOPLE'S PARK was the beginning of the Revolutionary Ecology Movement. It is the model of the struggle we are going to have to wage in the future if life is going to survive at all on this planet. In the Park we blended the new culture and the new politics that was developing in Berkeley for almost a decade. The revolutionary culture gives us new communal, eco-viable ways of organizing our lives, while people's politics gives us the means to resist the System.

Environmental rape is not only taking place in the large urban centers like New York and Los Angeles, but it's going on right here in Berkeley. . . . The rapists are trying to institute a sanitizing program of cultural genocide in the South Campus Community: drive out the longhairs, tear down the brown shingles, and put up plastic ticky-tackies for the technocrats. You kill two birds with one stone —provide the sort of sterile environment war researchers thrive on, and get rid of the troublemakers who often resist the University's defense complicity.

The projection along the BART [Bay Area Rapid Transit] strip is for new highrise apartments for commuter-swingers who work in San Francisco during the day and smoke dope and swap wives in Berkeley at night. There are plans for an industrial park in West Berkeley, which the black community is resisting. A convention center and medical school are also planned for the flatlands.

The people don't need any new people or buildings; we're not even using what we have now properly. Progress no longer means growth. We have to begin to use available land to produce food and create parks. We have to cut down on automobile traffic and liberate land by tearing up unnecessary streets and driveways.

Maybe we don't have enough living space if everyone has to have their own atomized apartment-cell, but when we start using the space we have communally and rationally we'll probably have more than we need. Communal ways of organizing our lives help to cut down on consumption, to provide for basic human needs more efficiently, to resist the system, to support ourselves and overcome the misery of atomized living.

What were once the utopian visions of the revolutionary drop-out culture are becoming means to survival. . . . Many of the ideas, projects and resources presented here are nothing new. They've been floating around Berkeley for a while now. What we have done is to pull together many of the best ideas and resources to give people a comprehensive look at what's possible for the community, to provide them with the beginnings of a resource handbook, and hopefully to provoke new ideas. . . .

Start getting it together with your sisters and brothers. Energy will be dispersed if everyone calls the resource people as individuals. When you've got

yourselves together in a group, avail yourselves of
the resources. . . .

I. Shelter

The organization of most of our living space is
based on assumptions which don't relate to our community. Partitions are arranged so that people won't
interfere with one another, so that we can proceed
with our private existence in order to produce and
consume more efficiently. Intercourse of all varieties
is discouraged. Rooms have well-defined functions
which reflect the fragmentation of our lives. Nuclear
families are still assumed to be the common living
arrangement.

In contrast, our needs are for space arranged to
encourage communalism and break down priva-
tization. Multi-purpose rooms are more efficient in
saving space, and can help to spacially integrate
our lives. With women's liberation, and a new communal morality the nuclear family is becoming
obsolete. And even where they remain families often
live together in communes rather than in separate
homes. Floor plans and housing arrangements don't
develop in isolation, they reflect the spirit of the
society, and the spirit of Free Berkeley is different
than that of America.

We can begin to reorder the construction of space
itself. Ticky-tackies have anywhere from four to
twelve tiny kitchens, none adequate, all cramped.
There is no reason why some of these cannot be

eliminated in a communal situation while others are
enlarged and put to more intensive use. Other
kitchens can be turned over to special needs such as
kiln rooms, bakeries, and canning factories when the
communal gardens are harvested. Shared storage
pantries can easily be established. Thus, kitchens

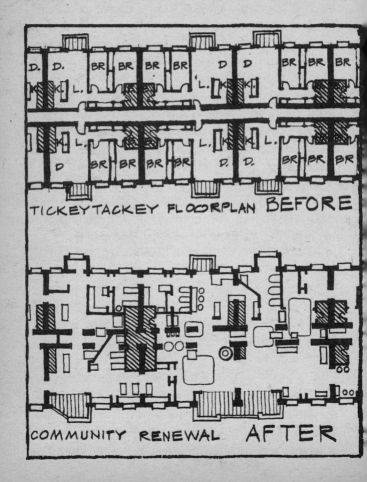

TICKEYTACKEY FLOORPLAN BEFORE

COMMUNITY RENEWAL   AFTER

can return to more social conditions by being larger, more traveled, with easier access. The bathroom has communal possibilities too.

To recapture the hallways and to break up their monotony, party walls can be relocated or removed (within reason). This new space can be added to existing rooms or pieces of it can be used as storage areas and darkrooms.

Within, walls can be remodeled to increase space and access to space. Larger rooms mean more interaction—such as communal dining rooms, meeting spaces and work areas. Sleeping areas can be arranged in alcoves around the edges of the larger spaces or made communal by concentrating them within the large room.

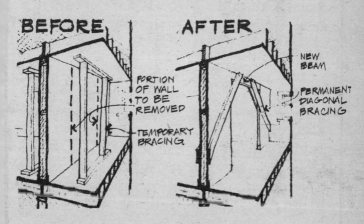

Ceilings can be opened up to turn our caves into something a little more cathedral-like, and walls can be altered too. . . . Basements can house the heavy machines of noisy cottage and barter industry,

hydroponic food growing and storage areas for re-
cyclable waste. The exterior upper walls and the
roof of your house can be turned into communi-
cating links with neighboring houses as as well as
providing space for gardens and social areas.
Gratings can be taken off balconies and they can be
reinforced and connected. Bridgeways can connect
buildings at the second and third stories. We can
live in the outdoors much more than we do.

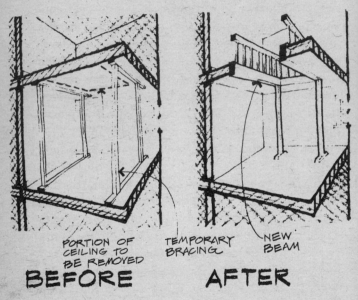

PORTION OF   TEMPORARY   NEW
CEILING TO   BRACING   BEAM
BE REMOVED

BEFORE   AFTER

II. Land

Older European rural and urban communities
were built quite differently from our modern city
grids. They consisted of clusters of dwellings

huddled together around dips and rises in the landscape, which were often left as open space and used communally for plazas, parks, markets, or gardens.

Only incidentally is this space a transportation center, since going *through* the neighborhood to get "somewhere else" was not regarded as more important than the life functions happening right then and there.

All land in Berkeley is treated purely as a marketable commodity. Space is parcelled into neat consumer packages. In between rows of land parcels are transportation "corridors" to keep people flowing from workplace to market. Fifty percent of the open space in Berkeley is devoted to the private automobile, and all planning about streets assumes that the private car will forever remain the dominant form of transportation in our community.

What has happened to *us?* Why do we have such difficulty in keeping together and protecting neighborhoods, communities, *communal space?* It is because the "efficiency" of a consumer society depends upon neat distinctions between public and private space, between home, job and market. The more separate we become, the more the economy "grows," and vice versa. This is "Progress."

BACKYARDS AND SIDEYARDS

If backyard and sideyard fences were dismantled, the interior of a whole block could become a park or garden. A backyard area formerly used as a parking lot might be best covered over with wood

chips as a play equipment area; other less com-
pacted grass-covered areas would be more easily
cultivated as vegetable gardens. . . .

Some garages which lie one behind the other
could have the roofs extended so as to join the two,
and the result utilized as a communal carpool re-
serve car "barn" to store unused vehicles. Other
garages could be dismantled and the structural
materials used to build an interhouse bridgeway, a
tool shed, or, with wood from two or three dismantled garages, a daycare shelter.

A platform "bridgeway" between two houses
would open up a lot of space possibilities, breaking
down the strict division between indoor and outdoor
space. If desired, the ground underneath could be
covered with discarded bricks, concrete, gravel,
wood chips, etc., to form a dry and/or hard surface
for a picnic table, tool storage bin, rainy day children's outdoor play area, car/bike port. Platforms
could be suspended from chains, or supported from
below with beams from dismantled buildings, railroad ties, etc. Driftwood recovered from the Bay is
nice building material too.

VACANT LOTS

If your neighbors aren't ready to tear down their
backyard fences yet, one way to start neighborhood
development of communal space is on a vacant lot.
All of the things we've suggested for the backyard
might be done on a lot. The next logical step would
be to try to integrate this public space into "private"

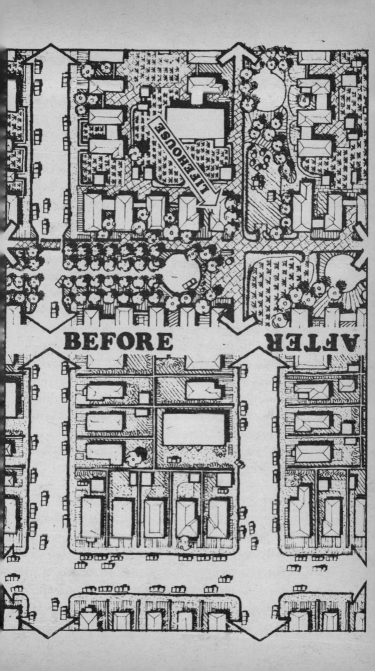

LIFEHOUSE

BEFORE

AFTER

space by tearing down an intervening fence, and letting things develop from there.

STREETS

Berkeley could function very well with half the streets closed off. This would stimulate collective transportation experiments, further cutting down traffic on residential streets. It would free *ten times more* land area for public use than we now have in park acreage. Intersections could become parks, gardens, plazas, with the paving material recovered and used to make artificial hills. Plazas in Europe serve as outdoor theaters and concert "halls" and as meeting places for action. Portable vegetable markets also set up shop in them two or three times a week. We could add flea markets, daycare centers, and frisbee festivals to the list.

This all points to some suggestive uses for the corner houses which would face these plazas. Corner houses are very often older, larger, more solid buildings which have been heavily subdivided, and which bring the landlord such a "healthy" income that he hasn't sold them yet to the Developers.

We offer the following idea: corner houses contain an older student and drop-out population which might be likely to initiate communal experimenting, possibly freeing front room or other space as a neighborhood Life House. If the plaza were created for neighborhood use, then the Life House on the corner might be the place to store portable structures for a market, daycare equipment, and other plaza-related things. The choice of which inter-

sections to close in a given neighborhood might be made after looking at the corner house situation.

Once we begin to close streets at one end, children can play more safely in front of houses; block parties can occur; stoop-sitting can become a lively way of passing time. . . .

PACK CREVICES WITH SANDY SOIL AND COMPOST. SEED WITH GRASSES. OR PLANT BERRY VINES OR IVY AT BASE OF WALL

ABOUT 3 OR 4 FEET

BROKEN ASPHALT OR CONCRETE

ABOUT 3 OR 4 FEET

DIG A SHALLOW TROUGH ABOUT 6 INCHES DEEP IN THE MIDDLE AND ABOUT 3 OR 4 FEET WIDE

MAKE RUBBLE MOUNDS & WALLS FROM THE ASPHALT ON THE STREET

III. Food

Commercially grown and packaged food is a rip-off in every conceivable way. Transitionally, the Berkeley community must begin to alter its food consumption patterns and begin to produce its own food. Ultimately, we must approach self-sufficiency where food is concerned.

THE FOOD CONSPIRACY

The Food Conspiracy provides organically grown foods at low prices in a communal way. Food Conspirators go as neighborhood groups and purchase goods at wholesale prices. The goods are distributed in the neighborhood where the members live.

The next step for the Food Conspiracy is a People's Market which will receive the organic products of rural communes and small farmers, and distribute them to the neighborhood conspiracies. Such a market place will have other uses—craftspeople can sell their wares there. The People's Market is a solid example of creative thinking about communal use of space. Its structure will be portable, and will be built in such a way as to serve neighborhood kids as play equipment on non-market days.

GROW YOUR OWN

Backyard Gardens: tearing down backyard fences allows many people to participate in the creation of a communal garden. Some free sources of organic waste for fertilizer and weed control are: sewage sludge from the Richmond Disposal Plant, manure from the Tilden Park Pony Rides, cocoa bean hulls from Ghirardelli's and Guittard chocolate factories, and sawdust from lumber companies. Also, your own organic garbage is a very important source.

You don't have to spend hours digging up the soil in preparation to plant. In fact, it's bad gardening because it turns the fertile layer of topsoil on to the bottom. Just clear the area of all inorganic materials. Spread aged manure and sewage sludge along closely spaded rows. Let them sit for at least a week. Water them lightly every day or two. In the meantime, start a few seedlings of your own in milk cartons and egg boxes. These should be primarily warm weather vegetables. They should be ready to transplant into your already growing garden in about four to six weeks. After about a week or two, take a hoe and chop up the fertilized rows, working the fertilizer into the earth. Rake the rows smooth and begin to plant the seeds of some of the cool weather vegetables directly into the ground.

When these seeds start to sprout above the ground, you can take milk cartons or other cardboard or paper containers and make stand-up collars along the rows to shield them from snails and cutworms. Planting a border of marigolds around your garden helps to control the bugs too.

COMPOSTING

Compost heaps are an excellent method of producing organic fertilizer and of recycling wastes. A compost heap consists of layers of natural wastes such as green yard-clippings and leaves, manure, kitchen wastes, wood chips and sawdust, bone meal, sewage sludge and just plain old earth. The pile is made in layers up to about five feet high and dampened down, but not saturated. Kitchen wastes should be chopped up well before adding them. The pile should be left uncovered and turned every three or four days, or it can be covered with a sheet of black plastic and left undisturbed to decompose by itself. Either way the result is a rich, fertile black humus-like mixture which is the most ideal fertilizer available. There are other ways of composting to be looked into, including the pit method. (Dig a hole; put it in; cover it up with earth.)

MULCHING

Mulching means covering the rows of already growing vegetables with cocoa bean hulls, straw, peatmoss, etc., to keep the ground moist and to prevent the growing of weeds. Mulch is spread all along the rows very loosely, up close to the base of each plant. When the growing season is over and you have already got all these natural organic materials all over the ground, simply add a layer of manure over the top and let it sit all winter. This is called sheet composting. When spring planting time comes again, the soil will be nourished, twice as rich and ready to plant in with hardly any preparation.

Other possibilities for food production are rooftop gardens, bee keeping and hydroponics.

COOPERATIVE RESOURCES

As more neighborhood gardens are started, we could use a tool and fertilizer cooperative for sharing expenses of such items as roto-tillers and shredders, bulk amounts of phosphate rock, bone and blood meal, cottonseed meal, seed, etc. One possibility is to outfit a large van or bus as a people's gardener, stocked with tools and fertilizer and a small organic gardening library.

BOOKS

Organic Gardening and Farming Magazine. Emmaus, Pennsylvania 18049

Turner, James S. *The Chemical Feast*. Grossman. 1970.

Hunter, B. *Gardening Without Poisons*. Houghton-Mifflin.

Rodale, J. I. *How to Grow Fruits and Vegetables by the Organic Method*. Rodale Association.

Douglas, W. *Wilderness Bill of Rights*. Little, Brown & Co.

DeBell, G. *The Environmental Handbook*. Ballantine.

IV. *Transportation*

The automotive-oil-steel-rubber related industries represent the essence of American capitalism. Planned obsolescence, pollution, exploitation, smog, tire dust, noise pollution, social disintegration, are all related to the automotive transportation system. The stop-gap solutions the system offers are a shuck. Clean cars, mass transportation, lead-free gas, industrial pollution control won't work. We must begin to question a society that necessitates this sort of transportation system.

Communal forms are essential for reducing our dependence on the automobile and the system it represents. As we begin to live and work in our communities, our needs to travel will decline. Get together with people in your building, your block, and your neighborhood. Try and localize as much of your living as you can.

Begin to think about working in your community. Make group arrangements to go shopping, to go to the laundry and to work. When you go some place, make sure your car is full. Then, begin to make communal decisions about your vans and cars. First, pool your cars and see what's available. You should find that your group doesn't need a third of what it owns. Sell the surplus and use the money to repair the remaining cars and to create local jobs for yourselves.

Along with the communalization of cars, we have to start communalizing their upkeep. The bloodsuckers from Detroit make more money on repairs because of planned obsolescence than on the actual sale of autos. Furthermore, since it is ecologically disastrous to produce any more cars, we're going to have to get the most out of the ones we have. Cars that are operating poorly cause more pollution than cars in good repair. While organizing your commune, landlord collective, block or whatever, find out who the mechanics are. Make arrangements with them to take care of the cars in return for services other members of your group have. There has also been talk of forming a mechanics' collective to service the whole community. At the community level, there is another possibility. We can form an expanded Taxi Unlimited by using several big checker cabs or vans. These cabs could continuously travel the most heavily used circuits in Berkeley. They could be waved down to pick you up at any point and could drop you off wherever you wanted along the route. The fare would be five or ten cents, depending on costs, regardless of how far you rode.

The best solution is to stop driving altogether. Walk or use a bike. If the distance is too great, hitch. To facilitate this we . . . ought to establish well identified hitching posts where people would make it a point to drive by and pick up their sisters and brothers. . . . Bulletin boards with hitching maps and reusable hitching signs, can be put at these points and mutual arrangements would be made to regularize rides among people going the same way at the same time.

V. *Community Services*

We've all been burned too many times by bureaucratic and centralized service institutions, public and private. Schools, hospitals, mental institutions, welfare, police—all promising to serve and protect—all part of the great propaganda and control machine exploiting us, keeping us weak and isolated, keeping us down. The more we learn about the ways we've been victimized the more important it becomes to develop our own communal and liberated means of dealing with our basic human needs.

People have been experimenting with countercultural, new and different ways of doing things for a long time. A quantum leap suggests itself: that small groups of neighbors mobilize resources and energy in order to cement fragmented neighborhoods back together and begin to take care of business (from child care and first aid to political education) on a local level and in an integrated way. Some concrete ideas:

CHILD CARE

The responsibility of caring for young children can be shared by many men and women in a neighborhood whether or not they have children of their own. A lot of inhibiting laws govern the establishment of formal day care centers, but no one can stop you from using your own home (the best place anyway) for sitting with a bunch of your neighbor's kids. If anyone comes to hassle you tell them it's an (un)birthday party. There is no need for separate facilities. The location of the center could be rotated among the empty homes of people who work during the days.

First aid and child care skills can be pooled and proliferated and materials can be collected from among the neighborhood surplus. Kids need lots of physical activity; outdoor ladders, slides and jungle gyms and indoor jump ropes, tumbling mats and bars to swing on

People who tend each others' children should exchange careful information about the kids—from what their allergies are to who their friends are on the block. This is important for emergencies and also generally helpful. Also important for emergencies are signed release statements so that a kid can get medical attention if his parent is not around. Even a signed form will not eliminate all hassles—it's probably best to simply lie. . . .

MEDICAL CARE

Bum trips, gonorrhea, malnutrition, infectious hepatitis, drug addiction, etc. . . . Too many of us are too weak or spaced out to build or fight. Starting in our own neighborhoods we can begin to help ourselves. Every one of us should know the fundamentals of medical care. . . . Each neighborhood could establish a small center where a stash of health information and supplies would be easily accessible *at all times.* Special effort should go into massing information on preventive medicine, prenatal care and other areas that most of us know little about. Maybe a local doctor could be persuaded to donate one afternoon a week to the neighborhood for free consultation and treatment.

The work of building communes, neighborhoods and communities demands that we trade old individualistic, neurotic, paranoid heads for new liberated ones. Also the pressures of trying to resist the system often become too much to bear alone. That means lots of real encounter with the people close to us. The Rap Center and the Free U. can both turn you on to people who know the ins and outs of ritualized communication and encounter and can offer advice on how to begin the process. . . .

A lot of these ideas suggest the need for a neighborhood focal point—some indoor public space given over to the functions that encourage the growth of the neighborhood. As neighborhoods begin to coalesce, and space is rationalized in a communal way, it will be possible to find a spare room or two or a shed or a garage to serve the purpose. Ecology Action first offered the idea of a Life House and has ideas about the ways in which they can help community ecology, recycling paper, cans and glass, composting, etc. The neighborhood Life House can also house bulletin boards, libraries on relevant and less relevant topics, community tools and bicycles. People who could dig the job would most likely be needed to keep the place in order and to watch the back door.

Whether we are talking about medical care, food, shelter or anything else we'll find that we can accomplish a lot by small rip-offs and by living off the waste of large institutions. But the people have a right to *all* the resources that disappear into those vacuum cleaners and will need those resources to take care of their own needs.

Contradictions inside those big institutions are acute these days. . . . There are demands coming down for community and worker control. As the people start to win those struggles the institutions can be de-centralized or dismantled and then integrated into the worklife of functioning neighborhoods.

Theodore Roszak. "Novum Organum"

> they are killing the whales . . .
> they are killing the whales . . .

Then come let us mourn for these leviathan
for great and lordly things degraded by
our vandal genius
                and for ourselves
who abuse the gift of our monkey cunning
to mock the brute magnificence of earth.
Maniacal craft
that devours the grace and goodness of our kind . . .
even the deep sea bottoms are stained with
unpitying insolence.
                    Narcissus-like,
we would not love what does not bear our image
if only the print of our butchering hand wiped
over all that is passive, dumb, and grandly
primordial.

Bacon, who gloried in "that right over
nature which belongs to us by
divine bequest," now acknowledge your progeny
sunk in this culture of busy despair,
vastly empowered, obsessed, and absurd.
What is this thing, your "New Philosophy"
but Old Adam's arrogance:
to name the beasts who need no names
and muse upon a serpent's squalid lie?

Kenneth Rexroth. From "The Signatures of All Things"

When I dragged the rotten log
From the bottom of the pool,
It seemed heavy as stone.
I let it lie in the sun
For a month; and then chopped it
Into sections, and split them
For kindling, and spread them out
To dry some more. Late that night,
After reading for hours,
While moths rattled at the lamp—
The saints and the philosophers
On the destiny of man—
I went out on my cabin porch,
And looked up through the black forest
At the swaying islands of stars.
Suddenly I saw at my feet,
Spread on the floor of night, ingots
Of quivering phosphorescence,
And all about were scattered chips
Of pale cold light that was alive.

From *Collected Shorter Poems* (New York: New Directions, 1949). Copyright 1949 by Kenneth Rexroth. Reprinted
by permission of the New Directions Publishing Corporation.

V. TRANSCENDENCE

Bid your soul travel to any land you choose and sooner than you bid it go, it will be there. Bid it fly up to heaven, and it will not lack for wings. Nothing can bar its way, neither the fiery heat of the sun, nor the swirl of the planet-spheres. Cleaving its way through all, it will fly up till it reaches the outermost of all corporeal things. And should you wish to break forth from the universe itself and gaze on the things outside the cosmos, even that is permitted to you. See what power, what quickness is yours.

Find your home in the haunts of every living creature. Make yourself higher than all heights and lower than all depths. Bring together in yourself all opposites of quality: heat and cold, dryness and fluidity. Think that you are everywhere at once, on land, at sea, in heaven. Think that you are not yet begotten, that you are in the womb, that you are young, that you are old, that you have died, that you are in the world beyond the grave. Grasp in your thought all this at once, all times and places, all substances and qualities and magnitudes together. Then you can apprehend God.

(From "The Divine Pymander" of Hermes Trismegistus.)

I recall a passage by Karl Marx; it appears in *The German Ideology*. In the course of only two paragraphs, the words "real" and "actual" are repeated over and over again, a dozen times or more. "We set out from *real*, active men and on the basis of their *real* life process. . . . Where speculation ends—in *real*

life—there *real* positive science begins. . . . Empty
talk about consciousness must cease and *real* knowledge takes its place. . . . This method starts out
from *real* premises. . . ."

Real . . . actual . . . real . . . actual. . . . Like
a hypnotic drumbeat meant to beguile subliminally:
"See *this! This* is *real;* this *alone* is *real*—what you
can touch, grasp, measure, *use,* only *this* is *really*
real." It is a concentrated dose of the constant
Marxian theme: to distinguish hard fact from mere
"phantoms formed in the human brain."

Magic: the art of "now-you-see-it-now-you-don't":
a conjuring up, and conjuring away of realities.
Marx was among the modern world's great
magicians. He knew: if the omega of politics is the
withering away of the State, the alpha is change of
consciousness. Not naked power, then, makes the
revolution, but power to adjudicate among realities:
to unearth the concealed foundations of thought,
speech, action, and to discover to mankind what
the words and symbols *really* mean. In this sense,
Shelley had named the poets "unacknowledged
legislators": those who "purge from our inward
sight the film of familiarity which obscures from us
the wonder of our being." Good magic: "to cleanse
the doors of perception." Bad magic: to block the
doors—and charge admission.

But it was no poet's reality Marx wanted. Rather,
he wanted an "empirically perceptible" politics, a
politics of matter and appetite: a *scientific* socialism,
hard to the touch as the iron and coal on which the

industrial captains built their power, a weapon graspable as a tool or a gun butt in the hand. The task, then, was to translate the transcendent images—sin, salvation, the heavenly city, the celestial splendors—into their secular equivalents: to haul them down from the clouds, to *materalize* and *historicize* aspiration. Heaven *on earth*—and no place else.

Boehme's lament: "O, dear children! Look in what a dungeon we are lying."

Pie-in-the-sky-when-you-die. That too was a conjuring act: priestly sleight-of-hand meant to dampen expectation. Revolutionary spirits—like Marx—easily showed up the trick. But their debunking carried too far. They failed to see: it was not the reference to transcendent experience that merited rejection, but its invidious employment and attendant obfuscation of consciousness. The evil lay in setting transcendence *against* the earth, the body, the city of man, *for the sake of* protecting criminal privilege.

We have many evils yet to expunge from the world, some as obvious and immediate as the massacre of the innocents. But beyond that, once again, the struggle will be against bad magic that undimensions the mind—and so against Marx as well as his capitalist adversary: against reductionist revolution as much as against the reductionist establishment. Our bad magic is scientized thought: the myth of depersonalized knowing which alienates and makes an absurdity of the noble human condition. Our bad magicians are the technical elites and those who employ them to intimidate by way of expertise. The artificiality of the industrial environment strengthens their hand against us. For how can we now do without them? Perhaps their intentions are even honorable: a despotism of beneficent technicians. Nonetheless, the technocrats clip the wings of imagination: that largeness of vision may seem to be a madness and the knowledge of God a betrayal of Reason. They must have a reality conveniently suited to keeping the Big System organized and well-oiled. But then what are they to do with those of us who   .

. . . would rather learn from one bird how to sing than teach ten thousand stars how not to dance? (e.e. cummings).

Like Uroboros, the alchemist's snake, this book's head takes hold of its tail and we come full circle. Probe to the depths of the person and you find the transcendent impulse: the unruly energy of the human adventure.

R. D. Laing. *Transcendental Experience*

The care of sick souls in our time falls—largely by default—to the psychotherapists. But is the soul possessed by transcendent longings "sick," or

From *The Politics of Experience* (London: Penguin Books, 1969). Reprinted by permission of the publisher.

struggling toward health of a higher order? For the most part, the psychiatrists—aspiring to scientific status—have seconded Freud's village atheism: religion, being an "illusion," has no proper future in the psychology of modern man. Jung dissented, insisting that the religious impulse be accepted as psychically central. The contemporary revival of mystical and occult traditions is much beholden to Jung's eclecticism which managed to keep at least one school of professional psychology free of reductive dogmatics.

Along rather different lines than Jung—in this case existentialist and phenomenological—the British psychiatrist R. D. Laing also postulates a "valid mysticism." The essay that follows is typical of the adventurousness that has made Laing one of the most controversial figures in his profession.

WE ARE living in an age in which the ground is shifting and the foundations are shaking. I cannot answer for other times and places. Perhaps it has always been so. We know it is true today.

In these circumstances, we have all reason to be insecure. When the ultimate basis of our world is in question, we run to different holes in the ground, we scurry into roles, statuses, identities, interpersonal relations. We attempt to live in castles that can only be in the air, because there is no firm ground in the social cosmos on which to build. We are all witnesses to this state of affairs. Each sometimes sees the same fragment of the whole situation differently; often our concern is with different presentations of the original catastrophe. . . .

I wish to relate the transcendental experiences that *sometimes* break through in psychosis, to those experiences of the divine that are the living fount of all religion. . . . If we can begin to understand sanity and madness in existential social terms, we shall be more able to see clearly the extent to which we all confront common problems and share common dilemmas.

Experience may be judged to be invalidly mad or to be validly mystical. The distinction is not easy. In either case, from a social point of view, such judgements characterize different forms of behaviour, regarded in our society as deviant. People behave in such ways because their experience of themselves is different. It is on the existential meaning of such unusual experience that I wish to focus.

Psychotic experience goes beyond the horizons of our common, that is, our communal sense.

What regions of experience does this lead to? It entails a loss of the usual foundations of the 'sense' of the world that we share with one another. Old purposes no longer seem viable: old meanings are senseless: the distinctions between imagination, dream, external perceptions often seem no longer to apply in the old way. External events may seem magically conjured up. Dreams may seem direct communications from others: imagination may seem to be objective reality.

But most radically of all the very ontological foundations are shaken. The being of phenomena shifts and the phenomena of being may no longer present itself to us as before. There are no supports, nothing to cling to, except perhaps some fragments from the wreck, a few memories, names, sounds, one or two objects, that retain a link with a world long lost. This void may not be empty. It may be peopled by visions and voices, ghosts, strange shapes and apparitions. No one who has not experienced how insubstantial the pageant of external reality can be, how it may fade, can fully realize the sublime and grotesque presences that can replace it, or that can exist alongside it.

When a person goes mad, a profound transposition of his position in relation to all domains of being occurs. His centre of experience moves from ego to Self. Mundane time becomes merely anecdotal, only the eternal matters. The madman is however confused. He muddles ego with self, inner with outer, natural and supernatural. Nevertheless, he often can be to us, even through his profound wretchedness and disintegration, the hierophant of the sacred. An exile from the scene of being as we know it, he is an alien, a stranger, signalling to us from the void in which he is foundering, a void which may be peopled by presences that we do not even dream of. They used to be called demons and spirits, and they used to be known and named. He has lost his sense of self, his feelings, his place in the world as we know it. He tells us he is dead. But we

are distracted from our cosy security by this mad
ghost that haunts us with his visions and voices
that seem so senseless and of which we feel impelled
to rid him, cleanse him, cure him.

Madness need not be all breakdown. It may also
be break-through. It is potentially liberation and
renewal as well as enslavement and existential
death.

There are now a growing number of accounts by
people who have been through the experience of
madness.

The following is part of one of the earlier contemporary accounts, as recorded by Karl Jaspers in
his *General Psychopathology* [Manchester, England: University Press, 1962].

I believe I caused the illness myself. In my attempt
to penetrate the other world I met its natural guardians,
the embodiment of my own weaknesses and faults. I
first thought these demons were lowly inhabitants of
the other world who could play me like a ball because
I went into these regions unprepared and lost my way.
Later I thought they were split-off parts of my own
mind (passions) which existed near me in free space
and thrived on my feelings. I believed everyone else
had these too but did not perceive them, thanks to the
protective and successful deceit of the feeling of personal existence. I thought the latter was an artefact of
memory, thought-complexes, etc., a doll that was nice
enough to look at from outside but nothing real inside it.
In my case the personal self had grown porous because of my dimmed consciousness. Through it I wanted
to bring myself closer to the higher sources of life. I
should have prepared myself for this over a long
period by invoking in me a higher, impersonal self, since

'nectar' is not for mortal lips. It acted destructively on the animal-human self, split it up into its parts. These gradually disintegrated, the doll was really broken and the body damaged. I had forced untimely access to the 'source of life', the curse of the 'gods' descended on me. I recognized too late that murky elements had taken a hand. I got to know them after they had already too much power. There was no way back. I now had the world of spirits I had wanted to see. The demons came up from the abyss, as guardian Cerberi, denying admission to the unauthorized. I decided to take up the life-and-death struggle. This meant for me in the end a decision to die, since I had to put aside everything that maintained the enemy, but this was also everything that maintained life. I wanted to enter death without going mad and stood before the Sphinx: either thou into the abyss or I!

Then came illumination. I fasted and so penetrated into the true nature of my seducers. They were pimps and deceivers of my dear personal self which seemed as much a thing of naught as they. A larger and more comprehensive self emerged and I could abandon the previous personality with its entire entourage. I saw this earlier personality could never enter transcendental realms. I felt as a result a terrible pain, like an annihilating blow, but I was rescued, the demons shrivelled, vanished and perished. A new life began for me and from now on I felt different from other people. A self that consisted of conventional lies, shams, self-deceptions, memory-images, a self just like that of other people, grew in me again but behind and above it stood a greater and more comprehensive self which impressed me with something of what is eternal, unchanging, immortal and inviolable and which ever since that time has been my protector and refuge. I believe it would be good for many if they were acquainted with such a higher self and that there are people who have attained this goal in fact by kinder means.

Jaspers comments:

Such self-interpretations are obviously made under the influence of delusion-like tendencies and deep psychic forces. They originate from profound experiences and the wealth of such schizophrenic experience calls on the observer as well as on the reflective patient not to take all this merely as a chaotic jumble of contents. Mind and spirit are present in the morbid psychic life as well as in the healthy. But interpretations of this sort must be divested of any causal importance. All they can do is to throw light on content and bring it into some sort of context.

This patient has described with a lucidity I could not improve upon, a very ancient quest, with its pitfalls and dangers. Jaspers still speaks of this experience as morbid, and tends to discount the patient's own construction. Yet both the experience and construction may be valid in their own terms.

Certain *transcendental experiences* seem to me to be the original well-spring of all religions. Some psychotic people have transcendental experiences. Often (to the best of their recollection), they have never had such experiences before, and frequently they will never have them again. I am not saying, however, that psychotic experience necessarily contains this element more manifestly than sane experience.

We experience in different modes. We perceive external realities, we dream, imagine, have semiconscious reveries. Some people have visions, hallucinations, experience faces transfigured, see auras, and so on. Most people most of the time experience themselves and others in one or other way that

I shall call egoic. That is, centrally or peripherally, they experience the world and themselves in terms of a consistent identity, a me-here over against a you-there, within a framework of certain ground structures of space and time, shared with other members of their society.

This identity-anchored, space-and-time-bound experience has been studied philosophically by Kant, and later by the phenomenologists, e.g., Husserl, Merleau-Ponty. Its historical and ontological relativity should be fully realized by any contemporary student of the human scene. Its cultural, socio-economic relativity has become a commonplace among anthropologists and a platitude to the Marxists and neo-Marxists. And yet, with the consensual and interpersonal confirmation it offers, it gives us a sense of ontological security, whose validity we *experience* as self-validating, although metaphysically - historically - ontologically - socio - economically - cultrally we know its apparent absolute validity as an illusion.

In fact all religious and all existential philosophies have agreed that such *egoic experience* is a preliminary illusion, a veil, a film of *maya*—a dream to Heraclitus, and to Lao-Tzu, the fundamental illusion of all Buddhism, a state of sleep, of death, of socially accepted madness, a womb state to which one has to die, from which one has to be born.

The person going through ego-less or transcendental experiences may or may not become in different ways confused. Then he might legitimately be regarded as mad. But to be mad is not necessarily to be ill, notwithstanding that in our culture the two categories have become confused. It is assumed that if a person is mad (whatever that means) then *ipso facto* he is ill (whatever that means). The experience that a person may be absorbed in while to others he appears simply ill-mad, may be for him veritable manna from heaven. The person's whole life may be changed, but it is difficult not to doubt the validity of such vision. Also, not everyone comes back to us again.

Are these experiences simply the effulgence of a pathological process, or of a particular alienation? I do not think they are.

In certain cases, a man blind from birth may have an operation performed which gives him his sight. The result—frequently misery, confusion, disorientation. The light that illumines the madman is an unearthly light. It is not always a distorted refraction of his mundane life situation. He may be irradiated by light from other worlds. It may burn him out.

This 'other' world is not essentially a battlefield wherein psychological forces, derived or diverted, displaced or sublimated from their original object-cathexes are engaged in an illusionary fight—although such forces may obscure these realities, just as they may obscure so-called external realities. When Ivan, in *The Brothers Karamazov* says, 'If God does not exist, everything is permissible,' he is *not* saying: 'If my super-ego, in projected form, can be abolished, I can do anything with a good

conscience.' He *is* saying: 'If there is *only* my conscience, then there is no ultimate validity for my
will.'

Among physicians and priests there should be
some who are guides, who can educt the person
from this world and induct him to the other. To
guide him in it: and to lead him back again.

One enters the other world by breaking a shell:
or through a door: through a partition: the cur-
tains part or rise: a veil is lifted. Seven veils: seven
seals, seven heavens.

The 'ego' is the instrument for living in *this* world.
If the 'ego' is broken up, or destroyed (by the insurmountable contradictions of certain life situations, by toxins, chemical changes, etc.), then the
person may be exposed to other worlds, 'real' in different ways from the more familiar territory of
dreams, imagination, perception or phantasy.

The world that one enters, one's capacity to experience it, seems to be partly conditional on the
state of one's 'ego.'

Our time has been distinguished, more than by
anything else, by a drive to control the external
world, and by an almost total forgetfulness of the
internal world. If one estimates human evolution
from the point of view of knowledge of the external
world, then we are in many respects progressing.

If our estimate is from the point of view of the
internal world, and of oneness of internal and external, then the judgement must be very different.

Phenomenologically the terms 'internal' and 'external' have little validity. But in this whole realm

one is reduced to mere verbal expedients—words are simply the finger pointing to the moon. One of the difficulties of talking in the present day of these matters is that the very existence of inner realities is now called in question.

By 'inner' I mean our way of seeing the external world and all those realities that have no "external', 'objective' presence—imagination, dreams, phantasies, trances, the realities of contemplative and meditative states, realities that modern man, for the most part, has not the slightest direct awareness of.

For example, nowhere in the Bible is there any argument about the *existence* of gods, demons, angels. People did not first 'believe in' God: they experienced his Presence, as was true of other spiritual agencies. The question was not whether God existed, but whether this particular God was the greatest god of all, or the only God; and what was the relation of the various spiritual agencies to each other. Today, there is a public debate, not as to the trustworthiness of God, the particular place in the spiritual hierarchy of different spirits, etc., but whether God or such spirits *even exist,* or ever have existed.

Sanity today appears to rest very largely on a capacity to adapt to the external world—the interpersonal world, and the realm of human collectivities.

As this external human world is almost completely and totally estranged from the inner, any personal direct awareness of the inner world has already grave risks.

But since society, without knowing it, is *starving* for the inner, the demands on people to evoke its presence in a 'safe' way, in a way that need not be taken seriously, etc., is tremendous—while the ambivalence is equally intense. Small wonder that the list of artists, in say the last 150 years, who have become shipwrecked on these reefs is so long— Hölderlin, John Clare, Rimbaud, Van Gogh, Nietzsche, Antonin Artaud. . . .

Those who survived have had exceptional qualities—a capacity for secrecy, slyness, cunning—a thoroughly realistic appraisal of the risks they run, not only from the spiritual realms that they frequent, but from the hatred of their fellows for anyone engaged in this pursuit.

Let us *cure* them. The poet who mistakes a real woman for his Muse and acts accordingly. . . . The young man who sets off in a yacht in search of God. . . .

The outer divorced from any illumination from the inner is in a state of darkness. We are in an age of darkness. The state of outer darkness is a state of sin—i.e. alienation or estrangement from the *inner light.* Certain actions lead to greater estrangement; certain others help one not to be so far removed. The former used to be called sinful.

The ways of losing one's way are legion. Madness is certainly not the least unambiguous. The countermadness of Kraepelinian psychiatry is the exact counterpart of 'official' psychosis. Literally, and absolutely seriously, it is as *mad,* if by madness we mean any radical estrangement from the totality of what is the case. Remember Kierkegaard's objective madness.

As we experience the world, so we act. We conduct ourselves in the light of our view of what is the case and what is not the case. That is, each person is a more or less naïve ontologist. Each person has views of what is, and what is not.

There is no doubt, it seems to me, that there have been profound changes in the experience of man in the last thousand years. In some ways this is more evident than changes in the patterns of his behaviour. There is everything to suggest that man experienced God. Faith was never a matter of believing he existed, but of trusting in the Presence that was experienced and known to exist as a self-validating datum. It seems likely that far more people in our time neither experience the Presence of God, nor the Presence of his absence, but the absence of his Presence.

We require a history of phenomena; not simply more phenomena of history.

As it is, the secular psychotherapist is often in the role of the blind leading the half-blind.

The fountain has not played itself out, the flame still shines, the river still flows, the spring still bubbles forth, the light has not faded. But between *us* and It there is a veil which is more like fifty feet of solid concrete. *Deus absconditus.* Or we have absconded.

Already everything in our time is directed to categorizing and segregating this reality from objective facts. This is precisely the concrete wall. Intellectually, emotionally, inter-personally, organizationally, intuitively, theoretically, we have to blast our way through the solid wall, even if at the risk of chaos, madness and death. For from *this* side of the wall, this is the risk. There are no assurances, no guarantees.

Many people are prepared to have faith in the sense of scientifically indefensible belief in an untested hypothesis. Few have trust enough to test it. Many people make believe what they experience. Few are made to believe by their experience. Paul of Tarsus was picked up by the scruff of the neck, thrown to the ground and blinded for three days. This direct experience was self-validating.

We live in a secular world. To adapt to this world the child abdicates its ecstasy. (*'L'enfant abdique son extase'*: Mallarmé.) Having lost our experience of the spirit, we are expected to have faith. But this faith comes to be a belief in a reality which is not evident. There is a prophecy in Amos that there will be a time when there will be a famine in the land, 'not a famine for bread, nor a thirst for water, but of *hearing* the words of the Lord.' That time has now come to pass. It is the present age.

From the alienated starting point of our pseudo-sanity, everything is equivocal. Our sanity is not 'true' sanity. Their madness is not 'true' madness. The madness of our patients is an artefact of the destruction wreaked on them by us, and by them on themselves. Let no one suppose that we meet 'true' madness any more than that we are truly sane. The madness that we encounter in 'patients' is a gross travesty, a mockery, a grotesque caricature of what the natural healing of that estranged integration we call sanity might be. True sanity entails in one way or another the dissolution of the normal ego, that false self competently adjusted to our alienated social reality: the emergence of the 'inner' archetypal mediators of divine power, and through this death a rebirth, and the eventual reestablishment of a new kind of ego-functioning, the ego now being the servant of the divine, no longer its betrayer.

Herbert Marcuse and Norman O. Brown. *Mystery and Mystification: An Exchange*

Norman O. Brown's *Love's Body* is indeed a work to be reckoned with: a prodigious effort to defend "the place of mystery in the life of the mind." Like James Joyce's *Finnegans Wake,* the book fathoms the great cultural motifs to their anagogical bottoms; anthropological, psychoanalytical, and mystical possibilities interpenetrate; historical episodes are played off against their dream meanings; learned philology and vulgar puns collaborate at lateral and free associative interpretation.

The whole is delivered in dithyrambic utterance: a mosaic of mind-teasing fragments whose purpose is to drive us below surface realities—logical and historical—the better to catch sight, as if by peripheral vision, of truths for which ordinary language will not serve. The balance is a delicate one, not easily held. Brown's peripheral vision is a fine bright line poised between eclectic pedantry and linguistic blur. But where the balance is kept, there is indeed illumination.

Herbert Marcuse's *Eros and Civilization* shares with Norman Brown's *Life Against Death* (and with the work of Philip Rieff) the distinction of inaugurating the contemporary reexamination of Freud. The books overlap deceptively; but Marcuse moves through Freud toward an enriched Marxism; Brown—as *Love's Body* makes vividly clear—strikes out toward Nietzsche, Jung, Joyce, Blake. The difference lies in the role of transcendence in the thinking of the two men. Marcuse, in the selection below reviewing *Love's Body* for *Commentary*, becomes the brave voice of secular humanism, clinging fast always to the demands of social justice. He will have nothing to do with a transcendence that flees worldly responsibilities as obvious as the cry of the oppressed. The way out is a "political task." One transcends the evils of the historical plane by generating a clean and just future: a horizontal movement forward in time.

Brown replies. He would keep the horizontal thrust, but also the vertical ascent. The two movements overlap for him to form, at every moment of time, the timeless cross: the emblem of resurrection, always present though much obscured by "the bourgeois cycle of repression and promiscuity."

I think in this reply, Brown adumbrates the *next* politics. But Marcuse's critique must be heard out and never in any jot or tiddle ignored.

Herbert Marcuse. *Love Mystified: A Critique of Norman O. Brown*

. . . sie hätte singen
nicht reden sollen diese neue Seele
—Stefan George, "Nietzsche"

FOR HERE is the "new soul," prophet of the new man—radical break with the past and with the present which is still the rule of the past. And this past is the archetypal one, in the individual as well as in the history of the species: the primal crime and the primal scene. Psychoanalysis in its most extreme and most advanced concepts guides Brown's interpretation of the history of men and of the human condition. Brown likes to quote Adorno: "In psychoanalysis, only the exaggerations are true." For only the exaggerations can shatter the normal complacency of common sense and scientific sense and

From "Love Mystified: A Critique of Norman O. Brown," *Commentary*, February 1967. Reprinted by permission of *Commentary* and the author. Copyright © 1967 by the American Jewish Committee.

their comforting limitations and illusions. Only the exaggerations can (perhaps), with the violence of a shock, elucidate the horror of the whole, the depth of the deception, and the incommunicable promise of a future which can come into being (can come into thought) only as the total annihilation of the past and present. Apocalypse and Pentecost: destruction of everything and the redemption of everything: final liberation of the repressed content —abolition of the reality principle, nay, abolition of reality. For what we call reality Brown calls illusion, lie, dream. We are asleep, and being asleep is being dead; we still live in the womb or return into the womb; our genital sexuality is regression to the state before birth; and we are still under the spell of the primal scene: we reenact the father whom we have introjected; our sex life is his, not ours, and our pleasure remains vicarious. Thus if all our life is dream and illusion, then the awakening to real life is the end of our life: death and resurrection in one. The way out of the womb, out of the dream cave is to die in order to be reborn.

Liberation is transubstantiation; resurrection of the body, but the body is "raised a spiritual or symbolic body." "The revolution, the revelation, the apocalypse, is vision; which pronounced a last judgment; and brings about the end." The cave and the womb, Plato and Freud, revolution and revelation, Marx and Christ: the grand union and communion of opposites, does it convey the image of liberation? Or is it again the past that asserts its power over the image of the future, the old in new

clothes? The attempt to answer this question involves heavy responsibility, for Norman Brown has
carried the burden of radical thought to the farthest
point: the point where sanity must appear as madness, where concepts must turn into fantasies, and
the truth must become ridiculous. Once again, the
tragedy of man as comedy, as the play of Satyre.
Norman Brown's book moves along the limits of
communication; he is on the search for a new
language, which can break through the falsifying,
stultifying, repressive universe of ordinary and academic discourse ("senatorial and senile"). In its
best parts, this book is a poem and a song, of the
beauty which is *nichts als des Schrecklichen Anfang,
den wir noch garde ertragen . . .* ["Nothing but
the beginning of terror we can just barely endure . . ."—Rilke, Duino Elegies (the translation is
by C. F. MacIntyre)—Ed.]. The form of the sentence, the proposition which freezes the content is
abandoned; the words, freed from the enchaining
form, recapture their explosive meaning, a hidden
truth.

The normal flux of ordinary and academic discourse is also broken—the argument is developed in
relatively self-sufficient fragments, short paragraphs,
aphorisms; their inner connection, the flow of the
argument is of a musical rather than conceptual
order: variations on a theme, progress through
repetition, dissonance as element of structural harmony and development. The right of the imagination as cognitive power is thus restored: released
from its senatorial and senile garb, thought becomes

play, *jeu interdit,* the scandal: the *esprit de serieux* gives way to the *gaya sciencia,* drunkenness and laughter. Hegel, the most serious of all serious philosophers, knew it well:

The true is thus the bacchanalian whirl in which no member is not drunken; and because each, as soon as it detaches itself, dissolves immediately—the whirl is just as much transparent and simple repose.

But then comes the hangover; the imagination falters, and the new language looks for support in the old. Support in quotations and references, which are to demonstrate or at least to illustrate the points made; support in returning to the primordial, elemental, subrational; to the infantile stages in the development of the individual and of the species. Psychoanalysis changes its direction and function: the latent content, the unconscious and its prehistory, serve not only as powers to be recognized, comprehended, conquered, but also (and increasingly so in the unfolding of the argument) as normative values, as ends. The grand leap into the realm of freedom and light is thus arrested and becomes a leap backward, into darkness.

Norman Brown's demonstrations and illustrations have yet another and very different significance. A large bulk of his references is to Holy Script, to Christ and his gospel. A few examples may show how central these references are:

The conclusion of the whole matter is, break down the boundaries, the walls. Down with defense mechanisms, character-armor; disarmament. Ephesians II, 14 . . .

The real world . . . is the world where thoughts are
omnipotent, where no distinction is drawn between
wish and deed. As in the New Testament . . .
The solution to the problem of identity is, get lost. Or
as it says in the New Testament . . .
The solution to the problem of war in the Eucharist
with transubstantiation . . .
But the unconscious is the true psychic reality; and
the unconscious is the Holy Spirit . . .
Real life is life after death, or resurrection . . . Colos-
sians III, 3 . . .
Fulfillment gathers up the past into the present in the
form of a recapitulation: that in the dispensation of
times there might be a recapitulation of all things in
Christ . . .
Then cometh the end, when he shall have put down all
rule and all authority and power. Mere anarchy is
loosed upon the world. I Corinthians XV, 24 . . .

Now Brown takes great pains to state again and
again that the religious symbolism is to be interpreted symbolically, in the other direction, as it
were. Sexual potency is restored at Pentecost;
speech resexualized; knowledge made carnal, copulation of subject and object; and the spirit is phallic
—merger of Christ and Dionysus. But the one stays
with the other, and the new emphasis does not
suffice to reverse the established direction: sexu-
alization of the spirit and also spiritualization of
sexuality, and sexuality itself becomes symbolic:
"everything is symbolic, including the sexual act."
Behind the veil of Brown's sexualized language,
desexualization prevails. The orgasm provides only
"vicarious gratification." Brown's consistent attempt
to convey, against overwhelming odds, the new

non-repressive interpretation of the old repressive symbols cannot undo the association of the spirit with the Spirit, the resurrection of the body with the Resurrection. Brown's images of fulfillment suggest total sublimation which drains the unsublimated dimension, Liberation in Nirvana; I like to believe that Norman Brown was aware of this goal of his voyage, and that he communicated his awareness to the reader: his first chapter is headed "Liberty" and his last, "Nothing."

Before examining the reasons for this failure, I shall review briefly the radical origin and intent of Brown's analysis prior to their mystification.

The truth of the human condition is hidden, repressed—not by a conspiracy of some sort, but by the actual course of history. The first aim, therefore, is the critical destruction of history, and of the manner in which history is written and understood. The facts stand for other facts in the depth of the individual and collective unconscious, and the repressed prehistory of mankind continues to make the history of man. The established facts are symbolic facts, derivatives and distortions of the latent content, which is the unexpurgated drama of sexuality. Consequently, history must be explained symbolically. All literal interpretation of history is falsification; the "modern historical consciousness is Protestant literalism which offends against the spirit, kills the spirit." Thus it becomes an "operation with ghosts (*Geisteswissenschaft*)" "We must rise from history to mystery"—here is the first mystification in Brown's analysis: the "mystery" is initially that of the primal crime and the ambivalent penitence for it; but then the mystery becomes that of the resurrection and redemption, transubstantiation, the Eucharist. The radical destruction of history terminates in the religious tale, in which history is, not *aufgehoben,* but simply negated, abolished. The beginning of Brown's book contained a very different promise: the refusal to accept any mystification, and the resolution to call things by their name, their real name, instead of canceling all names in the impossible unity and union of everything.

In line with this promise, Brown begins with the symbolic interpretation of politics:

In order to know the reality of politics we have to believe the myth, to believe what we were told as children. Roman history is the story of the brothers Romulus and Remus, the sons of the she-wolf; leaders of gangs of juvenile delinquents . . . ; who achieved the rape of the Sabine women; and whose festival is the Lupercalia; at which youth naked except for girdles made from the skin of victims ran wild through the city; . . . a season fit for killing. *Julius Caesar,* Act I.

And Brown continues, summing up the initial exposition: "Politics made out of delinquency. All brothers are brothers in crime; all equal as sinners" after the killing of the father, whom they restored in themselves and whom they continue to obey, the killing of each other. Myth or reality? Fictitious past, or factual history that is still with us? The stuff out of which history is made—the stuff of greatness and progress: Brown quotes Livy:

To expand the population, Romulus followed the model of other founders of cities: he opened an asylum for fugitives. The mob that came in was the first step to the city's future greatness. . . .

The City of Man—"a sanctuary" providing "immunity for a multitude of criminals" (Augustine). Here is the latent content in the notion of the social contract:

The social contract establishes corporate virtue as an asylum for individual sin, making a moral society out of immoral men; men whose natural inclination, according to Hobbes and Freud, is murder.

The foundation of the state is itself a crime, the primal crime, for the state is formed by the fraternity (here, Brown sides with Plato and Sparta against Aristotle and Athens), and it is the common crime that creates common solidarity—political, national solidarity. And after the primal crime, the endless struggle among the brothers—the "quarrel over the paternal inheritance": the original unity of the body politic now is divided into a multitude of segments, "moieties"; each acquiring private property, a self, group or individual self, fighting. Law only organizes this fight: "the Rule of Law is the Rule of Force"; and, as the classical myths tell us, right and wrong can be decided only "by an appeal to heaven, that is, by war and violence." The division stays with us: history is fratricide after the parricide. "Political parties are conspiracies to usurp the power of the father"; behind politics is the ritual of murder and sacrifice:

The comic wearing of the Indian mask, in the Boston Tea Party, or Tammany's Wigwam, is the lighter side of a game, a ritual, the darker side of which is fraternal genocide.

Brown then traces the development of the latent content in the historical step from absolute monarchy to representative government, from Hobbes to Locke. A step within the same continuum of fraud. The illusion in liberty and equality:

Locke allows no man the status of father, and makes all men sons of the Heavenly Father . . . Sonship and brotherhood are espoused against fatherhood: but without a father there can be no sons or brothers. Locke's sons, like Freud's, cannot free themselves from father psychology . . .

The father survives in the superego, and in the many new political leaders, now freely elected. The autonomous individual, the "person"—this cherished achievement of bourgeois society is a fraud, Hobbes's "artificial Person." In reality, a person is never himself but always another: he wears a mask, he is possessed by another, represented by another and representing another. And in all disguises, the other is always the father. In theory and in practice, it is always the Oedipus Complex: as in the Apocalypse, "pump, power, and politics is discovered to be sex"—perverted sex, sado-masochistic sex, striving for impossible satisfaction. For the desired object is the "combined object": frozen image of the primal scene—a "male female (vaginal father) or a female male (phallic mother)," "stuck together in eternal coitus, eternal lust, and eternal punishment." And this "could go on forever; there is eternal recurrence."

It must go on until we have overcome the Fall, which is the division of the original and total unity. The solution, the end of the drama of history is the restoration of original and total unity; unity of male and female, father and mother, subject and object, body and soul—absolution of the self, of mine and thine, abolition of the reality principle, of all boundaries. . . .

Perhaps only the most extreme imagery can elucidate the depth dimension of history, the web of pleasure and terror, truth and deception in eternal recurrence. But the imagery is not enough; it must become saturated with its reality: symbolism must recapture that which it symbolizes. The king must be shown not only as father but as king, that is to say, as master and lord; war and competition and communication must be shown not only as copulation but as war and business and speech. Unless the analysis takes the road of return from the symbolic to the literal, from the illusion to the reality of the illusion, it remains ideological, replacing one mystification with another.

Brown's concept of illusion (sleep, dream) covers, undifferentiated, the latent and overt content of history, or, it de-realizes reality. To him, the political kingdoms are "shadows," political power is a fraud: the emperor has no new clothes, he has no clothes at all. But unfortunately, he does: they are visible and tangible; they make history. In terms of the latent content, the kingdoms of the earth may be shadows; but unfortunately, they move real men and things, they kill, they persist and prevail in the sunlight as well as in the dark of night. The king may be an erected penis, and his relation to the community may be intercourse; but unfortunately, it is also something very different and less pleasant and more real. Brown skips the mediations which transform the latent into the overt content, sex into politics, the sub-rational into the rational. Thus he is stuck with the timehonored quandary of psychoanalysis: the airplane is a penis symbol, but it also gets you in a couple of hours from Berlin to Vienna.

The "lower depths," the "underworld" of the Unconscious moves the history of mankind without dissolving its reality, its rationality. The roots of repression are and remain real roots; consequently, their eradication remains a real and rational job. What is to be abolished is not the reality principle; not everything, but such particular things as business, politics, exploitation, poverty. Short of this recapture of reality and reason, Brown's purpose is defeated, and the critical destruction of history, the discovery of its latent and real content, turns into the mystification of the latent and real content. True, in the language which reveals the stuff out of which history is made, the established history of the Establishment, from Romulus and Remus to the Founding Fathers and their representative government, today appears as crime, deception, lie, illusion; we are asleep, we are dreaming, we are dead if we experience this as reality, as life, freedom, fulfillment. But this illusion is itself a historical fact and factor, and its negation, if any, is a historical, definitive negation: historical goal of historical practice. Outside and beyond the historical continuum, the solution is nothing (as Brown's last chapter indicates), and that means: it is not. And within the historical universe (the only one that, in any meaningful sense, can ever be the universe of freedom and fulfillment), there are divisions and boundaries that are real and will continue to exist even in the advent of freedom and fulfillment, because all pleasure and all happiness and all humanity originate and live in and with these divisions and boundaries. Such are the division into the sexes, the difference between male and female, between the penis and the vagina, between you and me, even between mine and thine, and they are, or can be, most enjoyable and most gratifying divisions; their abolition would be not only illusion but nightmare—the acme of repression. To be sure, this gratification is transitory, momentary and partial, but this does not make it "vicarious"—on the contrary! To be sure, *alle Lust will Ewigkeit,* but this eternity can only be that of the ever returning *moments* of joy, of the ever-returning solution of tension. Tension can be made non-aggressive, non-destructive, but it can never be eliminated, because (Freud knew it well) its elimination would be death—not in any symbolic but in a very real sense. And we still want to live, *within* our boundaries and divisions, which we want to make our own instead of leaving their determination to our fathers and leaders and representatives. For there is such a thing as the Self, the Person—it does not yet exist but it must be attained, fought for against all those who are preventing its emergence and who substitute for it an illusory self, namely, the subject of voluntary servitude in production and consumption, the subject of free enterprise and free election of masters. There is even such a thing as property which is a factor and ingredient of true freedom (Marx knew it well): that which is properly mine because I am different from you and can be with and for you only in this difference—boundaries to be enjoyed by you and by me. And there are "others," strangers who must remain strangers, must not enter my domain or yours because there is no pre-established harmony, and their otherness is not based on any economic position, social status, racial or national heritage but on their own self and own body with its own drives, pleasures, sorrows.

Here is the central fallacy, the mystification of Brown's vision. He obliterates the decisive difference between real and artificial, natural and political, fulfilling and repressive boundaries and divisions. Does the well-trained classicist not recognize the liberating truth in the concepts of *telos* and *mesotes?* Fulfillment becomes meaningless if everything is one, and one is everything. The sinister images of "burning" and "sacrifice" recur in Brown's vision: "The true sacrifice is total, a making holy of the whole"; "Love is all fire; and so heaven and hell are the same place. As in Augustine . . ."; "The true body is the body burnt up, the spiritual body"; "The reality adumbrated in all sacrifice, in animal sacrifice, is human sacrifice, the sacrifice of the human body, as an eternal truth." No symbolism can repulse the repressive connotation: one cannot love in fire—unless one is a Christian or Buddhist martyr. Acme of sublimation: the unsublimated realizations of Eros are burnt up, sacrificed —they evaporate. For Eros lives in the division and boundary between subject and object, man and nature; and precisely in its polymorphous-perverse manifestations, in its liberation from the "despotism of genital organization," the sexual instincts transform the object and the environment—without ever annihilating the object and the environment together with the subject.

Brown's logic is consistent: if the Fall was the division of the original unity which was total unity, then the redemption can only be the restoration of total unity:

Fusion: the distinction between inner self and outside world, between subject and object, overcome.

But such fusion would be the end of human life, in its instinctual as well as rational, sublimated as well as unsublimated expressions. The unity of subject and object is a hallmark of absolute idealism; however, even Hegel retained the tension between the two, the distinction. Brown goes beyond the Absolute Idea: "Fusion, mystical, participation." But mystical participation is not made less mystical if it is "freely" consummated, and magic does not become less magical if it is "conscious magic."

The last sentence of the last chapter: "Everything is only a metaphor; there is only poetry." To understand the reality of politics is to believe in the myth. We still don't believe in it; we don't understand; we are prisoners in the cave. "Turning and turning in the animal belly, the mineral belly, the belly of time. To find the way out: the poem." This is one of Brown's most advanced formulations: a vision of the truth. But poetry is made in history and makes history; and the poem which is "the way out" will be (if ever) written and sung and heard here on our earth. Brown had such a poem in mind, and he started to write it, but it became adumbrated by the ancient ghosts, by the symbols of sacrifice, death, transubstantiation. The concluding reference in his book contains the sentence:

Then the body of the Enlightened One becomes luminous in appearance, convincing and inspiring by its mere presence, while every word and every gesture, and even his silence, communicate the overwhelming reality of the Dharma.

This does not work, and no new symbolic interpretation can remove the impact of the many centuries of deception and exploitation which has defined the connotation of these words. To be sure, the sinister spell can be broken: by the power of the poet and singer, even before the historical, the real break with deception and exploitation has occurred. But the poet and singer can give to such words a new and revolutionary connotation only if his speech and song subvert the established meaning not merely symbolically but also literally, that is to say, if he cancels this meaning by translating the impossible into the possible, the mystical absurd into the real absurd, the metaphysical utopia into the historical utopia, the second into the first coming, redemption into liberation. Brown moves in the opposite direction. He begins with tearing the ideological veil; the "history of mankind goes from the natural cave to the artificial cave, from the underground cave to the aboveground underground." In such sentences, the symbolism names the reality as that which it is and thereby invokes revolution:

The revolution is from below, the lower classes, the underworld, the damned, the disreputable, the despised and rejected. Freud's revolutionary motto in *The Interpretation of Dreams: Flectere si nequeo Superos, Acherunta movebo.* If I cannot bend the higher powers, I will stir up the lower depths. Freud's discovery: the universal underworld.

But then, the very next paragraph opens with the statement: "Darkness at noon. A progressive darkening of the everyday world of common sense." Of common sense only? Or has the darkness also descended on the "way out" which Brown has opened? The equating sequence: revolution = revelation = redemption = resurrection strikes not only at common sense but at sense. True, it is not merely common sense that is false, thus it may be an indispensable, rational task to reduce words to nonsense, "to transcend the antinomy of sense and non-sense, silence and speech." However, this task, if it should help us to find "the way out," is a political task: the silence is not that of the Tibetan or any other monastery, nor of Zen, nor of mystical communion—it is the silence which precedes action, the liberating action, and it is broken by action. The rest is not silence but complacency, or despair, or escape. And when and where such action is barred, the task of reducing words to non-sense is the critique of the established language as the language of the Establishment which makes sense out of non-sense: the non-sense of its preservation and reproduction as its sole *raison d'etre*.

Brown's "way out" leaves the Establishment behind—that is, the way out is indeed mystical, mystification. The symbolic interpretation works both ways: it reveals the latent, the real content of reality, and it symbolizes the real content: it mystifies the possibilities of liberation. Revolution, freedom, fulfillment become in turns symbolic—symbolic goals and events. Symbolic of what? The answer remains, must remain, shrouded in mystery, because Brown envisions an absolute, a Totality, a Whole which swallows up all parts and divisions, all tensions and all needs, that is to say, all life. For such a totality does not exist in any sense or non-sense, and should not even be the vision of the free imagination because it is the negation of all freedom, and of all happiness (at least human happiness). To be sure, in dialectical logic, the whole is the truth, but a whole in which all parts and divisions have their place and stage. The relations between them, their specific function, the different levels and modes of reality, its inner development must be demonstrated and defined—only then, in the unending and subverting stream of mediations, appears the true as the bacchanalian whirl: sober drunkenness of the whole: Reason as Freedom. Critical, not absolute vision; a new rationality, not the simple negation of rationality.

In the beginning may have been the Uroboros: male and female, father and mother, mother and child, ego-id and outside world in one. But the Uroboros has busted a long time ago; the distinctions and divisions are our reality—real with all its symbols. In the light of its own possibilities, it may well be called a cave, and our life in it dream or death. Its horror has come to penetrate every part of it, every word and every vision. The way out may well be the subversion of this entire reality, but this subversion, in order to be real, must itself be real, look in the face of this reality, and not turn the head. Brown affirms the proposition on the need for changing the world instead of interpreting it. If there is one proposition which should not be understood symbolically, it is this one. And yet, in the development of Brown's argument, both the latent and the overt content of this proposition are being sublimated and mystified, and his vision of total change, of the final union at the end of history remains under the spell of the primordial Uroboros, the unity that is prior to all history.

The way out is also a way back: regression at a higher level, regression sanctified, liberated. Is it again a case of The God That Failed: from politics to a new Communion, from Liberty to Nothing? (When will we realize that there was no god that failed because there was no god, and that the failure was ours, and theirs?) Anyhow, his song of fulfillment ends in silence, not in the sensuous, audible, living silence at the end of the *Lied von der Erde*, but the silence under the cross, after the crucifixion; not the eternity of *Alle Lust will Ewigkeit* (the *"ewig"* which is the last word in the *Lied von der Erde*), but the eternity which is not of this world, the eternity of Nirvana in which all joy and all sorrow are fulfilled—annihilated.

We like to have a different idea of Love's Body, and we like to believe that Brown himself has a different idea:

To pass from the temple to the body is to perceive the body as the new temple, the true temple. The house is a woman, and the woman is a house, or palace. . . . The land is a woman, the virgin land; and the woman is a land, my America, my Newfoundland.

This is it. The woman, the land is here on earth, to be found here on earth, living and dying, female for male, distinguished, particular, tension to be renewed, Romeo's and Don Juan's, self and another, yours or mine, fulfillment in alienation. No Eucharist, no crucifixion, no resurrection, no mysticism. To find this woman, to free this land: *hic Rhodus, hic salta!* And don't jump into Nothing. Waking up from sleep, finding the way out of the cave is work within the cave; slow, painful work with and *against* the prisoners in the cave. Everywhere, even in your own land which is not yet found, not yet free, there are those who do this work, who risk their lives for it—they fight the real fight, the political fight. You have revealed the latent, the true content of politics—you know that the political fight is the fight for the whole: not the mystical whole, but the very unmystical, antagonistic whole of our life and that of our children—the only life that is.

Among the many sentences in Brown's book which I like best is the opening of the Preface: "At least in the life of the mind, ventures should be carried through to the end." He has not done so; this is not the end. He has reached a point of return; on a new way, return to the earth. *Bon voyage!*

Norman O. Brown. *A Reply to Herbert Marcuse*

MY FRIEND Marcuse and I: Romulus and Remus quarreling; which of them is the *real* "revolutionary."

He will not see the recurrence in revolution. Revolution is not a slate wiped clean, but a revolving cycle. Even newness is renewal. As it was in the beginning. The idea of progress is in question; the reality of Marx cannot hide the reality of Nietzsche. The thing is to change the world; but it is also

From "A Reply to Herbert Marcuse" *Commentary*, March 1967. Reprinted by permission of *Commentary* and the author. Copyright © 1967 by the American Jewish Committee.

true that everything remains always the same. The assignment then is (to put it simply) the simultaneous affirmation and rejection of what is; not in a system, as in Hegel, but in an instant, as in poetry.

There is eternal recurrence; there are "eternal objects" (Whitehead); archetypes. This is a hard lesson. There is a sense in which war cannot be abolished. Or, there is an eternal object of which literal war is a false image, or inadequate idea. The thing to be abolished is literalism; the worship of false images; idolatry. Allen Ginsberg saw it just the way it is: Moloch. A false idol fed with real victims. This is no joke. (Nor is fire; Heraclitean fire.) Idolatry is fetishism, mystification; demystification would be an end to idolatry. But an end to idolatry is not so easy. It is not the abolition of the temple, but the discovery of the true temple: Love's body. Karl Barth saw religion as idolatry; Karl Marx saw religion as the heart of a heartless world. The Sacred Heart. The thing is not to excise the heart but to put it where it belongs. The real atheism is to become divine. In a dialectical view, atheism becomes theurgy, god-making; demystification becomes the discovery of a new mystery; and everything remains the same.

There is another sense in which mystification must be affirmed. We have to surpass the Enlightenment notion that in the life of the species or of the individual there is a definitive change-over from darkness to light. Light is always light in darkness; that is what the unconscious is all about. Nor can the light become a current, always turned on, in ordinary prosaic language. Truth is always in poetic form; not literal but symbolic; hiding, or veiled; light in darkness. Yes, mysterious. Literalism is idolatry of words; the alternative to idolatry is mystery. And literalism reifies, makes of everything *things*, these tables and chairs, commodities. The alternative to reification is mystification. The world is actually not a collection of commodities;

> When silence
> Blooms in the house, all the para-
> phernalia of our existence
> Shed the twitterings of value and
> reappear as heraldic devices.
> —Robert Duncan

Heraldic devices: airplanes as penis symbols rather than "modern conveniences." One of the eternal verities is the human body as the measure of all things, including technology. The businessman does not have the last word; the real meaning of technology is its hidden relation to the human body; a symbolical or mystical relation.

With the whole world still in the bourgeois stage of competitive development and war, the thing to remember about Marx is that he was able to look beyond this world to another possible world, of union, communion, communism. What needs to be reiterated is not reassurance to the bourgeois that he will be able to carry his little old Self, Person, and Property into that world, but that the kingdom of heaven on earth is possible; and that other world, the negation of this jungle, cannot possibly be anything except Communitas. A higher form of chaos; instead of confusion, fusion (*Love's Body,* pp. 248, 253).

And, after Freud, we have to add that there is also a sexual revolution; which is not to be found in the bourgeois cycle of repression and promiscuity, but in a transformation of the human body, an abolition of genital organization. Indeed, *Love's Body* shows that genital organization is the same thing as Self, Person, Property; and, therefore, the abolition of genital organization, foretold by Marcuse in *Eros and Civilization,* turns out to mean what Marcuse calls the impossible unity and union of everything.

Yes, indeed, there was a God that failed; that mortal God, the great Leviathan; or Moloch; discovered to be not only mortal but also dead, an idol. From literalism to symbolism; the lesson of my life. The next generation needs to be told that the real fight is not the political fight, but to put an end to politics. From politics to meta-politics.

From politics to poetry. Legislation is not politics, nor philosophy, but poetry. Poetry, art, is not an epiphenomenal reflection of some other (political, economic) realm which is the "real thing"; nor a still contemplation of something else which is "real action"; nor a sublimation of something else which is the "real," carnal "act." Poetry, art, imagination, the creator spirit is life itself; the real revolutionary power to change the world; and to change the human body. To change the human body: here is the crisis, *hic Rhodus, hic salta;* which, as Hegel said, is to be translated "here is the Rose, here begin to dance." To begin to dance; who can tell the dancer from the dance; it is the impossible unity and union of everything.

From politics to life. And therefore revolution as creation; resurrection; renaissance instead of progress. To perceive in all human culture the hidden reality of the human body. This is to discover as Freud did, the Holy Communion as the basis of community; the Eucharist; the cannibalism, the hidden *eating;* one of the forms of which is war—making children pass through the fire unto Moloch. Go to the end of the road and that is what you will find. And so the God is not Freud's God Logis, abstract or disembodied Reason, but the Human Form Divine. And the language is the language not of reason but of love. Reason is power; powerful arguments; power-politics; *Realpolitik;* reality-principle. Love comes emptyhanded; the eternal proletariat; like Cordelia, bringing Nothing.

Lancelot Law Whyte. *Morphic Man*

If there is to be a science that transcends mechanistic reductionism, Lancelot Law Whyte will be counted among its founders. For more than a generation, he has been one of the leading pro-

From "Science and Our Understanding of Ourselves." Reprinted by permission of *Science and Public Affairs, the Bulletin of the Atomic Scientists.* Copyright © 1971 by the Educational Foundation for Nuclear Science.

ponents of a wholistic natural philosophy—meaning a science that unifies the fragmented specialties and which comprehends value as well as fact, sensuous immediacy as well as theoretical abstraction. The key to Whyte's vision of science is morphological sensibility: the Gestalt-like awareness of formative process and hierarchical order. Little wonder that his work has found as much of an audience among artists and designers as among philosophers of science. Further, his conception of an evolutionary "disassociation" between rationality and vital energy in man has been of great importance to the theoretical background of Gestalt therapy.

Nature, for Whyte, is primarily an inexhaustible shaping of organic and inorganic wholes and a building up of structures—from the nuclear "particle zoo" to the galactic clusters, with the organic structures scaled rather neatly to fit about midway between the micro- and macro-worlds. (Does that suggest a new cosmic centrality for life . . . ?) Far from being simply matter meaninglessly in motion, Whyte's nature is a maker of well-designed three-dimensional forms in space. To use his phrase, nature, like man, is "morphic" and indeed finds in the cultural creativity of the human mind its most perfect expression. All this comes within a hair's-breadth of saying that the universe has a direction, a *nonentropic* direction, if you will, a *purpose* to its activities. And "purpose," let us remember, is the dirtiest word our science knows. Yet, where purpose lacks, chaos and entropy reign supreme; the universe becomes a stage suited for nothing but the playing out of end games devised by Samuel Beckett.

What follows is a severely succinct resume of Whyte's worldview. Those who wish to follow him further should see his *Next Development in Man, The Unconscious Before Freud, Accent on Form,* or his more technical *The Atomic Problem.*

WHAT DO WE KNOW about the relation of man to physical, organic, psychological and social processes that can assist us now? My answer to this question is that present knowledge can help to restore belief in human nature and to unite all men in a common awareness on one condition: that we can see running through these four realms a principle which provides the basis for an adequate image of man.

Single items of knowledge are no use, for we need clarity on basic issues. What is man's supreme faculty? What is at the core of his mind? Are the fundamental laws for or against him? Can we see the logical germ of life and of mind in the most general laws, that is, in a feature present in all four realms?

At critical moments ultimate issues are crucial. Man is busy creating hell on earth, and if we are to hope we must see a possibility of history changing its direction. Man must be given a shock, be startled and fascinated by something he has never understood before. Old-style science plus love is not enough. Man must look deeper into nature and himself and find joy and strength in what he sees. This is much to expect, but less will not serve.

Moreover the jolt must come from an outlook coherent with science. Here we touch the core of present despair. This is, we say, an "age of science." That is a misleading half-truth. Ours is a transition period of an incomplete, unbalanced science lacking basic clarity. Science has not yet identified the fundamental laws of physics, biology, or psychology; and evolutionary theory needs an adjustment to allow for internal factors and morphic processes, as we shall see below. We are fundamental ignoramuses. A partial science hinders our gaining balanced self-knowledge, and this accounts for part of our troubles. There must exist a healthy organic core in our minds. But what is it like, and why has it failed us?

For a hundred years physical scientists have paid much attention to a class of processes which move toward states of greater dynamical disorder (thermal entropy), and little to any other natural tendency. As a result of this bias, influential scientists have even suggested that the physical universe displays only one tendency: toward disorder. (That was risky, in a world pervaded by opposites!) This entropy dogma was on many grounds unfortunate. For example, it implied that organisms, and so men, were arbitrary freaks or sports of nature with no roots in general laws.

The entropy curse troubled many. In a purely entropic universe man would be a misfit struggling to push things uphill, while the most powerful laws were everywhere driving them down. The idea is absurd. Billions of years of the successful emergence and evolution of organisms prove that man, with his partly unconscious ordering passion, is not a lonely Sisyphus, but one of a myriad successful species doing the same at their own levels.

In its extreme form the entropy dogma is wrong and even a milder form in common use is misleading. A few have always known this. By the 1930s warnings had been expressed, and by 1943 the contrary processes leading toward ordered structures in the organic realm had become so obvious that Schrödinger described them as intake of "negative entropy," now "structural negentropy." Today every physical scientist knows (or should know) that there are countless finite regions and processes, small and large, physical and organic, at many different levels in the hierarchies of nature, where there is a movement toward spatial order, generating ordered processes and structures.

There are more than 20 distinct types of processes, which, *prima facie*, display this movement toward spatial order, if we interpret this term in a wide sense. Here are some. In physics: the formation of nuclei, atoms, molecules, and crystals. In the transitional and organic realms: the formation of giant biomolecules, enzymes, membranes and so on, up to cells, organs, and organisms. In the evolutionary process: the formation of mutated genetic structures and their consequences. In the psychological and social realms: the formation of the brain modifications on which learning and social evolution depend, such as the ordered structures or processes underlying memory, imagination, judg-

ment and will. Then the formation of solar systems
and structured galaxies. And, not least of all, man-
made forms. All these, and many other processes,
display a spatial ordering tendency, though in some
cases we do not yet know how to describe the order
generated.

Thus the universe is the scene of the interplay
of two contrary tendencies: disordering and ordering. All the dominant pre-organic, evolutionary,
psychological, and social processes are in some
measure direct expressions of ordering tendencies
or, if you like, of one general ordering tendency
operating at many levels of the structural hierarchies of the inorganic and organic realms. This
is the continuity linking the four realms which
holds the key to human nature: when not pathological (a crucial restriction), man is the supreme
ordering instrument in the known universe. It
is these ordering processes which make it possible
for organisms to appear in an inorganic universe,
to grow, to evolve and to repair themselves, and
for man to imagine and to think, unconsciously
and consciously. This is the core of human nature
and of the healthy mind, and this is what man needs
to be told by science.

Then where is the difficulty? Alas! An awkward
mistiming has occurred. At this hour, when it is
urgently necessary not only to repair the damage
done by the unbalance of science, but to inspire
man anew, scientists do not yet know enough about
the various ordering processes to represent them in
a scientific notation as special cases of one class,

many of which operate continually inside every one of us. So this great category of formative processes which underlie life and mind has not yet entered the collective awareness of its supreme expression and instrument—man! The ordering processes are not yet recognized as being not merely as extensive as ordinary thermal entropy, but the very core of organisms and minds. Thus today, scientific self-knowledge is not possible.

In this emergency, to ease the development of a balanced science giving both tendencies their proper status, and in the meantime to provide an image of man more reliable than that of recent "scientific" humanism (which was not scientific, since it could not describe man correctly), I have introduced the scientific term "morphic." This designates the class of "dynamic" processes or tendencies in which spatial order, structure, or form is produced. "Morphogenetic" is a biological term, and "formative" is philosophical and too general. "Morphic" is short, Greek, unspoilt, suited to science, and timely.

I believe that only morphic man, having at his disposal a morphic science and aware of his intimate relation to and dependence on morphic processes, both inside and outside himself, can overcome present dangers. The science of the coming morphic age must take the form of a general morphology unifying our knowledge of spatial forms and of the morphic processes which generate them. We are entering a period in which morphic understanding is needed to lessen social lesions and personal neuroses. The human person can enjoy a no more inspiring vocation than to serve as the supreme instrument of the morphic powers of nature. Morphic man is not an anomaly. He sees the morphic laws of nature operating in himself: in his body (maintaining and restoring organic coordination) and in his mind (ordering the records of experience and shaping behavior). He recognizes the germ of life and of mind in morphic processes which under favorable conditions are more powerful than entropy.

In organisms the morphic processes develop and sustain the coordination of differentiated parts, and in the human brain-mind and behavior the union of contrasts in the erotic life, in the family, in all human groupings and in the imagination forging unities from differing parts. That is universally true and so does not tell us what to do now. Our union of contrasts in the late twentieth century, our special task today, I suggest, is to use understanding of the morphic processes to unify mankind, to unify knowledge, and to unify the personal life by dedication to these aims.

"Mankind faces dangers of unprecedented gravity." This platitude has radical consequences. It implies that a new kind of social instrument is necessary, preferably not a journal or society but a network of like minds, treating issues more fundamental than those with which existing political institutions and goodwill societies are concerned—not a world brain, but a world heart-judgment—exerting its will on primary matters, with the intellect its instrument. We must will to agree on an optimal and universally human attitude underlying all special issues and appropriate to 1971 to 2000 A.D. This is a superb undertaking. We, who already share intimations of this emergent attitude, must become aware of one another, strengthen our judgment by pooling ideas, collect allies by timely signals—this essay is one—and work gradually toward a program of action, for the dangers will not vanish before words.

We may be reaching a moment when what is authentic and timely will be unmistakable. Certainly if human values are to be preserved a consensus without precedent must rise soon from the morphic unconscious of millions of the younger generations in many lands. We should not waste our energies or insult our will by meditating on the chance of mankind achieving the necessary degree of social therapy in time. Such prognosis is, fortunately, beyond our powers. Enough that the new awareness is abroad, emerging simultaneously in many places like flowers in the spring, beneath the ugly wreckage of a past civilization. For the discontent of youth is, in my view, an expression of a widespread and growing determination to reconstruct our way of living in the light of a new and richer conception of what man is and should be.

Dane Rudhyar. *The Zodiac as a Dynamic Process*

The expanding interest in astrology—especially but by no means only among the young—inevitably proves to be an intolerable offense to intellectual respectability. For is this not one of the oldest and most discredited superstitions? Dane Rudhyar makes us think twice before we answer. For more than thirty years he has been writing on the occult margins of our society, shaping the astrological tradition into the vocabulary and symbolism of a uniquely persuasive wisdom literature. His work is a caution to us: the energies of transcendence may lie waiting for us in the most unlikely corners of our culture. Go back—and look again. Look with care.

IT IS BECAUSE astrology can be seen as a most remarkable technique for the understanding of the life-process of change in so many realms—and theoretically in every field—that its renaissance during the last two decades in the Western world is particularly important as a sign of the times. But this importance is conditioned upon a grasp of astrology which is truly modern. Nineteenth-century approaches and classical or medieval biases should

From *The Pulse of Life* (Berkeley, California: Shambala Publications, 1970). Reprinted by permission of the author.

be discarded in the light of the new twentieth-century understanding of physics and above all of psychology, in astrology as in every realm of thought. The emphasis should once more be placed on human experience, and away from the transcendent categories and mythological entities belonging to an ideology which today is, in the main, obsolete.

Astrology was born of the experience of order made manifest in the sky to primitive man immersed in the jungle and bewildered by the chaos of life on the prolific and wild surface of this planet. The search for order is one of the basic drives in man. At a later stage of evolution this search becomes intellectualized into science; but it has deep organic and instinctual roots. . . .

Man's experience is originally dual. He feels organic order within as such an absolute imperative that the slightest organic disturbance causes the most acute feeling of pain. Yet man also experiences what seems to him as chaos outside. All sorts of names have been given to this chaos, either to explain it away (as, for instance, Darwin's struggle for life, survival of the fittest, etc.), or to transfigure it into some kind of organic order (vitalistic philosophies), or to interpret it as one pole of a whole, the other pole of which is a noumental world of archetypes, perfect Ideas and the like (as when the Hindus called it *maya*). Every philosophical system, every religion, every science, every act and every pattern of social organization is only one thing: an attempt to explain disorder and to reconcile it with man's inner organic order.

Astrology is one of these attempts, the most ancient perhaps, or at least the one which has kept its vitality intact for the longest time, because the dualism of celestial order and terrestrial disorder is a universal and essential fact of human experience everywhere. In the sky, all events are regular, periodical, expectable within very small margins of irregularity. On the earth-surface (be it the primordial jungle, the countryside of medieval eras or the modern metropolis) there is relative chaos, unpredictable emotions, irrational conflicts, unexpected crises, wars and pestilence. Astrology is a method by means of which the ordered pattern of light in the sky can be used to prove the existence of a hidden, but real, order in all matters of human experience on the earth-surface.

It not only proves order by relating types, categories and sequence of events to the periods of celestial bodies (as moving points of light—and nothing else). It shows how events can be predicted and how fore-knowledge may be applied in social and personal matters. Fore-knowledge is the power to build a civilization out of the apparent chaos of earthly phenomena. All science is based on predictability. Astrology is the mother of all sciences, the mother of civilization; for it has been the first and most universal attempt by man to *find the hidden order behind or within the confusion of the earthly jungle—physical or psychological, as the case may be.* . . .

Every human experience is bi-polar. It is pulled by the attraction of the individual factor in experiencing, and also by that of the collective factor. These two pulls are varied relative strengths. Education (a collective factor) gives more strength to the collective aspect of experience; thus an educated man may not go as wild under the stress of emotional disturbance as an un-educated person who will kill if jealousy possesses him. But the strongly individualized artist may lose his emotional balance faster than the business man who is steeped in social respectability. To the Romantic artist the world at large may appear thus as a grandiose tragedy; but the English gentleman will drink his tea while the Empire crumbles, unconcerned to the last moment with the impact of chaos. . . .

Chaos is the path to a greater wholeness of being and consciousness: a path, a transition, a process. The Sage is he who, first of all, understands this process, feels its rhythm, realizes the meaning of its polar attractions and repulsions. He is the man who sees all nature as a cyclic interplay of energies between "lesser wholes" and "greater wholes." Within him as without, he witnesses individual pain transforming itself into collective peace, and collective fulfillment sacrificing itself into the inspiraation and guidance which those who are identified with the "greater whole" can bestow upon "lesser wholes" still struggling with the problems of their atomistic and painful relationships.

A cyclic interplay of polar energies: in this phrase can be found the key to an interpretation of human experience which does not produce irreconcilable dualities and the ever-present possibility of schizophrenia and nationalistic or class wars. Life is a cyclic interplay of polar energies. Every factor in experience is always present, but it manifests in an ever-varying degree of intensity. The waning of the energy of the one pole within the whole of experience is always associated with the waxing in strength of the other pole. Two forces are always active. Every conceivable mode of activity is always active within any organic whole, but some modes dominate, while others are so little active as to seem altogether inexistent. Yet nonexistence is a fiction, from our point of view. It should be called instead *latency*. No characteristic trait in the whole universe is ever totally absent from the experience of any whole. It is only latent. And latency is still, in a sense, activity of a sort. It is a negative, introverted kind of activity.

Such a philosophical approach to the problem of experience gives to astrology a meaning and a value which few contemporary thinkers suspect it to contain. Astrology can be seen, in the light of this world-philosophy, as a remarkable tool for the understanding of human experience considered as the field for a cyclic interplay of polar energies or attitudes. Astrology is a means to see human experience as an organic whole, a technique of interpretation, an "algebra of life." It uses the ordered pageant of planets (and to a lesser extent, of the stars) as a symbol of what can happen to a man who sees life whole. Every event in the experience of that man is part of an ordered sequence, as every piece of the jig-saw puzzle is part of a complete picture—and because of this, it acquires *meaning*.

It is not that the planets "influence" directly any particular person by flashing a special kind of a ray which will make the person happy or cause him to break his leg. The cycles of the planets and their relationships represent to man reality in an ordered state and in reference to the "greater whole" which we know as the solar system. Men are "lesser wholes" within this "greater whole." Men can only find peace and lasting integration as they relate themselves in consciousness to the "greater whole," as they identify their own cycles of experience with cycles of activity of the "greater whole," as they refer their meetings with other men to the total picture which only a perception of the "greater whole" can reveal. Every man is a whole—an individual. But to be an individual is meaningless except in reference to human society—or at the limit, to the universe. A man living on a desert island without any possibility of his ever being related to another man is not an individual, but only a solitary organism without meaning in terms of humanity. An individual is an individualized expression of collective (or generic) human nature. What he receives from the collective which existed before him, he must return to the collective which follows after him. No individual exists in a vacuum. There is no organic entity which is not contained within a "greater whole" and which does not contain "lesser wholes." To be an individual is a social status.

Every man is in latency a universal—or, as the Chinese said, a "Celestial." To bring out the latent into actuality, to transfigure the sphere of earthly man with the light, the rhythms and the integrated harmony which is of the "greater whole" and which the movements of celestial bodies conveniently picture—this is the goal for man.

Astrology opens to us a book of universal pictures. Each picture is born of order and has meaning. Every astrological birth-chart is a signature of the cosmos—or of God. It is the image of the completed jig-saw puzzle. Man, by understanding such images can fulfill his experience, because he can thus see this experience *objectively and structurally as an organic whole*. He can see it as a whole, yet as integrated within the cyclic process of universal change which is revealed clearly in the stars and the planets, and confusedly in the nearness of his earthly contacts. Nothing is static, and no life is absolutely divided. Life is a process, and every process is cyclic—if we believe our experience, instead of imposing intellectual categories and ethical dualisms upon this experience. Astrology is a study of cyclic processes.

All astrology is founded upon the Zodiac. Every factor used in astrology—Sun, Moon, planets, cusps of Houses, nodes, fixed stars, etc.—is referred to the Zodiac. But the Zodiac need not be considered as a thing mysterious, remote and occult. From the point of view above described, the Zodiac is simply the product of the realization by man that experience is a cyclic process; and first of all, that every manifestation of organic life obeys the law of rhythmic alternation—at one time impelled to activity by one directive principle, at another by its polar opposite.

Man acquires first this sense of rhythmic alternation by reflecting upon his daily experience which presents him with a regular sequence of day-time and of night-time, of light and darkness. But human life is too close to such a sequence, and human consciousness too involved in it, for it to appear as anything save a kind of fatality. It does so, because man normally does not keep conscious through the whole day-and-night cycle. He is confronted by a dualism which seems to him absolute, because it is not only a dualism of light and darkness but one which, from the point of view of consciousness, opposes being to non-being. Thus man is led to use this day-and-night cycle as a symbol to interpret the even greater mystery of life and death. The concept of reincarnation is nothing but a symbolic extension of the original experience common to all men of a regular alternation of days and nights; and so is the ancient Hindu idea of the "Days and Nights of Brahma," of cosmic periods of manifestation followed by periods of non-manifestations— *manvantaras* and *pralayas*.

The cycle of the year, particularly manifest in the seasonal condition of vegetation in temperate climates, offers to man's consideration an altogether different kind of regular sequence. There is no longer any question of one half of the cycle being associated with the idea of absolute non-existence.

Man remains active, as an experiencer, through the entire cycle. Indeed the year can be interpreted as a "cycle of experience" because the experiencer is experiencing through the whole of it—whereas the day-and-night cycle is not normally susceptible of such an interpretation, because during a large portion of it man ceases to be an experiencer.

The Zodiac is the symbolization of the cycle of the year. It is so, essentially, in the temperate regions of the Northern hemisphere where astrology was born. Zodiacal symbolism is the product of the experience of human races living in such regions: experience of the seasons, of the activities of nature and of man through the changing panorama of vegetation—vegetation being the very foundation of animal and human life on earth. As such races have been, during the last millennia, the *active* factor in the evolution of human consciousness, their experience has come to acquire a universal validity in the determination of cosmic meaning and human purpose. Civilization, as we know it today, is therefore centered in a Northern-hemisphere and temperate-climate kind of consciousness. It may conceivably not remain so in the future, but for the time being it is; and our present astrology interprets thus accurately its cyclic evolution.

The Zodiac which is used in our astrology has very little, if anything at all, to do with distant stars as entities in themselves. It is an ancient record of the cyclic series of transformations actually experienced by man throughout the year; a record written in symbolic language using the stars as a merely convenient, graphic way of building up symbolic images appealing to the imagination of a humanity child-like enough to be more impressed by pictures than by abstract and generalized processes of thought. The essential thing about the Zodiac is not the hieroglyphs drawn upon celestial maps; it is not the symbolical stories built up around Greek mythological themes—significant as these may be. It is the human experience of change. And for a humanity which once lived very close to the earth, the series of nature's "moods" throughout the year was the strongest representation of change; for the inner emotional and biological changes of man's nature did correspond very closely indeed to the outer changes in vegetation.

Humanity, however, has been evolving since the early days of Chaldea and Egypt. Such an evolution has meant basically one thing and one thing only: the translation, or transference, of man's ability to experience life significantly *from the biological to the psycho-mental level*. At first, mankind drew all its symbols and the structure of its meanings from biological experience. Man, experiencing life and change essentially as a bodily organism, sought to express his consciousness of purpose and meaning in terms of bodily experience. These terms were the only available common denominator upon which civilizations could be built. Even so-called "spiritual" teachings (for instance, the early forms of Yoga or Tantra in India) stressed sexual, and in general "vitalistic," symbols—and corresponding practices . . .

Today the remarkable rise to public attention of modern psychology offers to astrologers an opportunity for reformulating completely astrology and its symbols. Astrology can be made into a language, not of the individual ego, but of the total human personality. And, in a world rent with conflicts and made meaningless by the passion for analysis and differentiation at all costs, astrology can appear once more as a technique enabling man to grasp the meaning of his experience as a whole: physiological and psychological experience, body and psyche, collective and individual. Without fear of persecution—it is to be hoped—astrology can use the old vitalistic symbols of ancient astrology, the images derived from the serial changes in the yearly vegetation and from man's experiences with the powers latent in his generic and bodily nature.

These images are rich with the meaning of feelings and sensations common to all men since the dawn of civilization on earth. They are steeped in collective wisdom and organic instinct. They belong to the Root-nature of man, to "man's common humanity," the foundation upon which the later-date individual achievements of a rational and over-intellectualized humanity are built. Without the sustaining power of that Root-foundation man must ever collapse and disintegrate. And the very spectacle of such a collapse and disintegration is before our eyes in these dark days of mankind—days nevertheless pregnant with the seed of a new integration of human experience.

One cannot understand significantly the beginning

of any cycle unless one knows the general meaning
of the whole cycle. By the very definition of the
term "cycle," the beginning of a cycle marks also
the end of the preceding one. Beginning is conditioned by end, as the new vegetation is conditioned
by the seeds which were the product of the preceding yearly growth. To know the general meaning of a cycle is to know the nature of the two
basic forces which are at play throughout its course.
We must therefore define, first of all, the characteristics of the Day-force and the Night-force; and our
definitions will center around concepts of a psychological nature, because it is the purpose of this
book to establish astrological factors at the new
level at which modern man is now consciously and
deliberately operating: the psychomental level.

The Day-force is a *personalizing* energy. It forces
ideas, spiritual entities, abstractions into concrete
and particular actuality. It energizes the "descent
of spirit into a body" to use a familiar, though
dangerous, terminology. Thus it begins to grow in
power at Christmas, symbol of spiritual Incarnation;
but becomes only clearly visible in Aries, symbol of
germination—and in man, of adolescence. It is fulfilled in Cancer, symbol of "coming of age" and of
personal fulfillment through marriage and home-
responsibilities. The natural result of the action of
the Day-force is the stressing of that individual
uniqueness of human being which is known today as
"personality."

The Night-force is an *in-gathering* energy. It
brings personalities together. First, in Cancer (the

home) it integrates a man and a woman; in Leo, it adds the child; in Virgo, the servants, nurses, educators. But integration becomes public only in Libra, the symbol of social activity, of group activity toward the building of a cultural and spiritual community. With Scorpio, business and political enterprises flourish; with Sagittarius, philosophy, printing, long journeys. The Night-force reaches its apex of power with Capricorn, symbol of the State —the organized social whole. The natural result of the action of the Night-force is to emphasize all values related to "society."

Personality and Society—such are, indeed, the two polarities of the actual experience of human beings ever since we can trace the historical development of man. The two terms are the *concrete* manifestations, at the psychological level of modern man, of the two still more general concepts of "individual" and "collective." In every human experience these two factors are present with varying relative strengths. That this is so should never be forgotten. No man acts and feels solely as an individualized personality, or solely as a social being. It is never a question of "either-or" but of "more-or-less." It is a matter of point of view.

In a somewhat similar manner we may speak of our Sun as a "sun" or as a "star." It is a "sun" if considered as the center of an individualized and separate cosmic organism (a solar system); but it is a "star" if considered as a participant in the collective being of the Galaxy. In the first case, he is alone on his throne; in the second case, he is constantly related to his follow-stars within the boundaries of the "greater whole," the Galaxy. Man experiences the Sun as light-giver—as a "sun"—during daytime. At night, modern man realizes that this giver of light, this All-Father, is but one "star" in the companionship of the Galaxy. Overcome by light and heat, we worship the "sun" in devotion; in the silence and peace of the night we commune with the brotherhood of "stars." It is the same reality always, but we change our angle of approach to it— and the one reality divides into two phases of experience, and again into many more phases. The limit to the divisibility of our experience is only our ability to remain integrated as a person under this process of differentiation—our ability to remain sane; which is, to give an integral meaning to our experience as a *social personality*.

The dualism of personality and society becomes in another and more strictly psychological sense that of "conscious ego" and "Collective Unconscious." The realm of individualized consciousness is the realm of day-time, the realm of "sun." The realm of the Collective Unconscious is the night-realm, the realm of "stars." An understanding of these two realms is necessary in order to see how the waxing and waning of the two cyclic forces operate in a psychological manner.

To say simply that the Day-force begins to wane after the summer solstice does not give an accurate psychological picture of what happens within the human person. It is not only that the Day-force becomes less strong. More accurately still, the waning of the Day-force means that what was a positive, active force is becoming more and more withdrawn from the field of objectivity. *It becomes increasingly subjective and introverted; also more transcendent.* It operates from the point of view of unconscious motives, rather than from that of conscious ones.

Human experience is not only to be referred to consciousness and to the individual ego; for, if we do so, we have to give an ethical valuation to many of our experiences, which divides our total being into two conflicting entities. Thus some of our acts may have to be explained as proofs of our evil personality, others as manifestations of our heroic or saintly individuality; they *must* be given such interpretations if they are referred *only* to the conscious ego. But if we realize that our actions are partly the results of conscious endeavors, and partly the products of motivations emerging from an unconscious which is not "ours" (in an individualized way) but which is an ocean of racial and social energies unconcerned with ego-structures, ethics and reason—then we can explain human actions in another way; and man may know himself integral and undivided, a center of universal Life in its process of cyclic change.

From such a point of vantage man can see consciousness constantly interpenetrating unconsciousness, rationality rhythmically playing with irrationality—and not be disturbed, or frantically striving to be what he is not. Human experience is forever the outcome of this interplay of consciousness and unconsciousness, of individual and collective. Cyclic life pulsates through every human action, feeling or thought. Reality has a rhythmic heart. The systole and diastole of that heart create these beats of becoming which are birth and death, winter and summer, increase of light and crescendos of darkness. Gloriously, the dance of experience moves on in the hallways of nature's cycle. The Sage looks on, yet every phase of the dance pulsates through his awareness. He is spectator, yet he is partner to all protagonists in the universal dance; every lover knows him as beloved and his mind experiences the throb of every human heart. His vision encompasses all birthing and dying. Upon all things born of the pulsing and the dancing of cyclic Life, he bestows Meaning. And in that bestowal of Meaning, Man, total and free, creates reality.

Ronald V. Sampson. *The Vanity of Humanism*

The break with secular humanism . . . perhaps, if there is to be a new radicalism and it is to come into its own, this will be the most wrenching departure of all. For the secular humanists have been for so long the shock troops of civilized values in the struggle against obscurantism and oppression. They have given us a noble tradition,

From "The Vanity of Humanism," *The Nation*, 1969. Reprinted by permission of the publisher.

and moreover the only cultural vision wholly compatible with the dominant status of modern science. How neat a synthesis it has made!

God is dead? Good! We shall be better off without the superstitious cruelties of organized religion. *Écrasez l'infame!*

Man is alone in the universe? Good! The human condition becomes that much more heroic.

There are no absolute values? Good! We shall—in our freedom—make up even better values than tradition gives us.

There is no reality but this that science teaches? Good! We can at last get down to the business of making the earth more liveable.

Masters of our fate—captains of our soul. It takes a Tolstoyan sensibility—like that of the English political philosopher Ronald V. Sampson—to smell out the self-defeating vanity of such postures and to return us to the great question: *but where shall men and women find the strength of the good?* In a humanism, Sampson answers, which is not the child of intrepid despair.

SUSAN STEBBING wrote in 1941: "But it is also no illusion but uncontested fact that here and now we know that hatred, cruelty, intolerance and indifference to human misery are evil; that love, kindliness, tolerance, forgiveness and truth are good, so unquestionably good that we do not need God or heaven to assure us of their worth." When I first read this, it struck a responsive chord; I remember quoting it with approval a decade ago.

Virtue, I felt, was self-evident, beyond the possibility of sincere disputation; moreover, this was
all that was truly important: that we should get
on with the business of doing what we so clearly
knew. For if our lives were loving and honorable, if
we were kind, tolerant, forgiving and truthful, there
would be no problems of an urgent or serious kind.

Moreover, so it then seemed to me—it was not
merely that morality was self-sufficient and that discussion of the nature or existence of God was unnecessary. Theological discussion was positively
harmful. It was precisely when men began to dispute about the nature of God that they showed their
worst qualities, and for good reason. Men become
most bitter and intolerant at the point where the
touchstone of evidence, to which appeal can be
made, breaks down. In the absence of evidence
the will to self-assertion, the desire to subjugate
one's opponent, find free rein. "God" is such a nebu-
lous, unverifiable concept, meaning all things to all
men, I thought, that it is bound to be a bone of
inexhaustible contention. In morals, the appeal to
universal experience offers itself as an inescapable
arbiter; in theology, on the other hand, there is no
such arbiter, and so it is not surprising that religion
brings out the worst in man. . . .

In philosophy, molded largely by the 20th-century
reverence for science, concern has been with precision and clarity of linguistic usage. Tests of meaning of the most rigorous nature, acceptable to the
scientist, were devised. If a statement were neither
a definition nor verifiable by appeal to any pos-

sible sense of experience, it was held to be meaningless. Under attack, minor concessions were made to avoid manifest absurdity, but only to safeguard the purity of the central positivist principle. If God is to pass such a test before being admitted to the status of meaningful concepts, the onus is on the believer to supply evidence of God's transcendent reality. What evidence of a falsifiable nature can be adduced to prove that man is not alone in the universe, that God would still exist if the human species were to perish? In this way the whole 19th-century debate between immanentists and transcendentalists has been neatly headed off.

The theologians themselves have long been in full retreat before the positivist onslaught, bringing their teachings up to date, rethinking, rationalizing, salvaging what crumbs they could, or even—on the notorious principle that if you cannot beat your opponent, join him—producing ultra-sophistications of their own about what they are pleased to call the death of God. In short, the twin streams of the European Enlightenment, the liberal empiricist stream and the dialectical materialist stream, have united in an immensely powerful river to wash away the last remnants of man's traditional beliefs about the existence and nature of God. Since, however, most of us recognize that man cannot live without some guiding metaphysic, a new "religion," Humanism, is rapidly being evolved in the West and appears to be growing increasingly fashionable. The essential argument is admittedly persuasive and is implicit in the preceding analysis. Since the evidence is overwhelming that nothing is more difficult to secure than agreement among men concerning the nature of *reality*, and since it is a matter of urgency to secure some measure of agreement about the nature of *morality*, where common yardsticks of appeal are potentially within reach, let us put the religious debate into cold storage, if it is not possible to get rid of it altogether, so that we can get on with the practical and urgent business of hammering out an agreed morality. . . .

It is the purpose of this essay to deny this thesis, to argue that Humanism, be it agnostic or atheistic, is a false religion, . . . that the liberation from false metaphysics only to fall into new forms of error will not alleviate our existing grave situation, but will on the contrary produce even more deadly consequences; that morality is not an autonomous discipline, that the argument about the nature of reality is fundamental, that error about the nature and purpose of God must necessarily lead to avoidable suffering and death, and that the metaphysical debate, so far from being a luxury to be postponed indefinitely, is the most urgent task, now more than ever, confronting men. . . .

Let us return to the original quotation from Susan Stebbing and ask why, notwithstanding the fact that the distinction between good and evil is self-evident, men after millennia of struggle show as yet but faint signs of overcoming evil. We know here and now indisputably that "hatred, cruelty, intolerance and indifference to human misery are evil. . . ." Had Dr. Stebbing stopped there, none could gainsay her. But we must ask why, given this knowledge, we *appear* to be incapable of acting upon it. Is it that this knowledge has come to us only recently, that we have not had sufficient time to gird our loins? Clearly not. "War of any kind is evil," wrote Herodotus a very long time ago. But we wage it today with apparently undiminished zest. Sexual immorality and depravity also lead to great evil, but when theologians discuss morality solely in the context of sexual relations and to the exclusion of war, we rightly feel that there is something odd—that they are being less than honest to us, let alone to God.

Of the very many ills which afflict humanity one evil dwarfs all the others. Throughout human history men have lived in organized groups under governments which have feared and competed with one another by means of arms, and the resultant arms races have erupted at more or less regular intervals into wars. The present arms race is consuming $183 billion a year, and it is beyond the power of any human imagination to foresee the extent of the holocaust which will ensue if it continues until it erupts into war. In the childhood of our species it was no doubt possible to delude men that evil occurred because the gods were angry or because exceptionally wicked men held sway; but it is no longer possible to deceive in this way. Today, men know that when very great evil threatens to overtake them, it is and can only be because very large numbers of men are contributing their share to that evil, that is to say, are living their lives on a false and evil basis. And this, notwithstanding that we all know, indeed cannot *not* know, that "love, kindliness, tolerance, foregiveness and truth are good . . . unquestionably good." So where is all the evil coming from?

At this point I find it difficult not to resort to the first person singular, not because the evidence is in any way private or less than general but because it is more likely to touch the imagination when translated into the idiom in which we as individuals experience it. In my childhood it was the practice in my part of the world for children to go to day school on weekdays and to Sunday school on Sunday. It was in the latter school that I was first exposed to the four Gospels of the New Testament, and they immediately reached into my profoundest emotions—not the absurd and manifestly false tales about people rising physically from the dead, walking on the water and conjuring water into wine, but stories such as that of the woman taken in adultery, the good Samaritan, the prodigal son, and the lucid, yet poetic simplicity of the Beatitudes. But although these readings, repeated many times, were to make an ineffaceable impression, another and different lesson was also taught me, one that was the more powerful because it was never openly expressed. I noticed that while I was required to attend Sunday school and while interest was expressed if I received a prize for attendance or diligence in memorizing required lessons, the interest was nevertheless essentially polite. But the interest shown by everyone in my circle to success achieved in lessons and examinations at the day school was of the genuine variety which quickened the pulse.

In short, I learned that "religion" played in life some part that was never made plain beyond the fact that it was peripheral and wrapped around with much that was evidently irrational—dogma, miracle and ritual which inspired not respect but contempt. On the other hand, I learned that to make a successful career, that is to say, to "get on" in the world, was a matter of central and enduring importance, commanding the immediate and genuine respect of everyone I knew. That there might ever be a conflict between these two planes of experience never seriously occurred to me. That there had been such conflicts in history, I was of course aware, but that was on the public stage and in the past, and clearly had nothing to do with my own private, personal existence. The real purpose of life was to be successful, as the world and I measured success. As for virtue, that was something which largely took care of itself; one did as one's neighbor did and as professional standards required, and no one could pretend that such requirements were especially onerous. I knew, of course, that injustice and inequality existed in the world, and that this was wrong; but my obligations in that respect were wholly covered by my tacit membership in and support of the reformist party, which was working, admittedly slowly but nevertheless steadily—Rome was not built in a day—to

ჳot matters right. So I had been sedulously taught, and so I believed. . . .

In brief I had learned the ancient lesson that, while all human beings are more than adequately equipped to distinguish good from evil, nevertheless a price is to be paid for choosing the good rather than the evil. There is a reward, too, of course, in the shape of a tranquil conscience and the serenity of spirit that is alone born of a tranquil conscience; but most human beings appear to be more immediately impressed by the nature of the sacrifice than by the reality of the reward, for the former is tangible and the latter is not. And any discussion of the autonomy of ethics which fails to take this dilemma for mortal man adequately into account must be condemned as facile and not very helpful. It is not enough to know that kindliness is good and cruelty is bad. It is also necessary to be able to answer correctly the question: why am I alive and what is the purpose of this life that has been temporarily entrusted to me?

Every man must be bound by some conviction, conscious or unconscious, about the significance he attaches to his life in order to live it, to direct it, to make plans or merely to drift. Whatever a man may say, his behavior over a prolonged period will under close study inevitably reveal the real values sustaining it. And this metaphysic is the most important thing that we must know of a man if we need to assess his basic character or to predict how he will act in a given situation. Since every man is endowed with very powerful appetites, it is perfectly possible to find the meaning of one's life in a ceaseless pursuit of gratification. In practice, most of us are in varying degree aware both that appetites ceaselessly pampered are apt to cloy and that unrestrained egoism on the part of large numbers of individuals is calculated to bring about conditions of misery and discomfort to all concerned. Therefore a policy of unrelieved individualism is generally tempered to some degree by a further extension of this principle. That is to say, the individual finds the meaning of his life not solely in self-indulgence but also in satisfying the wants of a group or groups with which he identifies emotionally. The most universal form of ego identification with a group is of course with the family, but the principle extends in a lesser degree to schools, villages, social classes, religious and ethnic groups and political nationalities.

The difficulty with all these "goods" sought for oneself or one's group is that they are particularistic or exclusive; they displace a like good for somebody else or some other group. They are not compatible with the principle of universalism and therefore violate the principle of justice. They stimulate competition; they are keenly sought just because they confer privilege or special status; they differentiate favorably the successful from those who fail. They are therefore of the very stuff of strife, of envy, of the struggle for power, of the resentments of inferiority, of the war of all against all.

Unfortunately, the energies which are harnessed

to these secular goals are very powerful, and sustain the central efforts of a man's striving and struggle over a lifetime. If they are rejected as having morally indefensible consequences to mankind as a whole, inevitably an immense problem makes itself felt. To what is a man to devote his energies? What shall be the central goal of his life? If he ceases to find it in the quest for power, privilege, status, "authority," wealth, what substitute is there that *is* morally acceptable and which can realistically evoke a comparable single-mindedness and consistently sustained application of energy? In whatever way we seek to answer this question, one thing is certain: the first step consists in renouncing what have hitherto been powerfully felt desires, animating the individual's main aspirations and life goals. And such a task is calculated to daunt even strong people. Resistance cannot but be profound, as St. Augustine testified with a disarming candor and wry humor:

And when Thou didst on all sides shew me, that what Thou saidst was true, I, convicted by the truth, had nothing at all to answer but only those dull and drowsy words, "Anon, anon," "presently"; "leave me but a little." But "presently, presently" had no present, and my "little while" went on for a long while. . . .

But if it is difficult to acknowledge the truth and follow it, it is not impossible. To do what I will may not always lie within my power, but what surely does always lie within my power is the ability to will the good. And it is the peculiar and unique power of the truth that, if acknowledged freely and honestly, ultimately it will of its own accord rectify our existing false situation. Truth is impregnable against all forms of attack, all mockery, all satire; it is immune to self-contradiction; it is impervious to the emotions of cunning, deceit, self-doubt. It commands universal attention, and ultimately the obedience of all honest men. "Truth," wrote James Russell Lowell in the *Bigelow Papers,* "is quite beyond the reach of satire. There is so brave a simplicity in her, that she can no more be made ridiculous than an oak or a pine."

Nevertheless, truth is a hard taskmaster, for it demands as the first step in its service a willingness to transcend the claims of the self in the service of other selves. Its first and last law is that of renunciation, which though possible for man, does not come naturally to him. And the paradox is that insofar as a man succeeds in his aspiration to obey truth, he inevitably puts himself at the mercy of all who suffer from no such inhibitions and who accordingly take advantage of him. One man's truth has to confront another man's falsehood; one man's forbearance is met with another's will to dominion; the one's agony of conscience contends with him who is without scruple; the one man's love and nonviolence has to brave the threats of hatred and violence; the total vulnerability of the one stands against the bludgeon of a Cain or Raskolnikov.

In logic, the only possible remedy to the arms race based on fear is unilateral disarmament based on trust. The truth of renunciation which is the key to all goodness is pre-eminently demonstrated here, yet nowhere are there apparently so few willing takers. At no point does human skepticism and despair appear more intractable. The reason is to be found in the conviction, so deep in this world, that evil must inevitably triumph over good. . . .

"Had I no other proof of the immaterial nature of the soul," affirmed Rousseau's Savoyard vicar, "the triumph of the wicked and the oppression of the righteous in this world would be enough to convince me."

But on reflection we must surely see that there was no other way in which man could be taught the truth. If to avoid defeat we resist evil violently, we provide yet another alibi for wrongdoing, we do something dubious, we teach a wrong lesson. Men see only that a battle of wills is taking place, and they understand that well enough from long familiarity. It is essential that we show that we struggle not that our will should prevail but that the truth of justice or equality should prevail. *Not my will but Thy will!* Will it is that we must obey —and it is clearly not the will of organized men, nor is it the natural will of the individual. Then whose will? What is the will we follow in the quest for self-perfection? If it were our own will, would not the skeptics be right who accuse those who strive after perfectibility of vanity or self-righteousness?

We can abdicate all "power"—means of implementing our will, only if we have confidence that by following the way indicated by conscience and reason as the true way, thus paradoxically putting ourselves at the mercy of evil, good will ultimately be advanced and the truth prevail. *Not my will but Thy will!* But what confidence can we have in the presence of so much violence, a vast surrounding ocean of evil? Faith? Yes, perhaps, but not blind faith—it must be reasonable faith based on evidence and reasoning conducted as always by rigorous adherence to the logic of the argument to the end. After all, if we are to have faith, it may well cost us our lives. . . . Are we to sacrifice our all on the basis of blind faith, where reason would surely call at best for agnosticism?

It is inescapable that so long as one man survives who is willing to take advantage of his physically weaker brother to slay him, this world must remain the kingdom of power. But might it not be that an unknown X factor could, if found, trusted and relied upon, ultimately prevail over the forces of power, of evil, even in this world, the only world we know? But what if this X factor becomes efficacious only if we trust it even unto possible acceptance of a violent, premature and otherwise escapable death? And if such an X factor is found by all testable experience to exist, a factor before which power itself is rendered impotent by entirely nonpower-means, what name must we give it? Truth? Yes, but it is the very core of truth that we are seeking to define. *Magna est veritas et praevalebit.* Yes, indeed, if we always scrupulously follow it, but what is its essence and what is the evidence? What is the one thing that overcomes all our resistance, our pride, our self-love, our self-seeking, our power? Everyone knows the answer to this—it is love. . . .

But what is love? Again its inmost essence, its great strength, turns out to be powerlessness. When the barrier of our self-pride is broken down, when we become as little children, with the natural, naive humility of the child, it is then and only then, when power has fled us completely, that ultimately we move even the most hardened. . . .

If we turn back to the story of Jesus himself, we feel compelled to ask if it is mere coincidence that the account of the cursing of the fig tree because it failed to bear fruit out of season, and the hounding of the money changers out of the temple—both of them acts out of character and less than edifying —come immediately after Jesus' triumphant ride into Jerusalem, acclaimed by the multitude. Be that as it may, it is certainly not the success which has captured the imagination of the world for two millennia. What moves mankind is the vision of a child cradled in a cattle manger, because there was no room at the inn, which the well-to-do had already occupied. That was the significant beginning; the end was the crucifixion between two thieves. The man taught with unmistakable clarity: *Resist not evil,* and the forgiveness of sin. "Neither do I condemn thee. Go thy way and sin no more." And when Pilate marveled that a man being tried for his life, should make no attempt to defend himself, thrice called on him to answer, he met only with silence. "God forgive them, for they know not what they do." And indeed it is the case: we do not

know, we do not really know what it is we do, or
we could not inflict such astounding and unbelievable cruelties on one another. Men behold one another incomprehendingly. The Bishop of Linz confronted by the heroic Jägerstätter could see only
a young man with a lust for martyrdom; and Jägerstätter could in charity only conceive of the bishop
as one who had not received the grace to see things
as they really were.* But through it all runs the
consistent thread of the truth, simple, void of ambiguity, unmistakable to all with eyes to see. On
the one hand the sword of Caesar, the governor's
crown, the armed might of the centurion, the cry
for blood that arises when power feels itself threatened; and confronting it, *what*? An emaciated, dis-
armed, defenseless carpenter's son, whose only
crime has been the continuous, quiet yet impas-
sioned eloquence of his plea that we should love
one another.

To all of which no doubt the reply from those
who pride themselves on being what is called
"tough-minded" will be that emotion is emotion
and reason is reason, and reason indicates that,
whatever the truth of the foregoing, we have done
nothing to demonstrate that ethics is not an autonomous discipline. We have been discussing
morals, not theology. . . . Agnostics have never

---

* The reference here is to Franz Jägerstätter, the Austrian
peasant pacifist who was beheaded during World War II for
refusing to serve in the Nazi army, despite the pressure of
both church and state. Jägerstätter's remarkable story has
been saved from oblivion in an outstanding work by Gordon
Zahn, *In Solitary Witness* (New York, 1965)—Ed.

denied that morality exists, nor would they necessarily quarrel with this definition of the content of morality. The question at issue is whether or not morals are self-sufficient.

Let us recapitulate the central argument. It comes naturally to man to attend to what appear to be in his own interests or conducive to the pleasures of himself or the group with which he emotionally identifies. But all experience testifies that such conduct on the part of individuals and groups leads directly and inevitably to competition, strife, fear, hatred, rivalry, self-deception, greed, xenophobia. In short, it is destructive of man's real interests. Therefore the true form of conduct, which will promote man's genuine interests, is the opposite of self-interest. It consists in finding the meaning of one's life, not in the quest for wealth, power and prestige but in engaging in activities prompted by consideration of the needs of one's fellows. And this policy, although productive of great and enduring satisfaction, does not appear to come naturally and easily to man, although it is certainly possible for him to achieve it. The former metaphysic is the law of power and/or violence and leads to evil; the latter is the law of love and equality and leads to good. And the meaning of every individual's life consists in the choice which he is of necessity required to make between these alternatives. . . .

But the question remains: why should the individual choose the good, when it is a path full of difficulties and pitfalls, and may well lead him into a position of discomfort, hardship, persecution or even peril to his life? Because it is the good? But why should I prefer the good to my own immediate comfort, appetites and security? Even if I am capable of willing the good, why should I? Why should I not will what is "natural" to me? The good is clearly not the fruit of my own spontaneous will, nor is is it the will of nature, whose law is one that is indeed "red in tooth and claw"; still less is it will of human law, which is at all times and everywhere based on fear and violence. Then why should I obey this will? Whose will is it? I should obey it, because it is the will of God. There is no other possible answer. If God did not exist, I would have no reason for obeying this law; it would be no more than the idle dream, which is what vain, presumptuous and wicked men have always cynically claimed it to be.

Nor would this be all. If God did not exist, it would be possible to secure everlasting peace by mutual deterrence through the balance of terror— that is to say, to bring about good by doing evil, as the casuists and sophists would always have us believe. But it is not so possible. As men sow, so shall they always reap. Nothing and no one can disturb this law. And this is the answer to Man Friday's celebrated question to Robinson Crusoe: "Why God not kill the devil?" Man's only protection lies in his obedience to the moral law; were it possible to disobey it with impunity without bringing about evil consequences in its wake, the last barrier between the soul of man and his total depravity would go down. . . .

If God did not exist, then the individual's struggle to perfect himself would indeed be no more than a form of moral vanity or egocentric spiritual pride, which is how the enemies of perfectibility are so eager to construe it. When we fail in our moral striving, we are humbled, and that is good for us. When we succeed—and if success were impossible, aspiration itself would be fatally undermined—we are threatened by pride. When Bunyan was once complimented on the quality of the sermon he had just delivered, he replied: "You need not remind me of that. The Devil told me of it before I was out of the pulpit." If God did not exist, we would indeed be caught in a "double bind" from which no moral escape would be possible. But this is not so, as Job discovered when by his self-righteousness he brought upon himself the voice out of the whirlwind, whose awe-inspiring admonition left him no alternative but to acknowledge that he was "of small account," that he abhorred himself and repented "in dust and ashes."

Finally, if God did not exist, then ultimately we should unavoidably feel impelled to look not simply to our own truthfulness, integrity and humility but to our own *power* to implement the good and ward off the evil. And this quest for power, commonly disguised by what appear to be good or disinterested motives, is the primal source of the evil which we feel ourselves called upon to overcome. We can overcome it completely only if we can say with genuine conviction: *Not my will but Thy will!* . . .

Harold C. Goddard. *William Blake's Fourfold Vision*

More and more it becomes clear that the modern world's paramount prophet of revolution is William Blake. Only in his work do we find social justice and visionary splendor welded together; secular and spiritual liberation made inextricably members one of another. Here was a mind which could champion the wretched of the earth without casting away the transcendent dimension of life, that could celebrate the Jesus of Imagination without degrading the physical self. But in no respect was Blake more timely than in his recognition that the uglifying despair of our time traces to "single vision and Newton's sleep": the culture of science.

The whole and exact meaning of Blake eludes us still. His voice reverberates in the deep caves of the mind on too many levels for us to hear at once all that is there to be heard. The scholarship on Blake takes off in a dozen different directions; he seems to be a score of men with a score of messages. Yet for all the ambiguities, the force and fire of his conviction draws us on along his path . . . toward the *next* politics:

> I give you the end of a golden string,
> Only wind it into a ball,
> It will lead you in at Heaven's gate,
> Built in Jerusalem's wall.

From *Blake's Fourfold Vision*, Pendle Hill Pamphlet #86. Copyright © 1956 by Pendle Hill, Wallingford, Pa. 19086. Reprinted by permission of the publisher.

Then follow . . . follow. . . .

Here, in small space, Harold C. Goddard captures at least the spirit of the fourfold vision. For those who come new to Blake, it makes a fine introduction.

MAN HAS FALLEN from Eternity, from Innocence. How shall he return? That, and that only in the end, is the question we want Blake to answer. How?

Why, naturally, by reversing the process by which he fell, just as the ice in melting and rising as vapor reverses the process by which the cloud condensed into raindrops, and fell, and froze.

The fall and the return is the theme of Blake's so-called Prophetic Books, against which many critics bring the charge that they are chaotic and bewildering and marred by bizarre and arbitrary symbolism. They are—at first acquaintance. But what of it? Isn't darkness bewildering? Isn't the primeval forest? Isn't sunlight bewildering to him who has been born blind? Blake was a pioneer. He *is* unfinished. Yet the more you discover the keys to the Prophetic Books, the more you see them for what they are: an immense allegory of the human soul, a concrete and symbolic psychology that at times makes you wonder whether our "scientific" psychology isn't a mere bit of scaffolding in comparison. For Blake, like Dante and Dostoevsky, had *been there*. If his books are the history of Heaven and Hell, they are also his autobiography.

Of Blake's sublime and tremendous universe, his pantheon and pandemonium, I can give just one

glimpse, and then I shall try to translate its essence
into everyday experience. In Eternity four living
principles, or Zoas as Blake calls them: Urthona,
Luvah, Urizen and Tharmas, corresponding loosely
to Spirit, Emotions, Reason and the Senses, live
in harmony around the throne of God until Urizen,
Reason, rising in pride to rule over the others,
breaks the harmony and falls from Eternity into
Time, dragging the others with him. In Eternity,
Urizen was Light or Lucifer, the Light-Bearer.
When he falls, he becomes the rationalizing principle, still Lucifer by name, but in fact the Prince
of Darkness.

Now do not fancy, as is so easy, that all this is
just a bit of old mythology or outworn superstition. Nothing so venerable is just superstition. No,
it is around us, here and now. All history is little
else. Religion begins in revelation, and falls into
dogma and ecclesiasticism. Art begins in inspiration,
and falls into slavery to rules and technique, into
propaganda. Society begins in neighborliness, and
falls into law and the state, and finally into war.
Education begins in love of the child, and falls
into methods and regimentation. "I'll bring the boy
to reason," Blake's father probably said as he got
out his whip (literal or metaphorical) when the
child reported the tree full of angels; "I'll bring
him to his senses." How wise words are! But Blake's
mother intervened. Perhaps that's what mothers are
for: to prevent fathers from bringing little boys to
reason, to their senses.

*   *   *

Blake marks three stages in this universal fall and recognizes accordingly five worlds or states, counting the unfallen and the utterly fallen as two:

1. Eden (Innocence) or Eternity: the land of imagination, of pure creative activity, of Divine Love, whose symbol is the Sun.

2. Beulah: the region around or the state nearest Eternity, the land of sleep and dreams and human love, whose symbol is the Moon, because it reflects Eternity as the Moon does the Sun, as human love does Divine.

3. An intervening region, partly to be identified with Science, about which Blake says little, whose symbol is the Stars.

4. Generation, or Earthly Life: the prison of the senses, the region of physical love, whose symbol (as the name, Generation, implies) is Sex, which passes imperceptibly into

5. Ulro: the limit of opacity, frigidity, and contraction, whose symbol is Darkness, or Matter.

Because such is the fall, the return to Eternity is an ascent up a Jacob's Ladder through these same regions from Darkness to Vision. Above Darkness, then, there are four ascending or intensifying grades of vision.

> Now I a fourfold vision see,
> And a fourfold vision is given to me;
> 'Tis fourfold in my supreme delight
> And threefold in soft Beulah's night
> And twofold Always. May God us keep
> From Single vision and Newton's sleep!

The reach of this ladder of vision may be indicated by saying that roughly fourfold vision is to
single vision as ordinary eyesight is to blindness.

Now the entire value of what I have been trying
to say will turn on whether I can show you that
these types of vision are not arbitrary inventions
of Blake or even special gifts of his genius, but
that they fall, however rarely, incipiently, or frag-
mentarily, within the experience of us all, and that
wherever a man may happen to be on that ladder of
vision, he is alive to the degree in which he is bent
on climbing higher up it.

Single Vision is simply ordinary physical eyesight,
the eyesight of the average sensual rational man.
Everyone remembers Wordsworth's Peter Bell:

> A primrose by a river's brim
> A yellow primose was to him
> And it was nothing more.

That is single vision. We might call it Peter Bell
vision. The man who believes that a man is a man,
a tree a tree, that the sky is blue and grass green,
a foot twelve inches long and minute sixty seconds,
that you can find the essence of things by measuring
and weighing them, to whom Hesiod's statement
that a half is greater than the whole is nonsense, in
short, the hard-headed commonsense man to whom
things are what they seem is in a state of single
vision, or Newton's sleep, in the prison of his senses
or his reason or both.

But escape from this prison, take note, comes not
by rejecting the senses but by purifying them, not

by rejecting reason but by subjecting it to the imagination.

One day a man is standing in front of a fire. He has looked at a fire before and thought it was just something that was red and leaped up and burned you if you touched it. But today he notices how it was started by a spark from another fire, how, given fuel, it mounted up, burned hotly, began to subside, sank into embers, then into ashes, and, to all appearances, was gone; and suddenly he thinks: *My life is like a fire.* He has achieved a simile. But he doesn't stop there. Now he feels a kindling and warmth inside himself and he cries: *My life is fire.* He has achieved a metaphor. From this it is but a step to the omission of the "is." Life and fire have become synonyms. He can never see one without feeling the other; he can never feel one without imagining the other. He has achieved a symbol, a poetic image. With this hint he begins looking around him and realizes, astonished at his former blindness, that as still water gives back the image of his face, so everything around him gives back the image of his life: the path that goes up the hill and then down, the unseen wind that sails his boat, the tree that is two trees, one going down into the earth and the other up into the sky, the brook flowing past, always the same, never the same. "All things transient are but symbols," says Goethe. "I caught two fishes, as it were, on one hook," is Thoreau's homelier way of putting it. This is Blake's *Double Vision.* . . .

The Ghost of a Flea. Did you suppose, if you have

seen it, that this is the picture of a flea? It is. But it is also a picture of all blood-drinking parasites, insect or human, the world over. "As Poetry admits not a Letter that is Insignificant," says Blake, "so Painting admits not a Grain of Sand or a Blade of Grass." This is the language of things. The mother tongue, I like to call it, the language without which all your Greek and Latin, all your French and German and English, is so much mumbling. Imagination, as its name implies, begins in images. An image is simply a thought that has come to life.

For images are dynamic, and the moment they begin to interweave, to interplay, to form into constellations, to have love affairs, to marry and beget new images, we have *Threefold Vision*. There is no mystery about it. Whoever has had a beautiful dream and has said afterwards, as I heard someone say, "Even in my dream I held my breath, it was so lovely," understands threefold vision. At night our imagination takes the raw material of the previous day and reshapes it into patterns dictated by our hopes and fears. . . .

"The gods first appeared to men in dreams," says Lucretius.

> And yet, as Angels in some brighter dreams
>   Call to the soul, when man doth sleep:
> So some strange thoughts transcend our wonted
>   themes
>   And into glory peep.

That is Henry Vaughan. These are all great names. To come closer home, here is the dream of a college student—a girl in one of my classes a few years ago. "I was skimming along over hill and dale, particularly over snowy hilltops, and flying with me were three birds of an unearthly blue. Suddenly I exclaimed to anyone who might be listening, 'Why, we're going East!' One of the birds looked up rather saucily at me, and all at once the birds were cardinals of as bright a red as they had been a bright blue."

Many psychologists would explain that dream as repressed sex. That is all right if you are explaining the flower in terms of the root. (Personally I think a daisy resembles the sun, and a delphinium the blue sky, more than they do their respective roots, which, I daresay, are indistinguishable except to an expert.) But a lovelier and more profound explanation, it seems to me, would be to say that life in this dream is trying to ascend, to evolve human wings. Beautiful images are the wings of the soul. Psyche in art is always a winged girl. The girl who dreamed that dream was seeing with threefold vision, was in Blake's Beulah (the region just across the river in Bunyan from the Celestial City), the region through which, and through which alone, man finds his way back to Eternity or fourfold vision. Aeneas, you remember, returned to the upper world by the Ivory Gate of Dreams.

But it doesn't have to be at night. Our moods are merely our dreams by daylight, and whoever is ecstatically happy is at least in the neighborhood of Beulah. Whoever has known imaginative love, whoever has created a work of art and felt inspired at the moment he conceived it has an inkling of Blake's state of threefold vision.

> He who kisses the joy as it flies
> Lives in eternity's sun rise.

And how is the final step to *Fourfold Vision* taken? Why, simply by dreaming (or loving, or imagining—they are three forms of the same thing) with such intensity that the dream obliterates daylight as daylight ordinarily obliterates the dream. "Another morn risen on mid-noon." Milton's sublime phrase expresses it exactly. . . .

If the two worlds remain at odds, if the ship of dreams is wrecked on the rocks of reality, we have at the weakest daydreaming, at the strongest hallucination or insanity. But if the two coalesce, as it were, if the ship sails the seas of reality successfully, we have fourfold vision. This is the way Blake's pictures came. He saw them there before him in a light stronger and more vivid than daylight. (His famous "Ancient of Days" he saw at the head of a staircase.) That is why he could not tolerate a model.

"Our truest life is when we are in dreams awake," says Thoreau. We all know that from experience. "I'm dreaming. No, I'm not. I'm awake, it's really so!" Who hasn't said that at a moment of overpowering joy? "O brave new world," cries Miranda in *The Tempest*. And fourfold vision might be defined as the way the world would look if the state could be maintained of a man who has just fallen in love at first sight and found his love requited.

> And we are put on earth a little space,
> That we may learn to bear the beams of love,

says one of the *Songs of Innocence*.

Tolstoy has a memorable description of a man in this state. The world is touched with a celestial light. Pigeons flying from a roof, children playing in the street, even loaves of bread in a bake-shop window seem things not of this earth. He has to restrain himself from embracing everyone he meets. Everything is so beautiful that he laughs and cries for joy. "The heart at the center of the universe," says Emerson, "with every throb hurls the flood of happiness into every artery, vein and veinlet, so that the whole system is inundated with tides of joy. The plenty of the poorest place is too great; the harvest cannot be gathered. Every sound ends in music. The edge of every surface is tinged with prismatic rays."

But what even such seers as Emerson and Tolstoy perceive as light and ecstasy Blake in his supreme moments sees face to face. The bodily eye in evolving must have sensed light and color long before it saw the forms of objects and composed them into a world beyond itself. Vision, which is simply spiritual sensation, must pass through the same evolutionary stages. This explains Blake's at first perplexing quatrain:

> God Appears and God is Light
> To those poor Souls who dwell in Night,
> But does a Human Form Display
> To those who Dwell in Realms of day.

The world of single vision, of Error, or Creation, Blake declares, is "Burnt up the Moment Men cease to behold it." "I assert for My Self," he goes on,

that I do not behold the outward Creation and that to me it is hindrance and not Action . . . "What," it will be Question'd, "When the Sun rises, do you not see a round disk of fire somewhat like a Guinea?" O no, no, I see an Innumerable company of the Heavenly host crying, 'Holy, Holy, Holy is the Lord God Almighty.' I question not my Corporeal or Vegetative Eye any more than I would Question a Window concerning a Sight. I look thro' it and not with it.

Or, to think of it in more everyday terms, where is the darkness when the light comes?

Note that Blake, like Jesus, uses the image of the spiritual sword:

> Bring me my Bow of burning gold:
> Bring me my Arrows of desire:
> Bring me my Spear: O clouds unfold!
> Bring me my Chariot of fire.
> I will not cease from Mental Fight,
> Nor shall my Sword sleep in my hand
> Till we have built Jerusalem
> In England's green and pleasant Land.

Jerusalem means the City of Perfect Liberty. In other words, it is not just individual, but social ecstasy and vision that Blake seeks. Put more men, more often, into a more elevated state of imagination, and everything else follows.

> I give you the end of a golden string,
>   Only wind it into a ball,
> It will lead you in at Heaven's gate
>   Built in Jerusalem's wall.

That is Blake's faith. Our forefathers believed in individual salvation. We believe in social salvation. Either without the other is futile, Blake believes. Indeed "society" and "the individual" are simply two more of those abstractions of the Reason that he abhorred. Like Heaven and Hell they must be "married" before there can be creation. Social changes founded on anything else are sterile—or rather they are pure illusion. They undo themselves. What goes out the door comes in the window. Out go the capitalists, for example, and in come the bureaucrats. "Revolutions," says Bernard Shaw, "have never lightened the burden of tyranny: they have only shifted it to another shoulder." But not so with imaginative change. Why? Because Vision uncreates evil by forgiveness. This is the theme of Blake's last great poem, *Jerusalem*.

Dive down into your experience and I am sure you can bring up an incident to make this clear. Once upon a time something happened that brought you unadulterated joy. At almost the same time you chanced to be the victim of some unjust act or unprovoked attack. At an ordinary moment you would have retaliated hotly. But you were so happy you found it beyond your power to work up the wrath that all common morality called for. Blake is right. Imagination uncreates not only anger, but all the other seven deadly sins. A little of it mitigates evil. A little more forgives it. A little more yet forgets it. And still more uncreates it.

I use the word "uncreate" because "forgive" and "forget" are not strong enough terms. Imagination is Dante's River of Lethe in Purgatory. It can literally obliterate. Imagination can not only cause that-which-was-not, to be; it can cause that-which-was, not to be. It is this double power to annihilate and to create that makes imagination the sole instrument of genuine and lasting, in contrast with illusory and temporary, social change.

This is the clue to Blake's tremendous emphasis on art. (The word "art" has been so perverted by aesthetes that one almost hesitates to use it.) For art is the language of the imagination, the means by which the divine in man communicates with the divine in man, the coin that enables us to exchange LIFE, just as money enables us to exchange the goods of this world. And art, unless it is backed by celestial gold or celestial goods, is as valueless as the greenbacks of a bankrupt nation. Art is useless except for what it will buy. And what it will buy is Heaven. No man ever valued art less as an end in itself than Blake. No man ever valued it more as a means. "A Poet, a Painter, a Musician, an Architect," he declared: "the Man Or Woman who is not one of these is not a Christian." No remotest reference in that to professional or recognized artists or to anything the humblest person may not be, as is shown when he says, "The Poetic Genius is the True Man"; "Jesus and his Apostles and Disciples were all Artists." Everything Blake says of art is in the superlative degree: "You must leave Fathers and Mothers and Houses and Lands if they stand in the way of Art." "Art is the Tree of Life." "The Whole Business of Man Is The Arts." The business of redeemed

man, he means, just as the whole business of fallen
man is empire and war. "Empire against Art." Into
those three words Blake condenses his social and
political philosophy. Force cannot be overcome by
reason. Force can be overcome only by a higher
order of force. Imagination is that force. And
Blake believed from the bottom of his heart that if
a nation of warriors were confronted by a nation of
imaginative men the weapons of the former would
fall unlifted from their hands.

I believe William Blake was one of the wisest
men who ever lived. I believe in him for what he
thought, for what he saw, for what he wrote and
designed, and for what he was. But I believe in him
also because of the other men who confirm him.
When the greatest of the ages agree, if their agreement is not the truth, what is the truth? Take Dante,
for instance. When he exchanges Virgil for Beatrice
as guide he is dismissing Reason in favor of Imagination. His Paradise is simply Blake's fourfold vision
expressed with a sustained perfection to which
Blake could not pretend. Or Shakespeare. He went
through a longer period of rebellion and tragedy
than Blake. He, too, in his Hamlet stage, found life
"sicklied o'er with the pale cast of thought," but he
emerged in the end with an identical doctrine in
King Lear and *The Tempest*. In *The Tempest*, as I
read it, Prospero is the intellect, or reason, and
Ariel is the imagination. While Ariel is the slave of
Prospero, we have material wonders: the raising
and stilling of tempests, magic banquets, weapons
arrested in the air by unseen hands. But when Ariel

is set free and Prospero becomes *his* servant, the spiritual miracles of forgiveness and reconciliation begin.

And like Shakespeare before Blake, so Dostoevsky after him. I wish I could read you Dostoevsky's story of threefold and fourfold vision, "The Dream of a Ridiculous Man." What a story! Quite without any explanation of the context, listen to just these sentences at the end. You will catch the connection:

I will not and cannot believe that evil is the normal condition of mankind. And it is just this faith of mine that they laugh at. But how can I help believing it? I have seen the truth—it is not as though I had invented it with my mind, I have seen it, seen it, and *the living image* of it has filled my soul forever . . . though I cannot describe what I saw. But the scoffers do not understand that. It was a dream, they say, delirium, hallucination. . . . And is not our life a dream? I will say more. Suppose that this paradise will never come to pass (that I understand), yet I shall go on preaching it. And yet how simple it is; in one day, *in one hour* everything could be arranged at once! The chief thing is to love others like yourself, that's the great thing, and that's everything. . . . And yet it's an old truth which has been told and retold a billion times—but it has not formed part of our lives! [They say that] the consciousness of life is higher than life, the knowledge of the laws of happiness higher than happiness—that is what one must contend against.

How fortunate that we don't have to choose among the geniuses, that we can have them all. But if I *had* to choose there is another man whom I might be found preferring to Dante, and Shakespeare, and Dostoevsky, and Blake himself. He was

like Blake in being a sort of devil-angel. He had *his*
terrible rebellion. He too married Heaven and Hell.
He too ascended a Jacob's Ladder to fourfold vision.
The parallelism is astounding. Only his vision consisted less of images of eternity than of echoes.
Beethoven. Blake and Beethoven: the man who
could see, and the man who could hear. They both
died in 1827. What a year for Heaven!

Alan Watts. *Tao*

Alan Watts needs no introduction. As for the
Tao, who would name the unnameable? Nothing
to do but catch the mood of it . . . tone of the
voice . . . gleam in the eye. There is the philosophy which is words-in-a-book, words-in-the
head. And there is the philosophy whose word *we*
are every moment in every movement: the nervous giveaway twitch, the worried metabolism,
the smile and scowl in spite of ourselves, the
noble act, the compassionate gesture.

While you read these words, in a hundred
grubby, guilty corners of the world, good men
and women go down to death before murderers'
guns . . . children turn grey as ashes with
despair . . . the earth bleeds. Not much of this
evil happens at the hands of evil people—not
really—the villains among us are astonishingly
few. But there are so many who join in and go
along, having axes to grind, worlds to conquer,

From the *Alan Watts Journal*, August 1970 issue.

money to earn, planes to catch, bills to pay, history to make, duties to do, glories to win, fortunes to build, revolutions to achieve, advantages to reap, justice to establish, somewhere to get, much to do. At all costs, at any price, looking neither right nor left, and though the heavens fall.

Then what to do? What to do? For of course something *must* be done. Ah, but what if . . . what if all the endless *doing* is finally itself the problem. . . ?

So

    the Old Boy took to the woods
                        to do plenty of

                                  nothing

nothing nothing nothing at all
except
to grow ripe like the apples
wise like the trees
        knowing: rain drops are worth
                    more than money

nowhere to get
        nothing to do
                be still
and don't scare off the birds

home again

THE RED CHINESE characters which I have written on this page are the opening words of the Old Boy's Book of *The Way and its Power*, otherwise known as Lao-tzu's *Tao Te Ching*. I do not write Chinese very well; an oriental person looking at my writing knows at once that it was done by a Westerner.

非常道

道可道

Still, they sometimes say that my brushwork is pretty good (for a Westerner), and the young Japanese who are now using ball-point pens instead of brushes say I do it extraordinarily well. But they are a very polite people, and though I have played with the writing-brush for many years I am well aware that my technique is nowhere near that of the great masters.

Nevertheless, I have always been in love with Chinese writing. Each character, or ideogram, is an abstract picture of some feature of the process of nature—that is, of the Tao, the Way or Course of the universe. When translated very literally into English, Chinese reads like a telegram. "*Tao* can *tao* not eternal *Tao*," or "Way can speak-about not eternal Way." In contrast with English, and particularly German or Japanese, Chinese is the fastest and shortest way of saying things, both in speech and writing. If, as seems possible, Mao-tse Tung's people shift to an alphabetic form of writing, they will be at a great disadvantage, for, as their own proverb says, "one picture is worth a thousand words."

The very mechanics of writing Chinese is an aesthetic delight. It requires a pointed brush with a bamboo handle, the hairs of the brush being lightly impregnated with glue, and brushes come in a delicious variety of sizes and designs—from tiny twigs for writing characters like the footprints of spiders to immense three-inch wide swabbers for making posters. The ink comes in hard flattened sticks made, essentially, of carbon, glue, and perfume, and is embossed with dragons in the clouds or bamboos by the water, or with its brand name in gold characters. A fine old stick of Chinese or Korean ink may fetch as much as $500 on the Japanese market, and I am speaking of a small black object never much more than 6″ x 2″ x 1″. Why? Because of the aesthetic and meditative pleasure of rubbing a fine ink into liquid form upon an ink-stone, which is usually a black rectangular block with rounded corners like a small swimming-pool, with a short deep end and a long shallow end. Water is poured upon the stone, and the ink-stick is then rubbed gently and lovingly upon the shallow end until the mixture has just the right viscosity and color, for, under reflected light, the black pigment has to look blue, and the ink-stick has to slide through the water with a certain amiable greasiness. The rubbing takes at least fifteen minutes, and, with the perfume of sandalwood or aloeswood, an artist or calligrapher gets himself in the proper frame of mind to begin his work. Rubbing ink is a form of *za-zen* or Zen Buddhist meditation in which verbal and conceptual thinking is temporarily suspended. Inferior artists make their apprentices rub the ink. Truly vulgar and depraved artists use bottled ink.

There is a street in Kyoto named Tera-machi (i.e., Temple Street) where, from very small shops, one may buy implements for the tea-ceremony, ancient pottery, rosaries, mushrooms, second-hand books, and the most excellent tea in the world. There is also a British-style pub. But the largest shop on the street sells writing-brushes, ink, fine paper, and incense. It is one of my paradises, and whenever I get to Kyoto I go there immediately to buy aloes-wood (which has, as Dr. Suzuki told me, the essential smell of Buddhism), ink, and writing-brushes. I just can't resist them. Last time I found a small stick of vermillion ink covered with gold leaf. It should be rubbed on a window-sill, early in the morning, using a drop of dew for the water.

It is said to be "difficult" to master the art of Chinese writing, but this means only that the art must grow on you over many years. We use the word "difficult" for tasks which require extreme force or effort, and over which we must perspire, grunt, and groan. But the difficulty of writing Chinese with the brush is to make the brush write by itself, and the Taoists call this the art of *wu-wei*—which may be translated variously as "easy does it," "roll with the punch," "go with the stream," "don't force it," or, more literally, "not pushing." I suppose the Taoist way of life is the polar opposite of Billy Graham's muscular Christianity. *Wu-wei* is the understanding that energy is gravity, and thus that brush-writing, or dancing, or judo, or sailing, or pottery, or even sculpture is following patterns in the flow of liquid. Lao-tzu was perhaps the contemporary of that marvellous and neglected Greek philosopher, Heracleitus, and both taught exactly the same principles. *Panta rhei*—everything flows, and therefore the understanding of water is the understanding of life. Fire is water falling upwards. That is why I have written Lao-tzu's words in the color of flame.

Thus—another advantage of Chinese is that, although brief in form, it can say so many things at once. There must be at least eighty English translations of his book. All differ, and most are to some extent correct. Let us compare differing versions of these six first words:

The Way that can be described is not the eternal Way.

The Course that can be discoursed is not the eternal Course.

The Way that can be weighed is not the regular Way.

The Flow that can be followed is not the real Flow.

Energy which is energetic is not true energy.

Force forced isn't force.

The fourth and fifth characters appear, surprisingly, on planes and trains in the Far-East followed by a character which is simply a square, signifying "mouth" or "door." The three put together mean "Emergency exit." Thus:

The Go that can be gone is an emergency Go.

Most scholars translate the second use of the ideogram *tao* as "to speak about," although Duyvendak has argued that this is a late meaning of the word. But in my own feeling this kind of laconic and aphoristic Chinese is best translated by giving, in parallel, many of the different ways in which it may be understood: for it means all of them. Linear languages like English, German, and Sanskrit have to stretch out Chinese indefinitely. It has thus more or less come to the point where we have simply adopted the word *tao* into English (like karma and curry) and those who call it "tay-o" should realize that in Peking it is called "dow," in Canton "toe," and in Tokyo "daw," and of course Tokyo itself is something like "Tawkyaw."

Tao (which we shall therefore no longer print in different type as a foreign word) signifies the energy of the universe as a way, current, course, or flow which is at once intelligent and spontaneous, but not personal like a Western god. It would be absurd to worship or pray to the Tao because it's your own true self, the very energy and patterning of your bones, muscles, and nerves. Lao-tzu's first statement about it is that it cannot be defined—for the simple reason that you cannot make what is basically you and basically real an *object* of knowledge. You cannot stand aside from it and examine it as something out there. Although, then, we cannot define it, we must not assume that it is something bleary like the "blind energy" of 19th-century scientists. From our own points of view our heads themselves are blind-spots, but were it otherwise we should be looking only at neurons and dendrites and would never see mountains and trees. (But, of course, when neurons and dendrites are *seen from the inside* they become mountains and trees.)

Yet although Tao cannot be examined and pinned down it has a characteristic atmosphere which may be sensed in the life-styles of various Far-Eastern poets, artists, and sages, and which is indicated by the term *feng-liu* in Chinese and *furyu* in Japanese, and which means something like flowing with or following with the wind. It is also translated as elegance, which is not quite right, because in English an elegant person is refined and fussy, and perpetrates an atmosphere of haughty disdain— whereas the Chinese poet is sometimes amiably drunken, wandering aimlessly in the mountains, and laughing at falling leaves. One gathers that this sort of person is no longer allowed in China. But he is typified by Pu-tai, the fat, laughing, tramp-buddha who carries a gnarled staff and a huge bag of interesting rubbish which he gives away to children.

Poets like Su Tungp'o and Tu Fu were a little more on the side of elegance as we think of it, for they relished drinking fine tea on lazy afternoons, tea made with the best of clear waters from springs and wells, boiled over carefully chosen wood, and served in porcelain or in ceramic bowls with a glaze like jade. On the other hand, a young American Buddhist sought out an extremely holy and magical hermit in the mountains of Japan and, after finding him with extreme difficulty, was served hot water without tea. He had the sense to appreciate the high compliment which he had been offered. Frederic Spiegelberg, philosopher and orientalist, visited a Taoist hermit like Pu-tai on an island near Hong-kong. When he was introduced as an Ameri-

can university professor travelling under a Rocke-
feller grant to find out whether Asian spirituality
was still vital, the hermit began to chuckle very
gently, and this gradually developed into up-
roarious laughter at which his whole glutinous
mass shook like jelly. That was the end of the inter-
view.

A more ancient Taoist sage, whose name I forget,
was approached by the Chinese Emperor to be an
advisor to the government. He declined the offer

with extreme courtesy, but when the emissary had departed he washed out his ears—and also those of the donkey on which he customarily rode. There was also a Chinese Zen priest famed as a great painter, but who, unlike other priests, grew his hair long. After getting sufficiently drunk, he would dip his hair into a bowl of ink and then slosh it over a scroll of paper. The next day he would give himself a Rorschach Test on the splosh and see in it images of mountains, rivers, and forests which needed only a few touches of the brush to bring them out for all to see. When I was invited to the tea-ceremony by the artist and print-maker Saburo Hasegawa he pointed out the subtle beauty of cigarette-ash on a tile made by J. B. Blunk, which we were using for an ash-tray.

These are vignettes to give some suggestion of the atmosphere of flowing with the Tao. The principle of the thing is also recognized by our own surf-riders, some of whom know very well that their sport is a form of yoga or Taoist meditation in which the whole art is to generate immense energy from going with your environment, from the principle of *wu-wei*, or following the gravity of water and so making yourself one with it. For, as Lao-tzu himself said, "Gravity is the root of lightness."

Kathleen Raine. "The World"

It burns in the void,
Nothing upholds it.
Still it travels.

Travelling the void
Upheld by burning
Nothing is still.

Burning it travels.
The void upholds it.
Still it is nothing.

Nothing it travels
A burning void
Upheld by stillness.

From *Collected Poems* (London: Hamish Hamilton, 1956). Copyright © 1956, 1968 by Kathleen Raine. Reprinted by permission of the publisher.

Theodore Roszak. "Loyalty"

As bird
is no citizen of less than Wholeheaven,
nor fish
of less sea than Allocean,
swear no allegiance
to less than Mosthuman
meaning Muchloving
meaning Morepraising

Members all things one of another
so we of the beasts
and the beasts of the grass
and the grass of the earth
and the earth of the seas
and the seas of the rains
and the rains of the skies
and the skies of the spheres
without number or name
whose music (but listen!)
is the lovesong of God
for his creatures

Know no lesser anthem

And by it be known
as Woman by Man
in the innocent garden.
Be female-known, be seized, be possessed

There is no truth but makes increase of loyalty
nor true loyalty
but it ravish the heart

Instead of a Bibliography . . .
a Survival Kit.

I had planned to attach a bibliography to this reader. But that quickly proved impossible. In short order I had hundreds of titles and no way to draw the line between what got listed and what didn't. How do you make an exhaustive bibliography of the perennial wisdom? So I will leave it at this: an unapologetically personal selection—for whatever it may be worth to anyone else. Just to mention the twentieth-century figures that come first to mind as the sources that have meant the most in my education. For politics and economics: Tolstoy, Gandhi, Kropotkin, A. J. Muste, Paul Goodman, E. F. Schumacher, Danilo Dolci, Ronald V. Sampson. For the reexamination of science: Michael Polanyi, Lancelot Law Whyte, Owen Barfield, Charles Davy, Catherine Roberts, Theodor Schwenk, Seyyed Hossein Nasr. For a sense of the alternative realities: Bergson, Jung, Black Elk, Frank Waters's *Book of the Hopi*, Mircea Eliade, Lama Govinda, Idreis Shah, Alan Watts, Gary Snyder, Norman O. Brown. For things in general: Yeats, Joyce, AE, Johan Huizinga, Hermann Hesse, e.e. cummings, Martin Buber, Thomas Merton, the editor of *MANAS*, Antoine de Saint-Exupéry, and—especially—Lewis Mumford.

But another and more important reason for not

bothering to list the books: I suspect that many of those who trouble to sample the readings here—especially the younger readers—are in a life situation where bookishness is not what they most need to cultivate. Happily, we are (at least at the fringes of our society) getting away from the curse of being an inert and disembodied brain-culture where book-learning and facile articulation matter most. The proper vocabulary of values is action. The choice is not between "knowing the good" and "living the good"—a disastrous dichotomy; rather, one must live what one values, or one does not really know the values at all.

What many people now seek is a living, work-aday alternative to the wasteland, which means, if they haven't done so already, they need to join hands with others who are exploring the new ground. There are doors that lead out of this culture and into the next, though there are not always neon lights to point the way. In an appendix to the *revised edition* (1968) of *Toward a Psychology of Being*, Abraham Maslow collected all the good things he knew about into a "eupsychian network": the groups, publications, schools, experiments that were in touch with healthy possibilities. What follows is much the same kind of thing. But one should consult Maslow's listing too.

Needless to say, what I give here is hardly exhaustive. There is, in any case, a limit to what a book can do to help. By the time this reaches print, some of what I list here may have vanished, merged, absconded, or been transmuted. But there is really no need to be exhaustive in such matters. A network is a complex of interacting forces. Begin closest to home and follow the threads. One thing leads to another, and in time one finds one's own best medicine. This listing includes a scattering of European items for those who get around.

A number of people helped in assembling this part of the book. Thanks especially to James Hartz, Cynthia Merman, Pamela Portugal, Mihaly Czichszentmihaly, Lee and Carol Swenson, Gar Alperowitz, and the people at *Mother Earth News*.

1. *The Eupsychian Network.*

The "growth centers" started with the by-now much-publicized Esalen Institute at Big Sur, California. Esalen still offers the most innovative programs in affective education. For its brochure, write to 1776 Union St., San Franciso 94123. Reading the menu alone can be illuminating. Esalen also works with the San Francisco Zen Center; for the catalogue of their joint activities, write Box 31389, San Francisco 94131.

The Association for Humanistic Psychology (584 Page St., San Francisco 94117) issues a (non-endorsed) listing of growth centers throughout the US: e.g., Anthos in New York, Oasis in Chicago, Kairos and the Center for the Study of the Person in southern California, the Gestalt Therapy Institutes, and about eight dozen more. The Association also publishes the *Journal of Humanistic Psychology* and listings of growth centers abroad.

The National Training Laboratory (1201 16th St., N.W., Washington, D.C. 20036) is an important source of information on affective education.

Other groups I have come across: The Psychosynthesis Research Foundation, Room 314, 527 Lexington Ave., New York 10017; The Interscience Workshop (Reichian bioenergetics) Box 3218, Santa Monica, California 90403; The Institute of Bioenergetic Analysis (directors Alexander Lowen and John Pierrakos) 71 Park Ave., New York 10016. Alan Watts is director of The Society for Comparative Philosophy (Box 857, Sausalito, California 94965). Its monthly bulletin lists the many intriguing centers where Watts lectures: e.g., The Institute for Pleasure, Mann Ranch Community, Druid Heights Meditation Hermitage, etc.

Publications in the network include *The Journal of Transpersonal Psychology* (2637 Marshall Drive, Palo Alto, California 94303); *Bulletin of Structural Integration,* which features Ida Rolf's work (1334 23rd St., Santa Monica, California 90404); *Energy and Character,* the journal of bioenergetic research (Abbotsbury, Dorset, England).

Still the best introduction to Gestalt theory and practice: Frederick Perls, Paul Goodman, Ralph Hefferline, *Gestalt Therapy,* available in a Dell paperback. Also Perls's two recent books *Gestalt Therapy Verbatim* and *In and Out of the Garbage Can,* both from Real People Press and available through Esalen.

2. Rap Centers.

Rap Centers are grass-roots, do-it-yourself, group therapy, usually with a strong tendency toward communitarianism and political action. They provide a chance to talk it out and get it together with a minimum of professional intervention—or none at all. In particular, rap sessions have been of critical importance to the women's liberation movement as a method of consciousness-raising.

Number Nine (266 State St., New Haven, Connecticut 06511) is a good example of a well-developed Rap Center. It deals mainly with counter-culture casualties, has set up an alternative high school, and maintains a creative arts program. See the report in *The Radical Therapist* (see below: "Counter Institutions") Dec.–Jan. 1971, which presents a helpful model for organizing one's own center.

There is also the RaP Center connected with the Berkeley Free Clinic (1814 Haste St., Berekely, California).

The Radical Therapist has just assembled a directory of Rap Centers and therapeutic communes.

3. Communes: Guides and Handbooks.

Most communitarian groups are either too informal or too interested in privacy to be identified and located, which is all to the good. Nobody wants to live in a showcase, or to have his home marked out as a crash-pad for every needy or curious party passing through. On the other hand, some communities are willing to teach by example, offer help and advice, and reach out toward building a larger commonwealth. The Alternatives Foundation (P.O. Drawer A, Diamond Heights Station, San Francisco 94131) and the bimonthly journal *The Modern Utopian* (2441 LeConte Ave., Berkeley 94709) are important joint clearinghouses for American communitarian news and listings. Alternatives has done a "Commune Directory," available for $2.00, along with several other publications and newsletters.

The Questers Project (68801 D Street, Cathedral City, California 92234) has published Paul Marks's excellent handbook *A New Community: Format for Health, Contentment, Security,* which surveys a number of U.S. communes. The book includes much practical discussion of communes, plus a well-researched plan for financing and organizing communes along the lines of the Hunza villages of India. Cost: $4.00—worth the price and worth your attention. Questers also publishes a newsletter on their activities.

Community Fellowship has published *An Intentional Community Handbook* which includes a listing of and some reports on communes. Order from Box 243, Yellow Springs, Ohio 45387.

The Carleton Collective Communities Clearinghouse (Carleton College, Northfield, Minnesota) publishes a listing of communes which is available for $1.

For Europe, see the *Directory of Communes and Crash-Pads* available from the Commune Movement, 141 Westbourne Park Road, London W. 11. I am told the listing will be up-dated from time to time. It also contains a communitarian bibliography and a list of mystic-esoteric centers in Europe.

Two ways to link up with other communitarians: check the letters in the "Contact" section of *Mother Earth News* (see below: "Do It Yourself"); or write to the *People Directory*, published by the Alternatives Foundation (see above).

Also see *Finding Community: A Guide to Community Research and Action* by W. Ron Jones, Julia Cheever, and Jerry Ficklin (James E. Freel, publisher, 577 College Ave., Palo Alto, Calif. 94306) for advice about food, credit, welfare, health care, cops, etc.

4. Communes: Resource Groups and Publications.

Among the older communitarian stalwarts: School of Living (Lane's End Homestead, Brookville, Ohio 45309). The School is run by Mildred Loomis and has been a major center for propagating the back-to the-land philosophy of Ralph Borsodi (*This Ugly Civilization, Flight from the City;* Harper Colophon Books, 1972; etc.). The School publishes a newspaper, *The Green Revolution,* dealing with organic homesteading and self-help. Order from Heathcote Road, Freeland, Maryland 21053.

And then there is the well-seasoned communitarian workhorse, Community Service Inc. (Box 243, Yellow Springs, Ohio 45387), which has grown up around Arthur Morgan, former chairman of TVA and one of America's outstanding decentralist theorists. His books are basic reading for communitarians: *The Small Community* (Harper, 1942), *Nowhere Was Somewhere* (Chapel Hill, 1946), *The Community of the Future* (Community Service, 1957), etc. The Service puts out a good deal of extremely useful literature. See especially Morgan's *Industries for Small Communities* and *A Business of My Own*. The Service has offered support and advice to many small groups over the years, including American Indian and Third World efforts. It publishes a monthly journal, *Community Comments*.

The Cooperative League of the U.S.A. (59 E. VanBuren St., Chicago 60605) is the best source on the varieties of cooperation. Why don't we have more co-ops in America, especially in ghetto communities?

The Homer L. Morris Fund (Pendle Hill, Wallingford, Pennsylvania) specializes in short-term loans for operations—like communitarian businesses—which can find no orthodox financing.

Two successful communitarian efforts that are based on religious principles are the Society of Brothers (the Bruderhof movement) of Woodcrest, Rifton, New York, which survives by toymaking and farming; and Koinonia Farm (Route 2, Americus, Georgia 31709) which makes and mails the world's greatest Christmas fruit-cakes. Their experience, like that of the phenomenally successful Hutterites, is well worth examining.

Some useful periodicals: *The Modern Utopian* (as above); *Alternate Society* (published by the North Star Tribe, 10 Thomas St., St. Catherine's, Ontario, Canada); *Harrad,* on new life-styles (Box 841, Boston 02103); *Communes* covers the English and European scene (141 Westbourne Park Road, London W. 11); *Equality,* also for Europe (6 Frankfort Am Main, Postfach 3413, West Germany); *Cormallen,* on Dutch and continental communes, is an English language bimonthly (Postbus 10065, Amsterdam, Holland); for the French communities of work, see *Communauté Autogestion* (78 rue de Temple, Paris 3e, France); also *Communautés* (8 Allee Roland-Garros, 94 Orly, France).

Alternate Society (see above) is currently organizing a Community Settlement Service Land Inventory. The purpose is to locate promising sites for new communes.

The New England People's Coop (Route 123A, Alstead, New Hampshire 03602) helps communes to purchase tools, organic foods, books, etc. It has eight distribution centers and plans to become a producers' coop.

Among the many books worth looking at for practical advice: Clair Huchet Bishop's *All Things Common* (Harper, 1950) surveys the beginings of the French communities of work; Folkert Wilken's *The Liberation of Work* (London: Routledge, 1969) studies several experiments in producers' cooperatives; Darin Drabkin's *The Other Society* (London: Gollancz, 1962) is about the Israeli kibbutzim; Scott and Helen Nearing, *Living the Good Life*

(Schocken, 1970); Raymond Mungo, *Total Loss Farm: A Year in the Life* (Dutton, 1970).

The Multilateral Relations Study Group is (despite the title) a non-academic effort to collect reliable information from people experienced in group marriage. The approach is honest and intelligently helpful. If you want to assist with the survey, contact Joan and Larry Constantine, 23 Mohegan Road, Acton, Maryland 01720.

5. *Do-It-Yourself and Organic Homesteading.*

The Whole Earth Catalog (558 Santa Cruz Ave., Menlo Park, California 94021) is the do it yourself classic of our times; the Sears Catalog for practical drop-outs. The Catalog has ceased publication, but the back copies will continue to be useful for some years. Perhaps the Catalog's publishers, The Portola Institute (1115 Merrill St., Menlo Park, California 94025) will find other equally opportune things to do.

The Catalog leaves in its wake a Truck Store in Menlo Park and the Whole Earth Access Co., 2466 Shattuck Ave., Berkeley, California. Also a Canadian extension, *The Whole Earth Almanac* (Room 28, 341 Floor St., West, Toronto 181, Ontario).

The Mother Earth News (Box 38, Madison, Ohio 44057) picks up where the Catalog left off: organic homesteading, chicken farming, dressing rabbits, tools, handy hints, homey philosophy, survival on the land, etc. Like the Catalog, *Mother Earth News* is apt to become one of the important publications of the decade: a healthy sign of the times. *Mother Earth News* covers much of the ground this survival kit covers, but more fully and keeps its resources up to date. No college library should be without it. Six times yearly: $1 per issue. *Mother* is now planning a rural research center and is producing radio commentaries for local stations.

The Wood Heat Quarterly describes itself as "the quality guide to quality living." "Through the magnifying glass of love, *Wood Heat Quarterly* focuses on the practical arts of self-sufficient living . . . for the transcendental revolution of true living." Home building, organic growing, "working as worship," etc. Lowther Press, RD #1, Bristol, Vermont 05443.

On how to rig up your own dome and associated practicalities of life: The Lama Foundation (Box 444, San Cristobal, New Mexico 87564) issues Steve Baer's *Dome Cookbook* (price $1) and Pacific Domes (Box 1692, Los Gatos, California 95030) has published *Domebook One* (price $3): step-by-step instructions for dome building in several materials. A *Domebook Two* is scheduled to appear in 1971.

Ken Kern's *The Owner-Built Home* covers every aspect of home building and is something of a classic in the craft. Order from Kern: Sierra Route, Oakhurst, California 93644. Four volumes: $10.

Even the government can sometimes be helpful. The Engineering Experiment Station, Stillwater, Oklahoma 74074, issues the publication "How to

Build Your Own Home of Earth" (1943) and other
things on earth building blocks. The Department of
Agriculture issues "Building With Adobe and
Stabilized Earth Blocks" (Leaflet No. 535, Decem-
ber, 1965) and assorted items on adobe architecture;
also lots of pamphlets on farming.

On organic husbandry: the Rodale Press issue
several publications (including *Organic Gardening
and Farming*) from 33 E. Minor St., Emmaus, Pennsylvania 18049. *Organic Gardening* features a
"Farm Market" which lists homesteads for lease or
sale. Rodale compiled *The Encyclopedia of Organic
Gardening* (1145 pp. for $9.95). Another source:
The Biochemical Research Laboratory at Threefold
Farm, Spring Valley, New York 10977.

Biodynamics, the journal of the Biodynamic
Farming and Gardening Association, can be ordered
from RD #1, Stroudsburg, Pennsylvania 18360. A
long-established source of information on organics
is the Soil Association (Walnut Tree Manor, Haugh-
ley, Stowmarket, Sussex, England) which also
publishes a journal.

Juliette de Baïracli Levy's *Herbal Handbook*
(London: Faber & Faber) is a guide to the wilds
by an authentic gypsy. (Faber & Faber, 3 Queen
Square, London W.C. 1, puts out a large number of
well-selected books on wholefoods, nutrition, vege-
tarianism, etc. Send for their list.)

Mother Earth News keeps track of books on free-
for-the-eating wild foods and the ancient art of
foraging: e.g., things like Euell Gibbons's *Stalking
the Wild Asparagus.*

The Mildred Hatch Free Loan Library (8 Pine Street, St. Johnsbury, Vermont 05819) loans books on nutrition and health through the mail. Write for the catalog.

Natural Food Styles (Box 96, Woodstock, New York 12498) is a "hip natural food publication" emphasizing "survival information and macrobiotic recipes." Also *The Organic Morning Glory Message* (monthly from 71 Delmar Street, San Francisco, California 94117).

The Intermediate Technology Development Group Ltd. (9 King St., London W.C. 2) whose directors include E. F. Schumacher, gives shrewd advice on community scale economics and technology. Just ask. And write for a listing of its literature.

Teach Yourself Books (St. Paul's House, Warwick Lane, London E.C. 4) publishes useful do-it-yourself manuals for every practical craft: carpentry, brick-laying, household electrical installation, baking, house painting, etc., etc. There must be a similar series in the U.S., but I have not come across it.

Antaeus Books (Box 153, Granville, Massachusetts 01034) specializes in books on farming, gardening, nutrition, ecology, etc. Send for their list of new and out-of-print publications.

Joan Ranson Shortney's *How To Live on Nothing* (Pocket Books, 1968) is a basic guide to cheap living: handy hints and basic good sense.

For back-packing and getting around the wilderness, there is Colin Fletcher's *The Complete*

Walker (Knopf, 1968). And for those who really get stuck in the woods, there is Juliette de Baïracli Levy's *Natural Rearing of Children* (London: Faber, 1970) which will tell you how to make elder blossom pudding and how to drive away nightmares with sprigs of rosemary and sweet basil.

Alicia Bay Laurel's *Living on the Earth* (Vintage, 1971)—"celebrations, storm warnings, formulas, recipes, rumors and country dances"—is a long love lyric dedicated to voluntary primitivism as practiced at the Wheeler Ranch, and includes lots of survivalist good sense: sewing, composting, baking, building, childbirth, nature cures, soap-making, first aid, etc. Just lovely. (And hand-written, too.)

6. *Counter Institutions.*

Every profession has its dissenting faction these days—usually made up of younger near-drop-outs who have committed the heresy of taking their professional ethics to heart. The listing below is far from complete but will give some idea of how much is being done to create a new society within the shell of the old.

HEALTH SERVICES

The Health Policy Advisory Center (Health/PAC, 17 Murray St., New York 10007) has much to do with free clinics and principled medical practice. It publishes the monthly *Health/PAC Bulletin*. On free clinics, also see *The Free Clinic Journal* published by the Haight-Ashbury Medical Clinic,

San Francisco, which also issues *The Journal of Psychedelic Drugs*.

The Medical Committee for Human Rights (1951 Turk St., San Francisco 94115; also at 951 E. La-Fayette St., Detroit, Michigan) unites health workers concerned with community control of medicine. It publishes *The Body Politic*. There is also the Student Health Organization whose national headquarters is at 1613 E. 53rd St., Chicago, Illinois 60615. In New York City, the Health Revolutionary Unity Movement (HRUM) is an organization of black and Third World health workers.

PSYCHOTHERAPY

The Radical Therapist (P.O. Box 89, W. Somerville, Mass.) is indispensable for keeping up with the searching discussion of social responsibility in psychotherapy.

The Psychologists for a Democratic Society can be contacted at Box 427, Stuyvesant Station, New York 10009. In England, R. D. Laing's Philadelphia Association (1 Sherwood Court, London W.1) undertakes experiments in non-authoritarian therapy.

Dr. Thomas Szasz has organized the American Association for the Abolition of Involuntary Mental Hospitalization (116 Bradford Parkway, Syracuse, New York 13224) in order to combat the supposedly therapeutic incarceration of the supposedly mad by the supposedly sane—a practice that frequently masks simple injustice as psychiatry. Szasz is the leading crusader on this front; see his book *The Myth of Mental Illness* (Harper, 1961).

In London, the People Not Psychiatry group has organized a telephone network of "people offering themselves and their warmth as an alternative to treatment by straight psychiatry." Perhaps there are similar experiments in telephonic community in the US . . . possibly as an adjunct of a local Rap Center.

WELFARE AND SOCIAL SERVICES

Hotch-Pot, the National Journal for the Workers Movement in Human services (Box 2492, Cleveland, Ohio 44112) is an extremely valuable source of information on all aspects of counter institutions, but especially in health, law, and welfare rights.

The Social Welfare Workers Movement (1913 Pine St., Philadelphia, Pennsylvania 19103) aims at community control of welfare programs.

The National Welfare Rights Organization, with chapters in most cities, has its headquarters at 1419 H. St., N.W., Washington, D.C. 20005. Its journal is *The Welfare Fighter*.

HIGHER EDUCATION

This appendix could not even begin to survey the ferment on the campuses. Most schools are by now honey-combed with their own local dissenting groups, factions, and educational experiments. The New University Conference (622 W. Diversey, Room 403A, Chicago, Illinois 60614) is a good place to begin investigating the scene. Also, The Union for Experimenting Colleges and Universities (Antioch College, Yellow Springs, Ohio 45387). The

Radical Education Project (Box 561-A, Detroit, Michigan 48232) has a good selection of left-radical literature.

SCIENCE AND ENGINEERING

For a good survey of activity and a listing of contacts, see Martin Brown, ed., *The Social Responsibility of the Scientist* (New York, Free Press: 1971).

Science & Government Report (Box 21123, Washington, D.C. 20009) is a new journal offering sharp critical comment on the politics of the natural sciences. Expensive (24 issues per year for $25) but worth the price. It should be in every college library.

The leading national voice of dissenting natural scientists has long been the Society for Social Responsibility in Science (contact Franklin Miller, Jr., Kenyon College, Gambier, Ohio 43022). SSRS runs an occupations division for scientists with "job problems related to conscience"—meaning those who want to get out of bomb physics and such.

The Scientists and Engineers for Social and Political Action (SESPA) (Box 59, Arlington Heights, Massachusetts 02175) is just getting under way. Its journal is *Science for the People*.

SURVIVAL is an International organization of ethically concerned scientists. Information and its journal can be had from G. Edwards, 952 Portsmouth Ave., Kingston, Canada or contact W. Messing, Mathematics Dept., Princeton University.

The Scientists Institute for Public Information

(SIPI) is headquartered at Washington University
St. Louis, Missouri.

The Science Action Coordinating Committee
(SACC) started at the Massachusetts Institute of
Technology and has chapters around the country.

CONSUMERS AND BUSINESS

Ralph Nader and his raiders have now set up a
Clearinghouse for Professional Responsibility in
Washington, D.C. Its purpose is to encourage corporate and government technical personnel to volunteer information on how their employers bilk the
public.

The People's Coop Research Center at the University of Chicago tries to clarify obfuscating expertise for ordinary citizens and to make reliable
information available on important social issues.

The *Association Cooperative D'Economie Fa-
miliale* (ACEF) of Montreal approaches consumer
issues from a radical cooperators' angle. Contact
through Parallel Institute (see below: "City Planning").

CITY PLANNING

"Advocacy city planning" means planning *with*
people (not *for* them) and often *against* the urban
power structure. There are many such groups of
principled planners in our major cities. Urban
Planning Aid (407 Highland Ave., Somerville,
Massachusetts) is a good place to start asking for
information and basic reading.

People's Architecture (1940 Bonita Ave., Berkeley, California) works with communities at the logistics and politics of design and city planning. It has produced a wealth of bright ideas for the defense and reorganization of neighborhood life.

Richard Sennett's *The Uses of Disorder* (Vintage, 1971) is a good introduction to democratic neighborhood-building.

The Parallel Institute (C.P./P.O. Box 6, Station D, Montreal 104, Quebec) is seeking to build an autonomous, community-controlled economy in a blue-collar section of Montreal. The program is shrewd and ambitious: self-help, rehabilitation of old homes, producers' coops, a local housing corporation run by tenants. The approach could be used in a score of American cities.

RADICAL EXPERTISE

Most technical know-how winds up on the corporate-government payroll these days. But there are notable hold outs who stay independent and manage to combine radical social philosophy with sound expertise. The best known concentration of such talent is the Cambridge Institute (56 Boyleston St., Cambridge, Massachusetts 02138). An association of activists and intellectuals, it emphasizes studies and experiments in workers' control and community-based economics. Its publications and occasional papers are invaluable.

The Institute for Policy Studies (1520 New Hampshire Ave., N.W., Washington, D.C. 20036) offers critical examinations of public policy and major institions. Its publications are excellent.

The Center for Intercultural Development (Cuernavaca, Mexico) draws heavily on the ideas of Ivan Illich, a brilliant proponent of Third World development based on Third World (not Russian or American) priorities. His thought resembles that of Schumacher and the intermediate technologists: decentralism, village-based growth, community control, etc.

Counter institutions taper off into a twilight zone of secrecy and social sabotage. It is difficult to know how seriously to take the rumors. I hope there *isn't* an organization called "The Spreaders" working in university labs and government agencies to infiltrate the food supply with "pot high" fruits and vegetables—adulteration is adulteration. But I hope there really *is* a Society for the Abolition of Data Processing Machines boring from within IBM to drive the computers to distraction.

7. *The Law.*

The Center for Law and Education (38 Kirkland Avenue, Cambridge, Massachusetts 02138) offers every kind of legal back-up to libertarians who find themselves getting kicked out of school, hassled by the police, or suffering the administrative runaround. Especially helpful for information on law regarding schools and communes.

The American Civil Liberties Union (156 5th

Ave., New York 10010—but with many local branches) remains a reliable line of legal defense.

The National Lawyers Guild (5 Beekman St., New York 10038) is the dissenting fringe of the legal profession—important for radical legal talent.

Jean Strouse's *Up Against the Law: The Legal Rights of People Under 21* (Signet Books) is a basic guide for young people. Kathy Boudin's *Bust Book* (Grove Press) offers legal counsel from the hard-knocked victim's point of view.

Amnesty International (headquarters: Turnagain Lane, Farringdon St., London E.C. 4) is the best scheme so far for publicizing internationally the fate of political prisoners in all countries. There are over 800 Amnesty groups throughout the world, but very few in the U.S. There ought to be more.

8. *Drugs*.

Many cities now have a 24-hour underground switchboard network to provide aid and counsel regarding drugs (and numerous other subjects). Phone numbers can always be found in the local underground press.

The major experiment in addict self-help is, of course, Synanon, which has now grown into a veritable California institution rather lavishly head-quartered at Tomales Bay. Everybody I meet has a different opinion about Synanon, its leadership, and its highly-charged methods. (Lewis Yablonsky's *Synanon: The Tunnel Back* [Macmil-

lan] is a good study, but it dates from before 1965.)
The basic Synanon idea however—which is to have
addicts treated communally by former addicts—is
indisputably sound and has now traveled to the
Phoenix House Project. Phoenix House keeps about
fifteen centers in New York, plus a new adjunct in
London.

As long as drug use remains an illegal activity,
free clinics (or "freak clinics") like those in
Berkeley or San Francisco's Haight-Ashbury are going to be indispensable for treatment. Not only
because they are free of charge, but because they
put addicts in the hands of people they can trust.
(See *The Free Clinic Journal,* above: "Counter Institutions.")

The Do It Now Foundation (Box 3573, Holly-
wood, California 90028) is made up of "people who
think people from the street know more about the
street than the people who just drive by and look
at it." The emphasis is heavily on drug education,
mainly through the school system, and on rescuing
young casualties in general. (Also see Number
Nine in New Haven, above: "Rap Centers.")

John Dominick's *The Drug Bust* (The Light Company, French Road, Riverview, New York 12981)
tries "to reduce fear by providing information about
the operation of the narcotics agents, the police,
and the courts." Vic Pawlad's *Conscientious Guide
to Drug Abuse* (Mastodon Publishers, 4514 Fountain Ave., Los Angeles, California 90029) calls itself
a "crash program in drug survival."

9. Race and Poverty: Community Development.

The spectrum of action groups working for racial justice—from the Urban League to the Black Panthers and Young Lords—is too well-known to need mention here. What is perhaps more worth noting are the many local efforts to create CDCs: Community-based Development Corporations and Co-operatives. These experiments gain fewer headlines than talk of arming the ghetto, but they probably have more to do with achieving economic power for the poor—and with revolutionizing the surrounding society. I refer to efforts like FIGHT in Rochester New York (and its industrial adjunct Fight-On); Operation Bootstrap in Los Angeles (which manufactures Shindana Toys); Zion Non-profit in Philadelphia (a black investment group which distributes its capital among black-controlled shopping centers, factories, etc.); The Bedford-Stuyvesant Restoration Corporation in New York City; The Southwest Alabama Farmers Coop Association; The Home Education Livelihood Program Inc. in Albuquerque, New Mexico; etc.

Groups of this kind have formed a coalition called The National Economic Development Congress (c/o Center for Community Change, 1000 Wisconsin Ave., N.W., Washington, D.C.). Its purpose is to identify funding sources, to collect information, and to provide expert advice to new CDCs.

For a select list of CDCs, a good searching discussion of their experience and possibilities, and a
well-chosen bibliography, write to the Cambridge
Institute (see above: "Counter Institutions") for its
"Occasional Bulletin" No. 2, June 1970.

For information on all sorts of community-based
economics—including foreign models like the Israeli
kibbutz—write to: Librarian, Center for Community
Economic Development, c/o the Cambridge Institute.

Cesar Chavez's United Farm Workers Organizing Committee can be contacted at Box 130, Delano,
California.

The Indian Research & Development Association
(Box 4355, Ottawa 1, Ontario, Canada) is under-
taking to rewrite Indian history from the native
American viewpoint. It is asking for help in the task.

In general, the local offices of the American
Friends Service Committee can give up-to-date information and advice on local activities regarding
race and poverty. The Quakers are, in their own
quiet way, usually two or three generations ahead
of most radical ideologues.

10. *Ecology.*

*Ecotactics: The Sierra Club Handbook for En-
vironment Activists* (Pocket Books, 1970) is a good
place to begin searching the ecology scene. The
book surveys the many types of environmental politics, provides a roster of ecology organizations, a
bibliography, a list of relevant professional groups,

and even the names of key congressional contacts. The Sierra Club is always a reliable source of information and action. Its head office is 1050 Mills Tower, San Francisco 94104. There is also The Friends of the Earth (30 E. 42nd St., New York 10017): a Sierra Club off-shoot with a global view of ecology; and Environmental Action (2000 P. St., N.W., Washington, D.C. 20036) which publishes a biweekly newsletter.

An International Ecology University is being organized out of the University of California. Write to 3201 Claremont Ave., Berkeley, California 94705. IEU has published a brochure on its plans (price $1.50) and issues a good-looking monthly newsletter called *Ecosphere*. IEU is now compiling a directory of ecology organizations and setting up an "Information Clearing House."

The New Alchemy Institute (Box 432, Woods Hole, Massachusetts 02543; Box 376, Pescadero, California 94060) is an alliance of ecologists, artists, and humanists dedicated to creating ecologically balanced communes and pursuing harvest garden research. Its plans for polyculture economics sound brilliant. New and important.

The Ecology Center (2179 Allston Way, Berkeley 94704) and Ecology Action (Box 9334, Berkeley 94709) are two extremely active environmental groups. They can be helpful with literature and information.

The Center for Ecological Living (246 Center Ave., Pacheco, California 94553) publishes an excellent *Ecological Living Handbook*.

There are many good ecology periodicals available now. Among them: *Environmental Quality Magazine* (6355 Topanga Canyon Blvd., Suite 327, Woodland Hills, California 91364) and *The Ecologist* (73 Kew Green, Richmond, Surrey, England) which offers excellent international coverage. Also see *Environment* published by the Scientists Institute for Public Information, Washington University, St. Louis, Missouri.

The Christophers (12 E. 48th St., New York 10017) is a Christian ecology group. New Earth Communications Company (42 Sterling Ave., Tappan, New York 10983) specializes in making films for environmentalists.

There are reports that an investment brokerage firm (to be called ECO Inc.) is being pushed through the Security and Exchange Commission by environmental action groups. Its purpose will be to gather investment funds for ecologically sound small businesses to help them in their competition with the polluting giants.

Earthgaard (Box 12, 9690 Fjerritslev, Denmark) is an "environmental education center" run by an international staff as a branch of the Norden-Fjord World University.

Paul and Anne Ehrlich's *Population, Resources, Environment* (San Francisco: W. H. Freeman, 1970) is a fine handbook on basic ecology. Ward Shepard and Daniel McKinley's anthology *The Subversive Science* (Houghton-Mifflin, 1969) is a solid introduction to the field.

"Whales" (DelMar, California) is working to

save the whales from rapid extinction . . . though it looks like a losing fight. They have issued a long-playing record of deep-sea whale songs recorded by Dr. Roger Payne; the proceeds from the sales go toward keeping the surviving herds from being ground into pet food and shoe polish. The record is also available from "Whale Campaign," New York Zoological Society.

Zero Population Growth Inc. (Box 147, Old Mystic, Connecticut 06372) is Paul Ehrlich's world birth-control lobby.

11. Women's Liberation.

The appendices to Robin Morgan's excellent anthology *Sisterhood is Powerful* (Random House, 1970) offer much information on bibliography, organizations, movement contacts, abortion counseling, etc. Also see *Mushroom Effect,* a women's liberation directory (50¢) available from Box 6024, Albany, California 94706.

The Abortion Handbook for Responsible Women is not to be found in most bookstores. But it can be ordered for $3 from Contact Books, 6340 Coldwater Canyon, North Hollywood, California.

The National Organization of Women (NOW) can be contacted at Box 114, Cathedral Station, New York 10025. The more radical feminist groups are local, scattered, or underground. They are best located through newspapers like *Rat* (241 E. 14th St., New York) now run by an all-woman collective; *Off Our Backs* (2318 Ashmead Place, N.W.,

Washington, D.C. 20009); *It Ain't Me Babe* (2398 Bancroft Ave., Berkeley, California 94704); *Up From Under* (339 LaFayette St., New York 10012). A good library of articles, clippings, periodicals, and bibliographies is the Women's History Research Center, 2325 Oak St., Berkeley, California 94708.

The Radicalesbians can be contacted at the Women's Center, 36 W. 22nd St., New York 10011.

In the south, contact Women's Liberation Coalition (Box 19001, New Orleans, Louisiana 70119) and the periodical *Her Own Right* (1608 Milan St., Apt 6, New Orleans 70118).

12. *Schools.*

The New Schools Exchange (2840 Hidden Valley Lane, Santa Barbara, California 93103) is a clearing house for some 700 experimental schools. It publishes a weekly newsletter, a quarterly journal, and a directory.

The Big Rock Candy Mountain Catalogue of free schools is published by the Portola Institute (1115 Merrill Street, Menlo Park, California 94025). The Institute's *Whole Earth Catalog* for Spring 1969 gives a list of experimental schools on page 90 drawn up by John Holt, whose writings are basic reading. *The Modern Utopian* (see above) has also issued a *Directory of Free Schools*.

The Summerhill Society (6063 Margis, Los Angeles, California 90034) publishes a bulletin on A. S. Neill-type schools.

The appendix to George Dennison's *The Lives*

of Children (Random House, 1969) gives advice on starting an experimental school. There is also Frank Lindenfield's "How to Start a Free School" available from Vocations for Social Change, Canyon, California 94516.

Rasberry, Or How to Start Your Own Free School (Freestone Publishing Co., 440 Bohemian Highway, Freestone, California 95472—$3.95) by Salli Rasberry and Robert Greenway is useful in the same way: basic advice on laws, building codes, keeping health records, finances, etc.

The New Nation Seed Fund (Box 4026, Philadelphia, Pennsylvania 19118) solicits contributions "to help new schools get started and existing ones stay alive." The solicitors include Paul Goodman, John Holt, George Dennison.

The Teacher Drop Out Center relocates educators in distress. Contact Len Solo, School of Education, University of Massachusetts, Amherst, Massachusetts 01002.

The Education Development Center (55 Chapel Street, Newton, Massachusetts 02160) puts out a fine series of occasional papers and is experimenting with non-directive teaching techniques.

T. D. Lingo's Mountain Survival School (Laughing Coyote Mountain, Blackhawk, Colorado . . . with an address like that, it must be a good thing) teaches dropped out adolescents about mountaineering, meditation, and neural cybernetics.

Also see *This Magazine Is About Schools,* 56 Esplanada St., Suite 301, Toronto 1, Canada.

For college-level education: the Berkeley Free U

(2200 Parker St., Berkeley) is still in operation. But the Midpeninsula Free U (1061 El Camino Real, Menlo Park, California) must be the most active of them all. It publishes *The Free You*.

The Association of Humanistic Psychology (see above: "The Eupsychian Network") has produced a schools list for studies and degrees in the new psychology and related subjects.

Emerson College in Forest Row, Sussex, England draws a large number of questing young Americans by virtue of its highly imaginative curriculum. It maintains a school of Biodynamic Agriculture and Earth Sciences, along with its own experimental farm for organic husbandry.

Friends World College (Mitchel Gardens, Westbury, New York 11590) is Quaker-sponsored and non-sectarian; it stresses foreign work-study programs leading to the B.A.

13. Jobs.

Vocations for Social Change (Box 77, Canyon, California 94516) is an excellent and indispensible job counseling magazine for drop-outs. It should be placed in every college and university library. It is the work of the Canyon Collective. Check it for job possibilities in politically related projects, movement work, the arts, and for sound advice in general.

Job Generation (1124 Sutter, San Francisco, California) finds parttime work for drop-outs. There may be similar organizations in other cities. There *ought* to be.

Organization::Response (3233 P St., N.W., Washington, D.C. 20007) is a non-profit association for the study and improvement of educational institutions. It is conducting a new placement service for principled young professionals and college graduates. Its hope is to find niches in the system where people can work without selling their souls. The service is pricey: $35 to get on the files. So inquire carefully to see if this suits your needs.

Sociocom publishes concise resumés of jobseekers in social and economic development; Intercept is a counterpart service in higher education. Contact both through Mel Horwitch, Box 317, Harvard Square Post Office, Cambridge, Massachusetts 02138.

14. *The Cosmic Circuit.*

"COSMIC is a loosely-woven, worldwide fabric of small magazines and newspapers existing to facilitate cooperation between any Underground (radical and non-commercial), Upground (normal channel media) or Overground (celestially oriented and aspirational) magazines, for the promotion of the alternative society and the awakening of true consciousness in planetary man." I use the term here to cover religious, mystical, and occult literature and groups.

The Shambala Bookshop (Sather Gate Box 4336,

Berkeley, California 94704) publishes the journal
Maitreya "dedicated to the creative mutation and
evolution of all that is encompassed in the fabric
of life." It is a good-looking publication and may
serve to crystallize the widespread interest in occult and mystical studies. Also see *Pentagram* (68
Grove End Gardens, London, N.W. 8) which gives
a listing of other cosmic journals.

In London, John Watkins Ltd. (17 Cecil Court,
London, W.C. 2) has long been an outstanding
distributor of occult and religious books dating back
to Mme. Blavatsky. Its booklists and its own publications are well worth investigating. So too the lists
of Rider and Co. (178–202 Great Portland St.,
London, W.1) and The Wisdom of the East Series
(through Grove Press, 64 University Place, New
York 10003). Both contain outstanding works of
imagination and scholarship.

The Journal of Transpersonal Psychology (see
above: "The Eupsychian Network") No. 1, 1970,
lists several west coast oriental centers and schools.
Also in the west: The Zen Mountain Center, Tassa-
jara Springs, Monterey, California; The Buddhist
Fellowship, 814 Dartshire Way, Sunnyvale, California (Pure Land School); The Students' International Meditation Society, 2728 Channing Way,
Berkeley 94704.

The Lama Tarthang Tulku has recently established the Tibetan Nyingmapa Meditation Center in
Berkeley for the study of Tantric Buddhism.

The most sympathetic guide to some of the many
new spiritual movements is Jacob Needleman's

The New Religions (Doubleday, 1970): Zen, Subud, transcendental meditation, etc.

The Hare Krishna folk are still the happiest people I see on the streets of our grim cities. The International Society for Krishna Consciousness (ISKCON) maintains centers in most large cities in the U.S. and abroad, and will take in hungry adolescent downs-and-outs. Main U.S. headquarters is 40 N. Beacon St., Boston 02134. Otherwise check the telephone directory under ISKCON.

There is a very full guide to "Occult, Mystical, Religious, Magical London": it is the *Aquarian Guide* (Aquarian Press, 37 Margaret Street, London W.1). Centre House (10A Airlie Gardens, London W.8) is a rich source for material on religious, occult, and mystical studies throughout the world.

15. *Draft Resistance.*

The draft, as we all know, is scheduled to end the day after tomorrow: we have every assurance from Washington. But don't hold your breath till it happens.

Meanwhile, there are two ways around service in Caesar's legions: to become a CO or to resort to illegal resistance. Any competent draft counseling service can inform you of the range of options and their consequences. The established national counseling services—with many local offices—are The Central Committee for Conscientious Objectors, head office 2016 Walnut St., Philadelphia 19103; The War Resisters League, head office 339 La-

fayette St., New York 10012; and The American
Friends Service Committee, for which you can find
phone listings in most large cities. Contact any of
them for literature on resisting conscription. The
Union for National Draft Opposition (UNDO) is
at Princeton University, Princeton, New Jersey
08540.

There are any number of militant resistance
groups at the local or regional level; they can be
contacted on nearly every major university campus.
I will mention only a few here: CADRE, 519 W.
North Ave., Chicago 60610 and RESIST, 763 Massachusetts Ave., Cambridge, Massachusetts 02193. The
Resistance maintains many local centers; its headquarters is at 928 Chestnut St., Philadelphia 19107.

The *I-W Job Finder* lists job possibilities for
COs. Order from Dean Mitchell, CO Placement,
UUSC, 78 Beacon St., Boston 02108.

There are several Canadian groups aiding con-
scription-exiles. The American Deserters' Committee, 102 Villeneuve East, Montreal 151, Quebec,
Canada; Toronto Anti-Draft, Box 764, Adelaide
St. Station, Toronto 1, Canada; Committee to Aid
American War Objectors, Box 4231, Vancouver 9,
British Columbia. But check carefully with these
and others; the Canadian authorities have been
known to harass them.

LINK is the Serviceman's Link to Peace (Room
200, 1029 Vermont Avenue, N.W., Washington,
D.C. 20005). It is organizing war resisters already
in the armed forces. There is also the much harassed Movement for a Democratic Military, 429

J. St., San Diego, California 92101, which seeks to extend civil rights protection to soldiers for their political activities. The G.I. Counseling Services are at 339 Lafayette St., New York 10012.

The Underground Press Service (Box 26, Village P.O., New York 10014) can supply a list of some thirty G.I. underground publications.

16. Sundry Publications.

The most exhaustive list I have seen of underground-Liberation News Service and associated publications (for both the U.S. and Europe) appears in the appendix to Richard Neville's *Playpower* (Random House, 1971). No point in doing the job again here. But I will mention a few things that I have found to be especially valuable reading for one reason or another.

MANAS (Box 32112, El Sereno Station, Los Angeles, California 90032) is an indispensible philosophical weekly, and at $5 per year, the greatest bargain in periodical literature. *The Family Store: Directory of People's Resources* (10th and Howard, San Francisco, California 94103) is the "yellow pages of the cultural revolution": hip businesses, arts and crafts, head shops, health foods, etc. Mainly Bay Area, but as the second economy spreads, doubtless similar directories will appear in other regions.

The Canyon Collective (Box 77, Canyon, California 94516) covers lots of counter institutional news. The *Alan Watts Journal* (order from Human

Development Corporation, 200 Madison Avenue, New York 10016) is a thought from Alan Watts each month. *Country Senses* (Box 465, Woodbury, Connecticut 06798), "the east coast head magazine," is about agrarian communalism. *Our Generation* (3837 Boul. St. Laurent, Montreal 18, Quebec) carries lots of good, heavy, radical theory. *WIN* (339 Lafayette Street, New York 10012) manages to be radical without sacrifice of gentleness or intelligence. I understand that it too will soon become a commune and move on to the land in upstate New York. *The Homesteader* is published bimonthly at Oxford, New York 13829. *The Head Products Bulletin* (Box 165, Fulton, California 95439) puts handicraft producers in touch with head shop outlets, and vice versa.

Among British publications worth subscribing to: *Anarchy* (84B Whitechapel High Street, London, E. 1); *Peace News* (5 Caledonian Road, London, N. 1) is the oldest and best pacifist journalism around; *Resurgence* (24 Abercorn Place, St. Johns Wood, London, N.W. 8) has much to do with decentralism, human scale technology, anarchist theory: E. F. Schumacher is a frequent contributor; *Friends* (307 Portobello Road, London W. 10) is the best of the English underground press; *fire* (39 Randolph Avenue, London, W. 9) is put out by Joe Berke, an associate of R. D. Laing. *OZ* (52 Princedale Road, London, W. 11.)

Actuel (60 Rue de Richelieu, Paris 2e) is a new effort to bring the underground press to Paris . . . finally.

The Black Mountain Press (Box 1, Corinth, Vermont 05039) has a fine list of publications and reprints. Also People's Press (968 Valencia Street, San Francisco, California 94110). Consult both for radical print work.

There are several American Indian periodicals of interest. Among them: *Warpath* (United Native Americans Inc., Box 26149, San Francisco, California 94126); *Diné Baa-Hani* (Fort Defiance, Box 527, Navajo Nation 86504); *Cherokee Examiner* ("written by hostile American Indians," Box 687, South Pasadena, California 91030).

Katallagete (*Be Reconciled*) (Box 936, College Station, Berea, Kentucky 40403) is the journal of the Committee of Southern Churchmen and one of the few good religious publications I've come across.

Special Note

Subscriptions for school libraries: Many of you who read this will be students or teachers on a campus somewhere. A large number of campus library subscriptions to worthwhile underground or radical periodicals would be a great help to the cause. It takes little trouble to urge your library to subscribe; most will if they receive two or three requests. And besides the subscriptions will help put your school in touch with the real world. The following publications have become essential for any self-respecting school library:

The Mother Earth News (Box 38, Madison, Ohio 44057)

Manas (Box 32112, El Sereno Station, Los Angeles, California 90032)

The Radical Therapist (P.O. Box 89, W. Somerville, Mass.)

Vocations for Social Change (Box 77, Canyon, California 94516)

Hotch-Pot (Box 2492, Cleveland, Ohio 44112)

The Family Store (10th and Howard, San Francisco, California 94103)

WIN (P.O. Box 547, Rifton, N.Y. 12471)

The Modern Utopian (P.O. Drawer A, Diamond Heights Station, San Francisco, California 94131)

Plus at least one local underground newspaper, one American Indian paper, one radical black paper, one women's liberation paper.

17. *Miscellaneous Energy Centers.*

The Pacifica Foundation operates listener-subscription radio stations in Berkeley (KPFA), Los Angeles (KPFK), and New York (WBAI). Also KPFT in Houston which has been twice dynamited off the air by the city's crypto-patriots. The Bay Area station started from absolute zero and has survived gloriously for better than twenty years in a chronic state of near bankruptcy, thus proving how well the anarchist thing can be done. Organizing such stations in every town and city should be a top priority project for the radical community.

The Institute for the Study of Non-violence (Box 1001, Palo Alto, California 94302) reaches out in many directions—currently toward alternative institutions like a people's bank. Major sponsors are Joan Baez and David Harris. Also, for imaginative pacifist programs: The Peace Brigade (2400 Bancroft, Berkeley 94704); the War Resisters League (339 Lafayette St., New York 10012); the Atlanta Workshop in Nonviolence (Box 7477, Atlanta, Georgia 30309).

The Grail (Grailville, Loveland, Ohio 45140) is an international movement of women emphasizing "creative experimentation in community living, social action, the arts, worship and the search for the spiritual." The group owns bookstores (including an excellent one in Edinburgh, Scotland) and a well-equipped activities center on 300 acres of farmland outside Cincinnati where it sponsors advanced educational experiments. The Grail's secretariat is in Paris.

The Center for the Study of Democratic Institutions (Box 4068, Santa Barbara, California 93103) puts out an excellent line of high-powered publications.

The Council for Social Development (416 S. 11th St., Philadelphia 19147) works to combine encounter grouping with community organizing—an admirably broad-gauged program.

Survival International (Benjamin Franklin House, 36 Craven St, London W.C. 2) is the former Primitive People's Fund. Its purpose is to combat the developmental genocide which, it is estimated, will eradicate all remaining primitive cultures within the next two decades.

The People Power Clearinghouse (Sandrock &

Foster Memorial Foundation, Honey Ridge, Box 112, Altura, Minnesota 55910) is a scheme for living by exchange and barter between individuals or communes. I gather the idea is something like the Labor Gift exchange in Berkeley which seeks to eliminate the cash-commercial nexus between people. Instead, people volunteer goods and (especially) services to a central switchboard; other people then call in to draw on the offerings in return for a labor gift of their own.

Ecology Tool and Toy (Armory Road, Milford, New Hampshire 03055) is a collaborative effort by an electrical engineer and a psychiatrist whose purpose is "to create responsive, courteous environments." The emphasis in its design is on user participation and playfulness. Innovative and intellectually solid.

The New City Project is planning a genuine new town—meaning one that is something more than a real estate combine's idea of a sanitized suburb. The spirit of the enterprize is decentralist and communitarian, with democratic controls from the ground up. Projected size: about 30,000. The prospectus (which is also a strong critique of contemporary urban society) is available from the Cambridge Institute (see above).

Alan Chadwick's gardening projects at the University of California at Santa Cruz are, I am told, among the loveliest things happening in America— and among the most popular on the campus.

The best way to keep up with Buckminster Fuller's work is through John McHale at the World

Resources Inventory, Southern Illinois University, Carbondale, Illinois.

The Epic Book Shop (232 Xenia Ave., Yellow Springs, Ohio) is a local "survival tool" about which people tell me many nice things.

The Theater of All Possibilities (near Cerillos, New Mexico) is a commune which combines education and craft-skills with experimental theater.

This appendix has not found much to say about straight religion . . . though there must be something worthwhile going on in the churches. I probably just haven't heard Except, of course, for the "Jesus Freaks," whose most active congregations include the Submarine Church in Berkeley, California. But I think the Catholic Workers and Dorothy Day do a better job of keeping alive the Christianity of the catacombs. The Workers' main office is at 175 Chrystie Street, New York 10002.

Sri Aurobindo's Ashram (Pondicherry 2, India) is the organizing base for a World Union International Center and for Auroville, the first independent, international, planned city.

Lanza del Vasto's Community of the Ark, at La Borie Noble in southern France, is based on Gandhian non-violence, natural harmony, and handicraft —and has survived nicely for over 30 years. Del Vasto's 1936 autobiography *Return to the Source* has finally been translated by Rider & Co., London.

For those who visit England, BIT (141 Westbourne Park Road, London W. 11) is the all-purpose, underground information center, open 24 hours a day to give advice on accommodations,

legal hassles, survival, and amusement in general.
The phone number (as of summer 1971) is 229-8219
—or check the directory under BIT Information
Service. Richard Neville's *Playpower* has appendices on how to live cheap in London. A fuller
guide is Nicholas Saunders's *Alternative London*
(order from 65 Edith Grove, London S.W. 10: cost
$1 plus postage—and well worth the price): hous-
ing, jobs, drugs, food cults, legal aid, communes,
bargains, travel, etc. There ought to be similarly
competent handbooks for all major cities.